I0810225

Look Abroad, Angel

THE NEW SOUTHERN STUDIES

SERIES EDITOR

Riché Richardson, Cornell University

FOUNDING EDITOR

Jon Smith, Simon Fraser University

ADVISORY BOARD

Houston A. Baker Jr., Vanderbilt University

Leigh Anne Duck, The University of Mississippi

Jennifer Greeson, The University of Virginia

Trudier Harris, The University of Alabama

John T. Matthews, Boston University

Tara McPherson, The University of Southern California

Claudia Milian, Duke University

Look Abroad, Angel

THOMAS WOLFE AND THE GEOGRAPHIES OF LONGING

Jedidiah Evans

The University of
Georgia Press
ATHENS

Paperback edition, 2026
© 2020 by the University of Georgia Press
Athens, Georgia 30602
www.ugapress.org
All rights reserved
Set in 9.75/13 Warnock Pro by Kaelin Chappell Broaddus

Use of any part of this book in training for any artificial intelligence (AI), large language model (LLM), machine learning technologies, or similar generative language system without license is expressly prohibited.

EU Authorized Representative Easy Access System Europe—
Mustamäe tee 50, 10621 Tallinn, Estonia,
gpsr.requests@easproject.com

Printed digitally

Library of Congress Control Number: 2019042779
ISBN: 9780820356465 (hardcover)
ISBN: 9780820356457 (ebook)

Paperback ISBN: 978-0-8203-8131-2

For Renee

CONTENTS

ACKNOWLEDGMENTS

I would first like to thank my dear friend Lucas Thompson for his tireless support in reading drafts, corralling my scattered thoughts, and for helping guide this book toward completion. Lucas is what Stanley Cavell calls a "perfectionist friend," and he inspires me to be a better scholar and a better person. I am sure this book wouldn't exist without him.

I would like to thank the entire team at the University of Georgia Press, but particularly my acquisitions editor, Walter Biggins, for his generous and ongoing support of my project, and Thomas Roche, Beth Snead, and Jordan Stepp, for their help in the final stages. Thanks also to Daniel Simon for his careful editing of the final manuscript. I am especially grateful to Jon Smith and Riché Richardson for the inclusion of *Look Abroad, Angel* in their excellent series, the New Southern Studies, and am particularly indebted to Jon, who was kind enough to take my work seriously when I was ready to give up.

My doctoral supervisor, Paul Giles, saw this book in its earliest stages and provided invaluable support throughout my PhD candidature and beyond. The University of Sydney generously provided a series of grants and research support schemes that enabled me to visit the Thomas Wolfe archives at the Houghton Library and the Wilson Library. I am grateful to staff at both libraries for their support. Thanks also to the Princeton University Library, to the New York Public Library, and to the Deutsche Nationalbibliothek. Access to Wolfe's archives, along with permission to publish material from the William B. Wisdom collection, was made possible by Eugene Winick, administrator of the Thomas Wolfe Estate. A quotation from Wolfe's unpublished "A Letter on Homelessness" © 2019 by Eugene Winick, Administrator C.T.A. of the Estate of Thomas Wolfe, is reprinted with permission of McIntosh & Otis, Inc. Sections of Bradbury's poem "October" are reprinted by permission of Don Congdon Associates, Inc. © 1985 by Ray Bradbury. Three quotations from the Jack Kerouac Papers by Jack Kerouac, © 1940 and 1942 by Jack Kerouac, are used by permission of the Wylie Agency, LLC.

Parts of chapter 1 appeared in different form in "Thomas Wolfe and the Domestication of Culture," in *Portable Prose: The Novel and the Everyday*, edited by Jarrad Cogle, N. Cyril Fischer, Lydia Saleh Rofail, and Vanessa Smith (Lanham, MD: Lexington Books, 2019). Parts of chapter 5 originally appeared in different form as "Thomas Wolfe and the Really Deep South," in *The Thomas Wolfe Review* 38, nos. 1–2 (2014): 7–24. I am grateful to both publishers for permission to reuse this material in book form.

I have benefitted enormously from the advice, editorial revisions, and encouragement of numerous friends and colleagues. I am particularly indebted to Jon Eller, director at the Center for Ray Bradbury Studies, for his generous provision of manuscript material and his continuing support of this project. The members of the Thomas Wolfe Society have demonstrated extraordinary generosity since the beginning of my project, and I'm especially grateful for the William B. Wisdom Grant in Aid of Research, which enabled me to spend time in Wolfe's archives. Other significant help came from Robert Brown, Daniel Cobb, Vincent C. Frank-Steiner, Sarah Gleeson-White, Tim Marr, Vera Meyer, Scott Romine, Catherine Thompson, and Wilfried Weinke.

My family has provided a foundation of encouragement and support since well before I embarked on this project. Thanks to my parents, Ray and Cindy, and to my siblings, Jess and Tim. This book is dedicated to my wife, Renee, whose generous love, support, and deep encouragement is inexhaustible. Renee, I have encountered my fair share of exorbitant and effusive language studying the unrestrained novels of Wolfe, but there are not words enough to express my joy in knowing and loving you.

Look Abroad, Angel

INTRODUCTION

On October 18, 1929, Charles Scribner's Sons released the first novel of an unknown North Carolinian author named Thomas Wolfe. What the publisher could not have predicted was that just six days later, on the first of two "black" days, the New York Stock Exchange would experience its "most disastrous decline," followed shortly by a total collapse, in what became the most severe and prolonged economic depression of the twentieth century.[1] Had the novel been more conventional in structure, more narrow in scope, populated with more orthodox characters—in short, more typical—its release may well have been entirely overshadowed by such adverse economic conditions. But *Look Homeward, Angel* (1929) was anything but typical: Wolfe's first novel was acclaimed as a gargantuan, lyrical, sprawling work that would ultimately turn Wolfe into a literary celebrity and generate an interest so intense that it is startling when compared to Wolfe's current cultural status. Once regularly compared with three of his more familiar and enduring contemporaries—Fitzgerald, Hemingway, and Faulkner—Wolfe has in recent years been relegated, as a *Wall Street Journal* editorial put it, to the "mostly forgotten and little read" pile.[2] As Mark McGurl notes in *The Program Era* (2009), "these days Wolfe is likely to be confused with his near-namesake Tom Wolfe, dapper New Journalist and popular novelist of a later generation, and is no more likely than the younger Wolfe to be found on any college syllabus. [. . .] Thomas Wolfe is well on his way to becoming a footnote to American literary history."[3]

Overwhelmingly, Wolfe critics and enthusiasts have resignedly accepted such pronouncements. When the journal *Appalachian Heritage* ran a special issue on Wolfe in the fall of 2007, eminent Wolfe scholar John Idol Jr. acknowledged that "Wolfe's national and international reputation does not position him in the forefront of American or world writers," adding that his standing as "a regional author is more assured," particularly when scholars focus on the development of "southern Appalachian literature."[4] For scholars such as Idol, the priority has long been to salvage Wolfe as an object of critical study, even if that means reducing the scope of Wolfe's influence from international relevance to mere regional significance. Idol's assessment is a dramatic contrast to the sentiments of Stringfellow Barr, the editor of the *Virginia Quarterly Review* who founded the first "Great Books" program as president of St. John's College. Barr wrote in 1930 that *Look Homeward, Angel* was "the South's first contribution to world literature."[5] If these two characterizations of Wolfe's significance can be understood as bracketing the author's cultural relevance—from world writer to regional curio—my book is concerned with situating Wolfe within the global tradition of literature to which Barr points, while extricating his work from the safe confines of Idol's regionalism.

This book traces the trajectory of Wolfe's critical decline, and I will argue that regional essentialism was—and remains—a contributing factor in the author's waning popularity. Questions of regionalism within the study of the American South have been divisive in the last few decades: as recently as 2013, Leigh Anne Duck identified a persistent disagreement between two approaches to literature that is both from, and about, the southeastern United States, suggesting that "[s]ome, however, may still wish to argue for a thickly meaningful and binding regional culture, which I take to be a fairly stark dividing line between new southern studies and other scholars."[6] Increasingly, Wolfe's fiction has been tethered to a critical tradition that promotes his significance within a narrow, regional framework, while Wolfe's relevance to the broader development of American literature, as well as his global importance, has been largely overlooked.

Even those studies on Wolfe that explore his importance beyond his Appalachian heritage have been strikingly immune to the "spatial turn" in the study of American literature, which in Paul Giles's view should be seen as "no longer bound to the inner workings of any particular country or imagined organic community but instead as interwoven systematically with traversals between national territory and intercontinental space."[7] Much of this work has tended to focus on Wolfe's exceptional "American" character, implicitly following Alfred Kazin's 1942 pronouncement that Wolfe believed that "he himself was a prime symbol of American experience," without taking into account Kazin's corresponding assertion that it was "America as an idea," as an imaginary space, which Wolfe filled with the borrowed myths and symbols he accrued through multiple "traversals" across the Atlantic.[8] Critical studies that have sought to link Wolfe with southern or modernist literary traditions have also tended to unconsciously perpetuate such formulations as "the South" or "America," without noting Wolfe's own attempts to complicate and undermine these very abstractions.[9]

This book hopes to avoid the pitfalls of previous critical work on Wolfe by closely examining how Wolfe's work was received and understood by early readers. My attention to the reception and employment of Wolfe's fiction is a response to entreaties by scholars such as Rita Felski to attend to the ways literature is *used*, with "use" meaning more than simply ideological function but rather—in Felski's words—an engagement that is "extraordinarily varied, complex, and often unpredictable in kind."[10] Investigating how Wolfe's fiction has been used—popularly, critically, politically, imaginatively—opens up new terrain for attending to the meaning of the writer and his work, and moves away from the kind of literary analysis that relies solely on an attentiveness to aesthetic ingenuity or on readings that subordinate the text to the ideological prerogatives of the critic. Moreover, an attention to use can helpfully illuminate the very real ways in which worn-out conceptions of "southern" or "American" character *did* factor into how Wolfe was read, without treating those abstractions as if they are meaningful descriptors of some kind of coherent identity.

Of course, this project of reanimating Wolfe's oeuvre is subject to critique, particularly in the ways in which my interest in the historical use of Wolfe, following Felski, is an interest in the meaning of texts *for others*.[11] Wai Chee Dimock notes that the weakness of such a historical perspective is in its failure to say "why this text might still matter in the present, why, distanced from its original period, it nonetheless continues to signify, continues to invite other readings."[12] This book sets out to demonstrate that the ways in which Wolfe's work was used should interest us in the present, a project that involves reinscribing Wolfe's work as a cultural object: less the work of a genius than works of literature—books, even—whose various uses and reuses continue to signify. The early chapters in this book explore Wolfe's fiction within his most obvious and immediate contexts—as an American and southerner—but with a shift in focus. Rather than viewing Wolfe as a homegrown southern novelist, attempting to write the Great American Novel, my book emphasizes the reception of Wolfe and the culture that formed around him, arguing that in order to perceive Wolfe's critical relevance it is necessary to understand how he was *actually* read, and to observe the ways in which his work intersected with the cultural concerns of Depression America and beyond. Ted Atkinson undertook a similar revision of Faulkner in *Faulkner and the Great Depression* (2006), arguing that in order to move beyond "the boundaries of critical provincialism," a reassessment of writers from this period must incorporate "key conditions of historical and cultural context," confronting what Atkinson calls the "incoherence and upheaval that were Depression facts of life."[13]

While Atkinson still sees Faulkner's fiction as fundamentally "attuned to the American experience," my discussion of Wolfe also responds to Wai Chee Dimock's important thesis in *Through Other Continents* (2006), which suggests that although American literary studies began with the premise that literature is a "discrete entity," the "product of one nation and one nation alone, analyzable within its confines," what we call American literature is better seen as "a crisscrossing set of pathways, open-ended and ever multiplying, weaving in and out of other geographies, other languages and cultures."[14] The suggestion of "Looking Abroad" in the book's title implies a need for a shift away from the preoccupation with what is "homeward" in the novelist's oeuvre; the longing that characterizes so much of Wolfe's published work is not directed solely toward home or America but is instead fundamentally "open-ended and ever multiplying," ultimately insatiable. The multiple geographies identified by the title are also crucial to my argument; beginning with a discussion of the immediate aftermath of the U.S. publication of *Look Homeward, Angel* (1929), subsequent chapters will move increasingly outward, away from representations of the South in Wolfe's fiction to focus on the author's relationship with Germany and its literary culture. The final chapter reconsiders this movement on a temporal plane, tracing Wolfe's spectral presence in the work of other authors from the earliest appropriations into the current day. Also addressed in the last chapter are Wolfe's transpacific influence as well as his Martian reimagining in the work of Ray Bradbury. Ultimately, my book situates Wolfe within a global tradition of literature, revising the common critical reading of his work by revealing the complex ways in which his work was interpreted by readers far beyond the cloistered South.

Geographies of Longing

One obvious difficulty in this project of globalizing Wolfe is tethering my claims too firmly to an author in critical decline. Felski's analysis of the historical method includes the obvious critique that the reader, when she picks up a book from the past, does so "in the hope that it will speak to [her] in the present."[15] Beyond the manifold uses of Wolfe's fiction that function as the critical framework for this book, a corresponding analysis of longing in Wolfe's work—arguably the most recognizable feature of his fiction—will serve to highlight the ways in which that work continues to speak beyond the confines of a particular vision of the South. Although I will suggest that McGurl's description of Wolfe as a mere footnote is an obvious misreading—indeed, a misreading that follows a pattern established by the Agrarian critics shortly after Wolfe's death in 1938—this activity of reevaluating Wolfe serves to illuminate a wider "reconstruction of spatialized ontology" that Martyn Bone describes in *The Postsouthern Sense of Place in Contemporary Fiction* (2005).[16] Indeed, it is the very resistance of scholars to reading the writer's work outside of particular regional and national constraints that prompts such a reevaluation for Wolfe. Despite recent complaints that postsouthernists "lose the specific memories and meanings of the South in the name of a certain trend of globalism"—"memories" here serving as that persuasive yearning for the local, precapitalist, and authentic South that the Agrarians promulgated—few have seen Wolfe's work as anything other than rooted in the South.[17]

The unmooring of a "sense of place" that scholars either decry or celebrate is a central, if not *the* central, preoccupation of Wolfe's writing: an oeuvre that is endlessly embodying longing in spaces like *home*, *America*, *South*, and *geography*, while necessarily never arriving—that is, never satisfying the longing. It is no mistake that perhaps the most enduring legacy of Wolfe is the phrase "you can't go home again."[18] As only one recent example of the quote's ubiquity, I stumbled upon a reference while playing Dontnod Entertainment's award-winning episodic video game, *Life Is Strange* (2015). At the end of the first episode, "Chrysalis," the game's protagonist—time-altering Maxine Caulfield—has arrived back in her home town of Arcadia Bay in Oregon, unsurprisingly encountering the kind of small-mindedness she hoped she was leaving behind. Looking at a painting of her hometown, Max exclaims whimsically, "You can't go home again, said Thomas Wolfe."[19]

Given Wolfe's relative critical obscurity in the last few decades, this book offers a timely reappraisal that contemplates Wolfe's unique "spatialized ontology" as expressly connected to unsatisfiable longing. Despite the reluctance of scholars to engage with Wolfe in light of the spatial turn—a hesitancy that cannot be disentangled from the reality that, early on, Wolfe was championed as a distinctly southern writer by the hugely influential Louis D. Rubin—much of the recent work on southern literature is preoccupied, to some degree, with what Jon Smith has called the "*over*presence of the past," a construction that might just as easily have been the *over*presence of place.[20] In responding to these "*over*presences," my analysis is strongly informed by the German term for longing, *Sehnsucht*, which, in my theorization, serves a dual purpose. First, and most obviously, it links Wolfe's career-long preoccupation with longing—what I will label as his "ontology of longing"—within a broader transatlantic exchange of ideas surrounding homesickness, nostalgia, and longing. In "Look Homeward, Americans" (1940), Carson McCullers chose Wolfe's vision of homesickness as emblematic of an endemic *American* homesickness, perceiving it as being as "native to us as the roller-coaster or the jukebox." For McCullers, homesickness was a "national trait," expressing itself via an intense longing for "places we have never known."[21] The tendency to read Wolfe's expression of longing for home as identifiably American represents an approach that has been endlessly reproduced in the years following Wolfe's death, and it remains unchallenged even with the advent of fields like transnationalism and new southern studies, which have been deeply antagonistic toward such nationalizing imperatives.[22]

My use of *Sehnsucht* in this book is intentionally disruptive, identifying multiple centers for Wolfe's vision of alienation and longing—not just America or the South, but also those imaginatively rich spaces like Munich, Weimar, and Berlin that provided Wolfe with an alternate vision of home. The Romantic heritage of *Sehnsucht* recommends the term in discussions of Wolfe, since the writer's own descriptions of Germany in his notebooks and letters, written as he explored it between 1928 and 1936, demonstrate a deep indebtedness to German Romanticism and Weimar classicism, filled with representations that draw on a peculiarly Romantic vision of the German landscape and people. Deploying *Sehnsucht* in my analysis of Wolfe's ontology of longing also reveals a deeply idiosyncratic form of longing found in Wolfe's work, one that cannot be neatly or wholly contained within terms like *homesickness, nostalgia,* or even *longing. Sehnsucht* is thus a highly productive interpretive lens with which to understand Wolfe's obsession with "lostness" and insatiable longing, reconfiguring ideas around those more familiar expressions of desire to reveal Wolfe's underlying ontology of longing, and also to make the claim that it is very often this particular quality of Wolfe's work which has constituted his most enduring legacy—that is, why his work continues to be read, and why it ought to be.

Sehnsucht

Given the centrality of *Sehnsucht* to my analysis of Wolfe, and considering the constellations of longing-words that abound in his fiction as well as in critical discussions of his work, I want to offer a theorization of *Sehnsucht* before the close of this introduction. My hope is to bring a new perspective to one of the defining aspects of Wolfe's fiction and to articulate an approach to longing that could serve to unburden other studies of their reliance on overused critical terminology. Words have interpretive baggage, long histories of usage that have blurred their original distinctiveness or overlaid their meanings with richer and more nebulous implications. In a critical environment where words like *nostalgia, home,* and *place* have had much of their meaning wrung out through overuse, this theoretical lens of *Sehnsucht* (itself an overused word for German speakers, who are as likely to encounter it in travel advertisements as an American might read the ill-used *wanderlust*) offers an alternative vision of desire that dislocates "home" from "homesickness" and "place" from "nostalgia," instead identifying the productive capacity of Wolfe's ineffable and unfocused yearning.

The first word that intersects with my use of the term *Sehnsucht* is *longing.* In *On Longing* (1993), Susan Stewart writes that the location of desire is always "a future-past, a deferment of experience in the direction of origin and thus eschaton, the point where narrative begins/ends, both engendering and transcending the relation between materiality and meaning."[23] Longing in this sense is creative, engendering—in Wolfe's case, through narrative—

the object or place desired, but also always turned toward something beyond reach. Though longing need not always be construed as something so innately metaphysical, the expression of longing in Wolfe as it is discussed in this book closely resembles the "metaphysical desire" Emmanuel Lévinas describes in *Totality and Infinity* (1979): "Besides the hunger one satisfies, the thirst one quenches, and the senses one allays, metaphysics desires the other beyond satisfactions, where no gesture by the body to diminish the aspiration is possible, where it is not possible to sketch out any known caress nor invent any new caress. A desire without satisfaction which, precisely, *understands* the remoteness, the alterity, and the exteriority of the other."[24]

Desire without satisfaction and longing for something beyond reach are apt descriptions of the maddening and insatiable hunger that informs much of Wolfe's writing, in particular his long second novel, *Of Time and the River: A Legend of Man's Hunger in His Youth* (1935). *Of Time and the River* is full of unsatisfiable yearning, and it presents a picture of youthful longing that vacillates between the productive potential of such a hunger and the paralyzing force of loss: "It is to have the old unquiet mind, the famished heart, the restless soul; it is to lose hope, heart, and all joy utterly, and then to have them wake again, to have the old feeling return with overwhelming force that he is about to find the thing for which his life obscurely and desperately is groping for which all men on this earth have sought—one face out of the million faces, a wall, a door, a place of certitude and peace and wandering no more."[25]

The actual word *longing*, as a noun, stems from the now obsolete intransitive verb form *to long*, which means "to grow longer; to lengthen." This verb form was itself derived from the Old English word *langian*, which shares its etymological origin with the Middle Dutch *langen*, meaning "to 'think long' desire; to extend," and the Middle High German *langen*, "to reach, extend, suffice."[26] In light of these roots, the *OED* defines *longing* as "yearning desire," literally desire at its full extension.[27] Drew M. Dalton, in *Longing for the Other: Levinas and Metaphysical Desire* (2009), suggests that "all of these roots stress the passive nature of longing, the fact that it is not something which is done by someone, but is rather something which happens to someone."[28] However, the inherent compulsiveness of *longing* and its verb form *to long* seem to negate this passivity: *to long*, in its different permutations, can mean "to be restless or impatient (till something is attained)," "to grow weary," and in its adverbial permutation always implies "a verb of motion," as in "to long to go."[29] Revealingly, the *American Heritage Dictionary of the English Language* (2000) defines *longing* via an additional gloss on the *OED*'s "yearning desire" with the caveat: "Especially one that cannot be fulfilled."[30] Although longing is not for something *in particular*, the very experience of longing implies longing for *something*. The distinction made in the *American Heritage Dictionary* is fundamental: the weariness of *to long* is overcome by a yearning desire for something, apparently satisfying, that is beyond reach. Longing in this sense is an infinite reaching.

When home is the locus for this insatiable form of longing, the familiar notion of homesickness—a loan translation of the German *Heimweh*—is introduced. Unlike *longing*, which can be readily accepted as indeterminate and ineffable, *homesickness* necessarily implies an object: home. Both *home* and *homesickness* are terms worth distinguishing from *Sehnsucht*, in part because of the ways in which the home of Wolfe's fiction has so readily been identified as a concrete place: usually the mountains of North Carolina, and almost always somewhere in America. The history of homesickness in America is rooted in concrete expressions of loss and yearning. Susan J. Matt's *Homesickness: An American History* (2011) details the very tangible experiences of homesickness that have been a feature of American cultural identity since European colonization, describing the particular form of homesickness that was widespread during the antebellum period and received "systematic attention during the Civil War," where the malaise was so feared that "some army bands were prohibited from playing 'Home, Sweet Home' for fear the song might provoke the deadly illness in soldiers."[31] At the same time, the preponderance of the photographic image—often in the form of tintype portraits carried in jacket pockets—meant that American soldiers were effectively taking home with them onto the battlefield. According to Matt, as individualism solidified into cultural hegemony during the twentieth century, the imperative to move and so also to accept this sense of dislocation became a dominant metaphor of the modern age. With the advent of American modernism, homesickness as a physical malaise—as it was originally understood—was replaced with the new "religion" of mobility. Jonathan Flately has persuasively argued that modernity—in its "meanings as a particular experience of time and as a set of concrete transformations of the material world of everyday life"—is expressly related to an experience of loss.[32] Following the Great Depression, one concrete feature of dislocation and mobility in American culture was the introduction of the tramp figure—those many hundreds of thousands of individuals who rode the rails during the 1930s—providing a powerful new symbol of home*lessness*, which John Allen describes in *Homelessness in American Literature* (2004) as being alternately "romanticized or objectified" in literary representations.[33]

Of course, the prototypical figure of the American wanderer in the American literary imaginary predates the explosion of these wandering figures in the Depression era—in 1885 Huck Finn declared, "there warn't no home like a raft [. . .] we let her alone, and let her float wherever the current wanted her to"[34]—but during this period, the sight of young men riding freight trains was ubiquitous: a Depression-era report from the Children's Bureau noted that "the railroad men in Kansas City [. . .] estimated that every day approximately

1,500 men and boys went through that city riding the freights," suggesting that during the worst years of the Depression "perhaps a quarter of a million teenagers left home in search of opportunity, adventure, or escape."[35] In the figure of the tramp, home*sickness* shifts to home*lessness*, a dislocation from an identifiable home that has often informed literary discussions of homesickness in America.[36] In *Of Time and the River*, the word *homesickness* is always paired with *homelessness*, and the terms' synonymy in the novel reflects the author's impulse to regard specific forms of desire as universal. To think of home in Wolfe's fiction is also to acknowledge humankind's alienation, and home is always overlaid by what is lost.

An example of this more universal conception of home can be found in book 7 of *Of Time and the River*. Eugene Gant—Wolfe's protagonist and doppelgänger—has temporarily ceased wandering, finding quiet lodging in the French town of Tours. In a sequence that marks Wolfe's modernist experimentation with consciousness and time, Gant undergoes a "dream of time" marked by a phantasmal parade of "time-experiences": "Day passed into night, night merged into day again like the unbroken weaving of a magic web, and he stayed on, week after week, plunged in a strange and legendary spell of time that seemed suspended and detached from the world of measurable event, fixed in unmoving moment, unsilent silence, changeless change."[37]

In this spell of time, Gant thinks of home. In the pause from an unbroken "kaleidoscope of cafés, brothels, alcohol, and women," Gant encounters, afresh, "the terrible homelessness of a man for whom there can never be return." In this passage, homesickness bleeds into homelessness; the particular yearning for home that accompanies waking in a foreign land reminds Gant of the fundamental fickleness of that selfsame desire: "We are a phantom flare of grieved desire. The ghostling and phosphoric flicker of immortal time, a brevity of days haunted by the eternity of the earth."[38] One scholar has called such elegiac passages "dithyrambs to a vanished life," and they punctuate Wolfe's work as rhapsodies of loss.[39]

Wolfe's peripatetic heroes who "can't go home again" have been particularly amenable to critical appraisals that treat the South as the object of Wolfe's homesickness, but it is the nebulous character of home in Wolfe's novels that renders the idea of homesickness problematic: it is not simply "the South" or "America" that Wolfe's characters long for when they long for home.[40] Home is rarely a clearly defined place; in Wolfe's fiction, home often appears as existing on a transcendent plane, an "elsewhere," such that homesickness more closely approximates Lévinas's unsatisfiable, metaphysical desire. In *Look Homeward, Angel*, Wolfe introduced his romance of movement in the character of Eugene Gant, writing that the "vast Utopia of his loneliness" collided with the "hill-born [. . .] prison pent" nature of home. Wolfe adds that "to go alone, as he had gone, into strange cities; to meet strange people and to pass again before they could know him; to wander, like his own legend, across the earth—it seemed to him there could be no better thing than that."[41] In *Of Time and the River*, Wolfe extends this idea of homelessness to incorporate all Americans, stressing both its essential romance and despair: "It was the furious desire, unceasing, unassuaged, of wandering and forsaken man—the lost American—who longs forever for return—and who has no door to enter, no room to dwell in, no single handsbreadth of certain, consecrated earth upon that continent of wild houseless space, to which he can return."[42]

In an excised passage from *Of Time and the River* included in Richard Kennedy's *The Starwick Episodes* (1989), Wolfe noted the "growing evidence of homesickness and unrest in Eugene," which he called "that nameless bitter longing for return—return to God knows what, to God knows where—that bitter quenchless longing for an unknown home."[43] It is important to note that the very experience of longing for these multilocal home-places is itself often the desired emotion: the object of the longing is the experience of longing. Wolfe's commitment to longing thus also reflects the author's belief that longing itself was worthy of deep fictional investigation.

One final term that overlaps with my discussion of *Sehnsucht* in this book is the critically overladen word *nostalgia*. In a 1935 review of *Of Time and the River* for the *Saturday Review of Literature*, Henry Seidel Canby wrote that themes of restlessness and homesickness in Wolfe's novel were evidence of America's "impotence." Canby argued that Wolfe's American soul was impotent because "in three hundred years the American soul has not made itself a home." His article regularly returns to this idea, suggesting that "it is an impotence of wandering men at home," an "impotence of expression," while Wolfe's impotence was "exactly equivalent" to his inability to "control the theme."[44] Canby's description of Wolfe's central theme anticipates a persistent criticism of Wolfe's objectless longing and is also reminiscent of Civil War attitudes to homesickness. During that war, doctors had incorporated the European creation, *nostalgia*, into their pathology of homesickness, and as a diagnosable disease it quickly spread—over five thousand Union soldiers were recorded as "suffering" from the disease of nostalgia.[45] Responding to the preponderance of nostalgic soldiers, Theodore Calhoun, a military doctor, suggested that nostalgia was "a shameful disease that revealed a lack of manliness and unprogressive attitudes."[46] Calhoun's exasperation toward the condition was well-founded: Matt suggests that as many as seventy-four of those soldiers had succumbed to the allegedly fatal disease.[47]

The term *nostalgia* has incorporated numerous meanings since being coined by the Swiss doctor Johannes Hofer in 1688 as a new medical term for the disease of *Heimweh*, the German term for homesickness. In "The Idea of Nostalgia" (1966), Jean Starobinski notes that vague conceptions of home are ubiquitous in the history of nostalgia: "The attention which Johannes Hofer gave to *Heimweh* was decisive. First, he thought it proper to find a Greek word for it, as it was necessary in 1688 for a disease, originally designated by a common noun, to be invested with the appropriate classical trappings. Hofer had a happy touch: with the words return (νόστος) and sorrow (ἄλγος), he created nostalgia; a word which has had such success that we have completely forgotten its origin."[48]

The successes Starobinski refers to here are twofold. In *The Future of Nostalgia* (2001), Svetlana Boym contends that "Hofer's felicitous baptism of the new disease both helped to identify the existing condition and enhanced the epidemic, making it a widespread European phenomenon."[49] But the second implication of this rapid success was the gradual movement of nostalgia from the medical to the metaphysical, a movement that found its apotheosis in the Romantic period. Boym's thesis is as follows: "In response to the Enlightenment, with its emphasis on the universality of reason, romantics began to celebrate the particularism of the sentiment. Longing for home became a central trope of romantic nationalism. The romantics looked for 'memorative signs' and correspondences between their inner landscape and the shape of the world."[50]

Romantic tropes relating to nostalgia are reworked again and again within Wolfe's fiction—John Peale Bishop has called Wolfe's work "a culmination of the romantic spirit in America"[51]—and it is this quality that most closely approximates the notion of *Sehnsucht* that is discussed throughout this book. Boym's description of nostalgia as "a longing for a home that no longer exists or has never existed" echoes McCullers's contention that Americans are "homesick most for the places we have never known," and Wolfe's own 1931 assertion that "we're a homesick people, homesick for something we haven't here, and homesick still when we seek it abroad."[52] If there is a problem with nostalgia, it is that it is caught up with the variety of meanings attached to the term, due to the interpretive baggage that has accumulated around it since 1688. One example of this essential ambiguity can be found in *Love and Death in the American Novel* (1960), in which Leslie Fiedler dismisses Wolfe on the basis of his perceived nostalgia; Fiedler treats the sentiment as evidence that *Look Homeward, Angel* was a "lonely child" dream designed to recapture Wolfe's "lost, unknowable mother." Fiedler's analysis also argues that nostalgia was one of "Gant's protective devices" and that Wolfe's frustrated works ultimately find their place on "the shelf of masturbatory dreams."[53] This dismissal of nostalgia as an unproductive, even pathological, condition was not new in 1960; in an essay that analyzes case studies of nostalgia in nineteenth-century France, Michael Roth suggests that the disappearance of nostalgia as a medical pathology in France led to its almost immediate integration into psychoanalytic discourse. By the end of the nineteenth century, Roth contends, "The nostalgic, like the masochist, wants to protect his or her desire, wants to preserve the longing. Attachment to a lost object usually connects a person to the world because that attachment is the kernel of desire to refind the object. One weaves connections with the world because it offers so many imitations of the desired object. In the case of the nostalgic, however, attachment leads the sufferer to renounce the world as an illusory place made up of mere simulacra of the objects desired."[54]

By the start of the twentieth century, the notion that nostalgia could be a desirable sentiment, as it was for the Romantics, was largely dismissed. This attitude is obvious in contemporary responses to Wolfe's fiction, which only perceived the linguistic dimension of Wolfe's nostalgia, suggesting that the particular effects generated by his prose were achieved by "turning on the tap marked Purple" and, in Bernard DeVoto's scathing critique, through "tidal surges of rhetoric" and "psychic material" that the author did not have the discipline to shape into fiction, evidence of "borderline manic-depressive" behavior with its "classical accompaniment of obsessional neurosis" and "infantile regression."[55] Significantly, Wolfe did not employ the term *nostalgia* with anything like the frequency of words like *lost*, *hunger*, or *long*, and when he does it is almost wholly adjectival, often in relation to smell. In *Of Time and the River*, Eugene encounters the "pungent, haunting, spicy odor that pervades the atmosphere of pantries—a haunting and nostalgic fusion of delicious smells" as well as the "smoky pungency, the half-nostalgic savor of the Austrian ham" and a "faint nostalgic smell of tea."[56] Also invoked are "the citric nostalgia of oranges" and "the acrid and nostalgic fumes of French tobacco," all of which are attributed to Eugene's romantic proclivity to embrace what Wolfe calls the "sensual impact of this strange and fascinating world."[57] More recently, the significance of nostalgia within philosophical, sociological, historical, and literary discourse has been explored by theorists like Boym and Helmut Illbruck, reconfiguring and rehabilitating its interpretive potential.[58] In "You Can't Go Home Again: Re-Constructing Nostalgia in the American Imagination" (2006), for instance, Jennifer Scott argues that the use of nostalgia has become "more philosophical and polemical than clinical; it now carries connotations of political reaction as well as continued traces of pathology," although there nevertheless remains a need to "rediscover its lost transformative potential."[59]

A significant barrier for my own rehabilitation of *nostalgia* is the degree to which the term, along with the project of the "Old South," is inextricably linked to what Jon Smith labels a "Lacanian fantasy space, an antimodern populist world [. . .] overdetermined by symbolic investments in the future or the past," which he argues has been recently revived in scholarship that attempts to "reanimate agrarian melancholy."[60] Rather than relying on the multifarious and loaded meanings captured by these aforementioned terms, *Sehnsucht* provides a helpful alternative: moving away from both nostalgia and homesickness—both of which invariably promote a "U.S.-centric" interpretation of Wolfe's longing. *Sehnsucht* instead points to a more global expression of longing, while also speaking to the important German influence on Wolfe. Although DeVoto, in 1936, reduced Wolfe's wistful longing to infantile regression, across the Atlantic Martin Heidegger was arguing that *Heimweh* (homesickness) was the "fundamental attunement of philosophizing," an extension of the Romantic preoccupation with unsatisfiable longing and what he saw as "coming to be at home in one's own self."[61] Despite the bombast of Wolfe's declamatory prose, his commitment to articulating his characters' inchoate hunger for "coming to be at home" is undeniable, and indeed Heidegger's philosophizing comes with its own concomitant verbosity: linguistic tics that reveal the difficulty of expressing this mode of longing.

Heidegger frequently turned to Friedrich Schelling to articulate this reaching for the-thing-in-itself, particularly his *Philosophical Investigations into the Essence of Human Freedom* (1809), in which Schelling writes: "Since, however, nothing indeed can be outside of God, this contradiction can only be resolved by things having their ground in that which in God himself is not *He Himself*, that is, in that which is the ground of his existence. If we want to bring this way of being closer to us in human terms, we can say: it is the yearning [*Sehnsucht*] the eternal One feels to give birth to itself. The yearning [*Sehnsucht*] is not the One itself but is after all co-eternal with it. The yearning [*Sehnsucht*] wants to give birth to God, that is, unfathomable unity, but in this respect there is not yet unity in the yearning [*Sehnsucht*] itself."[62]

According to Heidegger, this conception of an incomprehensible and eternal God as eternally becoming means that "the being of things" can also only be understood as *becoming*, "since nothing which *is* can be thought as being absolutely outside of God." Schelling's image of "the ground" in God as *Sehnsucht* had enormous appeal for Heidegger, who revised Schelling's conception, wondering: "Is there not contained in longing [*Sehnsucht*] something which we have *no* reason to limit to man. [. . .] Is not longing [*Sehnsucht*] precisely the proof for the fact that man is something other than only a man?"[63]

David L. Clark makes the observation that Heidegger was in thrall to Schelling's expression of *Sehnsucht*, which "hungers for a knowledge about which it knows nothing," pointing out that this "rhetoric of proclivities and searching desires" has an infectious quality, something that pervades Heidegger's own writing on Schelling and marks much of Wolfe's prose.[64] This very quality can be detected in the following passage from Heidegger's *Schelling's Treatise on the Essence of Human Freedom*:

> Addiction is a striving and desiring, indeed, the addiction of longing [*Sehnsucht*], of being concerned with oneself. A double, contrary movement is contained in longing [*Sehnsucht*]: the striving away from itself to spread itself, and yet precisely back to itself. [. . .] In that the general nature of the will lies in desiring, longing [*Sehnsucht*] is a will in which what is striving wills itself in the in-

> determinate, that is, wills to find itself in itself and wills to present itself in the expanded breadth of itself. [. . .] Eternal longing [*Sehnsucht*] is a striving which itself, however, never admits of a stable formation because it always wants to remain longing [*Sehnsucht*]. As a striving without understanding, it has nothing which has been understood and is to be brought to stand and stability, nothing which it could call something definite, unified. It is "nameless"; it does not know any name; it is unable to name what it is striving for. It is lacking the possibility of words.[65]

In his essay "Building, Dwelling, Thinking" (1954), Heidegger builds on this notion of "striving without understanding" by arguing that the ineluctable homesickness (*Heimweh*) of man "consists in man's inability to think still of his *own, true* trouble in finding a place to live, his inability to think of it *as the* difficulty." Heidegger's solution to this ontological quandary, as with Schelling's call to consider *Sehnsucht* even in light of its unknowable object, lies in an individual's own reflections on "his *Heimatlessness*," suggesting that as soon as such reflection begins, "it stops being a misery. It is, thought of correctly and well remembered, the only consolation, which *calls* mortals into living."[66] The *Sehnsucht* that Heidegger identifies is strikingly similar to that developed in Wolfe's own ontology of longing. The frustration felt by Wolfe's protagonists resides in their inability to articulate such "nameless" desires—in Wolfe's parlance to speak what is "unspeakable"—and the novelist's project is precisely the consolation of Heidegger's philosophy of *Heimweh*, constantly reflecting on this nature of being—to "think about his *Heimatlessness*."

What Clark identifies as the addictive nature of this kind of rhetoric for Heidegger is precisely Wolfe's conundrum: dwelling on being lost and homesick—the project of Wolfe's ontology of longing—ultimately leads to an *addiction* to that very form of longing. This contention is central to this book's revision of Wolfe's fiction: it is not sufficient to see the longing of his writing as simple evidence of Romantic excess and waffle—perfectly symbolized by the image of Wolfe's work arriving by crate-load to the offices of Maxwell Perkins—but instead we should see that this longing, or *Sehnsucht*, operates both as the creative impulse behind Wolfe's fiction and the central object of the desires he fictionalizes. Thus, *Sehnsucht* exactly captures the intermingled nature of longing in Wolfe's fiction, which is not simply homesickness, nostalgia, or nihilism but, instead, an addiction to the very act of longing.

According to the *Deutsches Wörterbuch*, the verb *Sehnen* approximates the English "to long" or, more strongly, "to crave," and Jacob and Wilhelm Grimm use a number of quotations from German poets to gesture toward the insatiable nature of the longing.[67] In one example, Schiller's "The Triumph of Love" is cited: "*Sehnend an der Sternenbühne / Suchte die geheime Träne / Keine Götter noch*" (He pin'd not for the stars on high, / With yearning for a Deity / No tears in torrents broke), articulating the object of this longing as infinite or beyond grasp. The noun *Sucht*—which is combined with *Sehnen* to produce *Sehnsucht*—implied "physical illness" in its early usage but most nearly translates as "addiction."[68] *Sucht* entered the English lexicon briefly in the nineteenth century as part of a curious mental disease named *Grübelsucht,* which one psychiatrist described as "the obsession of the mind by an imperative mode of thought, taking the form of perpetual interrogation, a constant urgent morbid impulse to inquire into and investigate everything," or, more simply, as a form of "metaphysical insanity."[69] American philosopher and psychologist William James was also familiar with this term, deploying it in the psychiatric journal *Mind* in his observation that "it would practically be a case of *Grübelsucht,* if a ruffian were assaulting and drubbing my body, to spend much time in subtle speculation."[70] This psychiatric classification of *Sucht* adds an extra element of mania to its definition. *Sehnsucht,* the composite of these two concepts, is thus virtually untranslatable, but its suggestion of both an infinite and inarticulate yearning, as well as a compulsive addiction to the very experience of longing, provides a productive theoretical lens through which to perceive Wolfe's ontology of longing.

Locating this conception of *Sehnsucht* in German literature and noting the seriousness with which *Sehnsucht* is treated by the German philosophical tradition, it is unsurprising that Wolfe excited the interest of writers like Hermann Hesse, who wrote in 1933 that *Look Homeward, Angel* demonstrated the "loneliness and lostness of every man," suggesting that Eugene's "lust for life [. . .] often takes the form of extreme despair" and that he is on a "painful path to sublimation."[71] Indeed, Hesse considered *Look Homeward, Angel* to be "the most powerful piece of fiction from present-day America that I know."[72] *Sehnsucht* was a fundamental concept in the development of German Romantic thought; in *Novalis: Signs of Revolution* (1995), William O'Brien suggests that *Sehnsucht* demonstrated "the failure of signification," incessantly pointing to "an Absolute that hovers right there or right here, always transcendently and tantalizingly out of reach," while for German philosophers of Romanticism—like Schelling, Schlegel, and Novalis—yearning was always tempered by the impossibility of satisfaction.[73] Similarly, John M. Baker identifies the earlier significance of *Sehnsucht* for the understanding of consciousness in German idealism, pointing to Fichte's "typification of consciousness" as a yearning that "feels itself wanting, an activity without object."[74] In his entry on *Sehnsucht* for the *Dictionary of Untranslatables* (2014), Christian Helmreich suggests that *Sehnsucht,* for Fichte, was "a kind of vital principle" for all existence, a desire that can never be quenched and whose object, in Goethe's words, "can only be inaccessible."[75] In "The Musicality of the Past" (2007), Kiene Wurth links *Sehnsucht* to an eighteenth-century occupation with the sublime, pointing out the subsequent Romantic preoccupation with the infinite, and arguing that it performed a "simultaneity of pain and pleasure," unable to transcend the "double-bind that the infinite for which it longs is, so to speak, included in a past that is irrevocably lost."[76]

It is important to note here that though Wolfe never consciously employs *Sehnsucht* as a substitute for "longing" in his fiction, he was familiar with the term; Wolfe included a line in German from Mignon's song *Nur wer die Sehnsucht kennt—Nur wer die Sehnsucht kennt, Weiss was Ich leide* (Only they know my pain who know my yearning)—in *Look Homeward, Angel,* originally from Goethe's *Wilhelm Meisters Lehrjahre* (1795–96).[77] Wolfe's reading and incorporation of Weimar classicism and German Romantic thought in his work, as well as his fictional rendering of Weimar and Nazi Germany through an explicitly Romantic lens, reinforce the value of *Sehnsucht* as an interpretive tool for understanding Wolfe's ontology of longing. Germany looms large in the fiction of Wolfe, and a primary goal of this book is to offer a new perspective on Wolfe's indebtedness and involvement with German thought and culture as well as the more subtle ways in which Wolfe's fiction might shed new light on literary exchange between the United States and Nazi Germany.

It is not simply the German connection that makes the use of the term *Sehnsucht* productive in a discussion of Wolfe: the admixture of inarticulable longing and addiction implied by *Sehnsucht* is familiar to any reader of Wolfe's work. In *The Impossible Mourning of Jacques Derrida* (2006), Sean Gaston suggests that *Sehnsucht* is "a yearning sickness, a longing addiction that *displaces* any present, definite object and always leaves a gap. [. . .] Elusive, mercurial, always beyond one's grasp, *Sehnsucht* describes an *infinite* yearning for the *infinite*."[78] Gaston identifies the term's Romantic heritage, arguing that *Sehnsucht* is integral to Romanticism's central project, its "longing for *something* in the external world that only reveals a *deeper* yearning for a *hidden* internal world." For Gaston, *Sehnsucht* provides both the "genesis" and "structure" of Romantic transcendence, as an expression of both a yearning for "a hidden inner world" and a "longing for something outside" that provides the "possibility" for transcendence. Hence, *Sehnsucht* is at once creative and destructive, a yearning sickness: in Gaston's phrasing it is both a "torment *and* a marvel."[79] In *Musically Sublime: Indeterminacy, Infinity, Irresolvability* (2009), Kiene Wurth defines *Sehnsucht* as the "romantic, catastrophic longing for the infinite that can repeat itself infinitely," characterizing it as "a particular *configuration* of lack and endless movement" that figures prominently in both philosophical discourses of German idealism and German Romanticism. Wurth suggests that *Sehnsucht* describes a space of abject "suspension," the "suffering of a desire that constantly eludes its goal or destination," typified by "a purposeful purposelessness."[80] For the Romantic writer E. T. A. Hoffmann, this purposeful purposelessness, as for Gaston, is inextricably linked with inner torment.

Hoffmann evokes the myth of Tantalus in *The Life and Opinions of the Tomcat Murr* (1820–22) to describe Johannes Kreisler's experience of *Sehnsucht*: "I often feel a wild crazy longing [*Sehnsucht*] for something which I seek outside myself in restless activity, although it is hidden within me, a dark mystery, a confused, baffling dream of a paradise of the utmost contentment which even the dream cannot name, can only divine, and this idea plagues me with the torments of Tantalus."[81]

With its connotations of infinite yearning and torment, romance and addiction, *Sehnsucht* is richly suggestive of the form of longing that Wolfe's fiction regularly expresses. Employing it as a theoretical reference point within this book ultimately provides a new interpretive lens for investigating Wolfe's reception, rejection, and endurance in American literary history, offering a way out of the Appalachian hills. To take just one example of *Sehnsucht* here at the beginning of the book, in *Of Time and the River*, Wolfe describes his vision of Americans as people who "do not know to what [they] can return" and are thus "maddened" by a "smothering and incurable ache" for something they cannot identify:

> In that enchanted spell of time and silence, as men who gaze in visions across misty and illimitable seas, with the terrible homelessness of a man for whom there can never be return, with the terrible homelessness of a man who longs for home and has no home—with the impossible, hopeless, incurable and unutterable homesickness of the American, who is maddened by a longing for return, and does not know to what he can return, whose brain burns night and day with the maddened hope, whose heart aches night and day with the smothering and incurable ache of the houseless, homeless, and forsaken atom of the earth who has no goal or ending for his hunger, no final dwelling-place for his desire—he thought of home.[82]

The "longing for return" within this passage is described as an ache: something incurable, maddening, and ultimately insatiable, but also an emotional state that is fundamental to Wolfe's idea of identity. Those "men who gaze in visions across misty and illimitable seas"—among whom Wolfe always numbers himself—yearn with an "impossible, hopeless, incurable" homesickness that is "unutterable," but it is precisely Wolfe's *utterances*—his own lyric evocation of this ache—that function to imbue the "forsaken atom of the earth" with a purpose for being. Such passages reflect Heidegger's claim—which he discovered via Schelling—that *Sehnsucht* points to the very question of being, to an inarticulable longing for the unknowable that is central to the experience of being human. In "The Birth Pangs of the Absolute" (2010), Bettina Bergo describes *Sehnsucht* as "a restless yearning without an object, an *anxiousness* lying between an embodied sensation of disquiet and an affect that strives toward what it does not yet know."[83] Drawing on what Bergo calls "a horizon of unknowing," my own nuanced reading of *Sehnsucht* offers a valuable perspective for examining Wolfe's insistence that Americans are "lost, o lost" as in being indebted to a profoundly Romantic sentiment, but also as revealing a deeper insistence that humankind is essentially homeless, that *Sehnsucht* is a fundamental expression of being in the world.

It should be stated up front that a discussion which relies on the philosophy of Heidegger and the notion of man's essential homelessness in twentieth-century American culture invariably recalls related concerns of existentialism as well as Heidegger's own problematic legacy. Heidegger's relation to a peculiarly American version of existentialism has been explored in Martin Woessner's *Heidegger in America* (2011), which carefully articulates the need to historicize and contextualize the philosopher who is "destined to exist in a contested place" following his ideological championing of Nazi Germany.[84] Wolfe and Heidegger were strangers to each other's work, and it is their comparable expressions of *Sehnsucht* with which this book is concerned, particularly Heidegger's articulation of the essential value of *Sehnsucht* and Wolfe's Romantic vision of Germany, which became increasingly suspect during the period of National Socialism. While I will avoid conflating Heidegger's Nazism with Wolfe's wavering and complex allegiances, I suggest—particularly in the chapters on Germany—that Wolfe is closest to sympathy with National Socialism when he is most in the thrall of Germany's Romantic myths and heritage.

❖ ❖ ❖

Ultimately, the analysis of Wolfe in relation to *Sehnsucht* circles back to that other central aim of my book: situating Wolfe in light of his earliest critical and popular reception and use. The capacity of Wolfe to render this perceived spiritual malaise of the human soul in such vibrant prose was precisely what drew readers to him, and Wolfe's language of *Sehnsucht*—a lexicon of desire—endured, and endures, as an addictive quality of his work. Chapter 1 of this book focuses on Wolfe's complex reception history; building on Susan Hegeman's contention, in *Patterns for America: Modernism and the Concept of Culture* (1999), that new technologies of modernism in early twentieth-century culture prompted a dramatic reconception of the idea of culture in America, this chapter explores the many ways in which Wolfe's fiction addresses these very concerns and looks to both critical and popular reception histories to interrogate how his work was interpreted in light of this immediate context.[85] In addition, Wolfe's importance to myriad anxieties concerning mass publishing, his estrangement from the lost generation, as well as his earliest overseas reception are also briefly explored within an argument that ultimately positions the author as being at the center of several significant early twentieth-century debates around the idea of a distinct cultural identity.

Chapter 2 examines a particular formulation of the South that operates throughout both Wolfe's fiction and within the strain of criticism that has sought to position Wolfe's work as being emblematic of a distinctly southern literary tradition. This chapter emphasizes Wolfe's part in the modern invention of southern literature, arguing that his work problematizes simple conceptions of southern exceptionalism that rely on Wolfe's apparent homesickness for the Appalachian hills. Instead, Wolfe is positioned as a distinctly global author, reconfiguring his supposedly intractable homesickness for the American South through the lens of *Sehnsucht*, while shifting the terms of Wolfe's yearning from what has traditionally been understood as notions of "home" or "the South" toward an expression that is instead indeterminate and infinite.

Chapter 3 begins the exploration of Wolfe's crucial encounters with German culture, addressing Wolfe's *Sehnsucht* alongside the *Heimat* of the German Romantics, and demonstrating how German literature shaped his perspective on both Weimar and Nazi Germany as well as his own homesickness for America. What I designate as Wolfe's ontology of longing intersects with a discussion of early twentieth-century German philosophical investigations on the nature of *Sehnsucht* in art as well as an analysis of C. S. Lewis's theological understanding of *Sehnsucht* as spiritual longing. Chapter 4 continues this analysis of Wolfe's fiction in light of German literary culture, addressing his German reception as well as his influence on writers like Hermann Hesse and Heinrich Böll. Exploring the specter of German Nazism in Wolfe's work, I reconsider his most ardently anti-Nazi story, "I Have a Thing to Tell You" (1937). Significantly, I diverge from previous interpretations of this story by exploring its unlikely German-language translation during World War II by exiled Jewish novelist Rudolf Frank. These two chapters thus consider Wolfe in light of those "crisscrossing set[s] of pathways" to which Dimock refers, highlighting the fact that perceiving Wolfe's work as fundamentally "American" or "southern" misses this vital transatlantic link. Finally, chapter 5 identifies Wolfe's spectral literary presence, arguing that any dismissal of Wolfe must consider the profound and enduring effect his writing had on authors as diverse as Jack Kerouac and Stephen King. This chapter thus extends the influence of Wolfe into new territory, charting his impact on the works of Australian author Christopher Koch as well as exploring Wolfe's profound influence on the Martian romances of Ray Bradbury.

McGurl's assertion that Wolfe is well on the way to becoming a footnote to American literary history contains some truth, but his prediction is also deeply misleading. Wolfe's literary legacy lives on in increasingly small intellectual pockets, tethered to problematic and sometimes nostalgic interpretive frameworks that inadequately represent Wolfe's place in the history of literature, American or otherwise. The following chapters are not offered as an extended apology for an unfairly slighted author deserving recognition, but as a reappraisal of a writer whose work has profound implications for our understanding of the development of literature in America. My central contention is that Thomas Wolfe should not merely be seen as an overwhelmingly neglected Appalachian novelist but as an important—and fundamentally *global*—figure of American literature.

PART 1 Home

CHAPTER ONE

Unearthing the Buried Life

Wolfe's Readers and the Culture Crisis

Writing to Thomas Wolfe after the publication of *Look Homeward, Angel*, Maxwell Perkins—Wolfe's editor at Scribner's—noted that "if anyone were ever destined to write, that one is you."[1] Perkins's faith in Wolfe's literary gifts has become legendary, and Michael Grandage's film *Genius* (2016)—based on A. Scott Berg's biography *Max Perkins: Editor of Genius* (1978)—commits this relationship to celluloid in the persons of Jude Law (Wolfe) and Colin Firth (Perkins). Supposing that the film precipitates a reinvigorated interest in Wolfe's fiction in the United States, arguments around Wolfe's anonymity may well become moot, but for now it is fair to join the overwhelming number of voices saying that the novelist remains well on the path to obscurity. The purpose of this chapter is not to attempt a resurrection—arguing for the reevaluation of a critically *passé* author solely on the merit of his early fame—but to emphasize that the problems with reading Wolfe, and the causes behind his current obscurity, lie in how he is remembered, not in how he was forgotten. The reasons for Wolfe's critical decline have been well rehearsed by both acolytes and apologists, but what is rarely—if ever—considered is what Wolfe's fiction actually achieved within his lifetime and how his work fits within the broader cultural history of the Depression era.[2] With an oeuvre saturated with meditations on the impossibility of ever recapturing the past—"O lost, and by the wind grieved, ghost, come back again"[3]—it is highly curious that almost all the recently printed work on Wolfe has been reprints, unexpurgated editions, reissues of old critical studies, and biographical works, all of which stand testament to the resuscitating impulse animating Wolfe scholarship.[4] In this chapter, Wolfe's relevance within his historical moment will be comprehensively explored, with a particular focus on both the publication of his first novel, *Look Homeward, Angel* (1929), within the broader context of modernism's technological impact on publishing as well as his fiction's role in moving discussions of culture into the homes (and hands) of the American population. Taking its lead from McGurl's suggestion that a book can be seen as an "experiential commodity whose value to its readers is a transvaluation of the authorial labor that went into its making," this chapter situates Wolfe's work within an emerging culture market, arguing, *pace* McGurl, that the value of these novels "most often has little to do with the economic value of the pulp upon which it is pressed."[5] Wolfe's reception is also investigated, not only in terms of his perceived critical significance at the time, but also in light of his popular reception. Literary critics are often guilty of subordinating popular responses to novels in favor of reviews that appear in journals and newspapers—particularly when articulating an author's critical importance—but letters from fans frequently express something of the significance that contemporary readers attached to fiction, providing an invaluable glimpse into how fiction was actually read. Such unsolicited responses to *Look Homeward, Angel* describe the profound and even transcendent experiences that the novel provided for a young generation of readers.

# # #

For early readers and reviewers of *Look Homeward, Angel,* Wolfe's future decline into mere "footnote" status would have been unthinkable. After a modest initial print run of 5,540 copies, enthusiastic reviews prompted Scribner's to order a second printing of 3,000 copies, only two weeks after *Look Homeward, Angel*'s release.[6] Within just six months the hefty, 626-page *Look Homeward, Angel* had gone through five printings and 12,000 copies. These sales figures were relatively modest in comparison to those of Scribner's star author Ernest Hemingway, whose *A Farewell to Arms* (1929)—released in autumn of the same year—had "promptly sold 20,000 copies."[7] But the popularity of *A Farewell to Arms* ultimately highlights the sensation of Wolfe's maiden novel. Hemingway was already an established short-story writer, riding a wave of popular and critical success after the publication of his novel *The Sun Also Rises* (1926), while *A Farewell to Arms* had already been serialized in *Scribner's Magazine,* a literary periodical that represented a readership of 30,000.[8] Not only was a novel about the disillusionment of war perfectly situated to become a best seller—that same year Remarque's *All Quiet on the Western Front* (1929) sold 305,000 copies in its American edition—but Hemingway was also the epitome of the literary celebrity, whom the public, as Dorothy Parker noted in her *New Yorker* profile of the author, "want[ed] to hear things about [. . .] it is hard not to tell spectacular things."[9] Thomas Wolfe, on the other hand, was a comparatively unknown author who had penned something amounting to the antithesis of a Hemingway work, a deeply romantic and autobiographical novel described variously by reviewers as "a book of great drive and vigor,"[10] an "extraordinarily lavish"[11] work full of "monstrous torrential joy."[12] *Look Homeward, Angel* was, as Margaret Wallace begins in her *New York Times* review, "a novel of the sort one is too seldom privileged to welcome."[13] Andrew Turnbull, in his biography *Thomas Wolfe* (1967), reports that James Boyd, another Scribner's author, had written to Maxwell Perkins about Wolfe saying: "I have an uneasy feeling that the little fellows had better move over for this bird. But whether I mean the little fellows on Parnassus or on Blackwell's Island I don't yet know. I only know somebody's got to move. And on personal grounds there's no writer I'd rather move over or down for myself."[14]

One month after *Look Homeward, Angel* was published, the poet Kenneth Fearing reviewed Wolfe's novel in the *New York Evening Post*, reiterating Wallace's claim that it was the novel's originality and lack of precedent that constituted its immediate appeal: "For any variation in the few elementary patterns from which the majority of contemporary novels are cut, there is apt to be stirred in the reader [. . .] a feeling of either gratitude or annoyance. [. . .] 'Look Homeward, Angel' is such a performance."[15] This variation from the "elementary patterns" had initially proven problematic for Wolfe; the manuscript from which it was constructed, "O Lost," had already been rejected by three prior publishing houses (Boni and Liveright; Little, Brown; and Longmans, Green) before eventually finding its way into the offices of Charles Scribner's Sons.[16] The idiosyncrasy of Wolfe's work—its sprawling reach and size, the extraordinary exuberance of language, and the absence of an obvious precedent to a late 1920s reading public—swiftly became the central conceit behind *Look Homeward, Angel*'s marketing. Within just three months of its release, the *New York Times* ran one of many advertisements (figure 1) that contained this sensationalized retelling of the arrival of Wolfe's manuscript on the desk of Maxwell Perkins, his editor at Charles Scribner's Sons: "A year ago there came to Charles Scribner's Sons a bulky manuscript almost two feet high, more than a thousand closely type-written pages, ragged, weather-beaten, and showing signs that it had 'gone the rounds.' It was the first novel of a young Southerner whose identity and whereabouts were unknown. His written plea that his novel be given a hearing was a masterpiece in itself and as the readers, at first skeptical, turned over page after page of the story they became more and more sure that here was a great novel, a living, beautiful creation."[17]

After establishing the requisite mystery—a book without an author, a young novelist with the promise of genius—the advertisement emphasized the extraordinary nature of *Look Homeward, Angel*, heralding it as "a first novel by an unknown writer—at a time when every day brought the announcement of new books by popular American and English authors" and noting that any "*ordinary* novel" would have "dropped out of sight unnoticed."[18] Important too was Wolfe's "southern" designation: as Sarah Gardner has recently pointed out, the expanding book industry during the 1920s "manufactured and catered to a reading public hungry for literature about the exotic," and the South was in vogue.[19] Moreover, Gardner notes, literary reviews were voraciously read: "Just as influential as the writers, in the minds of the readers, were the national book

Look Homeward, Angel

THOMAS WOLFE
Author of
Look
Homeward,
Angel
© Doris Ulmann

A year ago there came to Charles Scribner's Sons a bulky manuscript almost two feet high, more than a thousand closely typewritten pages, ragged, weather-beaten, and showing the signs that it had "gone the rounds." It was the first novel of a young Southerner whose identity and whereabouts were unknown. His written plea that his novel be given a hearing was a masterpiece in itself and as the readers, at first sceptical, turned over page after page of the story they became more and more sure that here was a great novel, a living, beautiful creation. The most diverse tastes found in it rich and rare enjoyment. It had the richness and strangeness of the texture of life—its sin and terror, lust and cruelty, its health, sanity, and joy.

The news that his novel had been accepted reached the author in Vienna and a few months later he came to New York and started the editing that finally brought to its present form

Look Homeward, Angel

by Thomas Wolfe

The book was published on October 18, 1929—a first novel by an unknown writer—at a time when every day brought the announcement of new books by popular American and English authors. An ordinary novel would have dropped out of sight unnoticed. But here was the exception. Purposely announced without extravagant praise, this story of a Southern family became overnight the talk of literary New York. A feature review in the *New York Times* called it "as interesting and powerful a book as has ever been made out of the drab circumstances of American provincial life," and prophesied that "the final decision upon it, in all probability, rests with another generation than ours." Within ten days a first printing twice as large as that of the average first novel was completely exhausted and a second was necessary. Praise from individuals and from reviews poured in from every side.

In the South, the scene of the novel, the *Richmond Times-Dispatch*, said: " 'Look Homeward, Angel' has the good, rich, buoyant health of those roaring Elizabethan tales of Nash and Greene. It breathes the vigor of youth, bawdy, profane, soaring, depressed—but alive and real and full of meaning." John Chamberlain in *The Bookman* called it "a rich, positive grappling with life, a remembrance of things past untinged by the shadow of regret, of one who had found his youthful experiences full of savor. No more sensuous novel . . . has been written in the United States." A third big printing showed that the book had made its way into the heart of the reading public. During December it was one of the novels most frequently asked for at the leading bookstores, and the early days of the New Year bring reports of its continuing success.

The reason for this success is simple. "Look Homeward, Angel" has the humor, the sadness, the bright and dark sides of life itself. In the amazing Gant family and the myriad other characters of the book every reader will find a bit of his own existence. "It comes through to you like fumes or like one supreme mood of courage that you can never forget and with it is all the awe, the defilement, and grandeur of actual life," wrote Margery Latimer in the *New York Herald-Tribune*. "If I could create now one magic word that would make every one want to read the book I would write it down and be utterly satisfied."

When you read "Look Homeward, Angel" you know that it is not a book for to-day alone, but one that, as critical opinion has already stated, will stand for generations. The universality of its appeal, the magnificent breadth of its canvas, and the writer's opulent handling of his theme make it a novel for every reader.

Look Homeward, Angel

Third Printing *at all bookstores* 626 pages. $2.50

Charles Scribner's Sons **New York**

FIGURE 1. Display Ad 166, "Look Homeward, Angel," *New York Times*, January 12, 1930, 71.

reviewers who wrote for the intellectual weeklies, the Sunday book supplements, and the New York dailies."[20] Another advertisement, this time in Scribner's spring 1930 catalog, paid somewhat ironic tribute to Wolfe's success despite an absence of promotion: "This amazing book was published on October 18th, 1929, at the very height of the season, when books by famous 'names' were pouring from the presses in numbers sufficient to swamp the average first novel. But here was an exception. Without special promotion, it became overnight the talk of literary New York."[21] Following any such advertisement was always the mandatory list of favorable reviews—from the *New York Times*, the *Bookman*, the *New York Herald Tribune*, and the *New Republic*, among others—reinforcing *Look Homeward, Angel* as the publishing curiosity in autumn 1929 and as a critical success within trendsetting, "literary New York." Here, the critics and advertisers emphatically declared, was something new.

A Prophet in His Hometown

While *Look Homeward, Angel* continued to receive praise and esteem from readers across America, the press and public in Wolfe's hometown of Asheville, North Carolina, were having a dramatically different reaction to the novel. The autobiographical element that other reviewers had viewed as operating within a particular generic convention, or as a means of creative expression (aided by Wolfe's own admission at the beginning of the novel that "all serious work in fiction is autobiographical"),[22] was seen in Asheville as constituting a veritable *roman à clef*. Here was a story that had readily identifiable residents of Asheville scattered through its many pages, and the scandal this caused would deeply impact Wolfe and force him to delay returning home for many years. Writing in Wolfe's hometown newspaper, the *Asheville Citizen*, Walter Adams suggested both that "the book is written about Asheville and Asheville people in the plainest of plain language" and that "virtually all the characters are residents of this city."[23] According to Adams, Wolfe's feeble attempt to characterize all fiction as autobiography was merely an example of "clever twists of phrases," predicting that Asheville readers would soon discover for themselves the "intrinsic proof" indicating that *Look Homeward, Angel* was only a step away from reportage. Wolfe was thus recast as a scandal peddler; within the pages of his novel all the subterranean gossip of the small town was "dragged forth into the light," while those weaknesses of character that "more tolerant friends are considerate enough to overlook" were described in such a way as to suggest "the distinguishing characteristics of the persons."[24] Adams predicted that "the novel will be acclaimed to literary critics as a work of real distinction" but that Asheville citizens would be drawn to it because "it is the story told with bitterness and without compassion of many Asheville people." Indeed, within days, Asheville's bookstores were begging Scribner's to send more copies, and the novel was passed between residents eager to identify those characters who lived in their town.

This fabulous scene of townspeople walking head-down, noses in books, only peeking up to offer a wry smile or sneak a suspicious look at a neighbor, is surely unprecedented in modern American literary history. However overdrawn some stories of the reaction by Asheville residents might seem (Donald has one resident begging: "Do not let any influence persuade you to let his buckets of night soil sit on your shelves," while Andrew Turnbull notes the anonymous letters to Wolfe beginning, "Sir: You are a son-of-a-bitch"),[25] it is undeniable that *Look Homeward, Angel* was a sensation in Wolfe's hometown for all the wrong reasons. What is rarely, if ever, noted is that this violent initial reaction to the autobiographical nature of Wolfe's fiction was merely the most extreme form of a criticism now taken for granted; Wolfe, it is said *ad infinitum,* was unable to fashion a fictional world out of anything but his own self. McGurl points out that "As an apostle of 'self-expression,' Thomas Wolfe can be understood to have privileged the value of personal experience above all else, but the cluster of values surrounding 'creativity' was important, too: while he showed little interest in the act of fictionalizing—making things up—authorized by the rhetoric of creativity, the sense of cognitive self-sovereignty it carries in train was central to his sense of his own genius, and made even ordinary events in his life seem like emanations of an autochthonous artistic design."[26] In a letter to his mother dated November 6, 1929, Wolfe complained that the local reception represented "no way to read a book" and that "none of the reviewers in New York, or any where else besides Asheville" had mentioned anything about a "local angle."[27] Wolfe went on to explain that the very first page of his novel details that "we are born alone—all of us who ever lived or will live—that we live alone, and die alone, and that we are strangers to one another," a passage that, as Wolfe points out, "is not written about people in Asheville—it is written about people everywhere."[28] For McGurl, Wolfe's insistence in writing "what he knew" anticipates, to some degree, the explosion in output from the various creative writing programs that have enshrined that particular mantra of the creative process.[29]

Turning to the Book

Wolfe's novel arrived at a time in American history in which the very idea of culture—particularly a distinctly "American" culture—was being heavily contested, and when the technological organs of modernism—radio and print in particular—were enabling an unprecedented number of people to engage in these very debates. Writing in the year following the publication of *Look Homeward, Angel,* the American philosopher John Dewey suggested there had never been "a more lively and more widespread interest in ideas, in critical discussion, in all that forms an intellectual life, than ever before."[30] In *Patterns for America* (1993), Hegeman explains that in the early part of the twentieth century, America had seen the development and broad dissemination of the idea of culture, a term that emerged and was "elaborated upon in a diversity of interesting sites" during this period.[31] Culture and technology enjoyed both a reciprocal and problematic relationship in the early twentieth century. As advances in radio, print, and film ensured that ideas could be transmitted beyond the elite forums from which they emerged, anxieties surrounding the idea of "mass culture" encouraged an increasing number of groups and individuals to develop and defend their own ideas of an American culture. Warren I. Susman has argued that 1930s America saw the idea of culture "domesticated," and the history of Wolfe's writing overlaps with the beginning of a truly mass dissemination of the idea of culture in American homes.[32]

The novel was a crucial site in which the cultural idea was elaborated, inextricably linked as it was with the rising interest in culture and the development of mass printing technology. The idea of the "Great American Novel"—the search for which John William DeForest had famously initiated in the previous century—gained traction during this period of cultural debate, while for many people, particularly those looking for "the picture of the ordinary emotions and manners of American existence," they needed to look no further than Thomas Wolfe.[33] In a more stagnant publishing atmosphere with fewer headlining novels—an atmosphere that might have been reasonably expected after a financial crisis—the extent of Wolfe's popularity could be interpreted simply as a bright star in a dull literary environment. Indeed, writing on June 3, 1930, Maxwell Perkins admitted to Wolfe that he was glad that he "worked hard [. . .] to get out 'Look Homeward, Angel' before this collapse came."[34] But Perkins's anxiety was ultimately misplaced; in December 1929, only two months after the crash, the *Chicago Daily Tribune* ran a report suggesting that the state of the novel industry was anything but stagnant: "A few years ago any book that achieved a sale of one hundred thousand in one year was the talk of the town. [. . .] Doesn't it surprise you that *fifteen books* have sold over a hundred thousand copies this year?"[35] Though startling in retrospect, the success and desirability of books in the year of the Great Depression was taken for granted by the *New York Times*, which had run a feature-length article only three weeks before on "Books and Yet More Books for the Christmas Buyer," declaring: "Those who came out of the recent stock market debacle with sufficient cash to admit that Christmas implies more than the filling of a stocking with striped candy and animal crackers will, of course, turn to the book."[36] The popularity of the novel, even in the aftermath of an economic downturn, testifies to the cultural dominance of an art form that was in its heyday in the years following World War I. According to Christopher Wilson, from the turn of the century, professional authors—"social novelists, muckraking magazine writers and newspaper reporters"—achieved a "widely recognized place in American social and even political life."[37] Even in the midst of an economic crisis, books were still reliably bought and sold.

When considering the sheer number of books sold during this period as reported by the *Chicago Daily Tribune*, it is important to recognize the role that book clubs played in ensuring such a wide readership: nine out of the fifteen books that the *Tribune* reported as selling over one hundred thousand copies reached this sales figure as a direct result of book club choices.[38] Mail-order book clubs emerged during the 1920s as a solution to the problems of distribution for American trade publishers, and they were spectacularly successful. The two earliest American clubs, the Book-of-the-Month Club (founded in 1926) and the Literary Guild (founded later that same year), understood that the U.S. Postal Service could be adapted for literary dissemination; BOMC founder Harry Scherman identified the market potential of post offices, which at the time outnumbered traditional book outlets ten to one.[39] Particularly in their early years of operation, such clubs were panned by critics who bemoaned what they saw as their crass commercialism; *Time* magazine reported in 1946 that Harry Scherman had discovered the "ever-new old fact that Americans like to have culture sold to them."[40] For a novel like *Look Homeward, Angel*, the commercial success earned through such populist recognition would have been met with critical suspicion, and it is telling that in Geoffrey Hellmann's 1929 review of *Look Homeward, Angel* in the modernist magazine the *New Republic*, Hellmann approvingly emphasized the absence of any such affiliation with Wolfe's novel: "Unheralded, 'Look Homeward, Angel' will hardly remain unsung. Stamped with the approval of no book-of-the-moment club, lacking even the customary blurb-writer's accolade, it is an extraordinarily fine novel, not to be mentioned in the same breath with all the forgotten blue-ribbon winners of the past few years."[41]

The publishing history of *Look Homeward, Angel* intersects with the emergence of some of the new innovations in the mass circulation of literature ushered in during the twentieth century. Investigating this history reveals how Wolfe's maiden novel—and American fiction more broadly—participated in the domesticating process of culture, both in America and across the Atlantic. The rapid process of cultural exchange saw William Heinemann publish a UK edition of *Look Homeward, Angel* within nine months of its U.S. release, trimming some sections to correspond to the publisher's expectations of the British reading public.[42] By 1932, the first foreign edition, in German, had appeared, and in 1934 the Modern Library released an inexpensive Modern Library Giants edition (figure 2).[43] This reprint of *Look Homeward, Angel* is especially significant given the growing cultural importance of mass-publishing ventures like the Modern Library after World War I. Jay Satterfield, in *The World's Best Books: Taste, Culture, and the Modern Library* (2002), argues convincingly that

FIGURE 2. Thomas Wolfe, *Look Homeward, Angel* (New York: Modern Library, 1934). Photo courtesy of the Wilson Library, University of North Carolina at Chapel Hill.

the Modern Library symbolized the confluence of this growing sense of culture and the birth of mass-market dissemination in America during the 1930s. The appeal of the novel in this period is exemplified in the success of the Modern Library, which managed, in the deepening depression of 1930 alone, to sell over one million books.[44] Unlike the Book-of-the-Month-style clubs, which suffered from what Pierre Bourdieu has called a lack of "symbolic capital" due to their material success as "heteronomous cultural producers," the Modern Library provided an important bridge between the growing mass cultural market while still retaining an aura of "high" literary culture.[45] Lauded as "an invaluable cultural enterprise," it was avidly read by intellectuals, while writers themselves "feverishly desired to be a part" of it.[46] When Sherwood Anderson's *Poor White* was republished by the Modern Library in 1926, for instance, he remarked that it felt "a little like a countryman going to live in a great modern sophisticated city."[47] In a letter to his mother, Wolfe recounts his editor's reasoning behind Scribner's authorization of the Modern Library Giants reprint:

> Perkins thought it was a wise move to make for several reasons. First, because the *Modern Library* is a collection of famous works of famous writers, and he thinks the prestige of having the book printed in this series will be valuable. Also, although the royalty is much smaller, the chance of having a considerable

> sale now is much greater in this low priced edition. Another thing that should help us is that the people who buy the *Modern Library* books are likely to be people of higher intelligence and education than the average reading public, and Perkins feels this will be a very valuable audience to have.[48]

Over the course of the next decade or so, this edition of *Look Homeward, Angel* would sell over one hundred thousand copies.[49]

Wolfe's Popular Reception

While critics were debating the authors to which Wolfe could be compared—Melville, Whitman, and Joyce were popular contenders—the reading public was responding to Wolfe's novel as a quasi-religious revelation. When Leo Gurko wrote his social and literary account of the long 1930s in *The Angry Decade* (1947), he described the release of *Look Homeward, Angel* as "the nearest thing to a literary thunderbolt in the twentieth century," a pronouncement that seems all the more superlative in light of Wolfe's recent obscurity.[50] But Gurko's claim finds support in the popular response to Wolfe's novel: hundreds of letters from the general public—housed predominantly in the William B. Wisdom collection at the Houghton Library—contain statements reinforcing the claim that Wolfe was a veritable cultural prophet. In a letter dated January 29, 1934, one fan declares that her missives were "little prayers of thanksgiving to a living god," a sentiment of reverent praise that is representative of many letters Wolfe received.[51] One reader gushed that *Look Homeward, Angel* had gone "deeper than anything I know" in explaining the "pitiful sordidness and confusion, the beauty and ugliness of our muddled, mysterious lives."[52] Wolfe's prophetic status is regularly invoked: one fan described *Look Homeward, Angel* as the "greatest sermon that has been delivered since the Sermon on the Mount," while another adds, "I must tell you how I love *Look Homeward, Angel,* and of how much it has meant to me. I read it almost every day, pick it up and open it and read, just as I do the Bible."[53] For one particularly devoted couple, Wolfe's fiction even stood in the place of a regular dialogue, with the letter writer claiming that "tho' [we] couldn't speak [we] shared everything," and that Wolfe's books "said it for us—we used to think 'this is how I feel' or 'this is how we feel.'"[54]

In her essay "Main Street Reading *Main Street*" (2008), Amy Blair offers a caution in reading fan mail about books "everyone is talking about," noting the complicated slippages that occur between the private response and public disclosure: "even the most self-revelatory fan letter was, at least partially, a performance of reader reception."[55] Beyond mere adulation, such letters contain important insights into how Wolfe's fiction was initially read—or indeed how readers wanted Wolfe to perceive their reading—particularly in terms of a younger generation of readers. Eleanor Bodkin, a twenty-three-year-old New

York native, wrote that in light of contemporary novels that were "packed with hardness and unimagination," Wolfe's book was "a rare and broadening experience," offering herself as a "humble worshipper at the shrine of beauty."[56] Speaking on behalf of an entire generation, a Mexican reader of *Look Homeward, Angel* emphatically asserted that "the hunger of Eugene Gant is the eternal hunger of all of us who are still young."[57] Another letter from Nancy Tubiash—a reader for a Boston publisher—made a similar claim: "Dear Mr. Wolfe, to say that *Look Homeward, Angel* is the greatest book written since 1900 is not enough. To me it is more important that your book represents the present generation—the quintessence of the men and women in their early twenties. It speaks to us and of us and finds a profound and swelling echo within us. To me, *Look Homeward, Angel* means so much, that I'm frankly afraid to read *Of Time and the River*. [. . .] I don't dare to suppose that it will be to me what the first was, but I am looking forward to it as to something approximating a religious rite."[58]

This "quintessence" of youth is one of the most enduring claims made about Wolfe's work: namely, that it appeals to readers when they are young, then readers later discard it once they have reached an appropriate level of maturity and sophistication. For Doris Lessing, returning to Wolfe was less like reading about adolescence than a "re-experience [of] adolescence," suggesting that his gift lay in writing from within that youthful generation.[59] No writer and acolyte of Wolfe represents this youthful obsession more clearly than Jack Kerouac, whose *On the Road* (1957) would inspire a subsequent generation of young readers, enthralled as they were by Kerouac's unrelenting road trip across the American continent. While Kerouac never wrote fan mail to Wolfe such as those letters discussed above, his journals and letters similarly testify to the profound impact that Wolfe's novels had on him: a member of the generation of readers Wolfe first influenced. In a 1940 entry from his journal, Kerouac suggested an extraordinarily close correspondence between himself and Wolfe: "Thomas Wolfe lived and died. He is said to be one of [the] greatest writers. His different ideas are strikingly correspondent with mine. (Often, I foresee the next paragraph.) My mind, I think, is a small prototype of his. He found out; I shall benefit by his experience. He is my God (I shall use his philosophy)."[60]

The degree of Wolfe's impact on Kerouac is emblematic of the effect Wolfe's writing had on an entire generation of young writers—including Heinrich Böll, Ray Bradbury, Walker Percy, William Styron, Kurt Vonnegut, and Jessamyn West, among others—imbuing their work with a deep romanticism, while at the same time lingering as an embodiment of the youthful excess that such writers saw themselves as having cast off. While the extent of Wolfe's influence will be primarily explored in the final chapter of this book, it is worth lingering here on Kerouac, whose relationship with Wolfe seems prototypical of the familiar pattern of obsession and disavowal. For Kerouac, the shift in attitude from perceiving Wolfe as his "God" to something of an odious influence can be observed in his early work prior to the publication of *On the Road*. In 1949, while studying under Elbert Lenrow at Columbia, Kerouac failed to sit his English exam (being busy, it would later emerge, driving across the continent with Neal Cassady) and was instead asked to submit an essay on a topic of his choice. Kerouac's subsequent essay, "The Minimization of Thomas Wolfe in His Own Time," reveals his dedication to Wolfe as a writer of greatness, providing a picture of two emerging schools of criticism—Marxism and New Criticism—and their joint dismissal of Wolfe following World War II. Kerouac points out that the former school of criticism contends that "a work of art is only valuable insofar as it reflects the struggles of men to achieve material advantages," while the latter, with its "High Priest mood to over-emphasize the fashion of language, style, surface artfulness," had buried Wolfe in "an avalanche of critical disapproval."[61] For Kerouac himself, however, Wolfe was a literary mystic, wrestling with far more fundamental questions: "Concerned with the final human matters, as of God, and 'Dark time' in the midst of the hagglings of an intelligentsia that had never been as superficial as in the Twenties, and perhaps so in the Thirties from sheer desperate exhaustion, Wolfe was a Classicist writing in a Romanticist letter in a naturalistic atmosphere—a position of extreme loneliness in any case."[62]

In another essay from 1942, Kerouac argued that Wolfe's success lay in his work's essential vivacity: "It is a glorious panoply of movement, flashing fiery movement, the organic network of life weaving in and out of page after page, the whole consunmate [*sic*] fretting and jellying and writhing of Life."[63] It is difficult not to see a form of self-defense in Kerouac's devotion to Wolfe, partial as he was to the "wonder" present in books like *Look Homeward, Angel*, which he wrote "appears unblushingly in unblushing prose and gives itself no other name."[64] This project of weaving the "network of life" into narrative form informed Kerouac's own writing, while his first novel, *The Town and the City* (1950)—a name wholly reminiscent of a Wolfe title—was received by some critics as a Wolfean novel, with Douglas Brinkley pointing out that many critics of the time remarked that "Kerouac's talent was unoriginal and that he owed Wolfe a tremendous literary debt."[65] In *On the Road*, Kerouac was visibly trying to shake the influence of Wolfe, going so far as to have Carlo (Allen Ginsberg's fictional proxy) reproach Sal Paradise (Kerouac): "You're talking absolute bullshit and Wolfean romantic posh!"[66] In a 1968 interview, Kerouac—now far more famous than Wolfe—conceded that Wolfe's work had constituted "a torrent of American heaven and hell that opened my eyes to America as a subject in itself."[67] But despite his attempts at unshackling himself from Wolfe's influence, even in Kerouac's most famous passage on the "mad ones"—now regularly emblazoned on mugs and T-shirts—there is a clear distillation and echo of Wolfe's own philosophy in his description of the "ruined people": "The ruined people that we like are those who desperately have died, and lost their lives because they loved life dearly, and had that grandeur that makes such people spend prodigally the thing they love the best, and risk and lose their lives because life is so precious to them, and die at length because the seeds of life are in them. It is only the people that love life who die in this way—and these are the ruined people that we like."[68]

While Kerouac is one of the most prominent authors who demonstrate such a clear indebtedness to Wolfe's work, his voice is only one among a myriad of other literary voices that are discussed in the subsequent chapters of this book, revealing the extent to which Wolfe's literary legacy continues to endure.

The Provincial Novelist

Beyond a portrait of youthfulness in revolt—a point of praise that deteriorated into a criticism of naïveté in the years following Wolfe's death—*Look Homeward, Angel* also provided readers from small towns a familiar rendering of life, treated with a degree of philosophical and aesthetic seriousness that was thrilling. This provincial turn aligns the novel with an important trend in the growth of modern American literature at the beginning of the twentieth century. Sherwood Anderson published *Winesburg, Ohio* in 1919, a collection that cast an enormous shadow over the younger generation of American writers. According to Malcolm Bradbury, Anderson's book was a synthesis of what would become fundamental attributes of American fiction in the 1920s: it dealt with "an essential theme—the breaking free of the limitations of American small-town life and values—in an essential manner—a psychological and inward awareness of human need—with what was to become an essential technique—the method of prose symbolism."[69] In a letter to Anderson, Wolfe claimed that he had not been influenced by the older writer's work, but he enthusiastically positioned Anderson as "one of the most important writers of this country [. . .] you plowed another deep furrow in the American earth, revealed to us another beauty that we knew was there but that no one else had spoken."[70]

In spite of Wolfe's denial, Anderson's influence was apparent in the way *Look Homeward, Angel* was received, particularly in the vindication of the "beauty and ugliness" beneath the surface of America that Wolfe had credited Anderson with uncovering. Perhaps Anderson's most important gift to Wolfe was the suggestion of the universal within the particular, the belief that beauty could be located beneath the finicky, provincial ugliness of a small town. In a passage from *Look Homeward, Angel*, the balance of beauty and ugliness is illuminated by two competing light sources—a dim artificial light and moonlight: "He did not turn on the light, because he disliked seeing the raw blistered varnish of the dresser and the bent white iron of the bed. It sagged, and the light was dim—he hated dim lights, and the large moths, flapping blindly around on their dusty wings. He undressed in the moon. The moonlight fell upon the earth like a magic unearthly dawn. It wiped away all rawness, it hid all sores. It gave all common and familiar things—the sagging drift of the barn, the raw shed of the creamery, the rich curve of the lawyer's crab-apple trees—a uniform bloom of wonder."[71]

Here, Eugene's preference for moonlight matches Wolfe's own developing aesthetic ideal. The dim light of realism reveals blistering varnish and the sagging realities of Eugene's dilapidated home. But moonlight clothes the earth in wonder and invests the scene with a palpable *Sehnsucht.* At the end of the passage, Eugene falls asleep exultant in this new light, and the yearning sickness of *Sehnsucht*—whose object is always present and always beyond grasp—is present in the music of rustling leaves, the "distant elfin minstrelsy" of a rooster, and the specter of a dog's ghost howling.

This picture of small-town life, and the revolt against it, was also the focus of America's most critically successful novelist at the time, Sinclair Lewis. In many ways, Lewis's reputation has followed the same trajectory as Wolfe's: both authors are now rarely read and rarely taught.[72] However, from 1920 to 1930—after the publication of the immensely successful *Main Street* (1920)—Lewis found himself, in the words of James Hutchisson, "not only an overnight celebrity but also a national spokesman for a disillusioned postwar world."[73] And Lewis's success was not merely an economic one; his novel *Arrowsmith* (1925), described by a young Bernard DeVoto as "the most American novel of the generation [. . .] to endure with a few other great novels of America,"[74] won Lewis the Pulitzer Prize (which he famously refused), and in 1930 he became the first American to win the Nobel Prize in Literature. This latter achievement, according to Lewis's biographer Mark Schorer, was important "not merely in its putting American literature on a par with any other literature in the world" but also because it acknowledged that America was "a power that twenty years before it had not been, and that, until now, Europe had been reluctant to concede that it was."[75] In December 1930, Schorer suggests, "Sinclair Lewis was bigger than America knew."

Lewis's satirical renderings of the Midwest, most notably in *Main Street* (1920) and *Babbitt* (1922), were sociological explorations of an America beset by materialism, a world power still startlingly provincial. In his 1930 Nobel lecture, "The American Fear of Literature," Lewis spoke of an America that had "gone through the revolutionary change from rustic colony to world empire without having in the least altered the bucolic and Puritanic simplicity of Uncle Sam."[76] Lewis took the opportunity afforded him by the Nobel Prize to act as a spokesman of American authors, and in particular to decry the atrophied traditionalism of American academics, epitomized by the American Academy of Arts and Letters, writing: "Our American professors like their literature clear and cold and pure and very dead." As with Anderson, Lewis had been quick to praise the emerging talent of Thomas Wolfe, and when he looked at the current generation of unacknowledged authors in "American Fear," he singled out Thomas Wolfe as "a Gargantuan creature with great gusto of life" whose novel *Look Homeward, Angel* was "worthy to be compared with the *best* in our literary production."[77] In Wolfe's posthumous novel, *You Can't Go Home Again* (1940), he records a fictionalized version of the event, acknowledging the significance of Lewis's public recognition: "He was, of course, one of the chief figures in American letters, and now, at the zenith of his career, when he had won the greatest ovation one could win, he had seized the occasion, which most men would have employed for purposes of self-congratulation, to praise enthusiastically the work of an obscure young writer who was a total stranger to him and who had only written one book. [. . .] He had hailed the younger man as a future spokesman of his country's spirit, an evidence of a fruition that had come, of a continent that had been discovered."[78]

The implication of this acknowledgment was not merely the start of a new friendship between Lewis and Wolfe. When the papers reported the most significant literary event for America in 1930, they named Thomas Wolfe as the writer to watch.[79] Malcolm Cowley characterizes this period of American writing as a "diastolic period that admired breadth, observation, and social purpose," suggesting that Wolfe, though not nearly as penetrating an observer of society as Lewis, had managed to imbue the "rustic colony" with life.[80] In their book *What Is Philosophy?* (1991), Gilles Deleuze and Félix Guattari identify the novel form as having this peculiar capacity for imbuing apparently mediocre people with "greatness," finding an especially compelling example in Wolfe: "Whether mediocre or grandiose, they are too alive to be livable or lived. Thomas Wolfe extracts a giant from his father. [. . .] Wolfe may describe the people of old Catawba through their stupid opinions and their mania for discussion, but what he does is set up the secret monument of their solitude, their desert, their eternal earth, and their forgotten, unnoticed lives."[81]

At the beginning of the 1930s, Wolfe was one of the great young hopes of American literature, a writer whom Sinclair Lewis believed had the potential "to be the greatest American writer."[82] The American writer William Saroyan reinforced this view in a 1935 letter to Wolfe, in which he wrote: "I think your work more than the work of any other American is going to make the people of this continent aware of themselves. I think your work is going to influence the lives of Americans a hundred years from now."[83]

British Reception

Across the Atlantic and Pacific, by 1930, English-speaking readers had begun to respond to this unusual book and its enigmatic author, with the release of the Heinemann edition on July 14, 1930. On August 24, 1930, the *New York Times* reported that "Thomas Wolfe's first novel has received an unusual reception in England. [. . .] According to reports, 1,000 copies are being sold every four days."[84] Wolfe expressed delight at these figures in a letter to Maxwell Perkins, though his greatest pleasure was derived from a review by Richard Aldington, which he claimed "made me dizzy."[85] Aldington, a World War I poet who had published his first novel, *Death of a Hero*, in the same year as *Look Homeward, Angel*, reviewed Wolfe's first novel for the *Sunday Referee* in anticipation of its UK release. Aldington's praise was ecstatic. He saw Wolfe as operating within a modernist tradition, writing that: "[I]t is the one good book which has come from 'Ulysses,' because Mr. Wolfe is the first writer (so far as I know) to learn what Mr. Joyce has to teach without imitating him. I do not mention 'Ulysses' to disparage Mr. Wolfe, but to praise him, because I do not think anyone can write a large-scale and really modern novel until he has been through Joyce, until he has assimilated, mastered, and controlled all the technical revolution which Joyce has made."[86]

For Aldington, Wolfe's exuberant, immense, and fragmentary narrative represented a distinctly American transposition of Joycean technique; the "intellectual, minutely planned, static, and *au fond* life hating" *Ulysses* paled next to the vigorous *Look Homeward, Angel*, the product of "an immense exuberance, organic in its form, kinetic, and drenched with the love of life."[87] Aldington's review is particularly significant because, unlike American reviewers who saw Wolfe as merely having borrowed from the modernist tradition, Aldington instead articulated the idea that *Look Homeward, Angel* belonged to a distinctly American literary modernism.

Aldington's review also places *Look Homeward, Angel* within a broader sphere of transatlantic exchange: Wolfe represented the vitality of the New World, borrowing from a modernist tradition that would soon make a more permanent home in America, as Europe moved ever deeper into crisis. For Aldington, the stuffy confines of formal structure and plot were inadequate for Wolfe, since his novel "rejects the convenient devices of professional fiction and winds itself close to human life."[88] The criticism of "formlessness" is here ingeniously recast as evidence of a deeper and more organic form, the "complex but beautiful structure of something which has grown naturally." The poet's praise of Wolfe's structure is at odds with almost the entire body of critical response to Wolfe, which sees a lack of restraint in form as the defining feature of his oeuvre. Aldington's acknowledgment of modernist experimentation, and the sensitivity to rhythm and language, as guiding principles for structure in Wolfe's fiction, is evidence of the seriousness with which Wolfe's first novel was greeted in the UK. Importantly, it was Aldington who first compared these two texts—claiming that Wolfe's "native" Romanticism had energized the Joycean technique—but the tendency of critics ever since has been to employ Joyce as a way of gesturing toward linguistic excess, rather than ascribing any modernist virtuosity. For many critics writing on Wolfe and literary modernism, the "technical revolution" of Joyce established such techniques—or an appropriation of them—as essential for critical relevance, and nearly all attempts to incorporate Wolfe's fiction into literary modernism have relied on comparative analyses of Wolfe and Joyce.[89]

The London *Times Literary Supplement*, at the time the most influential review periodical in the UK, published a review of *Look Homeward, Angel* on July 24, 1930.[90] Like Aldington, the *TLS* reviewer emphasized Wolfe's resolutely American character: Wolfe's effusive language, whence words "come spouting up with all the force of a subterranean flood," demonstrated a "native force" that was "rare in England now." What excited the reviewer was Wolfe's boundless energy, along with a raw talent that was "so hard, so sensual, so unsentimental, so easily comprehending and describing every sordidness of the flesh and spirit, so proudly rising to the heights." Aided by a self-propagated and growing myth, the image of Wolfe as a gargantuan talent, an author who gorged himself on books, food, women, and experience and then crammed his novels with "honeydew and everything else under the sun," would become the most enduring image of the novelist over the coming decades. While the *TLS* review ends with the resounding praise that "if Mr. Wolfe can be wasted, there is no hope for to-day," this widespread narrative of a raw and untamable genius strongly informed popular depictions of Wolfe in the years following his death in 1938. In the most famous attack on this superfluity in Wolfe's fiction, Bernard DeVoto fumed in the *Saturday Review of Literature* about Wolfe's "raw gobs of emotion, aimless and quite meaningless jabber, claptrap, belches, grunts, and Tarzanlike screams."[91] What was unprecedented about Wolfe's fiction was also, for some, finally unpalatable.

As in America, the book's release in the UK prompted several prominent authors to rush to praise this exuberant new voice. In 1930 Hugh Walpole told the United Press that Wolfe's novel was "as nearly perfect as a novel can be. I feel it a duty as a literary man to say something in his favour. Let America awake to him, for he has the making of greatness."[92] Walpole was at the time a very successful middlebrow author, as famous in America as he was in England, having toured America five times as a lecturer over two decades.[93] The endorsement of *Look Homeward, Angel* by an English novelist was important for establishing Wolfe's international reputation, but Walpole's enthusiasm did not elicit the same exuberant response from Wolfe as other praise had. Wolfe himself had written to Walpole saying that it was "very fine for a man of your reputation to take such friendly interest in a young writer," and over the course of his writing career the two developed a friendship.[94] However, Wolfe would later admit to Maxwell Perkins that Walpole had "completely sold out to success" and, though a man with "much real friendliness and generous feeling in him towards other people," saw writing as "a necessary but rather tedious adjunct to the more pleasant occupation of being a successful popular novelist."[95]

It is worth briefly pausing here to consider Walpole as a point of comparison, in light of the literary culture in which both he and Wolfe emerged. Though Walpole was an established author before the release of *The Secret City* (1919), this book proved to be a watershed moment, winning the newly established James Tait Black Memorial Prize and setting him on a course of full-time writing that lasted until his death in 1941.[96] During these twenty-two years Walpole became a widely popular writer and received a knighthood for his services to literature in 1937, publishing a further thirty novels and numerous collections of criticism. In the midst of increasingly popular success—and diminishing critical fortune—Walpole established the Book Society in 1929, modeled on the American Book-of-the-Month Club, the first of its kind to operate in Britain. In 1935 Walpole had tried, to no avail, to persuade the Book Society to include Wolfe's *Of Time and the River*, and though Wolfe had indicated his interest in the possibility of extra sales, the eventual Book Society rejection of his novel ultimately helped Wolfe's critical reception in the UK, which was undergoing its own culture debates in light of the newly established category of "middlebrow" literature.[97] In 1932 Q. D. Leavis described the "efficient standardisation of taste" of the Book Society as "conferring authority on a taste for the second-rate" and perpetuating a "middlebrow standard of values" in the British reading public.[98] Leavis's criticism of the Book Society mirrored the critical antipathy toward American counterparts like the Book-of-the-Month Club, and though, as Nicola Humble has pointed out, the Book Society "offered rather more 'literary' choices than the more straightforwardly populist books," Walpole's association with middlebrow taste would eventually lead to his cultural obsolescence.[99] Just one day after his death, the *Times* published a vitriolic obituary that uncharitably described Walpole as a writer who could "tell a workmanlike story in good workmanlike English," labeling him "a sentimental egoist [. . .] not popular among his fellow-writers," who possessed the additional shortcoming of being "singularly sensitive to adverse criticism."[100] Walpole's decline was even more dramatic than Wolfe's, such that today almost all of his nearly fifty novels are out of print and there is almost no critical attention paid to his work.[101]

Where the novelists differ dramatically, however, is in the way their respective novels were received during their lifetimes. "Middlebrow," as Humble points out in *The Feminine Middlebrow Novel* (2004), "has always been a dirty word," a term by which Walpole and a slew of other popular authors who published in the four decades from the 1920s to the 1950s were readily disparaged.[102] In an unmailed letter to the *New Statesman* under the title "Middlebrow" (later collected in *The Death of the Moth and Other Essays* [1942]), Virginia Woolf characterized the middlebrow as "the man, or woman, of middlebred intelligence who ambles and saunters now on this side of the hedge, now on that, in pursuit of no single object, neither art itself nor life itself, but both mixed indistinguishably, and rather nastily, with money, fame, power, or prestige."[103] Though Humble's contention is that it was precisely such middlebrow authors—particularly female writers—whose novels sold tens of thousands of copies and "packed the shelves of lending libraries" and who produced the "literature of the middle classes," it is important to consider the cumulative impact of a critically acclaimed novel like *Look Homeward, Angel*, which went through multiple printings, editions, and adaptations in a publishing environment that was supposedly dominated by Book-of-the-Month lists.[104] Certainly, the crucial literary history of this middlebrow period must be read alongside overly privileged critical categories like "modernism" and "the lost generation," but for Wolfe these designations remain either inadequate or disputed. In light of his earliest reception, it would not be an exaggeration to call Wolfe a commercially successful novelist, deeply involved with literary modernism and concerned with the alienation of a "lost generation," who suffered the fate of a middlebrow author.

"Lost Generationers"

Before we continue to investigate the reception and use of Wolfe's fiction, it is worth briefly discussing Wolfe's involvement with the so-called lost generation. While I am hesitant to endorse this label as offering any coherent sense of literary community in the postwar period, it stands to reason that readers of Wolfe might fairly consider him a member of this group. The literary landscape in which Wolfe's book emerged was inhabited, so the narrative goes, by a generation of postwar, disillusioned, and rootless Americans, whom Gertrude Stein famously called the "lost generation" in a remark directed to Ernest Hemingway, a phrase she subsequently used as an epigraph for Hemingway's first novel, *The Sun Also Rises* (1926). Although Wolfe's ability to provide a voice for "lost" Americans was characteristic of the popular response to his fiction, his involvement with this particular literary coterie—in both contemporaneous and retrospective surveys—has been a point of contention. When Malcolm Cowley wrote *Exile's Return* (1934)—a famous and influential chronicle of a young literary generation linked together through similar journeys to Europe, experiences of the Great War, and a problematic return home—his narrative drew on the lives of Hemingway, Fitzgerald, Dos Passos, Hart Crane, Cummings, and others, who in Cowley's words, "went out into the world like the children in Grimm's fairy tales who ran away from a cruel stepmother. [. . .] They wandered for years in search of treasure and then came back like the grown children to dig for it at home."[105] Noticeably absent from Cowley's roll call was Thomas Wolfe, an author whom Cowley knew (he would later review Wolfe's *Of Time and the River* for the *New Republic* in 1935) and who in many ways typified the exilic experience of this "lost generation."[106] In 1951 Cowley added a prologue to *Exile's*

Return titled "The Lost Generation," in which he identified not only such writers' essential restlessness but also their homesickness as a defining characteristic of this literary generation, employing Wolfe's own expression of *Sehnsucht* as metonymic of the longing felt by an entire generation:

> They were seceding from the old and yet could adhere to nothing new; they groped their way toward another scheme of life, as yet undefined; in the midst of their doubts and uneasy gestures of defiance they felt homesick for the certainties of childhood. It was not by accident that their early books were almost all nostalgic, full of the wish to recapture some remembered thing. In Paris or Pamplona, writing, drinking, watching bullfights or making love, they continued to desire a Kentucky hill cabin, a farmhouse in Iowa or Wisconsin, the Michigan woods, the blue Juniata, a country they had "lost, ah, lost," as Thomas Wolfe kept saying; a home to which they couldn't go back.[107]

In the epilogue to *Exile's Return*—also added in 1951—Cowley offered a feeble justification for omitting Wolfe from his original work, explaining that Wolfe differed from the other exiles in "preferring Germany to France."[108] Wolfe's admiration for German culture in the 1930s sharply differentiates him from contemporaries like Hemingway and Fitzgerald, not only in terms of the lost generation label but also, it is important to note, highlighting that not every famed American writer of this period deplored the German regime after the collapse of the Weimar Republic. In response to Cowley's definition of this generation, Philip Young laments: "Perhaps the trouble with me, among others, is literal- or narrow-mindedness. But it does seem to me that to qualify for membership in this group a writer should 1) have had experience of World War I—at least osmotic from having been on the scene of some of it and 2) have spent some bohemian period in Paris. If we accept that, then [. . .] exactly three qualify: Cummings, Dos Passos, and Hemingway. Some generation. If we ease up a little and require only one of these criteria, we still eliminate Faulkner and Wolfe as a minimum."[109]

While Paris provides an essential point of reference for the lost generation authors, Wolfe's exclusion is commensurate with the odd tendency to characterize the group's concerns in terms frequently applied to Wolfe's fiction.[110] In Craig Monk's *Writing the Lost Generation* (2008), for instance, the writers he is interested in all have a "persistent desire" to "chronicle their experiences abroad," are aware of the emergence of "the Lost Generation as a phrase with undeniable currency," and produce "self-conscious writing" in response to the "critical impulse" of a nascent modernism.[111] That *Look Homeward, Angel* is popularly accepted as an example of autobiographical fiction, loudly promoting the influence of Joyce's "self-conscious" modernism and overflowing with a chronicle of a young man's "experiences abroad," was evidently not enough to persuade Monk to include Wolfe in his study. Wolfe's absence here is symptomatic of his absence in almost all critical discussion of this generation of writers.[112]

Certainly not all "lost generation" authors have benefitted from this label in terms of the longevity of their critical appreciation, but exclusion from this group, for Wolfe, mirrors his larger exclusion from other considerations of American modernism. Wolfe's early reputation and association with the lost generation authors accentuated his outsider status after his death: seen as lacking relevance to the literary movement of his own historical moment, Wolfe's work was gradually relegated to a more "regional" subset of American literature. Though Monk warns that "American modernism must not simply be equated with the Lost Generation," he later concedes that the notion of the lost generation is "inexorably implicated" with literary modernism in America.[113] The two other famous writers with whom Wolfe shared an editor at Scribner's—F. Scott Fitzgerald and Ernest Hemingway—were both visitors to Gertrude Stein's studio at 27, rue de Fleurus, both literary exiles in Paris, and both members of the generation for which Hemingway popularized a label, and for which Fitzgerald named the age. As early as 1930, Wolfe was aware of his exclusion, and he expressed his feelings in an embittered letter to Alfred Dashiell that is worth quoting at length:

> I have been shy and silent before these liars and fools far too long—I have eaten crow and swallowed my pride for ten years before the wastelanders, the lost generationers, the bitter-bitters, the futility people, and all other cheap literary fakes sicklied o'er with a pale cast of Stein-shit—but now I will hold my tongue no longer: I know what I know, and I have learned it with blood and sweat. I have lived alone in a foreign land until I could not sleep for thinking of the sights and sounds and colors—the whole intolerable memory of America—its violence, savagery, immensity, beauty, ugliness, and glory—and I tell you I know it as if it were my child, as if it had been distilled from my blood and marrow: I know it from the look and smell of the railway ties to the thousand sounds and odors of the wilderness—and I tell you I had rather have ten years more of life there than fifty years of continental weak tea and smothering in this woolly and lethargic air, than a hundred years of shitty expatriatism: you have seen them in Paris sitting on their rumps around the café tables and pretending to know France and Europe—they know nothing and as for the superior European "culture" some of them profess their love for—how many of them do you think give one good God damn for it: they do not know either Europe or France[,] their life is a vile cardboard affair, the French hate and despise them and they know it—but they are like pimps who will endure slaps, insults, and mockery so long as they can have their whore.[114]

Though Wolfe ultimately distanced himself from what he regarded as the anomie of a solipsistic generation of Hamlets, whose work is "sicklied o'er with a pale cast of Stein-shit," what he shared with such writers was a sense of alienation engendered by modernity along with a recurrent desire, which surfaced most often while in exile, to write about the "intolerable memory of America."[115] The *longing* of the lost generation found its most eloquent—if sometimes unceasing—voice in Thomas Wolfe, whose fiction centered on questions of home and longing, often obsessing over the "lostness" that marked much of the fiction of his literary generation. In his wide-ranging study *America as a Civilization* (1957), Max Lerner suggested that the prevailing mood of the generation was "the sense of being ravaged and lost," pointing out that Wolfe himself proposed the "theme of deprivation and search that echoes in the repetitions of 'Lost, lost' [. . .] his tortured quest for an authority principle in a world of unremitting flux."[116] As Lerner later points out, however, the final theme of American life is an organic optimism: an unwillingness to adopt the mood of fatalism or tragic pessimism that he saw as characteristically European.[117] Wolfe's "tortured quest" is organically optimistic, and this is, in part, why I am compelled to think in terms of *Sehnsucht* over lostness. *Sehnsucht* encompasses the kind of longing Wolfe refers to in his letter: aesthetic, sensuous, and productive, even in its lack of fulfillment.

In an unpublished chapter titled "A Letter on Homelessness" from the *You Can't Go Home Again* manuscript, Wolfe described "lost generationism" as "only a kind of convenient term by which to lump together those people who exist in every generation who are embittered by the present while vaguely mourning for the past."[118] In spring 1938, Wolfe was invited to speak at Purdue University's annual Literary Award Banquet, in which he took the opportunity to elucidate his views on the vocation of writing and to explicitly reject any attempt to connect him with the lost generation:

> One of [my friends] not more than three or four years my senior, is very fixed in his assertion of what he calls "the lost generation"—a generation of which he has been quite vociferously a member, and in which he has tried enthusiastically to include me. "You belong to it, too," he used to say. "You came along at the same time. You can't get away from it. You're a part of it whether you want to be or not"—to which my vulgar response would be: "Don't you you-hoo me!" If my friend *wants* to belong to the Lost Generation—and it really is astonishing with what fond eagerness those people hug the ghost of desolation to their breast—that's *his* affair. But he can't have me. If I have been elected, it has been against my will; and I hereby resign. I don't feel that I belong to a lost generation, and I have never felt so. Furthermore, I doubt very much the existence of a lost generation, except insofar as every generation, groping, must be lost.[119]

While Wolfe rejects the label—which he associates with a nihilistic impulse to "hug the ghost of desolation"—he reclaims for his own fiction the broader experience of being "lost." Rather than simply employing such desolate longing, which Wolfe regards merely as a form of despair, his novels are suffused with an insatiable longing for a homeplace, with what I interpret as evidence of Wolfe's deeply idiosyncratic exploration of *Sehnsucht*. Unlike Fitzgerald's longing in a novel such as *The Great Gatsby* (1925), which was predominantly directed toward objects and bodies, Wolfe's longing has a distinct spatial embodiment: such loci as *home, America, South*, and *geography* that are permanently beyond reach.[120] What emerges instead is an intermingling of the modernist dilemma—what John Frow describes as "ontological homelessness," which became a "key metaphor for the condition of modernity"[121]—with the *Sehnsucht* of Wolfe. Wolfe's narratives frequently oscillate between these two poles of desire: a Romantic *Sehnsucht* that informs the movement of Wolfe's protagonists across a mystical vision of the American continent, accompanied by an overwhelming sense of bitter and inconsolable loss. When *homesickness* is evoked in Wolfe's fiction, it necessarily combines the rootlessness that Frow identifies as a key metaphor of modernity with the Romantic proclivity to dwell on, and validate, the emotional experience of *Sehnsucht*. Wolfe provides a succinct summary of this experience of *Sehnsucht*—and his own attempt to explicate it through fiction—in his description of Eugene Gant's own written chronicle of wandering in *Of Time and the River*:

> And in those words was packed the whole image of his bitter homelessness, his intolerable desire, his maddened longing for return. In those wild and broken phrases was packed the whole bitter burden of his famished, driven, overladen spirit—all the longing of the wanderer, all the impossible and unutterable homesickness that the American, or any man on earth, can know.
>
> They were all there—without coherence, scheme, or reason—flung down upon paper like figures blasted by the spirit's lightning stoke, and in them was the huge chronicle of the billion forms, the million names, the huge, single, and incomparable substance of America.[122]

The "homesickness" to which Wolfe refers ultimately points toward an impossibility, a longing for return to a place that does not satisfy what is already an "unutterable" desire for home—Wolfe's unsatisfiable addiction to the experience and expression of *Sehnsucht*.

Books as Weapons

Following Wolfe's early death in 1938, it was the romance and exuberance of his *Sehnsucht* for the American continent—rather than the implicit bitterness and "lostness" in his addiction to longing—that framed the author's legacy for a nation on the cusp of war. As America entered World War II, the cultural significance of books—particularly as a means by which ideas of culture could be disseminated in the first half of the twentieth century—was reaffirmed in one

FIGURE 3. Thomas Wolfe, *Look Homeward, Angel* (New York: Editions for the Armed Services, 1944). AC8.A6 NO. 0-31, 1929, Special Collections, University of Virginia, Charlottesville.

particular aspect of the American war effort. In 1944 *Look Homeward, Angel* was released in a trim volume of 512 pages as an Armed Services Edition (figure 3). (In *American Pulp* [2014], Paula Rabinowicz recounts a letter between serviceman Leo Meltzer and Philip Van Doren Stern—historian, editor, and general manager in charge of distributing the Armed Services Editions—in which Meltzer had apparently requested *Look Homeward, Angel* on the basis that not enough "literary" books were circulating among the forces.)[123] Historians credit the Armed Services Editions with introducing books to soldiers who had previously read very little and also for helping fuel the paperback boom in the postwar years.[124] Rabinowicz writes that "the ASEs can be seen as part of the postwar drive to educate GIs that resulted in new forms of engagement with books and with the readers of books," adding that "pulp—as a literal form used to transmit new sensibilities—brought modernist literature to the 'near-illiterate' GI Joes, and eventually their Janes, of America. This wartime ephemera spread ideas and images that ultimately contributed to postwar countercultures."[125]

The Armed Services Editions represented "the greatest mass publishing enterprise of all history," with nearly 123 million copies of 1,322 titles being distributed to defense force personnel.[126] John B. Hench notes that "like the landing of the troops on D-Day, this invasion of books was intended to effect a liberation, in this case, the unfettering of people's minds."[127] This mass publication of books during a period of unprecedented censorship gave a political dimension to the supply of books, highlighting the cultural significance that books had attained by the middle of the twentieth century.

The Council on Books in Wartime (CBW), a nonprofit organization founded by publishers, booksellers, librarians, and authors, adopted the W. W. Norton slogan (later given wide circulation by Roosevelt): "Books are weapons in the war of ideas."[128] Though this publication added very little profit to Wolfe's estate (royalties were half a cent per copy), it is highly significant that Wolfe's novel, then over fifteen years old, was embedded within a political program that emphatically promoted the moral value of reading. *Look Homeward, Angel*—together with the rest of Wolfe's oeuvre—had clearly attained symbolic significance as embodying the romantic myth of America.

This transformation of Wolfe into the voice of America is routinely overlooked today, but such a position is vital in understanding the author's place in American literary history. While Holliday has argued for Wolfe's inclusion in the canon of high modernism, his amenability to popular forms—particularly radio—saw the author evolve into a popular and mythic voice for America.[129] Indeed, this understanding of Wolfe as a mythmaker was already popular during his lifetime; by the time Alfred Kazin wrote his seminal *On Native Grounds* (1942), this particular reading of Wolfe had become the status quo.[130] Wolfe's vision of lost Americans who "walk the streets of life alone" was in many ways a perfect counterpart to Kazin's criticism, which emphasized the "terrible estrangement" and "nameless yearning for a world no one really ever possessed" in the fiction of modern American writers.[131] For Kazin, the myth of America in Wolfe's fiction was the "necessary consequence of his situation and his understanding," stemming from Wolfe's belief that he was a "prime symbol of American experience" with the ability to speak for "all America itself."[132] While Kazin ultimately dismissed Wolfe as a "gargantuan boy," full of romantic naïveté, this notion of the author speaking for Americans had already been reinforced by the Literary Guild of America's publication of a collection of his most "poetical passages" only a year after his death, grandly titled *The Face of a Nation* (1939). John Hall Wheelock—an early advocate of Wolfe at Scribner's who worked closely with him on manuscript revisions—wrote in the introduction to *The Face of a Nation* that Wolfe's major achievement lay in articulating the "American spirit and the American earth of our day."[133]

Radio producers, sensitive to this poetic power of articulation, also helped propagate this version of Thomas Wolfe; within six months of his death, CBS—which would broadcast a number of dramatized versions of Wolfe's writing over the following years—contacted Maxwell Perkins for permission to broadcast Wolfe's final letter written to Perkins, within in a segment called "Words Without Music."[134] Even before *Look Homeward, Angel* had assisted the war effort via its Armed Services Editions reprinting, Wolfe's vision of America had been co-opted by the U.S. Treasury for the purpose of selling war bonds, sponsoring a radio play adaptation of Wolfe's "The Face of America" in 1942. What all these adaptations have in common was the collation of those scattered paeans to America strewn throughout Wolfe's work, such as declamatory passages like the following from *Of Time and the River* (1935), which was used prominently in this example of the treasury's campaign for war bonds: "It is the place of the howling winds, the hurrying of the leaves in old October, the hard clean falling to the earth of acorns. The place of the storm-tossed moaning of the wintry mountainside, where the young men cry out in their throats and feel the savage vigor, the rude strong energies; the place also where the trains cross rivers. It is a fabulous country, the only fabulous country; it is the one place where miracles not only happen, but where they happen all the time."[135]

Through both print media and radio, Wolfe's artistic portrayal of America was disseminated to a broader population after his death, in the belief that his romantic vision represented a nation worth fighting for. His novels, full of yearning and ecstatic nationalism, were valorized for their nostalgic power in a period dominated by economic crisis, as if the America they expressed was fragile and in need of protection. The opening of the radio play "The Face of America" offers an insight into how Wolfe's writing had come to be understood chiefly in terms of the vision of America it promoted: "Ladies and gentlemen—it is with a sense of reverence that we turn to the pages of one of America's greatest writers. He was known as a novelist—but often he wrote as a poet, and spoke with the poet's burning vision and gift of prophecy. Thomas Wolfe wrote about America; and tonight . . . he speaks to us *of* America!"[136]

Ironically, this relationship between Wolfe's fiction and American nationalism was reproduced in Nazi Germany. Just as *Look Homeward, Angel* had imbued American soldiers with a sense of civility and hope, the German edition, *Schau heimwärts, Engel!* (1932), was one of the books that could be found sitting on a shelf in Dachau's prison library.[137] Wolfe's writing, apparently so clear in its promotion of the myth of America, had also spoken to German readers, with the novelist ultimately attaining a celebrity in Germany that outshone his reception at home. This transnational relationship between Wolfe and Germany—particularly in terms of the influence of German Romanticism on Wolfe's version of longing, and the degree to which, as historian Michaela Hoenicke Moore argues, "Wolfe's [. . .] novels offer a catalog of the central themes that characterized the American debate on the Third Reich"[138]—is discussed at length in the third and fourth chapters.

Reception in the Global Deep South

This chapter has so far been predominantly interested in Wolfe's national reception, focusing on the writer's place within the American consciousness, while also acknowledging some of the transatlantic exchange of Wolfe's work and ideas. As an Australian scholar, I am interested in a hitherto unexplored sphere of reception for Wolfe's earliest novel, in part because this investigation expands the framework with which to approach the fiction of Thomas Wolfe, but also because it anticipates the transnational modes of influence that characterize the remainder of this book. While Wolfe is now virtually unknown and unread in Australia—and I can testify to the difficulty in acquiring his work through bookstores or libraries across Australia—*Look Homeward, Angel* encountered a modest, though enthusiastic, transpacific reception. In 1930 the *Sydney Morning Herald* characterized Wolfe's novel as "a strange book with a strange title," which was ultimately closer to being a "forerunner of further work of strength" rather than a work of genius.[139] Unlike the novel's American reception, however, Wolfe's vision of provincial life seemed too aggrandized in the mind of the Australian reviewer: there was not enough narrative to justify the verbose portrait of uncomfortable and "mean relations," a "drunken father [. . .] a penurious, avaricious mother," and a principal character filled with "repressed desires and fantastic dreaming."[140] The *Brisbane Courier* suggested that "the novel would have been better if there had been a rigorous condensation,"[141] while the *Queenslander*, in a column on American writers, reprinted F. Tennyson Jesse's backhanded compliment that Wolfe's was a "vital though turgid book."[142] The most thoughtful review of *Look Homeward, Angel* came from the *West Australian*. While the reviewer acknowledges the aforementioned criticisms of Wolfe—conceding that his novel is "immensely diffuse" and conceived on so large a scale that "his canvas strikes the reader as being overcrowded with characters"—the unnamed reviewer goes on to praise his "spaciousness of style, a manifest gusto in the use of words, and, above all, a method by which he expresses himself in prose which not infrequently nearly approaches perfection."[143] While such reviews are in many ways reprising the American critical consensus—namely that Wolfe's fiction was overdrawn and verbose but that it also contained exquisitely lyrical passages—what is important to note is the very existence of this reception history in Australia, which has not been acknowledged in any of the criticism on Wolfe since his death.

Including this Australian perspective does not merely add another theater of reception but instead reveals a broader tendency within American literary studies to exclude transpacific reception histories. In American studies, the focus on Wolfe's German connection has been a fruitful avenue for reconceptualizing Wolfe within a global perspective—most recently in Waldemar Zacharasiewicz, *Images of Germany in American Literature* (2007) and Robert H. Brinkmeyer Jr., *The Fourth Ghost: White Southern Writers and European Fascism, 1930–1950* (2009)—though the overwhelming critical impulse has been to read him inside rigid southern—or even Appalachian—boundaries.[144] Further extending Wolfe's boundaries of influence to what I have termed the "really deep South" is not intended to confer an exceptional status on Australia but to demonstrate the influence of Wolfe's fiction beyond his native soil.[145] Although there has been scholarship on Wolfe outside of Europe and America—for instance, in 2000 an anthology of articles by Japanese scholars, *Studies in Thomas Wolfe* (2000), was released for Wolfe's centennial, while in 2010 an essay appeared in *Thomas Wolfe Studies* by Lan-Ming Wang discussing a recent Chinese translation of *Look Homeward, Angel*—such studies have often been limited investigations into Wolfe's global impact.[146] Discussing work in translation is often problematic—in the case of Wolfe's Chinese legacy, there have been at least four translations of *Look Homeward, Angel* since 1987—but in Australia, readers encountered Wolfe as he was published in the Heinemann editions, while he was also a fixture in the literary news.

For Leon Gellert, the South Australian poet and journalist, those Australians who had reached their "imperturbable period of your existence—your mid-thirties" by 1947 would remember the arrival of *Look Homeward, Angel* as a period in which "there flamed above your literary horizon a new and brilliant star."[147] Wolfe's impact on this young generation, according to Gellert, induced "a strange excitement" that shed a "warm light on unsuspected burgeonings in the mind's undergrowth." Wolfe's writing took "the commonplace things and spread them out like toys, and [made] them splendid for our reawakened delight." Beyond the regular reviews, there are some more superficial examples of Wolfe's lexicon entering the popular imagination in Australia: the familiarity with his work was such that a local paper like the *Goulburn Evening Post* could borrow "Look Homeward, Angel" as an ironic title for its front-page story about a woman leaving her husband for an evangelical preacher, while Douglas Wilkie, on May 9, 1950, chose the same title for his story on atomic power in the *Advertiser* (Adelaide, SA).[148] Beyond such examples, Wolfe's deeper impact is palpable in the later work of one particularly influential Australian author, Christopher Koch.[149] Investigating this influence—and locating what might be considered "Wolfean" themes within an Australian context—is one focus of the final chapter of the book, offering further justification for exploring Wolfe within a global milieu.

Reading the Autopoet

This chapter has outlined the cultural and historical importance attributed to Wolfe's fiction following the publication of *Look Homeward, Angel* in 1929. It has, I hope, offered a much-needed concrete picture of Wolfe's early significance, which is necessary to challenge and redirect the current attitude of critical apathy. It is worth amending Mark McGurl's pronouncement at this point, that Wolfe is on his way to becoming a "footnote to American literary history," by noting that this shift away from Wolfe has been gradual and, for many critics, imperceptible. The most productive critical work done on Wolfe in recent years—which situates him within a particular historical moment in American culture and identifies the "global" nature of the South within which Wolfe lived and recorded his experience—has been set forth in Mark McGurl's *The Program Era: Postwar Fiction and the Rise of Creative Writing* (2009) and in Robert H. Brinkmeyer Jr., *The Fourth Ghost: White Southern Writers and European Fascism, 1930–1950* (2009), the latter of which is explored more deeply in subsequent chapters. Having begun this book with McGurl's insistence on Wolfe's declining star, I wanted to end this chapter with a brief reflection on *The Program Era*'s treatment of Wolfe.

Wolfe is a perfect example of the author prototype that McGurl associates with creative writing programs, an "autopoet" who practiced the central tenet of literary self-expression: "Write what you know."[150] Wolfe satisfies McGurl's criterion of institutional influence, having not only maintained a "prolonged intimacy with institutions of higher education" but also having taken part in George Pierce Baker's Drama 47 Workshop, which was "among the first creative writing classes ever offered at the graduate level."[151] Although McGurl notes the irony that "the careening decline of Wolfe's reputation" can be traced to "his brazen flouting of the idea of painstaking craft that the postwar creative writing program would do so much to institutionalize," ultimately Wolfe allows McGurl to pry open the deeper conflicts at work in progressive education theory, meaning that this reduction of the writer to a self-aggrandized figure goes ultimately unchallenged. Just as McGurl recounts stories of writing programs holding out Wolfe's work as an example of "bad writing," there is palpable distaste in the way Wolfe's work is handled, and ultimately dismissed, as simply "expressing himself full time."[152] While *The Program Era* does concede that all fiction in the postwar period was "explicitly or not [. . .] on one level, a portrait of the artist," and that such works "resonate[d] broadly with the concerns of serious readers everywhere, living, as they do, multiply institutionalized and indeed self-reflexive lives," the "autobardolatry" of Wolfe is interpreted in light of an alleged narcissistic obsession, rather than its profound effect on the reading public.[153] Wolfe's belief that "all fiction is autobiography," stated at the beginning of *Look Homeward, Angel*, along with his resonance for readers in the 1930s, anticipated the literary trend that McGurl traces through the postwar period. Fredric Jameson identifies a similar shortcoming in McGurl's treatment of Wolfe: rather than perceiving the actual historical importance assigned to Wolfe—reminding us that Faulkner "once considered [him] the greatest writer of his time"[154]—the analysis presupposes "an allegorical structure, a system of levels," whereby Wolfe is ultimately the recipient of McGurl's own "anti-intellectualism."[155] Jameson suggests that there are many compelling reasons for a critical reevaluation of Wolfe, particularly in light of his early influences, "which have considerable historical and structural interest for us still." Jameson's suggestion that Wolfe's fiction has considerable interest "for us still"—a rare faith in contemporary American literary studies—animates my discussion in subsequent chapters.

CHAPTER TWO

Homesick for Unknown Places

Longing and the Imagined South

Thomas Wolfe was nineteen years old when he left Asheville, North Carolina, for graduate study at Harvard University. It was the first time that Wolfe had left the South, with his journals from these Harvard years revealing his profound awareness of being an alien in a northern city. In one undated entry, Wolfe reflected that a "Southerner in northern states soon learns what is expected of him," namely to act like a hillbilly romantic whose "words crawl and drip with syrupy reluctance," adding that if one is not careful, one "is apt to [refer] to his own father as 'the colonel.'"[1] Just a few years earlier, H. L. Mencken published his notorious essay "The Sahara of the Bozart" (1917), arguing that the South possessed a "curious and almost pathological estrangement from everything that makes for a civilized culture."[2] Mencken's attack—which was representative of a larger view of southern alterity at the beginning of the twentieth century—provoked the young Wolfe to wonder whether "the desire to create an art in the South today arise[s] from a passionate desire to create beauty, or from chagrin at our barrenness and a desire to 'get back' at H. L. Mencken?"[3] In the same journal entry, Wolfe predicted that the South would "witness an awakening of culture and [. . .] make its own particular and local contribution to the creative arts," a belief later vindicated by what southern literary historians came to call the Southern Renaissance, in which Wolfe himself would play an important role. In *The Burden of Southern History* (1960), C. Vann Woodward identified the year of 1929 as a possible origin of this so-called renaissance, the same year that both Faulkner's *The Sound and the Fury* and Wolfe's *Look Homeward, Angel* were published.[4] "Of all American novels," wrote Woodward, "no one who read [*Look Homeward, Angel*] in his youth will forget the strange excitement of the experience." From the earliest definitions of a distinct modern literature in the southeastern states of America—which Michael Kreyling has called the "invention of Southern literature"[5]—Thomas Wolfe's fiction has been included.

Contemporary literary critics, however, have devoted far more time to the study of William Faulkner—the coinheritor in Woodward's southern origin myth—than Thomas Wolfe. Though, in recent years, southern studies has undergone a vast proliferation, using insights from fields like transnationalism, postcolonialism, and new southern studies to challenge the very notion of southern exceptionalism, Wolfe's fiction is regrettably still tethered to an increasingly problematic understanding of notions of southern identity. Wolfe's position within the study of the American South reflects a division that exists between what is loosely called "new southern studies" and a more "exceptionalist" approach to southern studies whose origins can be traced to the postwar project of the Agrarian critics and later proponents of southern distinctiveness in developing a canon of southern literature. In *Finding Purple America* (2013), Jon Smith argues that this group of critics, aligned with what he terms "old southern studies," makes the fundamental error of conflating the "presence of the past"—which it sees as "opposed to the imagined absence of any past"—with the "pathological, melancholy *over*presence of the past, of the loved lost object."[6] Since the postwar period, it has predominantly been the "old southern studies" scholars who have taken up the task of interpreting Wolfe, a situation that has led, in part, to the exclusion of his work from current theoretical discussion around the very notion of the South. Often, the strictly regional nature of Wolfe's fiction has been emphasized or assumed, which ultimately reduces it to the status of a nostalgic curiosity—a favorite regional author of halcyon days.[7] This chapter argues that Wolfe's fiction played a significant role in those very debates that shaped the modern "invention" of southern literature, contending that Wolfe's fiction problematizes those early conceptions of a distinct "South" that still govern the interpretation of his work. I will also continue to explore *Sehnsucht* as a way of challenging the peculiar exceptionalism that demands a southern locus for Wolfe's longing. There is a clear historic precedent for the appropriation of an author's words for their purely symbolic power—a body of work for which Wolfe's rhetoric proves surprisingly amenable—and understanding how his fiction has been employed as both "southern" and "American" underscores Wolfe's relevance to discussions of the imagined South.

Thomas Wolfe and the Invention of Southern Literature

The brief period in which Wolfe's work was published—roughly 1929 to 1938—corresponded with a significant period in southern literary history, in which the South experienced a burgeoning of cultural output. As the broader United States was encountering the idea of culture en masse, the South saw an increasing number of cultural commentators elucidate a vision of the South distinct from the rest of America. Southern authors and critics who had a significant impact on postwar literary culture, such as John Crowe Ransom, Allen Tate, and Robert Penn Warren—all signatories to the Southern Agrarian manifesto *I'll Take My Stand* (1930) and all early supporters of regional distinctiveness—saw their ideas whisked from small literary magazines like the *Fugitive* into nationwide circulation on the coattails of the New Criticism. Many authors now popularly associated with the renaissance also began to emerge—William Faulkner, Zora Neale Hurston, James Agee, and Lillian Smith, to name just a few—prompting C. Vann Woodward to declare that it was southern novelists (implicitly, white male southern novelists) whose work was able to "penetrate the romantic haze of an older generation as well as the cynical stereotypes of our own," adding, in an uncharacteristic act of deference, that the southern historian must "abandon temporarily the standoffishness of his guild and make his bow to the Southern men of letters."[8] Michael Denning argues that this so-called Southern Renaissance was also part of the larger "southernization" of American culture, which had a dramatic impact on national culture in the years following World War II: massive internal migration led to southern "race" and "hillbilly" musical genres being "renamed as 'rhythm and blues' and 'country,'" while a "regional writer whose works were largely out of print at the end of the war, William Faulkner, became recognized as the leading 'national' novelist."[9] In short, the southern voices that H. L. Mencken had mocked as being "almost as sterile, artistically, intellectually, culturally, as the Sahara Desert," migrated from the periphery to the very center of U.S. literary culture.[10]

This perception of "southernization" or "renaissance," however, does not capture the complex ways in which the South was constructed in the years surrounding the Great Depression. As Leigh Anne Duck points out in *The Nation's Region* (2006), "southern traditionalism was increasingly seen as a threatening chronotype; no longer an effective container for the nation's disavowed antiliberalism, the trope of the backward South began to comprise an image of what the United States could become."[11] For Duck and other southern literary scholars, the dominant perception of the South during this period was strongly informed by ideas of cultural alterity—"the South" was a category entirely distinct from "the nation." Several southern literary historians—observing both the productivity of writers during this period and this implicit cultural dichotomy—have instead chosen to reinforce alterity in the guise of regional distinctiveness, flouting what Tara McPherson calls "tired old clichés of southernness" that work to "*preserve* the South [. . .] rather than to pursue it in relation to national or global contexts."[12] While regional distinctiveness was a vital and imaginatively rich platform for writers and critics in a period of modernization, mass culture, and latent national antagonisms, it is also important to emphasize the degree to which it was a fabrication. Stressing the inventedness of "southernness" in Wolfe's fiction also highlights his relevance to—and finally his problematic confinement within—the development of the traditional canon of modern southern literature. Challenging this view of an exceptional "South" operates in two directions, exposing the uncritical biases within a depoliticized, romantic South in the regionalist perception while also admitting that those antiliberal and backward characteristics of the South—such as interwar sympathy with racial biology—were also part of the broader national experience.

Wolfe and the Agrarians

One of the earliest and most influential attempts to imagine the South can be found in the Agrarian manifesto *I'll Take My Stand* (1930), the culmination of the literary and cultural movement during the 1920s and 1930s led by the Vanderbilt Agrarians. *I'll Take My Stand* outlined a southern tradition that the authors believed was vital for southerners to grasp hold of in the wake of "younger Southerners" being "converted frequently to the industrial gospel," a gospel of the "new South" that they perceived as "an undistinguished replica of the usual industrial community."[13] In *The Nation's Region*, Duck argues that during the Depression era, regionalists saw the modern American "nation"—that coherent cultural ideal whose dissemination was being accelerated via mass publishing, radio, and film—as relying on the local, seeing "the possibility that local cultures could provide a needed counterbalance for the national collective."[14] The problem with this particular view of regionalism, as Duck acknowledges, was the degree to which all regionalisms were often equated—by outsiders—with the more conservative groups who saw their different regional cultures "not as a supplement but as an alternative to that of the United States." With specific regard to the South, Duck identifies the vociferous group of southern Agrarians as emblematic of this antagonism of the region toward the nation, pointing out that the "Agrarian argument sought to retain a stark temporal division between the South and the larger United States."[15] The relationship between Wolfe and the southern Agrarians was, according to David Herbert Donald, "curiously ambivalent," suggesting that "they sensed that Wolfe was in some ways a kindred spirit," while at the same time dealing Wolfe significant critical blows in reviews of his fiction.[16] In considering Wolfe's significance to these early constructions of southern identity, it is worth briefly exploring the Agrarian response to his work. Not only were these figures Wolfe's contemporaries, being among the first to read and critique his fiction, but their interpretations of Wolfe's work reveal some of the deeper, latent anxieties the Agrarians had about the impact of modernity on the "southern" way of life, along with their prescriptions for southern literature.

The first published Agrarian critique of Wolfe came in a review of *Look Homeward, Angel* in 1930 by Donald Davidson, writing in the *Nashville Tennessean*, the literary section of which he edited. An enthusiastic regionalist, his impassioned view on regionalism as "the symbol of all [that] is worth fighting for in the reconstruction of American literature" was later expanded in his own manifesto, *Regionalism and Nationalism in the United States* (1938).[17] Davidson was also an ardent segregationist, whose beliefs about white supremacy would eventually lead to his estrangement from a number of the other Agrarian writers, particularly Ransom, Warren, and Tate.[18] Davidson initially conceded that Wolfe's "performance is superb" but drily adds that it represented the kind of novel that captivates "an entire chorus of New York reviews into warm twitterings."[19] In *Regionalism and Nationalism*, Davidson characterized the centralizing nationalism he perceived in the U.S. publishing industry as tyrannical; Wolfe's success in New York is here taken as evidence of the novelist's amenability to the expectations and demands of a northern audience.[20] Jennifer Rae Greeson argues that it is precisely this "Northern metropolitan apex of U.S. cultural production" that needs to be "reinsert[ed] into our consideration of writing about the southeastern United States," pointing out that the southern novelist—no matter how distinct or "regional"—was almost always bound by the monopoly of northern presses and their audiences.[21] Further, as Sarah Gardner has shown, depressed literacy and maldistribution of books in the 1920s led to what amounted to a crisis of nonreaders in the southeastern states.[22] For Agrarians like Davidson, Wolfe's success in New York reinforced the precarious position of southern letters in the early part of the twentieth century as well as the threat of being subsumed into a national (read: *northern*) literary culture.

Later in his review of *Look Homeward, Angel*, Davidson bemoaned the fact that Wolfe was really writing a novel of "Why Young Men Leave the South," an experience that was increasingly common for many young artists born in the southeastern states at the beginning of the twentieth century, a "tragic condition of mind for an ambitious and able novelist" according to Davidson.[23] Davidson believed that since Wolfe was working with the materials of southern life, he had a responsibility to use his substantial talents to promote an ennobling image of the South and to identify ways in which various systems of industrialism—against which Agrarianism explicitly stood—had negatively impacted the southern way of life. The fact that critics had already embraced Wolfe as an American polemicist was at stark odds with Davidson's vision of southern literature as providing cultural propaganda; Wolfe ought to have been promoting "the South," not America. Furthermore, the lack of adherence to a system in Wolfe's novel—the youthful narcissism of Eugene Gant prompts Wolfe to write that he was "content with any system which might give him comfort"[24]—infuriated the ardent ideologue in Davidson, who argued that while the fictional character might survive this indifference, the author could not separate his art from life.[25]

Davidson's review is illustrative of his personal sense of urgency within the southern Agrarian movement and the extent to which this project was taken seriously as retrieving an alternative "southern" cultural ideal: in his letters to Allen Tate from 1929, Davidson warned Tate about separate humanist and progressive symposia that threatened to establish their movements before *I'll Take My Stand* was complete: "Will we let the Progressives [. . .] capture the field and walk off with public opinion [?] But they have great strength on their side [. . .] they may even cut the ground out from under us."[26] Written in the "rhetoric of battle," Davidson's concern was that the southern intellectual movement be systematized in order to, in Kreyling's reading, "control and define the South in the process of cultural contest," a work that *Look Homeward, Angel* was frustratingly ambivalent toward.[27] Here Davidson obliquely acknowledges the imaginative process of the Agrarian movement in inventing a "South" in light of challenges from other groups—such as Howard Odum's "progressives"—who were equally involved in a contest of cultural definition. The perception of the southern states in the wake of events like the *Scopes* trial in 1925 had given added impetus for groups like the Agrarians to promote a version of the South that could achieve currency in the minds of the nation. Within the terms of this project, *Look Homeward, Angel*—and therefore also Wolfe himself—was deemed a failure, unwilling to endorse agrarian living and traditionalism in light of impinging modernization and too indeterminate in constructing a cohesive and vital picture of bountiful southern life. The closing scene of *Look Homeward, Angel* can be read as emblematic of Wolfe's failure to focus on the South: standing on the porch of his father's store, Eugene "was like a man who stands upon a hill above the town he has left, yet does not say 'The town is near,' but turns his eyes upon the distant soaring ranges."[28] Wolfe's wavering geographical focus, the constant impulse within his fiction to turn away from the South along with the reiteration that return is impossible, frustrated the Agrarians' commitment to promoting a romanticized picture of southern life.

John Donald Wade's review, in the inaugural edition of the *Southern Review*, was even more venomous than Davidson's. The *Southern Review* was and is an influential literary and cultural journal published out of Louisiana, with two of its founding editors—Robert Penn Warren and Cleanth Brooks—being early advocates for the exceptionalist view of southern culture.[29] Warren had initially hoped for a submission from Wolfe, but when none was forthcoming he chose instead to publish Wade's damning critique of Wolfe's second novel. Wade was a Vanderbilt colleague of Ransom and Davidson, and his own submission to *I'll Take My Stand* had taken the form of an allegorical narrative titled "The Life and Death of Cousin Lucius" that traced the impact of modernism on the decline of dependable social (white, male) hierarchies.[30] Wolfe's second novel covers the journey of Eugene Gant from the southern town of Altamont to study at Harvard, and then on to New York, with an internal opposition between the North and the South occupying a prominent position in the early stages of the narrative. Nervously anxious about the prospect of leaving home, Eugene "dreamed and hungered for the proud unknown North with that wild ecstasy, that intolerable and wordless joy of longing and desire, which only a Southerner can feel," a sentiment that Wade read as evidence of Wolfe's interpretation of a "southern" way of life.[31] Wade's first point of contention with Wolfe's novel is its absence of true religious sentiment, in spite of Wolfe's "gusty paeans about catholicity," an unwillingness to invest his myth of the South with what John Crowe Ransom saw as bearing irreducible traces of religious doctrine.[32] Wade joins Davidson in praising Wolfe's "monumental performance," claiming that the novel represented a work of "stupendous gusto and energy"—"performer" *not* "artist" was the resounding implication—taking great pleasure in Wolfe's satirical "[Sinclair] Lewis-like episodes" lampooning the "leprous intellectuals around Harvard University" with its culture of "stupid mincingness, its inane irrelevancy, its dead and rotten bawdiness."[33] Wolfe, if only momentarily, had succeeded in identifying the northern threat to southern intellectualism that, according to Wade, had a "sad bearing upon the development and damnation of us all, and of this nation."

The particular section of *Of Time and the River* to which Wade refers contains an episode set at Harvard, in which Eugene is surrounded by other young men who worry about being "modern" and who "dispose of most of the established figures with a few well-chosen words of contempt."[34] Wade's focus on the "inane irrelevancy" of Harvard intellectuals, however, missed the wider implication of Wolfe's satire of university life in the 1920s—the mounting pressure on young writers and intellectuals, such as the Agrarians, to "brand oneself in the esteem of the group":

> Intuitively he saw that their jargon formed a pattern by which they might be placed and recognized; that, to young men most of all, to be placed in a previous discarded pattern was unendurable disgrace. It represented to them the mark of intellectual development, just as in a sophomore's philosophy, the belief that God is an old man with a long beard brings ridicule and odium upon the believer, but the belief that God is an ocean without limit, or an all-pervasive and inclusive substance, or some other equally naïve and extraordinary idea, is regarded as a certain sign of bold enlightenment. Thus, it often happens, when one thinks he has extended the limits of his life, broken the bonds, and liberated himself in the wider ether, he has done no more than to exchange a new superstition for an old one, to forsake a beautiful myth for an ugly one.[35]

Wade's most revealing criticism concerns Eugene's idealization of America from the vantage of Europe, along with his conviction that home can be found everywhere and nowhere. For the Agrarian critics, such ambivalence toward the notion of home cut to the very heart of the "southern way of life," signaling a shift away from what they considered the concrete South. Pausing his narrative on a dusty sand-clay road in South Carolina, Wolfe writes that as the "immortal visage of the earth" reveals itself to Eugene, it spoke "instantly, intolerably, exultantly, not of home, return, and settlement but of one image [. . .] the image of the enchanted city, in which, it now seemed, all the frenzy and unrest of his spirit would find a certain goal and triumph." It was precisely such evocations of *Sehnsucht* that prompted Wade to breathlessly proclaim: "So much for those who feel it necessary to think of home in terms of a continent [. . .] it would be as practical to think of the continent in terms of a cottage."[36] Eugene's *Sehnsucht* for the "enchanted city" is resolutely not for an Agrarian vision of the South, leading Wade to conclude his lengthy review with a caution to the author: if "*Oh, lost, lost!* is the refrain constantly echoed, that this man from Old Catawba, immured now in Brooklyn, N.Y., cries piteously," then Wolfe would do well to realize that to "live validly and with satisfying peace," he should seek "reconciliation with his origins [. . .] should be obliged [. . .] to make room for the people who bred him."[37] That is, in the mind of this Agrarian critic, Wolfe's longing could be cured if he just went home again.

Wade's frustration with Wolfe's unwillingness to define a concrete home-place—and his suggestion that the novelist's intolerable homesickness could be cured by simply returning to the South—is investigated later in this chapter, since it is central to my broader project of repositioning Wolfe in relation to an imaginary South. Carson McCullers—a fellow southerner who also left her home to take up residence in the same Brooklyn neighborhood where Wolfe had lived—characterized this homesickness as emblematic of a national longing for "places we have never known," while elsewhere admitting that the South represented "a homeland within a homeland" to which Wolfe was inexorably bound.[38] For McCullers, the South was inherently "other," a home-place within a nation that was geographically bound but imaginatively separate, while the longing that Wolfe expressed was neither for the South nor for America but rather for "places we have never known."[39] There are thus two distinct inflections given to *Sehnsucht* throughout Wolfe's fiction—expressing both a concrete and an undefinable home—but for Wade such nuances were reduced to mere sentiment, to a yearning capable of being satisfied via a stronger identification with his native soil.

Wolfe and the "Real South"

Wolfe's native soil was, of course, Appalachia. The Agrarian idealism of southern farming did not reflect Wolfe's childhood—he was the son of business owners—nor was the imaginative landscape of his youth suitably bucolic. In this way, Wolfe was doubly excluded: not only did his fiction fail to sufficiently romanticize the Agrarian South, but Wolfe's Appalachian South was wholly distinct from the region esteemed by the southern Agrarians. David E. Whisnant, in his cultural history of Appalachia, further complicates this relationship by noting that the Appalachian region was itself being colonized by northeastern capital—"most of the coal and timber land was bought by northeastern-based entrepreneurs and corporations"—and that a history of intervention by those who acted to "preserve" or "revive" mountain culture meant that the supposed culture of Appalachia was in many ways a "selection, an arrangement, an accommodation to preconceptions."[40] In Whisnant's terms, the southern Agrarians were "cultural interveners," and the southern culture that they wished to preserve was not evident in the pages of Wolfe's fiction. Scott Romine, in *The Real South* (2008), describes this complex and conflicted vision of the "real South" as the "real"/"South," a "set of anxious, transient, even artificial intersections, sutures, or common surfaces between two concepts that are themselves remarkably fluid."[41] Eugene Gant's mountain hamlet in Altamont—modeled on his hometown of Asheville—did not inhabit the southern space of Wade's "wise old bird" farmer Cousin Lucius, and their divergent southern homesickness is evidence of this fluid figure of the South. It is important to note that the capital "colonizing" Appalachia was not peculiar to this region of the South. In his essay "Place as Everywhere," Michael O'Brien describes the tendency to think of the "pre-1941 South" as a world that was "isolated and backward," rather than recognizing that "the entanglement of the South with international markets has been fairly continuous since the seventeenth century, [. . .] foreign investment in the southern economy has long been commonplace," and the economic changes at the heart of Agrarian anxieties "should be seen less as an unprecedented innovation and more as the resumption of normal service."[42]

Competing ideas of "home" and "region" routinely intertwine in studies of the American South, such that a displacement of this understanding of home is not only vital in interrogating the global significance of Wolfe's fiction but also in understanding the affront that Wolfe's picture of the South registered in the minds of these early regionalist critics, as well as contributing to present concerns around ideas of "place." But it is also important to acknowledge that Wolfe did have more fruitful encounters with the southern Agrarians. In a letter to Dixon Wecter, Wolfe recounted a "very pleasant evening" spent with "Red Warren, Allen Tate, Caroline Gordon, John Crowe Ransom," who were in Richmond for an MLA meeting, joking that he "did almost everything except become a Southern Agrarian."[43] Robert Penn Warren and Wolfe had already met the previous year at a writers' conference in Boulder, and Warren later wrote to Wolfe on a number of occasions, requesting a submission for his inaugural edition of the *Southern Review*. Warren's collection of short stories by southern writers, *A Southern Harvest* (1937), included Wolfe's "The House of the Far and Lost," though in *Understanding Fiction* (1943), Warren's American college textbook co-edited with Cleanth Brooks, Wolfe's work was noticeably absent. Stark Young—another southern novelist published by Charles Scribner's Sons and a contributor to *I'll Take My Stand*—also struck up a friendship with Wolfe, with one of the few direct references to an idea of "the South" occurring in a letter between the two writers within an ongoing conversation on Faulkner. Wolfe concurred with Young's suggestion that Faulkner wrote fiction that "is not like the South," yet "the South is *in* his books, and in the spirit that creates them."[44] Young later included Wolfe's story "Circus at Dawn" in his edited collection *Southern Treasury of Life and Literature* (1937), though he too was skeptical of Wolfe's "southern" status, writing to a friend that Wolfe was "scarcely Southern," since he came from "a German family from Pennsylvania transplanted to N.C. on the wrong side of the tracks."[45]

Wolfe wrote an oblique response to the Agrarians' handling of his fiction in *The Web and the Rock* (1939), a posthumously released novel that contains his most blatant condemnation of such critics. Wolfe characterized the Agrarians as the "refined young gentlemen of the New Confederacy," who, having found their lives and art severed from "the living inspiration of [their] source [. . .] what [they] had begun to call roots," retreated "haughtily into the South, to the academic security of a teaching appointment at one of the universities, from which they could issue in quarterly installments very small and very precious magazines which celebrated the advantages of an agrarian society."[46] George Webber, the novel's protagonist and yet another of Wolfe's fictional counterparts, finds the Agrarian critics puzzling in their renunciation of "aesthetic cliques" in whose membership they seemed to belong, arguing that the merits of "a return to an agrarian way of life" was always couched within language that "assuredly few dwellers on the soil [. . .] could understand." Wolfe adds that for Webber, "one who was himself derived from generations of mountain farmers who had struggled year by year to make a patch of corn grow," it "came as a mild surprise to be informed by the lily-handed intellectuals of a Southern university that what he needed most of all was a return to the earthly and benevolent virtues of the society which had produced him."[47] Wolfe, who was famously thin-skinned, was here clearly responding to Wade's suggestion that the novelist's duty was to reconcile with his origins, but he was also rejecting what he perceived as a fundamentally cloistered vision of the South, a retrogressive nostalgia peddled by a group of effete, "lily-handed" intellectuals who were "too tender and inept" to deal with the challenges of city living.

While Wolfe simplistically contends that the Agrarian ideology was merely a return to the "Old South" ways of the Confederacy, his skepticism toward their exceptionalist rhetoric and characterization of these men as intellectuals writing in small literary magazines reflects the fact that the main forum where their ideas had a real and lasting impact was in the development of southern literature. Addressing this very role of *I'll Take My Stand*, John M. Grammer contends: "It is the book that, whether they [southern intellectuals] liked its arguments or not, defined their role in the national literary community, the touchstone that any commentator on Southern letters or culture must acknowledge in some way."[48] Challenging their view of a detached South, Wolfe emphasized his own essential "southernness," pointing to his ancestry and his masculine determination to "do his best [as a southerner] when the odds are against him," staying committed to remaining a southerner in a northern city.[49] Wolfe's view had an unlikely ally in H. L. Mencken, who in 1935 suggested that such Agrarians made the error of social reformers "at all times and everywhere [. . .] conjur[ing] up a beautiful Utopia" of the bucolic South without recognizing its inextricable ties to the very society from which they wished to extricate themselves.[50]

Extending his tirade in *The Web and the Rock,* Wolfe reflects on the experience of the southerner within "the howling maelstrom of the city's life," which he took to be the vital and vigorous symbol of American life.[51] The picture of the South conjured by George Webber is precisely the image the Agrarians wanted to alter, prompting one critic to suggest that Wolfe "spat upon" the South:

> He saw an old house, set far back from the travelled highway, and many passed along that road, and the troops went by, the dust rose, and the war was over. And no one passed along that road again. He saw an old man go along the path, away from the road, into the house; and the path was overgrown with grass and weeds, with thorny tangle, and with underbrush until the path was lost. And no one ever used that path again. And the man who went into that house never came out of it again. And the house stayed on. It shone faintly through that tangled growth like its own ruined specter, its doors and windows black as eyeless sockets. That was the South.[52]

Regarding this specific passage, Michael O'Brien remarks that "this is a quotation I used in my first (and very bad) article on the South," overly persuaded, at the time, of the South's insularity—the South as a "shuttered mansion." While O'Brien takes for granted that Wolfe's image is "deeply misleading"—yet another rehearsal of southern exceptionalism—his contention that the South needs to be reconfigured within a global framework (not escaping "old structures of power," but "devis[ing] new structures that must [. . .] interact with those old structures and thereby transform them") is central to the project of this book.[53] Wolfe's backward glance to the "ruined specter" of the antebellum South needs to be read in light of his ontology of longing—as a yearning for a nonplace that is endlessly enticing—bearing in mind the ways this same *Sehnsucht* for a supposed "South" is indefinite, multilocal, and fundamentally global. Rather than reading Wolfe's work as the tangled path in this excerpt—a way back to an unaltered, provincial vision of small-town southern life—it is worth mobilizing Wolfe's own metaphor of the "web" as a means of understanding the transnational trajectory of his work and influence as it moves outward: extends, threads, and crisscrosses, "engulfed again in the everlasting web and weaving of this great earth."[54]

Wolfe as the Voice of Patriotism

Moving from the Agrarian treatment of Wolfe, it is worth returning to a central contention of this book: that the way Wolfe's fiction was *used* is at least as revelatory as careful attention to his writing. One instance in which approaching Wolfe's fiction as a cultural artifact reveals the problem of his regional identification is in the publication of an anthology titled *American Harvest* (1942). *American Harvest* was an anthology of American creative writing edited by Allen Tate and John Peale Bishop. The editors decreed that "for the first time in the history of this country it is possible to produce an anthology [that] represents what is, properly speaking, a literature," adding that *American Harvest* demonstrated that "from our experience of Europe [. . .] we learned first to be Americans and then how to be American writers."[55] Wolfe's inclusion in this anthology is curious. Allen Tate never published his own criticism of Wolfe, and in lectures he had told students that the author "not only did harm to the novel, but moral damage to his readers."[56] Bishop's only essay on Wolfe, written for John Crowe Ransom's inaugural issue of the *Kenyon Review*, attacked Wolfe's formlessness and immaturity, concluding that Wolfe had "achieved probably the utmost intensity of which incoherent writing is capable."[57]

That these two editors would choose an author they apparently loathed as representative of "a literature in the sense in which the French understand the word" is in reality indicative of the way that Wolfe's fiction was widely adopted as nationalist propaganda, a reminder of the importance of approaching his fiction within a broader geographical frame. Revealingly, the Office of Inter-American Affairs (CIAA)—a U.S. State Department agency committed to "unify[ing] the American Hemisphere on a multilateral basis against possible aggression from outside"—had sponsored the publication of *American Harvest* as a form of soft diplomacy, which they characterized as a "cultural relations" project.[58] The CIAA was formed in response to concerns of a Nazi influence in Latin America—concerning potential ideological allegiances and a raw materials trade—with one of its more famous projects being the Walt Disney Studios productions *Saludos Amigos* (1942) and *The Three Caballeros* (1945), which, in the words of one prominent commentator, "did more to cement a community of interest between peoples of the Americas in a few months than the State Department had in fifty years."[59] In the process of editing Wolfe's story for the state-sponsored collection, Tate had chastised Bishop for his fifty-page selection, writing that his own was only nine pages, "making it about 5½ times as good as yours. Zero would be perfect."[60] According to the CIAA, Wolfe's romantic vision of America, however much its formlessness irked the editors, was particularly amenable to cultural propaganda within Latin America, and so the story was included.

It is clear that from as early as 1939, Thomas Wolfe's fiction was excised, altered, emended, and reconfigured to serve as a symbol for America—a job Wolfe himself facilitated through the project of taking the "billion forms, the million names, the huge, single, and incomparable substance of America" and making it the substance of his art.[61] What is routinely overlooked, however, are the ways in which the amenability of Wolfe's work to propagandizing a legend of "America" has strongly influenced Wolfe's reception, particularly in the tendency to treat him as a symbolic writer or even as a propagandist himself. Thus, certain southern critics can perceive the ubiquitous symbols of "the South" and brand Wolfe a regionalist, while the CIAA, the Council for Books in Wartime, and CBS, among others, can be attracted to the prevailing symbol of "America" in his work. As I mentioned in chapter 1, radio writers quickly seized on the aural riches of Wolfe's language, particularly his prose portraits of the great continent of *America*. One CBS Radio Workshop episode, which aired in 1957, exemplified this approach to Wolfe's writing: in a segment called "1489 words," in which 1489 words were lifted from a literary text to challenge the old adage about pictures painting a thousand words, 398 of those came from "The Thunder of Imperial Names," a patriotic piece with musical accompaniment that composer Jerry Goldsmith took from *Of Time and the River*.[62] The piece is almost solely taken up with a roll call of names—names of men and battles, states and rivers—but in Wolfe's original version it is a self-consciously poetic creation, frequently interrupted by myth and evocations of British balladry.[63]

In this particular section of *Of Time and the River*, the poet Alfred Tennyson stands by the rivers of time, hearing "the horns of Elfland faintly blowing" (a line from Tennyson's "Bugle song")[64] and watching the rivers of America unfurl before him: the Potomac—central to the southern American imaginary—is called "Father Tiber," and the Hudson is recast as the "gently flowing Thames," referencing Spenser's *Prothalamion* (1596) in its refrain: "Sweet Thames, flow gently till I end my song."[65] The narrative continues listing river names—"the Monongahela, the Colorado, the Rio Grande, the Columbia"—with the river names accruing like an incantation, conjuring actual water, flooding over "the mighty rails that bind the nation."[66] A kind of central railway station where all the lines and rivers meet is submerged, whose ruined cities and Greek corpses Wolfe likens to the drowned men in Shakespeare's *The Tempest*: "Full fathom five the carcass of old man Lype is lying (of his bones is coral made)."[67] The "thunder of imperial names," as it originally appeared in *Of Time and the River*, mythologizes the American continent, tracing the immutability of time as it unearths the detritus of other great civilizations—Roman and British—ultimately evoking the finite nature of man: "We are a phantom flare of grieved desire, the ghostling and phosphoric flicker of immortal time, a brevity of days haunted by the eternity of the earth. [. . .] We are the dupes of time." Goldsmith's radio appropriation of the passage—re-recorded in 2006 by the U.S. Air Force Tactical Command Band—alters the passage so much that all textual and mythic references are omitted, with what is left serving merely to highlight the grand picture of America suggested through Wolfe's accumulation of names: "These are a few of their great, proud, glittering names, fit for the immense and lonely land that they inhabit."[68] Here Wolfe's words serve a purpose beyond their original use, and it is important to reiterate that his susceptibility to these kinds of propagandistic transformations—along with his cultural position as a voice of the South—is further evidence of how Wolfe's fiction has been employed in history, not evidence of Wolfe as a propagandist or regionalist.

Wolfe, Racism, and Eugenics

While Wolfe did not live long enough to see his work co-opted as propaganda, in the 1930s his fiction was not identified with Agrarianism, nor was the author interested in aligning himself with a movement that he considered to have fascist sympathies.[69] It is crucial to note that this exclusion from Agrarian circles does not liberate Wolfe from some of the charges leveled at the Agrarians since the publication of *I'll Take My Stand*. Southern Agrarians may have rejected Wolfe's vision of the South, but the criticisms of conservatism, fascism, racism, misogyny, and anti-Semitism that *I'll Take My Stand* has met with are strikingly similar to Wolfe's own views. In the 1960s, Paschal Reeves illuminated Wolfe's ideological indebtedness to nineteenth-century values like "racial superiority, exclusiveness, veneration for established tradition, distrust of unassimilated cultural patterns, and suspicion of urban values."[70] Brinkmeyer, likewise, argues that Wolfe's racial beliefs, "bound up with his troubled attitudes toward women and sexuality," combined a "characteristic white southern prejudice against blacks with hardcore American nativism" like that found in the work of Madison Grant and Lothrop Stoddard, which advocated for a "hereditary interpretation of history."[71] Importantly, both Brinkmeyer and Reeves acknowledge the relatively mainstream nature of these prejudices, not only in the Jim Crow South—where eugenics and racial biology were readily adapted in segregationist policy—but broadly circulating in America during the 1920s and '30s. Where Brinkmeyer and Reeves differ is in their interpretation of Wolfe's developing sense of social responsibility, his firsthand witness of oppression in Nazi Germany, and his advocacy for a "brotherhood of man" that characterizes his later work, particularly Wolfe's "Credo" at the end of *You Can't Go Home Again* (1940), which imagines America's "everlasting, living dream" as the "discovery of our own democracy." For Reeves, Wolfe's "espousal of the brotherhood of man" at the end of his career ultimately signified a renewed, liberal vision preceding his untimely death; for Brinkmeyer, Wolfe's "racialist thinking continued to befoul, and to betray, his larger, more hopeful vision."[72]

In my later chapters on Germany and Wolfe, I will contend that Wolfe's clarity around issues of racial injustice—particularly in his attitude toward Nazism—is muddied by his corresponding *Sehnsucht* for an imagined Germany. Much like Nazism's own reliance on myths of homeland and a heroic past, Wolfe's supposed "liberal vision" is marred by his unwillingness to see what is in front of him. Wolfe's broader engagement with racial identity, especially for a writer whose supposed project was a panorama of American life, is also shockingly narrow. His work is filled with racist epithets and essentializing portraits, and even when Wolfe creates a more fully realized nonwhite character, as in the case of Nebraska Crane in *The Web and the Rock*, the novelist obsesses over qualities that mark them as other. Whenever Crane's Cherokee identity is mentioned, for instance, it is evoked as a mythic force, inextricably connected with his capacity for violence: "His black eyes shone like agate in his head, the Cherokee in him had been awakened, he was set to kill."[73] Similarly, when Wolfe dedicates a chapter to the exploits of Dick Prosser, a young black man employed as a family servant in the story "The Child by Tiger," the story centers on violence: in this case, Dick's murderous rampage and eventual murder at the hands of a lynch mob.

"The Child by Tiger," originally published in the *Saturday Evening Post* in 1937, is closely modeled on a terrible episode from 1906 that Wolfe remembered from his childhood in Asheville. Prosser's real-life counterpart was Will Harris, a twenty-two-year-old man from Mecklenburg County who had escaped prison in Raleigh in 1903, having served three months of a twenty-five-year sentence for burglary, larceny, and assault.[74] On the night of November 13, 1906, following his purchase of a rifle and ammunition from a local pawnbroker, Harris was reported as having an altercation with an acquaintance, Toney Johnson, which led to Johnson alerting the police to Harris's whereabouts. Fleeing arrest, Harris embarked on a shooting spree, in which three onlookers—all black men—were shot and killed by Harris, as were two white police officers who were in pursuit. Local papers reported sensational calls for "another Ku-Klux," and on November 14—armed by the same pawnbroker that sold Harris his gun and emboldened by a privately funded reward of $1,200—armed citizens formed squads with police and began the hunt for Harris.[75] When Harris was finally caught the following day, the *Washington Post* front page read: "Outlaw dies fighting—Slayer of Asheville Policeman Riddled with Bullets—Run Down by Band of Fifty" (figure 4).[76] There were fears that the angry mob, which swelled as the procession returned to the town square, would steal and burn the body, and as a concession the coroner allowed the bullet-riddled corpse of Harris to be displayed in a window. The *Post* reported that onlookers streamed in and out of the undertakers' room for more than

OUTLAW DIES FIGHTING

Slayer of Asheville Policeman Riddled with Bullets.

RUN DOWN BY BAND OF FIFTY

Driven to Bay in Woods After a Long Chase—Two Members of the Posse Wounded in Encounter—Crowd at Asheville Gaze on the Dead Body. Threat of Burning Not Carried Out.

FIGURE 4.
"OUTLAW DIES FIGHTING."
Washington Post, November 16, 1906.
The sensational story of Will Harris's capture and death that formed the basis of Wolfe's story "The Child by Tiger" ran on the front page of the *Post*.

three hours. Wolfe's version viscerally recalls Harris's body, which he refers to merely as a *thing*: "It was this way, bullet-riddled, shot to pieces, open to the vengeful and morbid gaze of all, that Dick came back to town. The mob came back right to its starting point in South Dean Street. They halted there before an undertaking parlor, not twenty yards away from where Dick had killed John Chapman. They took that ghastly mutilated thing and hung it in the window of the undertaker's place, for every woman, man, and child in town to see."[77]

The story of Will Harris illuminates structures of power that were present in Asheville at the turn of the century. The mob that formed and the private subscriptions that bolstered the reward money reveal the state-sanctioned threat of public violence that accompanied black crime in Asheville. In the year following the massacre, a superior court judge from North Carolina was at pains to correct the *Washington Post*'s designation of "lynching" in the case of Harris, writing that "I had duly outlawed the man known as Will Harris [who] was shot by a posse after he had failed to surrender and while he was firing upon his pursuers."[78] Terence Finnegan writes that whites "often regarded lynching as the appropriate response" when the crimes involved "a convict or outlaw," highlighting the belief that the "recidivist had proven himself impenetrable to white criminal justice, hence lynching was necessary to preserve civil and social order."[79] At the end of "The Child by Tiger," Wolfe remains baffled by the violence of his story and its source, incapable of registering its relationship to racism or structural inequality. Instead, Wolfe's sees the origins of Prosser's violence—and so also Will Harris's—as a dark (read: black) secret. Wolfe fills his final passage in language that stresses the alterity of dark skin and reinforces the white prejudice that blackness is other, primordial, untamed, even demonic: "He came from darkness. He came out of the heart of darkness, from the dark heart of the secret and undiscovered South. He came by night, just as he passed by night. He was night's child and partner, a token of the other side of man's dark soul, a symbol of those things that pass by darkness and that still remain, a symbol of man's evil innocence, and the token of his mystery, a projection of his own unfathomed quality, a friend, a brother, and a mortal enemy, an unknown demon, two worlds together—a tiger and a child."[80]

# # #

If we return to the ways in which Wolfe's fiction was used, there are examples of appropriation by individuals and groups whose broader message conflicted with Wolfe's own latent antagonisms and, in a number of instances, his racialist thinking. Even with his "befouled vision," for instance, some adopted the author's vision of American hope and democracy in support of race relations. Eleanor Roosevelt—a figure who, according to Harvard Sitkoff, "did more to alter the relationship between the New Deal and the cause of civil rights" than any other individual—appropriated the sentiment of democratic change expressed in Wolfe's "Credo" ("a wind is rising and the rivers flow") to declare, in a 1941 speech, that "a wind is rising throughout the world of free men everywhere, and they will not be kept in bondage."[81] Four years later, a section of the same speech, together with a more overt reference to Wolfe's quotation, was used as an epigraph and inspiration for Walter White's *A Rising Wind* (1945), the NAACP leader's exposé on the discrimination of black soldiers during World War II.[82] Nevertheless, I am more sympathetic to Brinkmeyer's analysis, which reads Wolfe's racialist thinking—specifically attributed to Grant and Stoddard—as deeply at odds with his supposed liberal vision. Brinkmeyer's thesis concerning the relevance of Grant and Stoddard to Wolfe's racial politics reveals the complex ways in which such politics were developing in the 1920s, demonstrating the degree to which Wolfe's problematic racism was an echo of popular belief. While Brinkmeyer concedes that it is not known whether Wolfe actually read these authors' works, their mutual insistence on the primacy of blood—and therefore also genetics—in determining the expression of society and culture through history is indicative of a popular and widespread belief in hereditary and racial superiority.[83]

Although eugenics and the hereditarianism of Grant and Stoddard should not necessarily be conflated, Alexandra Stern points out that in the 1920s, as the eugenics movement achieved its greatest national visibility, it was "virtually synonymous with biological racism and modern degenerationism," and other critics have suggested that the American public learned about heredity "primarily from the eugenics movement."[84] The year after Lothrop Stoddard published his influential *The Rising Tide of Color* (1920) under the auspices of Wolfe's publisher, Charles Scribner's Sons (and publicly endorsed by President Warren G. Harding), the American Natural History Museum hosted the Second International Eugenics Congress (1921), attended by over three hundred global delegates including future president Herbert Hoover and Alexander Graham Bell (honorary president of the congress), as well as Madison Grant (treasurer) and Stoddard (in charge of publicity).[85] In an article covering the conference, the *New York Times* reported the comments of Major Leonard Darwin—son of Charles Darwin—that the "sound and fit and superior people should, by a campaign of patriotism, be induced to raise larger families. [. . .] Racial deterioration seems evident among all highly civilized peoples [. . .] because of the thinning out of the descendants of highly endowed stock and the multiplication of those of inferior endowment."[86] By the time of the conference, the American eugenics movement was already the world's largest and best funded, with support from the Carnegie Institution, the Rockefeller Foundation, and Kellogg's Race Betterment Foundation, with speakers representing some of America's most prestigious centers of learning, including Johns Hopkins, Columbia, Princeton, Cornell, MIT, NYU, Harvard University, the U.S. Department of Agriculture, the Wistar Institute, and the Peabody Museum.[87] In his book *The Nazi Connection* (1994), Stefan Kühl uncovers the extensive financial support from American foundations that underwrote eugenic research in Germany, arguing that "the Rockefeller Foundation played the central role in establishing and sponsoring major eugenic institutes in Germany, including the Kaiser Wilhelm Institute for Psychiatry and the Kaiser Wilhelm Institute for Anthropology, Eugenics, and Human Heredity," noting that the foundation continued to support eugenicists "even after the National Socialists had gained control over German science."[88]

In 1939, just as Wolfe had done three years earlier, Lothrop Stoddard visited Nazi Germany as a celebrated American author, reflecting on his experiences in *Into the Darkness* (1940). Stoddard—a Massachusetts-born Harvard alumnus—traveled in an official capacity as a journalist for the North American Newspaper Alliance, using the reputation of his previous work on racial anthropology to gain access to high-level German officials, included Heinrich Himmler and Adolf Hitler. He reported that "Nazi Germany's eugenic program is the most ambitious and far-reaching experiment in eugenics ever attempted," a response to what Stoddard saw as a nation "biologically in a bad way" when the Nazis first came to power.[89] Wolfe's familiarity with Stoddard goes beyond Brinkmeyer's assertion that the only evidence lies in Wolfe's own racial taxonomy. Not only did Wolfe's publisher, Charles Scribner's Sons, publish eight of Stoddard's books between 1920 and 1935, but in May 1934 Stoddard and Wolfe both had pieces published in the same edition of *Scribner's Magazine*.[90] Moreover, Stoddard was certainly known to Wolfe's friend F. Scott

Fitzgerald, whose character Tom Buchanan, in *The Great Gatsby* (1925), extolls the virtues of *The Rising Tide of Color*:

> "Civilization's going to pieces," broke out Tom violently. "I've gotten to be a terrible pessimist about things. Have you read 'The Rise of the Colored Empires' by this man Goddard?" [. . .] "Well, it's a fine book, and everybody ought to read it. The idea is if we don't look out the white race will be—will be utterly submerged. It's all scientific stuff; it's been proved." [. . .] "Well these books are all scientific," insisted Tom. [. . .] "This fellow has worked out the whole thing. It's up to us, who are the dominant race, to watch out or these other races will have control of things." [. . .] "This idea is that we're Nordics. I am, and you are, and you are, and—" After an infinitesimal hesitation he included Daisy with a slight nod, and she winked at me again. "—and we've produced all the things that go to make civilization—oh, science and art, and all that. Do you see?"[91]

It would have been no surprise that a man like Tom Buchanan—or Thomas Wolfe—had access to Stoddard and Grant's notions of racial superiority. Not only was *The Rising Tide of Color* a publishing success in 1920, but, in that same year, Henry Ford began a propaganda campaign against Jews, while the *Saturday Evening Post*—in 1920 the most widely read magazine in the United States—urgently commended Grant's doctrines to its readers.[92] Daylanne English argues that in the 1920s, "eugenics emerged as a central national ideology [. . .] most of all because it so effectively addressed that crisis of modern American subjectivity."[93]

The history of racialism in the Jim Crow South, and the centrality of race to regional identity, is fundamental to discussions concerning both the imagined figure of the South and the invention of southern literature.[94] Within the context of the Agrarian movement, the steadfast belief held by white southern men of the South as the true embodiment of the American spirit insisted on segregation as an essential condition of the southern way of life. As Leigh Anne Duck rightly points out, concerns with southern poverty and racism only intensified in light of fascism's expansion throughout Europe, serving to "highlight the contradiction between southern apartheid and democratic governance."[95] Proponents of the new southern studies over the past few decades have properly insisted on foregrounding race and gender within discussions of the South as an imagined space, working to extricate "representations of the South [. . .] from a possessive investment in a version of southernness that makes it hard to account for other Souths. [. . .] Put simply, we need a southern studies that is not only for white southerners."[96] Crucially, Wolfe's fiction not only embodies aspects of this problematic nativism but has also been discussed by critics in these exceptionalist terms, alienating his fiction from almost every significant publication on southern literature in the last two decades. It is important to recognize that the racial politics Wolfe developed—although codified and enduring in the South—were also present in the rest of America. Duck notes that as early as the end of the 1930s, the nation/South dichotomy was being critically scrutinized, as "writers and activists exposed the degree to which southern racial practices corresponded, rather than conflicted, with those of the larger nation."[97] Wolfe's fiction cannot be unmoored from his racialist thinking, and rather than sidestep this innate ugliness within his oeuvre, subsequent chapters will consider the ways in which his *Sehnsucht* for Germany undermined the universalist vision that constitutes part of Wolfe's enduring legacy.

Wolfe and New Southern Studies

When Wolfe published *Look Homeward, Angel* (1929) at the age of twenty-nine, his southern identity was not considered an essential element of his writing by most readers. Wolfe had already lived in North Carolina, Massachusetts, New York, and England, crossed the Atlantic four times, and spent (in total) roughly two years abroad between 1924 and 1929. As with many other writers from the southeastern United States, Wolfe followed the pattern of internal migration from south to north, moving from Asheville, North Carolina, to Harvard, and then on to Brooklyn. Though his itinerancy did not directly correlate to his fictional counterpart Eugene Gant in *Look Homeward, Angel*—ending as it does before the hero leaves his hometown—Wolfe's subsequent fictional outpouring tracks a northward course and crisscrosses the Atlantic as his doppelgängers attempt to satisfy their unquenchable *Sehnsucht* for "elsewhere" places. Wolfe's profoundly autobiographical fiction romanticized the movement and travel that characterized his early writing years. While almost all early reviews of *Look Homeward, Angel* acknowledged Wolfe and his fictional family, the Gants, as southerners, very few paused to consider the importance of region to Wolfe's writing. In 1929 there was not yet any Agrarian manifesto, no *Southern Review* or *Kenyon Review*, and no established canon of modern southern literature. In fact, the perspective of one southern critic, Stringfellow Barr, offered an important counterargument to Agrarian dissatisfactions with *Look Homeward, Angel*, identifying Wolfe's rejection of southern insularity as healthy, while also positioning the author as an early example of a global southern writer.

In the early 1930s, Barr edited the influential *Virginia Quarterly Review*, which played an important role in voicing New Critical concerns, publishing early work by Cleanth Brooks, Allen Tate, and Robert Penn Warren. Unlike other journals that published early instances of New Criticism, Wolfe's fiction found a sympathetic, critical ear in Barr at *VQR*. Barr greatly admired Wolfe's novel, inviting him to speak at the University of Virginia on two separate occasions, while his review of *Look Homeward, Angel*, "The Dandridges and the

Gants" (1930), was the most significant scholarly treatment of the book to date. In his essay, Barr compares Wolfe's *Look Homeward, Angel* with Stark Young's *River House* (1929), published by Charles Scribner's Sons in the same year that it released Wolfe's maiden novel. Young was a contributor to the Agrarian manifesto *I'll Take My Stand,* and his novel *River House*—out of print since 1930—is preoccupied with the notion of the "Old South" as a culture in crisis. For Barr, the two novels couldn't be more different in their treatments of the South: he claims that "a foreigner would not readily discover in the two books reflections of the same civilization."[98] While Barr reads *River House* as "a backward glance at a dying culture submerged and overwhelmed not merely by America but by its own Americanized youth," *Look Homeward, Angel* was "the saga of a human soul, the soul of a boy who happened to grow up in North Carolina."

While "northern" critics like Maxwell Geismar would later be criticized for suggesting that Wolfe's place of birth was incidental to his fiction, Stringfellow Barr was the first southern critic to emphasize the necessity of reading Wolfe as an international, not merely southern, author.[99] Barr not only anticipated the friction that would arise between Wolfe and the Agrarians but also identified a central problem of Wolfe criticism that endures to the present day. Only in recent years have scholars described the concept of the South in terms that allow for invention and flux, realizing that from the beginning, groups like the Agrarians "deliberately presented a fabricated South," seeing the South instead as a crucial point of intersection for connections of U.S. literature, incorporating "broader narratives of the Western journey into modernity."[100] Barr presciently intuited Wolfe's place amid a new generation of southern novelists, having grown up "sufficiently outside of River House to look with a child's eyes at the life about him."[101] According to Barr, the problem of the South that Young and his fellow Agrarians were trying to preserve was ultimately "unable to recapture a social synthesis that Reconstruction had destroyed, it had not the heart, or the stomach either, to adopt frankly the American solution of life."[102] In Wolfe's case, Barr suggests that the author hadn't just adopted a specifically "American" solution but had instead gone even further, invoking a universal conflict: "His conflict is no longer the political conflict of the South and the North but the artistic conflict of his own spirit with the souls about him. With 'Look Homeward, Angel' the South has contributed to the literature of the world a novel, strongly provincial in its flavor, universal in its terrible tragedy."

This reading of Wolfe as a "global" southern writer is an important anomaly in a field that has increasingly sequestered his fiction within a definably southern tradition. Barr's essay, however, was ultimately unable to prevent the eventual relegation of Wolfe to a mere "footnote" within southern literary history.

In his influential *The Mind of the South* (1941), W. J. Cash wrote that while southern heritage could never be "the sole determinant in shaping the writers to whom I refer," for a writer like Wolfe the extravagance and enormity of his characters had a "good deal to do with [. . .] the fact that he was a Southerner."[103] That Wolfe's experiences in the South inform his view of time and longing is undeniable, but the insistence of critics in aligning Wolfe's longing with his regional identity is typical of arguments that presume an a priori regional distinctiveness. The larger reimagining of the literature of the South that has emerged in the last few decades has been directly antagonistic to these sorts of claims and to the literature, like Wolfe's, that seems most amenable to such exceptionalism. In an essay reviewing three books published under the mantle of "new southern studies"—an umbrella label for this critical turn—Richard H. King suggests that this reconceptualization of the South is an inevitable result of several lingering questions—What is the South? What is Southern literature?—and that the new southern studies is now, primarily, "an exploration of the way the South has been thought about."[104] This reimagining, as King suggests, is not about an *actual* South—that is, the coherent, homogeneous, matter-of-fact, *old* South—but with images or representations of the South; in King's words, "there's no South there, only 'the South.'"

Following on from Kreyling's *Inventing Southern Literature*, other critical works on the construction of southern literature have raised questions about the validity of an assumed or commonsense set of qualities that, historically, have been said to constitute the South.[105] New southern studies' intersection with hemispheric and transnational studies has, in McKee and Trefzer's phrasing, "unmoor[ed] the South from its national harbor [where] it becomes a floating signifier in a sea of globalism."[106] Likewise, in Greeson's *Our South* (2010), "the South" appears in quotation marks, regarded first and foremost as "an ideological concept rather than a place." Greeson views "the South" as a cultural construct that has persisted since U.S. independence, firmly rooted in the development of national identity and inextricably linked with the United States writ large, as its "internal other."[107] Greeson borrows Raymond Williams's term *ideological juxtaposition*, suggesting that the United States and "the South" are understood by reference, or in opposition, to the other. In this formulation, Greeson offers one particular justification for what she sees as the disproportionate interest of writers and readers with the southeastern states in light of their "actual role" in the "body politic at a given historical moment": not only were southern authors writing for a northern audience because of publishing constraints, but the "South" of their fiction was a site of national imagining, an internal other that was "materially peripheral to the modern nation" but "symbolically central to it."[108]

While one apparent result of the new extension of southern borders into an American imaginary is that the South ceases to be a region characterized by its exceptionality—now falling in with other constructions like "the nation" or "the North" or "America"—scholars in new southern studies have been careful to point out that the status of the imagined South, as it has been historically understood, has also been highly peculiar. Harilaos Stecopoulos suggests that while scholars have been hesitant to make exceptional claims about this region, the South's "national status renders it especially valuable for a post-nationalist American studies eager to question and destabilize normative boundaries"—a national status identified by Stecopoulos as both "hybrid" and "alien."[109] As Duck demonstrates in *The Nation's Region*, Depression-era reviews of experimental southern fiction reflected "an interpretive community convinced that the South constituted a site of profound cultural alterity," while the legacy of this period in the field of southern studies has been an enduring focus on "regional distinctiveness."[110] While arguments employing a priori assumptions around "southernness" are disregarded or treated as suspect within the discourse of new southern studies, one challenge lies in how to talk about this very tangible belief in the South's exceptional status when it is embedded in those texts that constitute the traditional southern canon. This challenge is further magnified when those texts that have traditionally been regarded as examples of self-evidently southern fiction fail—for a variety of reasons—to be incorporated into this new critical framework. Michael Kreyling has suggested that in some instances this challenge has necessitated critical decisions tantamount to willful forgetting: "There is an imperative to think new; on the other hand, one must not leave behind the old, enduring South, for doing that mounts to a kind of cultural suicide, a forfeiture of identity. Memory struggles with amnesia: what to remember and what to forget, and most importantly at what cost to whom."[111]

Kreyling's construction of a "forfeiture of identity" has been deployed most recently in *The South That Wasn't There* (2010), in which he employs a "Moebius strip of memory-and-history" as an interpretive framework for the study of southern literature, a coupling that even Kreyling admits is overused in southern studies.[112] Following Jon Smith, who has suggested that Kreyling's book is representative of an "old South" mentality that is "overdetermined by symbolic investments in the future or the past," my claim is that a core problem in Wolfe studies is precisely this insistence on nostalgically remembering Wolfe instead of attending to his actual reception and to the culture that formed around him.[113] While Wolfe remains tethered to a critical tradition that continues to interpret his fiction within such narrow parameters, his fiction is also overlooked within the "new" southern school of criticism. In *Disturbing Calculations* (2008)—one of the few books in this school to mention Wolfe—Melanie Benson argues that *Look Homeward, Angel* "turns a mirror on [. . .] an aspirant white underclass" but soon shifts the focus to Wolfe's cultivation of "an innate superiority": an unsavory "narcissistic reverie" that Benson dismissively concludes is "bent upon inflating the final product."[114] More recently, Tara Powell identifies Wolfe as one of a group of "beleaguered" southern intellectuals in *The Intellectual in Twentieth-Century Southern Literature* (2012), but she ultimately concedes that Wolfe has been "routed in the southern canon" by Faulkner.[115] My argument, following Greeson in *Our South*, is that "rather than furnishing something so simple as a site of domestic regional variation for U.S. literature," as a generation of southern literary historians has done, in order to "grasp the workings" of Wolfe's South, it is essential to incorporate a "comparative, transnational geographic frame."[116]

Longing for Home

At this point in the chapter, it is fair to ask: What precisely *is* Wolfe's vision of home, if it is not the typical, crumbling vision of an identifiable "South"? In an interview with the *Boston Evening Transcript* in 1931, Wolfe reflected on the nature of American homesickness: "I learned this curious thing about myself in those years of wandering, and I think it is true of Americans as a whole. We're a homesick people, homesick for something we haven't here, and homesick still when we seek it abroad."[117] In "Look Homeward, Americans," reflecting from the vantage of her room overlooking the Brooklyn Bridge, Carson McCullers echoed Wolfe's sentiment, writing that "our literature is stamped with a quality of longing and unrest, and our writers have been great wanderers."[118] As McCullers described the distant view of the Manhattan skyline, with its "pastel mauve and yellow" skyscrapers that "rise up sharp as stalagmites against the sky," she remembered that this vista was once shared by Thomas Wolfe and Hart Crane; looking out, McCullers is "homesick in a way that they were often homesick." As previously noted, this particular kind of homesickness is, for McCullers, peculiarly *American*: "It is a curious emotion, this certain homesickness I have in mind. With Americans, it is a national trait, as native to us as the roller coaster or the jukebox. It is not simply longing for the home town or the country of our birth. The emotion is Janus-faced: we are torn between a nostalgia for the familiar and an urge for the foreign and strange. As often as not, we are homesick most for the places we have never known."

McCullers's description of an American homesickness is an intentional evocation of Wolfe's first novel, *Look Homeward, Angel*, the sprawling and romantic bildungsroman that is preoccupied, and indeed saturated, with *Sehnsucht*. Writing at the age of twenty-three and having just published *The Heart Is a Lonely Hunter* (1940), it would be too easy to characterize this social critique as merely the reflected Romanticism of those whom McCullers mentions as being indicative of the same youthful exuberance that has led many writers to be in thrall to Wolfe at eighteen, only to renounce him after college for more "serious" fiction. However, McCullers's avoidance of a specific home "place," while still evoking the idea of homesickness, offers a valuable frame for reinterpreting Wolfe within the context of imaginary and global Souths.[119]

As I have been arguing, Wolfe's *Sehnsucht*—particularly as it took on the form of a kind of infinite homesickness—is often presented as an inevitable outcome of being in the world, a universal longing for something imagined and unattainable: "And everywhere that year there was something secret, lonely, and immense that waited, that impended, that was still. Something that promised numbly, hugely, in the fog-numb air, and that never broke to any open sharpness, and that was almost keen and frosty October in remembered hills—oh, there was something there incredibly near and most familiar, only a word, a stride, a room, a door away—only a door away and never opened, only a door away and never found."[120]

The accumulation of declaratives—"that waited, that impended, that was still [. . .] that promised"—reinforces the latent possibility of such yearning, and the cavalcade of words such as "secret," "lonely," "numbly," "hugely," and "fog-numb," highlights the impossibility of attainment. The home conjured by Wolfe's "remembered hills"—always in the forlorn and mournful month of October—is both "near" and "most familiar" while also, necessarily, "a stride, a room, a door away." Wolfe's homesickness is for no place, or perhaps a no-place: a home that is not southern or northern but always yet unvisited, and thus the nostalgic glance is turned impossibly forward. This expression of *Sehnsucht* resides at the core of Wolfe's ontology of longing. While southern literary historians comfortably characterized Wolfe's expression of *Sehnsucht* as homesickness for the South, or as a particularly *southern* sensitivity to memory, in Wolfe's other professed homeland of Germany, Martin Heidegger was lecturing on the essential nature of *Sehnsucht*, calling it "something which rather gives us occasion to understand it as that in which we humans are freed *beyond* ourselves."[121] While this longing "beyond" did not stop Wolfe from nationalizing his experience, writing about longing as a distinctly American experience, Wolfe's ontology of longing embraces various frames of reference, not all of them immured within the United States. In a later lecture delivered at the University of Freiburg in 1942, while National Socialism was steadily enacting its weltanschauung across Europe, Heidegger identified the necessary implication of this fundamental experience of *Sehnsucht* through an analysis of Hölderlin's hymn "The Ister," which he interpreted as an indication that we are *not yet* at home: "This *coming to be* at home in one's own self in itself entails that human beings are initially, and for a long time, and sometimes forever, not at home."[122]

Within the context of Wolfe's writing on the South, his universalizing imperative in describing an ontology of longing—an experience that exists for all persons everywhere, as Wolfe conceives it—is often linked with narratives that engage directly with the imaginative differentiation of "America" and "South." Wolfe's protagonists can long for "home" even while they are in the South, reinforcing McCullers's claim that for Wolfe there was a homeland within a homeland. Beyond this distinction, the South also serves as a symbol for dislocated longing, offering a rich imaginative language for exploring this ontology of longing, as a focal point for the insatiable and unnamable *Sehnsucht* that pervades so much of his work. Indeed, if "the South" can be properly understood first as a concept, then it is clear how the figure of "the South" provides Wolfe with one of the loci of his hero's intolerable longing. Wolfe's typically *southern* longing must be reframed as an engagement with the imaginative potential of the South as an ideological concept in order to challenge the regionalist approach to his work, and also to suggest how reconceptualizing home and homesickness in Wolfe's fiction provides new interpretive strategies for approaching this same preoccupation in the fiction of his contemporaries.

❋ ❋ ❋

Following the introduction of *Sehnsucht* and Heidegger's existential grappling with *Heimweh*, the specter of Germany invariably looms large in this book. The following discussion of Wolfe and Germany explores and expands this vital relationship, further complicating previous treatments of Wolfe within the confines of the American continent as well as offering a compelling case study in the complex transnational exchange between German and American literary cultures. Wolfe's relationship to Germany, his indebtedness to German Romanticism and classicism, and his reception in Germany at a time in which fellow American writers fled to Paris offer an original and highly revealing approach to an important figure in the development of modern American literature. When the German émigré philosopher Ernst Bloch was reaching for a quote to summarize a tragic vision of universal homelessness at the conclusion of his monumental study *The Principle of Hope* (1959)—written in the United States between 1938 and 1947—he turned to Thomas Wolfe, quoting from the epigraph to *You Can't Go Home Again*: "There came to him an image of man's whole life upon the earth. It seemed to him that all man's life was like a tiny spurt of flame that blazed out briefly in an illimitable and terrifying darkness, and that all man's grandeur, tragic dignity, his heroic glory, came from the brevity and smallness of this flame. He knew his life was little and would be extinguished, and that only darkness was immense and everlasting."[123]

Bloch viewed this passage as symptomatic of an ontological hopelessness—the insatiability of *Sehnsucht*—and his interpretation gestures toward the complex relationship of exchange and reception that Wolfe's fiction underwent across the Atlantic, which will be discussed in the following chapters.

PART 2 Abroad

CHAPTER THREE

"The Measureless Realm of Elfland"

Wolfe, Germany, and *Sehnsucht*

On May 23, 1935, Wolfe sat down with Martha Dodd, the daughter of the American ambassador in Germany, and dictated a long letter to his editor, Maxwell Perkins. Writing from the Wartburg castle, Wolfe enthusiastically relayed that he was staying on the "great legendary kind of hill" where Richard Wagner had been inspired to write his opera *Tannhäuser und der Sängerkrieg auf Wartburg* (1845).[1] The location was particularly evocative for Wolfe, who had just visited Goethe's home in Weimar and the crypt in which both Goethe and Schiller were buried, telling Perkins that he seemed to have uncovered "the spirit of the great Germany and the great and noble spirit of freedom." The landscape from Weimar to the Wartburg castle was for Wolfe "the most indescribably lovely and magical landscape I have ever seen," adding, "I have not space or power enough here to tell you how beautiful and fine and magical this trip has been." Wolfe's letter to Perkins traces his pilgrimage to these literary sacred sites, which are all the more enchanting in light of the author's warm reception in Germany, of which he adds: "I have heard it said that Lord Byron awoke one morning at twenty-four to find himself famous. Well, I arrived in Berlin one night, when I was thirty-four, and got up the next morning and went to the American Express and for the last two weeks at least I have been famous in Berlin." Almost ten years earlier, in a letter to Aline Bernstein—the well-known American set and costume designer with whom Wolfe had a long, turbulent affair—Wolfe predicted that Germany would ultimately be the nation in which his own "strange life" would "find a home."[2] More than almost any other American novelist of his generation, Wolfe filled his novels with Germany, both his reflections on its culture and the influences of its traditions on his work.

The important relationship between Wolfe and Nazi Germany has informed several recent and significant books dealing with American literature and the transatlantic exchange of culture and myth, most notably Brinkmeyer's study on the specter of European fascism in the work of white southern writers, *The Fourth Ghost* (2009), in which he dedicates a chapter to Wolfe, arguing that "perhaps no southern writer was influenced as deeply as Thomas Wolfe by the rise of Nazi Germany."[3] In one important study detailing the history of the "intellectual side of the American war effort against Nazi Germany," Michaela Moore sees Wolfe's work as emblematic of the American response to Nazism, pointing out that "in a striking illustration of literature prefiguring political and historical analysis, Wolfe's two prewar novels offer a catalog of the central themes that characterized the American debate on the Third Reich."[4] Waldemar Zacharasiewicz also locates Germany at the center of Wolfe's fiction, arguing that both Germany and Austria served as "counterimages and foils to capitalistic American society," and that by the end of his life Wolfe belonged to "the group of chroniclers of the fateful turn of events in Germany."[5] Where this current study diverges from these works is in identifying the degree to which the imaginative figure of Germany, like the figure of "the South," was a creatively rich resource for Wolfe—an elsewhere place that operates as surrogate home for the wandering heroes of Wolfe's fiction. Just as Wolfe was developing an ontology of longing within the confines of the American continent, his engagement with ideas of home and *Sehnsucht* held a striking resonance with attitudes that were developing in Weimar Germany and which saw their final fruition in the *Volksgemeinschaft* of the 1930s and 1940s. Significantly, German classicism and the Romantic movement—so deeply tied to German nationalism during and after the Weimar period—had a lasting impact on Wolfe's own expression of *Sehnsucht* and homesickness, an influence that challenges the notion of "endemic homesickness" that Carson McCullers, and many others, have identified as a central element of Wolfe's fiction.

The following two chapters explore the vital relationship between Wolfe and Germany, divided between the literary and philosophical exchanges, on one hand, and Wolfe's German reception, translation, and growing political awareness on the other. Chapter 3 offers a comprehensive investigation of Wolfe's problematic relationship with Germany, exploring how literature shaped Wolfe's earliest conception of Germany and its imaginative representation in his fiction as well as demonstrating that the imagined "home" of Wolfe's South should be considered in light of the German notion of *Heimat*. Turning briefly to the work of C. S. Lewis, this chapter also explores an alternative manifestation of *Sehnsucht* that is indebted to German Romanticism, comparing Lewis's spiritual longing with Wolfe's unutterable and insatiable yearning. In short, this chapter continues to argue that the German notion of *Sehnsucht* offers a crystallizing metaphor for what critics have previously perceived to be a diffuse and aimless yearning. Chapter 4 addresses Wolfe's reception in Germany and his influence on German writers like Hermann Hesse and Heinrich Böll. Contributing to the work on the specter of German Nazism in Wolfe's work, the story "I Have a Thing to Tell You" (1937) is also reconsidered; this story has already received significant scrutiny in discussions of Wolfe and Germany—as the narrative contains Wolfe's most coherent rejection of Nazism in Germany—but scholars have not yet explored its unlikely German-language translation during World War II by Rudolf Frank, an exiled writer and German Jew who was forced to flee to Switzerland. Focusing on this peculiar reception history, chapter 4 revitalizes discussion around Wolfe as a global figure of American literature.

There's No Place Like Heimat

At the close of the previous chapter I included a reference to Wolfe from Ernst Bloch's *The Principle of Hope*, a sprawling work of philosophy that explores, among other things, utopian desire and its connection to a homeland. Bloch's use of Wolfe is interesting not only because it offers an example of Wolfe's thought being taken seriously but because Bloch reads Wolfe as offering a vision of hopelessness: a denunciation of hope that is at odds with Bloch's own *Sehnsucht* for a concrete utopia. In the final paragraph of *The Principle of Hope*, Bloch describes this longing as being specifically anchored to a "homeland": "Once the person has grasped himself and established what is his, without expropriation and alienation, in real democracy, there arises in the world something which shines into the childhood of all and in which no one has yet been: homeland."[6] The idea of "homeland" is notable in this extract, given the history and relative untranslatability of the German term *Heimat* (homeland), which became foundational in National Socialist policy. Much like the Agrarian criticism of Wolfe, the longing of Wolfe unmoored from land is what leads to hopelessness, and Bloch's insistence on linking longing to homeland is fundamental for understanding the politics of *Sehnsucht* in the time of Wolfe's writing, particularly given the ideological connotations and uses of *Heimat* between 1933 and 1945 under the Nazi regime.[7] The concept of *Heimat* played a crucial role in the literature and the public sphere of the Third Reich, not only in legitimizing plans of racial cleansing and territorial expansion but also operating as a central conceit in the film and literature of the Nazi period.[8]

According to Alon Confino, the recent historiography of *Heimat* demonstrates that the idea is a "sophisticated cultural artefact" that—though it has roots in the late eighteenth century—was "engineered anew in the wake of the 1871 national unification as a way to reconcile the local, regional, and national identities."[9] Confino points to Celia Applegate's groundbreaking study *A Nation of Provincials* (1990), which mapped the abstract idea of *Heimat* onto regional contexts, taking what Applegate called the "particularities of regionality and the generalities of nationality" to rest on "what both region and nation have in common: the effort, for better or for worse, to maintain 'community' against the economic, political, and cultural forces that would scatter it."[10] Following on from the discussion of "the South" in the previous chapter, these recent shifts in the critical discussion of *Heimat* reflect the similar skepticism surrounding concrete expressions of "southernness" by scholars in new southern studies, focusing instead on the inventedness of these ideas while still recognizing their centrality in discourses of place, belonging, and identity.[11] This is not to conflate the complex and multitudinous connotations of *Heimat* with "the South," but simply to suggest that the various cultural, literary, national, and ideological manifestations of *Heimat* that have been discussed in the last few decades bear a resemblance to the reimagining of the South across the Atlantic.

In their work on *Heimat*, Szejnmann and Umbach describe a recent shift in critical discussions of *Heimat* in which the concept is "portrayed as a mechanism for participation" that enabled "people to imagine their attachment to a place as a vehicle for their membership in a wider 'imagined community.'"[12] In a statement of caution that is similarly applicable to proponents of southern studies—and broadly relevant to present discussions around nativism and America-first politics—Szejnmann and Umbach warn that such histories are susceptible to "overlooking or downplaying the political realities behind these cultural imaginaries." In one telling example that links the critical preoccupation with the South and *Heimat*, the region-focused collection *Appalachia Inside Out* (1995) at one point conflates *Heimat* and the Appalachian mountains, notably Wolfe's place of birth.[13] The editors argue that "Appalachia is perhaps one of the few places in the country where the concept of homeland still has great vitality. For those raised among them, the mountains are the *Heimat*, in the true German sense of the word, with its connotations of an inexpressible quality which is both a gift to and a claim upon its constituents." As a favorite son of Appalachian literature, it is Wolfe whom the editors perceive as an example of an "Appalachian" who left the mountains, only to continually feel "the tug of home[land] in his fiction."[14]

Heimat, according to Applegate, "is the word Germans reach for to express the attachments of place," but though it is evoked as a *particular* place, a "particular set of associations in both spatial and temporal terms," *Heimat* actually refers to a "collection of particularities," demonstrating a "multiplicity of German places."[15] In talking about *Sehnsucht* in Wolfe, it is essential to recognize this same impulse toward spatial metaphors—home, the South, America, Germany, etc.—without demanding that any of these places, or geographies, reign as the ultimate locus of desire. Indeed, as Szejnmann and Umbach argue, the political career of "the Heimat idea" only took off when "it was applied instead to the abstract sphere of the nation."[16] "Heimat," Szejnmann and Umbach note, "became a way of making one's attachment to the nation thinkable, configuring identity not as the property of an individual but as a cultural construct emerging at the intersection of people and space." It is possible for *Sehn-*

sucht to point to multiple geographies of desire, and in the case of Wolfe the attachment to a German *Heimat* is as obvious and significant as his yearning for a mythic American homeland. German "spaces" in Wolfe's fiction and correspondences are notably romanticized; in a journey entry from August 24, 1928, Wolfe describes Germany as the "measureless realm of Elfland."[17] Importantly, Wolfe's nearness to fascism is most apparent in his *Sehnsucht* for a German "Elfland," as it reflects the familiar permeation of fascist language with spatial metaphors—what Szejnmann and Umbach call the "spatialization of political language."[18] Linking Wolfe with the Germany literary tradition, particularly in light of the expression of *Sehnsucht* in his work, sheds light on the author's unusual attraction to a nation that was, increasingly, in the throes of a fascist dictatorship.

Wolfe and the German Literary Tradition

Right at the beginning of *Of Time and the River*, Eugene prepares to leave his "mountain town of Altamont" and head north, where the "tower-masted island of Manhattan beckons," with Wolfe describing the "fury of youth" in the language of *Sehnsucht*:

> It may have been a rock, a stone, a leaf, the moths of golden light as warm and moving in a place of magic green, it may have been the storm-wind howling in the barren trees, the ancient fading light of day in some forgotten summer, the huge unfolding mystery of undulant, on-coming night. Oh, it might have been all this in the April and most lilac darkness of some forgotten morning as he saw the clean line of the East cleave into morning at the mountain's ridge. It may have been the first light, bird-song, an end to labor and the sweet ache and pure fatigue of the lightened shoulder as he came home at morning hearing the single lonely hoof, the jinking bottles, and the wheel upon the street again, and smelled the early morning breakfast smells, the smoking wheat-cakes, and the pungent sausages, the steaks, biscuits, grits, and fried green apples, and the brains and eggs. It may have been the coil of pungent smoke upcurling from his father's chimney, the clean sweet gardens and the peach-bloom, apples, crinkled lettuce wet with dew, bloom and cherry bloom down drifting in their magic snow within his father's orchard.[19]

Such passages abound in Wolfe's work, but more than merely being instances of purple prose or vivid description, they gesture to Wolfe's grappling with the incoherence of such an experience of desire: hence, the accumulation of possible points of desire, all of which "may" or "might" illuminate the object of *Sehnsucht*. In fact, it is precisely these moments of inchoate desire that mark the yearning of Wolfe's writing as characteristic of *Sehnsucht*. In "Longing and Form," György Lukács suggests that it is the "stammering" quality of *Sehnsucht* that constitutes its essentially inexpressible quality: "They always say that Germany is the land of *Sehnsucht*, of longing, and German longing is so strong, they say, that it destroys all form, so overpowering that one cannot express it except by stammering."[20] Lothar Hönnighausen points out that these kinds of descriptive passages—which employ what he calls "magic" language—are particularly abundant in Wolfe's German scenes, evoking a Romanticism that informs both his picture of the "immense and lonely land" of America and what Wolfe called the "faery" land of Germany.[21]

After pointing out Wolfe's spellbound writing on Germany, Hönnighausen traces a familiar narrative of Wolfe's shift from a naïvely romantic view of Germany to a recognition of Nazi brutality, then a subsequent renewal of his faith in American democracy. This perspective on Wolfe's political trajectory characterizes much of the scholarship on Wolfe that has sought to redress his obscurity in the last few decades.[22] Even Brinkmeyer, who rightly asserts that Wolfe's democratic project was finally undone by his unrepentant racialist thinking, argues that Wolfe's story "I Have a Thing to Tell You" (1937) signaled "a reconfiguration in Wolfe's thinking and art, away from the fierce Romantic individualism that had shaped *Look Homeward, Angel* and *Of Time and the River* and toward [. . .] Wolfe's democratic 'social consciousness.'"[23] Because Wolfe described a picture of Nazi Germany that "reconfigured" his thinking at the end of his career, most critical appraisals tend to privilege Wolfe's "social consciousness" as it relates to Nazi Germany, while overlooking the *Sehnsucht* that characterizes the two major novels published during Wolfe's lifetime, for which he was most widely praised and imitated. If, as I will argue, Wolfe's *Sehnsucht* for an imagined Germany moves him nearest to a fascist spatialization of political language, it is essential to interrogate those literary antecedents that colored Wolfe's view of modern Germany with a too-rosy hue.

Goethe

What led Wolfe to Germany in the first place was his own romanticized vision, his *Sehnsucht* for what *The Web and the Rock* calls "that staggering superflux of German culture."[24] In the same passage, which derives from a section titled "Oktoberfest," Wolfe describes the hunger for Germany in the precise terms of *Sehnsucht*: George Webber wanders in "a kind of German heaven," an "enchanted land," trying to satiate himself "upon that which was itself unable to be fed," and to come to "the end of all Unendlichkeit"—that is, to possess and fathom the infinite, which Wolfe notes "was in itself unpossessable, unfathomable, and unutterable."[25] In his story "Dark in the Forest, Strange as Time" (1934), Wolfe describes the "dark enchantment of the forest of Germany" as something "more than trees," suggesting that they represent "a spell, a magic, and a sorcery, filling the hearts of men [. . .] with a dark music, a haunting memory, never wholly to be captured."[26] *Sehnsucht* was a central conceit of German classicism and Romanticism, and when Wolfe engaged directly with these texts it was frequently in order to reinforce the romance of his scenes, to evoke *Sehnsucht*. As mentioned in the introduction, Wolfe's familiarity with *Sehnsucht* is evident in his use of the word in *Look Homeward, Angel*, where Wolfe includes:

> *Nur wer die Sehnsucht kennt*
> *Weiss was Ich leide*
> (Only they know my pain
> Who know my yearning).

This line is from Mignon's song "*Nur wer die Sehnsucht kennt*" in Goethe's *Wilhelm Meister's Apprenticeship*. Mignon's song was one of eight songs in *Wilhelm Meister's Apprenticeship* that had an accompanying melody written by Johann Friedrich Reichardt, and Jack Stein notes that the song "exercised a fatal fascination on composers" since it appeared, listing as many as fifty-six separate settings of the piece up to 1970, including arrangements by Beethoven, Schubert, Schumann, Liszt, Tchaikovsky, and Hugo Wolf.[27] In a now-famous essay on music and Romanticism, "Beethoven's Instrumental Music" (1814), E. T. A. Hoffmann suggested that music—specifically Beethoven's "instrumental music"—should be understood as "the most romantic of all the arts [. . .] since its subject matter is infinity."[28] The *Sehnsucht* of *Wilhelm Meister's Apprenticeship* offered a perfect platform for Romantic composers like Beethoven, whose music, Hoffmann argued, "sets in motion the machinery of awe, of fear, of terror, of pain, and awakens that infinite yearning which is the essence of Romanticism." Hoffmann believed music could transmit "the deeper mysteries [which] can never be spoken of in ordinary words."[29] It was during November 1928 that Wolfe first encountered these lyrics from Mignon's song, when he visited a concert hall in Vienna and heard Schubert's version of "*Nur wer die Sehnsucht kennt*" performed.[30] The performance of "*Nur wer die Sehnsucht kennt*" had a lasting impact on Wolfe: he told Aline Bernstein that it contained "the most beautiful lyrics I have ever read." He had included Mignon's song in its original German in his letter to Aline and asked whether she might be able to translate it for him.

Wolfe's inclusion of Goethe's "*Nur wer die Sehnsucht kennt*" in *Look Homeward, Angel* occurs during a scene that introduces the "patroness of all the arts," Mrs. Franz Wilhelm Von Zeck. Frau Von Zeck appears only briefly in the story, and Wolfe's use of the line "*Nur wer die Sehnsucht kennt / Weiss was Ich leide*" is initially unclear, occurring as an isolated sentence after Von Zeck's arrival and abrupt departure.[31] Initially, Goethe's lyric of *Sehnsucht* simply points to her innate "Germanness"—Wolfe also mentions her "Wagnerian breasts"—but the phrase, and its connection to Von Zeck, prefigures an important expression of *Sehnsucht* that occurs at the end of the novel. In chapter 38 of *Look Homeward, Angel*—the only other mention of Von Zeck—Eugene reflects on his desire to be an artist, wondering: "What [. . .] can I be, besides a genius?"[32] In that moment of reflection, Eugene remembers that "sometimes Mrs. Von Zeck [. . .] sends a genius or two off to New York to study," a recollection that encourages Eugene to imagine that he might yet find "new life—and new lands," with this conjuration of Von Zeck recalling her first appearance and Goethe's evocation of painful yearning.[33] Goethe's lyric captures the spirit of Eugene's grasping for escape, the "lost land-end into heaven" and "an unfound door" that stand as symbols of longing throughout *Look Homeward, Angel* and that are forever unobtainable—the very pain of *Sehnsucht.* Perkins, Wolfe's editor, had originally cut this scene incorporating Goethe's quotation, but Wolfe wrote to John Hall Wheelock—an editor at Scribner's who worked closely on the manuscript with Wolfe—insisting that it was important to keep the section, arguing that Von Zeck's German heritage had meaningful implications in a scene discussing World War I, while also reinforcing the varied "pattern of race, culture, background, etc. even in a small town."[34] Since Wheelock was fluent in German, Wolfe regularly deferred to his expertise for checking such quotations. Wolfe's interest in *Wilhelm Meister's Apprenticeship,* and his reliance on Goethe for endowing his narrative with *Sehnsucht,* was reinforced in his inclusion of another song of Mignon—*Kennst du das Land* (Know you the land)—as a poetic dedication at the start of *Of Time and the River.* Even though Wolfe owned Carlyle's popular translation of *Wilhelm Meister's Apprenticeship* and was not fluent in the German language, he chose to include the entire poem in German, as the first thing a reader encounters after the book's title page.[35]

Of Time and the River, more than any of Wolfe's other novels and stories, is an extended meditation on longing, full of expressions of *Sehnsucht* as his protagonist, Eugene, wanders across America and Europe looking for the satisfaction and full investigation of his yearning. The novel completes the two-part *Künstlerroman* that begins with *Look Homeward, Angel,* with these narratives reflecting Goethe's own famous *Künstlerroman*s—particularly *The Sufferings of Young Werther* and *Wilhelm Meister's Apprenticeship*—as well as inviting comparisons with the German writer, whom Stanley Corngold has identified as a recurring, Romantic type: the self-absorbed, provincial youth writing a narrative of the "late-adolescent, elite-educated, hormone-besotted, rebellious youth with artistic inclinations."[36] The poem from *Wilhelm Meister's Apprenticeship* that Wolfe reproduced in *Of Time and the River* is *Kennst du das Land,* a lyric that had an even more impressive impact on classical composers than *Nur wer die Sehnsucht kennt,* with as many as eighty-four settings by 1970.[37] Significantly for Wolfe, the poem is evocative of the wandering yearning that fills his novels with *Sehnsucht. Kennst du das Land* begins with a question—"Know you the land where the lemon blossoms blow?"—with each stanza repeating the same pattern: "Know you the house? Roof pillars over it," and "Know you the mountain and its cloudy trails?"[38] The poem ends with a rejoinder:

> You know it, yes? Oh there, oh there
> Our path goes on.

For Wolfe, this song evoked the magical landscape and yearning he encountered in Germany, while Wolfe's own Romantic imaginings of the American landscape—"the enchanted promise of the golden cities" and the "enchanted, time-far hills [. . .] and mournful mystery of the South" that he wrote of in his notebook[39]—was informed by the faery magic Wolfe saw in this other homeland, "the measureless realm of Elfland."[40]

Schiller

In Wolfe's compulsive list-making, Friedrich Schiller was another German writer whom he made frequent reference to—regularly alongside Goethe—and it must have seemed appropriate to Wolfe that both authors were interred side by side in Weimar. Though Wolfe refrained from quoting Schiller directly, *Wilhelm Tell* (1804) is explicitly discussed in relation to Eugene Gant's artistic development at the hands of the Margaret Leonard and the Altamont Fitting School in *Look Homeward, Angel.* The period of Wolfe's own life to which this section refers—four years at the North State Fitting School under the tutelage of J. M. and Margaret Roberts—was significant for the author, who later wrote that Margaret "succeeded in getting under my skull an appreciation of what is fine and beautiful in literature."[41] In the novel, Eugene—in his fifteenth year—is developing the unutterable desires that would mark his romantic quest for "a stone, a leaf, an unfound door," and Margaret Leonard is the "light" to which Eugene turns: "She saw the unholy fires that cast their sword-dance on his face, she saw the hunger and the pain, and she fed him [. . .] on poetry."[42] Eugene's desire for poetry—"which burned up from the page [. . .] like lamps for him"—develops almost as a form of gluttony, and it is in this spirit that Wolfe refers to his reading of Schiller: "He possessed them to their living core, not in a handful of scattered quotations, but almost line for line. His thirst was drunken, insatiate: he added to his hoard entire scenes from Schiller's *Wilhelm Tell,* which he read by himself in German."[43] It is under the far more prosaic tutelage of Margaret's husband, John Dorsey Leonard—a teacher whom Wolfe characterizes as a "bad sailor" who "hated exploration" and "distrusted voyages"—that *Wilhelm Tell* is subsequently referenced in the following chapter of *Look Homeward, Angel.* Wolfe identifies one scene from Schiller's play, the "unearthly siren song to the fisher-boy," which haunts the young Eugene with "its faery music"; though Eugene and his classmates recognize, wearily, that much of Schiller is "Great Literature" with his "embattled Swiss" who "bounded ponderously from crag to crag, invoking [. . .] [Liberty] in windy speeches," they cannot help but "[bend] eagerly to the apple-shooting scene, and the escape by boat."[44] More importantly, when John Dorsey grandiosely identifies Schiller's mountains as broadly emblematic of the "traditional seat of Liberty," the Romantic Eugene "turns his face toward the western ranges" and in a moment of *Sehnsucht* hears his own "siren song": "Far off, a whistle, a remote, thunder on the rails."

The "unearthly siren song to the fisher-boy" that opens Schiller's *Wilhelm Tell* is closely related to the German expressions of *Sehnsucht* and *Heimweh.* Before the curtain rises, the *Kühreihen* or *ranz-des-Vaches* is heard: a traditional Swiss melody—involving horns and cowbells—used by herdsmen to drive their animals from the valleys to pastures high up on the Alps. By Schiller's time the *ranz-des-Vaches* was already considered a major cause of nostalgia; Charles Zwingmann recounts: "According to one report, a whole battalion of Swiss mercenaries in the service of the King of France took to their heels at hearing cowbells in the pastures," while Rousseau noted in his *Dictionnaire de musique* (1767) that it was "forbidden to be play'd in their troops under pain of death, because it made them burst into tears, desert, or die, whoever heard it."[45] Upon reading this opening section of *Wilhelm Tell,* Goethe wrote to Schiller on January 13, 1804, and offered a reassessment of the impact of the *ranz-des-Vaches*: "The Swiss does not feel homesickness because he hears the *ranz des Vaches* at a different place, for that is not blown, as much as I know, at any other place; rather, he feels homesickness because he does not hear it, because his ears are deprived of an adolescent need."[46] Helmut Illbruck argues that Goethe's reframing of the *ranz-des-Vaches* intuits that the "nostalgia of the Swiss is essentially a nostalgia for particularity," a nostalgia "for the distinctive thusness of the original sound, for the alphorn he first heard on the hilltop of his youth. [. . .] The sound and experience the nostalgic truly hankers for [. . .] is what Baudrillard will call 'radical otherness,' an otherness definable only by virtue of its absolute resistance to comparison."[47] The fisher-boy's song tells of "a sweet music / of flutes in a dream," while buried within the music is a voice calling "Come hither to me, / My spell's on the dreamer."[48] For Wolfe, the song is another instance of this "radical otherness," an intimation of the infinite and an object for Eugene's *Sehnsucht,* which he calls an "unearthly siren song." Wolfe's evocation of the fisher-boy's song transposes the "faery music" of Schiller onto the American landscape, likening the nostalgic pull of the *Kühreihen* to the whistle of a train. In *Of Time and the River,* Wolfe aligns the *ranz-des-Vaches* found in Schiller—now simply "a cow-bell broken by the wind"—with "the lonely whistle of a departing train," a sound that reverberates through his oeuvre and might fairly be considered Wolfe's transposition of the *ranz-des-Vaches* into an American literary imagination:

> And finally, the immortal visage of the earth itself with the soaring and limitless undulations of its blue ranges, the great bulk of the autumn hills, immense and near, the rugged, homely, and familiar trees [. . .] the homely look of the old red clay—the unforgettable and indescribable naturalness of that earth—with its rudeness, wildness, richness, rawness, ugliness, fathomless mystery and utter familiarity, and finally the lonely, haunting, and enchanted music that it made—the strange spirit of time and solitude that hovered above it eternally, and which can never be described, but which may be evoked by a cow-bell broken by the wind in distant valleys, the lonely whistle of a departing train, or simply a sinuous gust of wind that smokes its way across coarse mountain grasses when spring comes—all this, which Eugene had felt and known in his childhood, and yet had never had a tongue to utter, he seemed now to know and understand so well that he had himself become its tongue and utterance.[49]

Heine

The final German writer to have an important impact on Wolfe's yearning for Germany was the poet Heinrich Heine. Heine was a German-Jewish writer who wrote much of his poetry in exile. His later disavowal by the Nazi Party complicates Wolfe's admiration for Heine, given the correspondence between Wolfe's *Sehnsucht* for a Romantic vision of Germany and the Nazi repurposing of *Heimat.* Wolfe's peripatetic heroes often draw from the German Romantic figure of the wanderer—epitomized in Caspar David Friedrich's 1818 painting, *Wanderer above the Sea of Fog*—and Heine's influence is recognizable in Wolfe's familiar evocation of wandering. One scholar has suggested that the implication of the word *ziehn* in Goethe's *Kennst du das Land*—which Coleridge translates as "wend," Carlyle as "go," and Hal Draper most recently as "fare"—invokes the Romantic trope of the "'Wanderer' and of 'Wandering' as Romantic mode of existence," arguing that Wolfe "takes up these suggestions of German Romanticism" in his opening prose poem, which begins: "Of wandering forever and the earth again. [. . .] Where shall the weary rest? [. . .] What doors are open for the wanderer?"[50] What appears more likely, however, is the suggestion that Wolfe's prose poem was self-consciously rephrasing Heinrich Heine, whose gravestone bears the quote: "*Wo wird einst des Wandermüden / Letzte Ruhestätte Sein*" (Where will the last resting place of the weary wanderer be?).[51] Wolfe had jotted down this refrain in his notebook from August 12, 1930, and though the source for the quotation that the editors of the notebook identify—Heine's 1827 *Buch der Lieder* (Book of Songs)—is incorrect (the poem was unpublished at the time of Heine's death), it seems probable that Wolfe had copied the quote from Heine's gravestone in Montmartre where he had been only days before—just as he later visited the crypt of Goethe and Schiller in completion of a kind of Romantic pilgrimage. The work of Heine is important in tracing the German influence on Wolfe's expression of *Sehnsucht*, and the poet turns up on a number of occasions in his notebooks and novels, listed among the greatest German poets and in notes reminding himself to purchase more of Heine's poetry.[52] At the end of *Look Homeward, Angel*, Wolfe notes that Heine had a face on which "life had fed," a face "wasted by the vulture, Thought [. . .] seared and hollowed by the flame of Beauty."[53]

Wolfe owned a copy of Heine's *Buch der Lieder*, and in the notes for *O Lost* the Bruccolis note that Eugene's German parody, "Du bist wie eine bum-me," in *Look Homeward, Angel*—which he wrote in answer to a classmate's message—is almost certainly an alteration of Heine's *Du bist wie eine blume* (Thou art like a flower), originally from the poem cycle *Die Heimkehr* (The homecoming) and later republished in *Buch der Lieder*.[54] While the line is offered in jest, the section of the book in which it occurs is focused on the early moments of Eugene's Romantic education—Wolfe writes that during this time Eugene's heart is opened as if "had been [a] locket"[55]—and it is significant that it is Heine's *Die Heimkehr* that Wolfe is alluding to. In a letter to Aline from November 9, 1926, the month before his first ever visit, Wolfe imagines a Germany in which "upon the rocks Lorelei comb their hair," referring to Heine's popular poem *Die Lorelei*, the second poem in the *Die Heimkehr* cycle.[56] In *Die Lorelei*, a boatman moves up the Rhine listening to "the song of the Lorelei" who is

> reclining
> in wondrous beauty there;
> Her golden jewels are shining,
> She combs her golden hair.[57]

The "magical melody" of the Lorelei causes "Wild-aching passions" to fill the boatman, and Wolfe's reference to Heine as he imagines the enchanted Germany that he will visit prefigures his own faery journey up the Rhine two years later. When Wolfe finally took this journey, he wrote to Aline Bernstein about the "Lorelei magic" of the Rhine, noting that "you can understand all the fables that have come out of this region. [. . .] The river flows and winds through it like a magic thread."[58] It is important to note that the magic of Germany for Wolfe, inspired and enriched by Heine's sirens, endures well into a historical moment that saw Heine's work banned and burned, and the poet himself demonized more often than any other Jewish writer in the pages of *Völkischer Beobachter*, the Nazi newspaper.[59] While the Rhine reminds Wolfe of Heine's enchanted river, elsewhere in Heine's own writing the Rhine is explicitly overlaid with

Jewish identity—apparently invisible to Wolfe—as well as narratives of emancipation, as in Heine's unfinished *Der Rabbi von Bacherach* (1840): "Then the Rhine seemed to murmur the melodies of the *Agade*, and from its waters the pictures, large as life and in strange exaggerated guise, came forth one by one. There was the patriarch Abraham frightfully smashing the idols, which pieced themselves together ever anew; the Mitzri fiercely defending himself against an enraged Moses; Mount Sinai in lightning and flames; Pharaoh swimming in the Red Sea, holding his zigzagged gold crown tight in his teeth, frogs with men's faces swimming behind him, and the waves foaming and roaring, while a dark giant-hand rises threatening from the deep."[60]

For Wolfe, however, it is Heine's Lorelei—divorced from their creator's fate—that evoke the mystical Germany through which he, and his protagonists, experience *Sehnsucht*. The Lorelei are a presence in both Wolfe's biographical and fictional visions of Germany, and they appear once more, this time in the novella *The Party at Jack's* (1995), which had been originally released posthumously as a story in 1939, later incorporated into *You Can't Go Home Again*, and finally reedited and released by Suzanne Stutman and John L. Idol Jr. according to a chronological scheme set down by Wolfe near the end of his life.[61] The opening of *The Party at Jack's* begins with a dream; Frederick Jack imagines he has returned home to Germany after twenty years to discover that his family still treat him as if he were a child. It is not simply the "indignity and injury" of being mollycoddled, nor the "interminable family gatherings" and "reunions, funerals, gossip, visits and receptions" that upset Jack, but a deeper fear that "[h]is life was passing like a dream under the strange and terrible visages of time."[62] What follows are shifting scenes of what Wolfe calls a "dream of time": Jack with his family in the old house in the Weinfass Gasse, Jack walking along an ancient cobbled street toward an impending meeting with the schoolmates of his youth, Jack standing with his mother on the Rhine boat landing, all disjointed moments that arrive and depart before Jack finally wakes—back in reality—on the day of the party.[63] The dream centers on a profound sense of loneliness and loss—Jack "long[s] for some goal and home and harbor, and had nowhere to go"—and the sequence is permeated with a mythic vision of Germany, evoked through the cobbled streets and "old gabled houses" with a look of "old witch-haggery," and through the siren-song of the Lorelei.[64] Stutman and Idol note that this section of the narrative was likely completed around 1930, with Wolfe's own dream of Germany still fresh in his mind, just before the takeover by Hitler's National Socialist party.[65]

In the midst of this "dream of time," Wolfe imagined yet another dream haunting Jack: the yearning of *Sehnsucht*, which "had come to him a thousand times in the first years of poverty and exile to fortify his soul with its triumphant music" and which will not leave when he wakes.[66] Jack wants to recount this dream to the ghostly remembrances of his old schoolmates, suddenly free to share with these spectral presences "the secret dreams and visions of his youth which he had never told to anyone." In his haunting vision, Jack relates that he is in another cobbled street, but this time there is an "old and elfin house" where a woman lives who has the "face and figure of a young woman he had seen in Bonn."[67] In Jack's recollection, the woman has transmogrified into one of the Lorelei, whom he hears "singing as she combed her long blonde hair," her bewitching song "as rich, as strange and haunting as any songs that sirens sing from fabled rocks." As the "dream of time" shifts away from the schoolmate reunion to the Rhine River, Jack finishes recalling this hidden vision of *Sehnsucht*, but the remembrance has stirred "an immense and nameless excitement" and a "sense of incommunicable sadness": as the boat "feathered against dark flowing waters," Jack thinks he hears "the mermaids singing." Upon waking, Jack still hears the lingering music, now sad and "defunctive," and he begins the day with this spectral memory of his yearning, "out of the dream of time into the dream of time," as though his *Sehnsucht* has dissolved the boundary between waking and dreaming.[68]

Wolfe and the English Romantics

Of course, German Romanticism was not the only Romantic literature that influenced Wolfe. English Romanticism provided an even greater stockpile of language and quotation that the author drew from—having read and studied them more—but the difference for Wolfe was that the Germany he visited during the 1920s and 1930s retained tangible evidence of its Romantic past in the author's mind, while England did not. In a letter to Aline Bernstein, Wolfe suggested that "England is a sad, cold, desperate country," a view of England most clearly demonstrated through his dismal account of British food in *Of Time and the River*, which diverges radically from his tendency toward sensuous and sumptuous description. While it might seem unusual to point to Wolfe's culinary reflections as evidence of an unromantic view of England, it is important to recognize that food—particularly the overladen tables of Eugene's youth—is a common trigger for nostalgia in Wolfe's fiction.[69] In fact, some of Wolfe's descriptions of food are among his most enduring writing, anthologized in Linda Wolfe's *The Literary Gourmet* (1989), Oxford University Press's *Food: An Oxford Anthology* (1994), and Library of America's *American Food Writing: An Anthology* (2007).[70] The description of English food in *Of Time and the River* follows his pattern of cumulative descriptive detail, creating a kind of cornucopia of blandness:

> The food looked very good, and was, according to the genius of the nation, tasteless. How they ever did it he could never tell: everything was of the highest quality and you chewed upon it mournfully, wearily, swallowing it with the

dreary patience of a man who has been condemned forever to an exclusive diet of boiled unseasoned spinach. There was a kind of evil sorcery, a desolate and fathomless mystery in the way they could take the choicest meats and vegetables and extract all the succulence and native flavor from them, and then serve them up to you magnificently with every atom of their former life reduced to the general character of stewed hay or well-boiled flannel.

> There would be a thick heavy soup of dark mahogany, a piece of boiled fish covered with a nameless, tasteless sauce of glutinous white, roast beef that had been done to death in dish-water, and solid, perfect, lovely brussels sprouts for whose taste there was no name whatever. It might have been the taste of boiled wet ashes, or the taste of stewed green leaves, with all the bitterness left out, pressed almost dry of moisture, or simply the taste of boiled clouds and rain and fog.[71]

Wolfe does not extend this unromantic view to the *literature* of England, however, and this is where his distinction between German and English Romanticism is most pronounced. While both literary traditions furnished Wolfe with the language of Romanticism, the concrete place of Germany, where Wolfe believed his "strange life shall find a home," is inextricably linked to his numerous expressions of *Sehnsucht*. Germany looms large, both in terms of its Romantic traditions but also as the faery-land of Goethe, Schiller, and Heine, as the place where "the winds about the castle crags at night are full of demon voices; and the gabled houses of the toyland towns are full of rich and gluttonous warmth."[72] While the land of Germany reinforced Wolfe's Romantic expectations, the geography of Wolfe's *Sehnsucht* did not extend to England as place. For the English Romantics, Wolfe perceived that it was the particular "quality of *lack*" that had enabled these writers to write so convincingly of beauty and desire, suggesting that—as with *Sehnsucht*—the absence of the thing desired manifested a yearning that was itself desirable:

> Now it seemed to him that these people had written so magnificently about good food not because they always had it, but because they had it rarely and therefore made great dreams and fantasies about it, and it seemed to him that this same quality—the quality of *lack* rather than of *possession*, of desire rather than fulfilment—had got into everything they did, and made them dream great dreams, and do heroic acts, and had enriched their lives immeasurably. [. . .] Their poems were so full of the essential quality of sunlight because their lives had known sunlight briefly, and so shot through with the massy substance of essential gold [. . .] because their lives had known so much fog and rain, so little gold. And they had spoken best of April because April was so brief with them.
>
> Thus from the grim gray of their skies they had alchemied gold, and from their hunger, glorious food, and from the raw bleakness of their lives and weathers they had drawn magic.[73]

This expression of a palpable absence is evident in the reference to Matthew Arnold's "The Buried Life" (1852), which Wolfe included in the full title of *Look Homeward, Angel: A Story of the Buried Life.* Arnold's poem describes humankind's concealment of thoughts and its distance from a "genuine self," an unregarded "river of our life" that flows on indiscernibly, "Eddying at large in blind uncertainty / Though driving on with it eternally."[74] The yearning in Arnold's poem is for the "knowledge of our buried life" that rises up as "an unspeakable desire":

> A longing to inquire
> Into the mystery of this heart which beats
> So wild, so deep in us—to know
> Whence our lives come and where they go.

For Arnold, as for Wolfe, these "nameless feelings" course on "forever unexpressed," and people find themselves stupefied by a power that "benumb[s] us at our call."[75] As with the train whistle or the *ranz-des-Vaches* that stirs *Sehnsucht* in the listener, Arnold suggests that "from time to time, vague and forlorn [. . .] airs" come from an "infinitely distant land," "floating echoes" that convey "a melancholy into all our day." The specter of Germany in Wolfe's first two novels conforms to this idea of "an infinitely distant land," like the Elfland of Lord Dunsany's *The King of Elfland's Daughter* (1924), whose twilight frontier ebbs away from those who seek it, leaving only the faintly blowing "elfin horns" to pierce "the barrier of dim light and silence with the magical resonance of their silver note."[76] There are a number of instances, in fact, where Wolfe explicitly characterizes Germany as "Elfland": he writes to Aline about a "big German city," with a famous quarter "full of those Elfland houses that Albert Dürer painted," and in later letters of the "Old Town" near Goethe's house that was "as close to Elfland as we'll ever come."[77] The Elfland that Wolfe uncovered in Germany—that "measureless realm of Elfland" he encountered up the Rhine—was yet another manifestation of his notion of *Sehnsucht. O Lost* contains a passage excised from the final version of *Look Homeward, Angel,* in which Wolfe wrote that after "the slow drift of magic back into the nighttime actual world, [he] heard through his elfland spirit the whistles wail again far down the river, thought of escape in darkness in the high cab of a lunging engine [. . .] the ecstasy of avoiding capture, and pearl dawn through ghostly fields beyond the hills. There were new lands."[78]

C. S. Lewis and His Reconceptualization of *Sehnsucht*

Before I turn to Wolfe and the Germany of his contemporaries, I want to identify one other enduring exploration of *Sehnsucht* in English, in part because if the word is used today outside of its German heritage, it is most frequently in connection with C. S. Lewis. Although English Romantics had encountered the German idea of *Sehnsucht* before Wolfe—Arnold wrote about "the German *Sehnsucht*" as "a wistful, soft, tearful longing" in his *On the Study of Celtic Literature* (1867)[79]—the word was rarely used in English or American publications over the course of the twentieth century. One notable exception is *The Varieties of Religious Experience* (1902), by William James, in which he makes a passing reference to *Sehnsucht* in a section exploring the "mystical experience."[80] James suggests that "single words, and conjunctions of words, effects of light on land and sea, odors and musical sounds, all bring it [the mystical experience] when the mind is tuned aright," recollecting that "an excellent old German lady [. . .] used to describe to me her *Sehnsucht* that she might yet visit 'Philadelphia,' whose wondrous name had always haunted her imagination."[81] It was in the work of C. S. Lewis, however, that this idea of *Sehnsucht* was most profoundly reimagined, and like Wolfe it was a central theme of the writer's work.[82] The term is frequently associated with Lewis; in 2007 the Arizona C. S. Lewis Society began publishing *Sehnsucht: The C. S. Lewis Journal*, while in the wake of Corbin Carnell's *Bright Shadow of Reality* (1974)—a study of the role of *Sehnsucht* in Lewis's work—many critics have turned to the word that Lewis himself used to describe longing in his autobiography, *Surprised by Joy* (1955): "Every day there were what we call 'the Green Hills'; that is, the low line of the Castlereagh Hills which we saw from the nursery windows. They were not very far off but they were, to children, quite unattainable. They taught me longing—*Sehnsucht*."[83] As early as 1933, Lewis began to work out his theme of *Sehnsucht* in *The Pilgrim's Regress* (1933), his revision of Bunyan that follows the character John—a young man brought up in a rigorous, rules-based tradition of faith—through the philosophical landscape of the early twentieth century, and whose quest begins when he is awakened to "Sweet Desire."[84] Lewis's explanation of this desire, in a preface written ten years later, constitutes his most precise definition of *Sehnsucht*:

> The experience is one of intense longing. It is distinguished from other longings by two things. In the first place, though the sense of want is acute and even painful, yet the mere wanting is felt to be somehow a delight. Other desires are felt as pleasures only if satisfaction is expected in the near future: hunger is pleasant only while we know (or believe) that we are soon going to eat. But this desire, even when there is no hope of possible satisfaction, continues to be prized, and even to be preferred to anything else in the world, by those who have once felt it. This hunger is better than any other fullness; this poverty better than all other wealth. And thus it comes about, that if the desire is long absent, it may itself be desired, and that new desiring becomes a new instance of the original desire, though the subject may not at once recognise the fact and thus cries out for his lost youth of soul at the very moment in which he is be-

> ing rejuvenated. [. . .] For this sweet Desire cuts across our ordinary distinctions between wanting and having. To have it is, by definition, a want: to want it, we find, is to have it.[85]

Lewis's revision of *Sehnsucht* reinforces the pleasure of the act of desiring, suggesting that the addictive quality inherent in *Sehnsucht* is not simply "tearful," as Arnold suggested, or solely a sickness, but also a pleasure *in the very act of desiring,* since desiring is tantamount to having. The second distinction Lewis offers is in describing the object of this desire:

> Every one of these supposed *objects* for the Desire is inadequate to it. An easy experiment will show that by going to the far hillside you will get either nothing, or else a recurrence of the same desire which sent you thither. A rather more difficult, but still possible, study of your own memories, will prove that by returning to the past you could not find, as a possession, that ecstasy which some sudden reminder of the past now moves you to desire. [. . .] But what has [this] to do with that unnameable something, desire for which pierces us like a rapier at the smell of a bonfire, the sound of wild ducks flying overhead, the title of *The Well at the World's End,* the opening lines of *Kubla Khan,* the morning cobwebs in late summer, or the noise of falling waves? It appeared to me therefore that if a man diligently followed this desire, pursing the false objects until their falsity appeared and then resolutely abandoning them, he must come out at last into the clear knowledge that the human soul was made to enjoy some object that is never fully given.[86]

Lewis's definition is both a rejection and a defense of Romanticism. Lewis subscribed to T. E. Hulme's proclamation, in "Romanticism and Classicism" (1911), that Romanticism was a "spilt religion," while he later suggested that this longing was evidence for a broader spiritual reality: "The books or the music in which we thought the beauty was located will betray us if we trust to them; it was not *in* them, it only came *through* them, and what came through them was longing. These things—the beauty, the memory of our own past—are good images of what we really desire; but if they are mistaken for the thing itself they turn into dumb idols, breaking the hearts of their worshippers. For they are not the thing itself; they are only the scent of a flower we have not found, the echo of a tune we have not heard, news from a country we have never yet visited."[87]

Lewis defended the significance of this experience of longing; in an essay titled "Christianity and Culture" (1940), where he uses the term *Sehnsucht* to describe his early experiences of joy in longing, he writes that "the dangers of romantic *Sehnsucht* are very great. Eroticism and even occultism lie in wait for it. On this subject I can only give my own experience for what it is worth [. . .] in this process I have not (or not yet) reached a point at which I can honestly repent of my early experiences of romantic *Sehnsucht*."[88] In a revision of this statement he adds: "I am quite ready to describe *Sehnsucht* as 'spilled religion,' provided it is not forgotten that the spilled drops may be full of blessing to the unconverted man who licks them up, and therefore begins to search for the cup whence they were spilled."[89] Lewis would later admit in *Surprised by Joy* that the experience of *Sehnsucht* colored his whole childhood and foreshadowed his later conversion experience: "It is difficult for me to find words strong enough for the sensation which came over me; Milton's 'enormous bliss' of Eden [. . .] comes somewhere near it. It was a sensation, of course, of desire; but desire for what? [. . .] Before I knew what I desired, the desire itself was gone, the whole glimpse withdrawn, the world turned commonplace again, or only stirred by a longing for the longing that had just ceased. It had taken only a moment of time; and in a certain sense everything else that had ever happened to me was insignificant in comparison."[90]

The expression of *Sehnsucht* in the work of C. S. Lewis as an acute and painful longing for the infinite—where "to want it, we find, is to have it"—articulates the same character of desire that was prevalent in the works of Thomas Wolfe: longing for the sake of longing. Like Wolfe, Lewis was also interested in German Romanticism, and he admits in *Surprised by Joy* that he was "a votary of the Blue Flower," pointing to the *blaue Blume* that is among the most readily identifiable symbols of Romantic *Sehnsucht,* most famously found in the opening of Novalis's *Heinrich von Ofterdingen* (1802): "The youth lay restless on his bed and thought about the stranger and his stories. 'There is no greed in my heart; but I yearn to get a glimpse of the blue flower.'"[91]

The German influence on Lewis's understanding of *Sehnsucht,* particularly in light of spiritual longing, can be seen through the impact of the Scottish writer George MacDonald. MacDonald's impact on Lewis is well documented; Lewis compiled a selection of MacDonald's writings in 1946 titled *George MacDonald: An Anthology,* in which he wrote: "I have never concealed the fact that I regarded him as my master; indeed I fancy I have never written a book in which I did not quote from him."[92] Lewis recalls purchasing a copy of MacDonald's fantasy romance *Phantastes* (1858), noting that having already been "waist-deep in Romanticism," *Phantastes* was "romantic enough in all conscience; but there was a difference. [. . .] What it actually did to me was to convert, even to baptize [. . .] my imagination."[93] MacDonald's romantic vision, anchored to a spiritual reality, enabled Lewis to see that "the quality which had enchanted me in his imaginative works turned out to be the quality of the real universe, the divine, magical, terrifying, and ecstatic reality in which we all live [. . .] that elusive Form which if once seen must inevitably be desired with all but sensuous desire—the thing (in Sappho's phrase) 'more gold than gold.'"[94] For MacDonald, the German Romantic Novalis was a formative influence on his own romantic vision, particularly evident in the bildungsroman of Anodos in *Phantastes,* whose journey through Fairy Land traces the young man's quest to locate the true source and fulfillment of Romantic *Sehnsucht.* (MacDonald includes several quotations from Novalis in *Phantastes,* including a German epigraph on the qualities of a "true" fairy tale.)[95]

Kerry Dearborn argues that Novalis's "passionate hunger and thirst for God, and for meaning beyond this life," was instrumental in MacDonald's deep appreciation for the Romantic author.[96] Indeed, MacDonald eventually translated Novalis's *Hymns to the Night* and *Spiritual Songs* in his anthology of European poems and hymns titled *Rampolli* (1897), in which he discovered that Novalis's proclamation of "the fleeting, extinguished life" of "endless longing [*Sehnsucht*]" has been turned finally to "the beloved Jesus":

> A dream will dash our chains apart,
> And lay us on the Father's heart.[97]

In 1930 Lewis reflected on his reading of *Heinrich von Ofterdingen,* writing that it was a "very Macdonaldy book," full of "'holiness,' gloriously German-romantic," and this reading prompted Lewis to conclude that "Novalis is perhaps the greatest single influence on Macdonald."[98] The vital difference between Wolfe and Lewis in their expression of *Sehnsucht* can be traced back to the influence of MacDonald; in *Phantastes,* after Anodos dies, MacDonald noted that "if my passions were dead, the souls of those passions, those essential mysteries of the spirit which had embodied themselves in the passions, and had given to them all their glory and wonderment, yet lived, yet glowed, with a pure, undying fire. They rose above their vanishing earthly garments."[99] For Lewis, *Sehnsucht* ultimately pointed to a theological solution to insatiable hunger, observing in *Mere Christianity* (1952): "If I find in myself desires which nothing in this world can satisfy, the most probable explanation is that I was made for another world."[100] Though Lewis and Wolfe were both at Oxford in 1926—while Wolfe was working on the first version of *Look Homeward, Angel*—there is no indication the two authors met. Lewis himself never visited the United States, though in response to a letter from Mary Van Deusen—a regular correspondent from Hendersonville, North Carolina, who would often include photos of the local American landscape—Lewis wrote that "the new photos raise extreme *Sehnsucht:* each a landscape as fulfils my dreams. *That* is the America I wd. like to see."[101] Moreover, Joy Davidman—the American poet and writer who later married C. S. Lewis—wrote about her own conversion experience in 1949, published two years later as the essay "The Longest Way Round" (1951), where she invokes Wolfe as a writer of "the undiscovered country": "There is a myth that has always haunted mankind, the legend of the Way Out. 'A stone, a leaf, an unfound door,' wrote Thomas Wolfe—the door leading out of time and space into Somewhere Else. [. . .] The symbol varies with different men; for some, the door itself is important; for others, the undiscovered country beyond it—the never-never land, Saint Brendan's Island, the Land of Heart's Desire."[102]

Davidman suggests that it was C. S. Lewis and *The Pilgrim's Regress* that taught her the meaning of this "never-never land," contending that the myth of Wolfe's unfound door actually pointed to a broader spiritual need for a home "more our home than any earthly country." In the same way that Lewis identified the object of his *Sehnsucht* as having a spiritual source, Davidman sees the clues of a spiritual reality in Wolfe's "legend of the Way Out," and just as MacDonald's romances helped clarify for Lewis that what he desired was "goodness," Lewis in turn provides the spiritual meaning for Davidman's own indefinable yearning. Davidman completed this essay before having ever contacted Lewis, and it stands as the earliest instance of connection between Lewis's and Wolfe's expressions of *Sehnsucht*.[103] While Lewis would eventually give a theological inflection to his reading of *Sehnsucht*, Wolfe never provided a way out for his unutterable yearning; instead, he committed to dwelling on what both Schelling and Heidegger perceived in *Sehnsucht*: that in longing we *are*.

Wolfe, Weimar, and Werfel

Wolfe's *Sehnsucht* for Germany was allayed, in part, through the four separate trips to Germany he took in 1926, 1927, 1928, and 1930, before his final two visits to the nation under National Socialist rule in 1935 and 1936. Brinkmeyer points out that over the course of these trips, Wolfe was forced, increasingly, to confront the real Germany, particularly as his deeply ingrained feelings about race were "made manifest in the Nazi system," compelling the writer to "reevaluate his thinking, including his political and artistic commitments."[104] Even in 1936, however, when Wolfe gave an interview to the *Berliner Tageblatt*, it was Goethe whom the author said "personifies for me the idea of world literature," suggesting: "If there were no Germany, it would be necessary to invent one. It is a magical country. I know Hildesheim, Nuremberg, Munich, the architecture of Germany, the soul of the place, the glory of her history and art."[105] David Durst points out that the Weimar Republic had intentionally relocated the center of Germany to the home of Goethe and Schiller, "the revered members of classical German humanism, of German culture as an institution of national unity and conciliation," implying that for Wolfe the signs of the past cultural glories on the modern landscape of Nazi Germany were still visible.[106] It was Weimar that Wolfe and Martha Dodd—the daughter of the ambassador to Germany—visited in 1935 and which impressed Wolfe with this same spirit of German culture. Dodd recalls the trip in her memoir, *My Years in Germany* (1939):

> The trip was a joy and a revelation. We were made conscious again of the Germany of the past; great, deep, courageous chapters in the history of literature and progress were unfolded. I think I learned at this time, once and for all, not to confuse the real German character and people with their present oppressors.

Hitler will undoubtedly have a role in history, but it will be an unsavoury one, one which the inheritors of the great literary, artistic, philosophic traditions of giant men will detest remembering.

Tom left soon after, with many of his illusions intact, though some were wavering.[107]

Peter Gay argues that there were two Germanys in the Weimar Republic: "Germany which remained as it always was: undemocratic, conservative, broken up into party factions, and the other Germany: the humane and free Germany."[108] This was the same conflict that Wolfe perceived in the years following the dissolution of Weimar and the takeover by the National Socialists, when he explained to Perkins the reason behind his long, lyrical account of his experience in Germany: "I do not see how anyone who comes here as I have come could possibly fail to love the country, its noble Gothic beauty and its lyrical loveliness, or to like the German people who are I think the cleanest, the kindest, the warmest-hearted, and the most honorable people I have met in Europe. I tell you this because I think a full and generous recognition must be made of all these facts and because I have been told and felt things here which you and I can never live or stand for and which if they are true, as by every reason of intuition and faith and belief in the people with whom I have talked I must believe, are damnable."[109]

The conflict between the spirit of Weimar and the Republic of Weimar, according to Gay, led to the period's "hunger for wholeness," which found its most "poignant expression" in German youth and the youth movement (*Wandervogel*) that flourished throughout the 1920s.[110] Wolfe's own hunger for wholeness led the author to cross the Atlantic again and again, seeking in Germany an object for his Romantic *Sehnsucht.* Wolf Lepenies identifies a tendency within German culture to be seduced by a notion of "Culture" as a "noble substitute for politics," writing: "If there is anything that can be called a specific German ideology, it consists in playing off Romanticism against the Enlightenment, the Middle Ages against the modern world, culture against civilization, and *Gemeinschaft* against *Gesellschaft.*"[111] Wolfe too was similarly afflicted by this cultural seduction, and the Elfland echoes of Germany and its "noble gothic beauty" form part of his initial reluctance and resistance to acknowledge the dangers of Nazi Germany.

❖ ❖ ❖

There is one reference in *Look Homeward, Angel* that elucidates Wolfe's position within the broader German context in which he actually took part, as distinct from the Romantic visions of Germany that have characterized this chapter. In one section of *Look Homeward, Angel,* Eugene Gant is loafing with a schoolmate, George Graves, while outside voices of their small town overlap with the discussion; predictions of America's involvement in World War I intermingle with the boy's own enthusiasm about the Wheeler boys, two brothers who went off to fight in the Foreign Legion. Eugene imagines the fate of Clifton Wheeler—"they thought he was a sissy," Graves warns him—and wonders what his own "chance of glory" might be, at which point Wolfe inserts the line "*Ich bin ja noch ein Kind*" (I am still a child) in parentheses next to this statement, as if to remind his protagonist—and himself—that there is still time.[112] The source of this quotation has been a matter of contention for scholars; Arlyn and Matthew J. Bruccoli suggest that it was drawn from Jakob Michael Reinhold Lenz's *Der Hofmeister* (*The Tutor*, 1774).[113] Not only is the context of this line from *Der Hofmeister* implausible—it is spoken by a young woman, Gustchen, who is pledging an ill-founded oath of love to her cousin Fritz before he leaves for university—but Lenz's play seems an entirely unlikely candidate as there is no evidence of Wolfe's awareness of Lenz or his play.[114] In the most recent, annotated German translation of the novel, *Schau heimwärts, Engel* (2009), the editors suggest that Wolfe might have been referring to an 1847 preface to a German edition of Alexandre Weill's village tales by Heinrich Heine, where he writes "*Ach! ich bin ja noch ein Kind der Vergangenheit*," a more likely suggestion because Wolfe had certainly read Heine, but the implication of *Vergangenheit*—a child of *the past*—likewise does not cohere with Wolfe's use of the quotation.[115]

What is far more likely is that Wolfe was referring to Franz Werfel's poem, titled *Ich bin ja noch ein Kind*, which appeared in his expressionist collection of poems *Wir Sind* (1913) and centers on a young man pleading to God for life's tortures and trials so as to justify the exorbitant grace of his savior.[116] Klaus Weissenberger writes that Werfel's poem addressed "the alienation of man from any communal structure as a result of the particularism and anonymity of modern society," suggesting that he "proclaimed the brotherhood of mankind as the only way to overcome the existential loneliness and isolation of man."[117] Werfel (1890–1945) was a novelist, playwright, and poet whose earliest poetic contributions *Der Weltfreund* (the philanthropist; 1911), *Wir Sind* (we are; 1913), *Einander* (each other; 1915) and *Der Gerichtstag* (the day of judgment; 1919) were, according to Hans Wagener, "hailed as the beginning of a new era in literature, known today as Expressionism." Werfel was born in Prague—then the district capital of Bohemia—and his parents were progressive, German-speaking Jews for whom "religion was little more than a matter of form."[118] Sent to a Piarist Catholic elementary school—which Rainer Maria Rilke had attended a few years earlier—Werfel later attended the German University of Prague and completed his obligatory year in the Royal and Imperial Army, during which Werfel befriended other young Prague literati including Franz Janowitz and Franz Kafka. Kafka would later write to Felice Bauer that "Werfel is really a miracle. [. . .] That man is capable of tremendous things," while Rainer Maria Rilke wrote in his essay "On the Young Poet" (1912): "For the author [Rilke] the generally happy occupation with Franz Werfel's poems was in some way the prerequisite for this work."[119] Werfel completed most of his early work in Austria but fled after the Anschluss in 1938, eventually immigrating to Los Angeles where he completed *The Song of Bernadette* (1941) and toyed with the possibility of Catholic conversion. Wolfe was familiar with Werfel; he had written to Aline Bernstein in 1926 asking whether her theater guild had performed Werfel's *Paulus unter den Juden* (Paul among the Jews; 1926) and had included Werfel, a number of times, in his notebook lists of great German writers.[120] In addition, Werfel was also aware of Wolfe; Peter Jungk, in his biography of Werfel, points out that Wolfe was Werfel's "favorite American author."[121]

In identifying the source of this quotation, it is tempting to read Werfel and Wolfe as analogous in their reactions to Nazism, at least in their literary outputs. Werfel was among those artists and writers forced out of the Prussian Academy of Art in 1933—among them Heinrich Mann, Alfred Döblin, and Thomas Mann—and his novel about the Armenian genocide, *The Forty Days of Musa Dagh* (1933), "did more than anything else to publicize the mass murder of the Armenian community in Turkey during World War I and was subsequently banned by Hitler."[122] As with Wolfe's own political ambiguity, however, Werfel's writing was characterized as much by evasion and conservatism as it was by its political nuance, and Lionel Steiman points out that the "abandonment of the political for the mystical is characteristic [for Werfel]." Just as in Wolfe's later writing, Steiman writes that Werfel saw the division between good and evil as running through "the middle of every human heart," and so his analysis of the interwar political climate—as was the case for Wolfe—"tends to reduce political, social, and economic conflict to the point that the only real choice is between what is oriented toward transcendent reality and what is bound to natural appetite."[123] For Wolfe, the romance of Germany—and the seduction of German culture—fed an early political ambiguity that was not particular to the naïve American novelist. As Moore points out, Wolfe's work "captured in stirring images Germany's 'spiritual disease' and its dual character," though it was not simply his later reservations about National Socialism but also his appropriation and indebtedness to the Romantic view of Germany that is vital to understanding his relationship to Germany as well as his international relevance and significance.[124] Wolfe's reception and reinterpretation within Germany, along with what is roundly characterized as his political awakening in light of the growing threat of Nazism, is the focus of the following chapter.

CHAPTER FOUR

"The Geography of Heart's Desire"

German Writers, Fascism, and the Translation of Thomas Wolfe

In an article titled "The Last Time I Saw Berlin" (1947), American journalist and broadcaster Dorothy Thompson recalled a reunion with old friends in Berlin on her initial return to Germany since she became the first journalist to be expelled by the National Socialist regime in 1934. Thompson was one of the most prominent American commentators on Germany during the 1930s and 1940s and, according to Michaela Moore, was the "first well-known journalist to warn of developments in Germany during the final phase of the Weimar Republic."[1] Thompson wrote that "the unbridgeable chasm between myself and them was the chasm which would exist between people who had been to hell and those who had not," and as the friends sat together vainly trying to take up "the thread of an uninterrupted conversation" in an effort to "turn the clock back, back to 1934," they found themselves discussing the "tragically early death of Thomas Wolfe."[2] Walking down the Kurfürstendamm in Berlin during the 1930s, it would not have been surprising to hear Wolfe's name among the murmur of café chatter; the author had attained a level of celebrity in Germany even beyond his American reception. *Look Homeward, Angel* had been translated as *Schau heimwärts, Engel!* in 1932 by the expressionist poet Hans Schiebelhuth, whose excellent version of Wolfe's novel—roundly praised as both accurate and poetically beautiful—was a significant contribution to Wolfe's German reputation.[3] As William W. Pusey III noted in "The German Vogue of Thomas Wolfe" (1948), not only did the release of Schiebelhuth's next translation—*Von Zeit und Strom* (1936), his version of *Of Time and the River*—closely follow the author's publicized trip to Berlin in 1935, but the publication interval of Wolfe's two novels represented a substantially shorter break than in America.[4] This fact, Pusey notes, "added to the cultural darkness that was enveloping Germany" and also to Wolfe's "enormous personal appeal to the Germans," helping consolidate "his popularity in Germany and [giving] it in a period of some six years a concentrated intensity which it did not obtain in the United States."

Considering the scant critical attention paid to Wolfe in general, there has been an impressive output of work focused on this central relationship between the author and Germany in recent years. As previously noted, Brinkmeyer's study *The Fourth Ghost* (2010) represents the most significant scholarly account of Wolfe's relationship with Nazi Germany so far, but this fundamental connection has also appeared in broader studies linking America and Germany during the period of National Socialism, including Shareen Blair Brysac's *Resisting Hitler: Mildred Harnack and the Red Orchestra* (2000), Michaela Moore's *Know Your Enemy* (2010), Erik Larson's *In the Garden of Beasts* (2011), and Andrew Nargorski's *Hitlerland: American Eyewitnesses to the Nazi Rise to Power* (2012).[5] Lawrence D. Stokes, a historian who, before his death in 2007, was working on a comprehensive study of the relationship between Wolfe and Germany, has provided the most exacting account of Wolfe's early reception in Germany in his article "The Translation and Reception of Thomas Wolfe's Works in Nazi Germany, 1933–1938" (2003). Oliver Lubrich highlights Wolfe's own reportage of this relationship in his collection *Travels in the Reich, 1933–1945: Foreign Authors Report from Germany* (2010)—originally published in German in 2004—that includes Wolfe's novella "I Have a Thing to Tell You," (1937), which Lubrich notes had "remained undiscovered in Germany."[6] What all of these critics have identified is the unmistakable fact that Thomas Wolfe was both an important American eyewitness to the changing political climate of Germany and an author who enjoyed significant acclaim in those same years of unrest, upheaval, and Nazi takeover. As Moore points out, during the years 1933–45 "the United States never achieved a politically coherent consensus on whether the enemy was the Nazi regime or the German nation [. . .] nor was there agreement on the ideological front," and "only in retrospect did the war effort against the Third Reich take on a clear purpose."[7] In light of this reality, Wolfe's privileged and problematic witness offers an invaluable perspective on this vexed relationship.

This chapter draws together the disparate discussions of Wolfe and Germany in order to problematize an accepted narrative trajectory of political naïveté to awakening that has developed since his death, arguing that Wolfe's romanticized vision of Germany was not replaced by a critical realism in response to Nazism but instead operated in conjunction with his growing sense of unease. Exploring the German concept of the *Volk*—which underpinned Nazi ideology—this chapter illuminates aspects of Wolfe's fiction that directly engage with such ideas, suggesting that Wolfe's appeal to German readers needs to be read in light of these historical concerns. Extending the previous discussion of the influence of German literature on Wolfe, this chapter also explores Wolfe's reception and transmission in the works of German authors such as Klaus Mann, Hermann Hesse, and Heinrich Böll, among others, addressing the inherent appeal of Wolfe's exuberant picture of America during a time of artistic decline in Nazi Germany as well as Wolfe's themes of exile and alienation, which corresponded with the actual lives of many authors forced to flee their home. Importantly, this chapter also reexamines Wolfe's most frequently discussed—and most ardently antifascist—story, "I Have a Thing to Tell You" (1937), engaging with Rudolf Frank's forgotten 1942 German edition of *You Can't Go Home Again* (*Es führt kein Weg zurück*) and identifying the exiled author's translation of "I Have a Thing to Tell You" that appears under the new title "*Der Andere Weg*" (The Other Way).[8] Although English-speaking critics have been aware of this translation since 1948, none have drawn attention to the significance of both the translator and the wartime date of translation.[9] Following the 2013 retrospective exhibition celebrating the life and works of this nearly forgotten actor, director, critic, writer, and translator—a Jewish exile who saw his own books burned just as Wolfe was enjoying popular success in Germany—it is an appropriate moment to reconsider his translation in light of its ramifications for understanding Wolfe's reception history.[10]

Over the course of his visits to Germany, Wolfe's professed liberalism was thrown into stark relief through an encounter with fascist ideology that epitomized attitudes toward race and art that Wolfe, at times, embodied in his own work. As Brinkmeyer has written, Wolfe's "deeply ingrained thoughts and feelings about race, including his bitter anti-Semitism," were central to Wolfe's complicated response to Nazi ideology.[11] These beliefs, which included a combination of "white southern prejudice against blacks" and a nativism that embraced the racial taxonomies popularized in the work of Grant and Stoddard, were "made manifest in the Nazi system," and this "pressured him [Wolfe] to reevaluate his thinking, including his political and artistic commitments." As highlighted in chapter 2, such an adherence to racialism was not peculiar to Wolfe or the South in early twentieth-century America, and though Brinkmeyer is right to identify the congruence of Wolfe's thinking with "a dictatorial regime that made real, by law and fiat, many of Wolfe's racialist thoughts," his ultimate characterization of Wolfe as being "mired in a morass of filthy racism" is a view that must be understood in light of how Wolfe was read and received in Germany.[12] Certainly, Wolfe's attempt at a fundamentally democratic "American" project is utterly undermined by his unapologetic racism and anti-Semitism. But the circulation of Wolfe's fiction in Germany and his engagement with German literature and culture goes beyond shared racial attitudes. Trying to understand and clarify Wolfe's complex involvement with Germany under National Socialism, particularly his political ambivalence and the profound lateness of anything approaching awakening, is the purpose of this chapter.

Wolfe and Fascism

In an oft-quoted section of Wolfe's notebooks from 1936, the author included a brief defense of "Freedom of Speech and Thought" in America, in which he pithily summarizes the popular view that "we say in America that we are free to speak and write and think as we please," while in fascist Germany "people can not speak and write and think as they please."[13] Wolfe's contention is that there are many degrees of freedom, and that while Germans "are free to speak and write that you do not like Jews and that you think Jews are bad, corrupt, and unpleasant people," Americans "are not free to say this." Brinkmeyer argues that—beyond the obvious fact of Wolfe's rampant anti-Semitism—Wolfe believed that unreasoned political discussion, along with any form of press suppression, was similarly evidence of totalitarianism, insisting that an open dialogue about fascism was better than the stifling conversation of democratic ideologues.[14] Wolfe designated these sorts of people as "slot-machines," whose views he summarized as follows:

> The Slot Machine
> We can make any criticism we like, however violent, about the inhabitants of the state of Kansas. But it is very dangerous to make any criticism, even a mild one, about Jews.
>
> Nothing good can be said about the Italian or German dictatorships. If one suggests that benefits from the dictatorships have been considerable, the slot-machine answer, with a slight sneer, is, "Oh yes, we know—the streets are clean and the trains run on time, but do you think these blessings compensate for the loss of human liberties, freedom of speech, etc., etc."
>
> It is useless to tell the Slot-Machines that the benefits of the Fascist Dictatorships have resulted in far more considerable benefits than "clean streets and trains on time," and that if we are really going to combat the evil of Fascism, we must first begin by understanding its good.[15]

In a letter originally addressed to Donald Ogden Stewart and the League of American Writers, Wolfe responded to the question "Are you for, or are you against Franco and Fascism?" by providing a further explanation of his position regarding Germany under Nazism: "About Germany today we must be very true. And the reason that we must be very true is that the thing we are against is false: we cannot turn the other cheek to wrong, but also we cannot be wrong about wrong. We cannot meet wrong with wrong: we must be right about it. And we cannot meet lies and falsehood with lies and falsehood, although there are people who argue that we must."[16]

After his experiences in 1936, which would shape his story "I Have a Thing to Tell You"—the publication that Wolfe believed would finally sever his ties with his other homeland of Germany—Wolfe's defense of fascism wavered under the weight of the actual suppression and fear that he had witnessed. Wolfe wrote to his agent, Elizabeth Nowell, on September 14, 1936, to inform her that "I've written a good piece over here—I'm afraid it may mean that I can't come back to the place where I am liked best and have the most friends."[17] As Wolfe predicted, he never again returned to Germany after his story was published in 1937. While many scholars, including Brinkmeyer, have identified the publication of this story as the catalyst for Wolfe's break with Germany, it is important to note that Wolfe's books were not removed from German libraries or bookstores until the wholesale removal of American books following the declaration of war.[18] George R. Preston Jr., in his 1943 bibliographical study of Thomas Wolfe, points out that following the publication of this story in the *New Republic*, Wolfe's books were "placed on the black list for several months," though the ban was lifted when "it was decided that the circulation of the *New Republic* was not such as to foment any considerable anti-Nazi sentiment."[19] While Stokes reports that the Reich Chamber of Literature has no record of any such ban, both Stokes and Pusey note that it was Will Vesper, the Nazi literary critic and publisher of *Die neue Literatur*, who reacted most virulently to Wolfe's story, naming it as part of the American "spiritual cesspool of humankind extruded by a hotchpotch of peoples and civilizations."[20] Vesper was an active member of the Nazi Party and had given a speech at the infamous Dresden book-burnings in 1933. Wolfe was among esteemed company as the object of his indignation; in a letter to Thomas Mann, Hermann Hesse wrote that the "hack, W. Vesper" was determined to "discredit me completely," to which Mann later replied: "Vesper has always been one of the worst nationalist idiots. [. . .] Those people's hearts and minds are utterly corrupt. We can only hope [. . .] that side by side with them a better, spiritually sounder Germany is holding itself in reserve."[21]

Since "I Have a Thing to Tell You" is referred to many times throughout this chapter, it is important to provide a brief synopsis of the story as well as an explanation of its complicated publication history. On a train journey out of Germany in 1936, Wolfe witnessed the terror of Nazism firsthand after guards arrested a Jewish man who was apparently attempting to leave the country with more money than the currency restrictions allowed. Wolfe had volunteered to take the money for the man (only ten marks), and his story afforded an opportunity to describe the trauma of that moment, in Brinkmeyer's words "lashing together Nazi repression with his silent complicity."[22] Wolfe writes:

> They had him. [. . .] Slowly the train moved from the station. We rolled right past him, very slowly. They had him. They surrounded him. He stood among them, protesting volubly, talking with his hands now, insisting all could be explained. And they said nothing. They had him. [. . .] He lifted his eyes to us, his pasty face, and he was silent for a moment. And we looked at him for the last time, and he at us—this time, more direct and steadfastly. And in that glance there was all the slice of man's mortal anguish. And we were all somehow naked and ashamed, and somehow guilty. We all felt somehow that we were saying

> farewell, not to a man but to humanity; not to some nameless little cipher out of life, but to the fading image of a brother's face.[23]

This experience encouraged Wolfe to publish his story, with its overt criticism of National Socialism, fully aware that it would likely mean never returning to Germany again, and it was released in three installments in March 1937 by the *New Republic* with the title repeated in German translation: *"Nun Will Ich Ihnen 'Was Sagen."*[24] The story was later expanded for its inclusion in the posthumously published *You Can't Go Home Again* by Wolfe's new editor, Edward Aswell, where it was reformed as Book Six under the title "I Have a Thing to Tell You (*Nun Will Ich Ihnen 'Was Sagen*)." In this version, Aswell introduced a new opening section he titled "The Dark Messiah"—a name Wolfe used for Hitler—which the editor compiled from material found in an unpublished letter to the League of American Writers called "The Spanish Letter." As Francis Skipp points out, Aswell included some extra material from "Wolfe's writings on fame and the poet," supplied his own introduction, and added in some "transitional paragraphs."[25] Finally, Aswell chopped the final section of the *New Republic* version of the story and inserted it as the "Credo" at the end of *You Can't Go Home Again*, where it has since been interpreted as a clarion call for democracy. This novelized version of the story is significant for the later discussion of the German translation of *You Can't Go Home Again*.

Apart from the section describing the train journey and subsequent arrest—which predominates the narrative—Wolfe's original published story opens with a long conversation between Paul Spangler (later changed to George Webber) and Franz Hartmann (later changed to Franz Heilig) that details the intrusion of the Nazi system in the life of an ordinary German like Hartmann. As with most of Wolfe's material, this conversation drew on several real encounters, in this case with Heinrich Maria Ledig-Rowohlt, the son of Wolfe's German publisher and his contact and friend in Berlin. In an article published after Wolfe's death, Ledig-Rowohlt explained the fear he felt upon reading the "atrocity stories" that Wolfe had worked over with "phonographic exactness" for "I Have a Thing to Tell You":

> Though I appeared as a librarian under the name of Franz Heilig, and spoke a dry, schooled-on-Shakespeare English, all my personal circumstances were described exactly. Reading it took my breath away and brought the tears to my eyes. Wolfe had spitted me with his pen, had given a merciless X-ray picture of me with all the constraint, all the inner contradictions that the tactical juggling of those years involved and that he, as an American, simply could not understand. If these facts became known, if some unfriendly contemporary revealed the secret of Franz Heilig, then my fate was sealed. [. . .] The latent fear in which we were living then became a naked terror. [. . .] I thought everyone must rec-

> ognize who Franz Heilig was. I could no longer sleep peacefully [. . .] I thought my last hour had come indeed when Gestapo officials appeared at the office one afternoon. [. . .] It did not occur to the Gestapo to look for the original of Franz Heilig. But Franz Heilig was often close by me.[26]

Although *You Can't Go Home Again* was not translated and published in Germany until after the war, Ledig-Rowohlt notes that the *New Republic* was "read and 'gutted' in Goebbels's Propaganda Ministry," with his concern showing that Wolfe's anticipation of a ban was not unfounded.

Based on the publication of this story, Wolfe scholars have identified a shift toward a new social consciousness, with Brinkmeyer noting that after 1936, Wolfe's politics were "largely leftist" as he became increasingly vocal in his criticism of "monopoly capitalism and particularly of the power wielded by corporations to shape economic and social policy."[27] Indeed, the credo at the end of *You Can't Go Home Again* is taken to be representative of the new "social democrat" Wolfe, and it was this passage that Dorothy Thompson used to encourage the Yugoslav Partisans who formed an anti-Nazi resistance movement during World War II: "To the Yugoslav guerrillas, fighting in the mountains, this testament from America's great writer, Thomas Wolfe, who above us all understood the dynamics of these times: 'To lose the earth you know, for greater knowing; to lose the life you have for great life; to find a land [. . .] more large than earth—toward which the conscience of the world is tending—and wind is rising, and the rivers flow.'"[28]

In approaching Wolfe's fiction, the popular narrative of cultural seduction to redemption—or fascism to democratic socialism—is problematic in a number of ways: it is unwieldy in both its oversimplification of fascist ideology and its emphasis on unpublished or posthumously published work by the author. While Brinkmeyer qualifies Wolfe's political change by identifying his failure to escape his "virulent racism"—a fact that most other scholars continue to overlook—he fails to articulate one central intellectual and ideological factor in German fascism that characterized aspects of Wolfe's fiction and is useful in understanding Wolfe's earliest attraction to Germany: the *Volk*.[29]

Folk and Volk

In T*he Crisis of German Ideology: Intellectual Origins of the Third Reich* (1966), George Mosse outlined the meaning of *Volk* as it has been historically understood in Germany: "'Volk' is a much more comprehensive term than 'people,' for to German thinkers ever since the birth of German Romanticism in the late eighteenth century 'Volk' signified the union of a group of people with a transcendental 'essence.' This 'essence' might be called 'nature' or 'cosmos' or 'mythos,' but in each instance it was fused to man's innermost nature, and represented the source of his creativity, his depth of feeling, his individuality, and his unity with other members of the Volk."[30]

As highlighted in the previous chapter, it was the romanticized vision of Germany in which Wolfe believed his "strange life [would] find a home," while the resonance of Wolfe's vision of longing for home with the *Volksgemeinschaft* employed in Nazi ideology—and its philosophical framework—marks his work as being indebted to the history of *völkisch* thought. Just as Wolfe's doppelgängers sought out this "essence," they, like Wolfe, found "the other part of his heart's home [. . .] a magic domain of fulfillment" in Germany.[31] Although *You Can't Go Home Again* seems to end with that vision of Germany crumbling—since, after all, you can't go home again—his vision shifts back to his other equally mythic homeland and "the true discovery of America," an equally *völkisch* obsession as Wolfe's Americans search for the "fulfillment of our spirit, of our people, of our mighty and immortal land."[32] For the German critic Wolfgang von Einseidel, Wolfe's fiction—particularly *Of Time and the River*—dealt with "the creative 'I' in the modern world," while "the reassuring and warning aspect of his novel" is contained within "the experienced and shaped experience, that helps the 'I' not only to resist the impersonal dragging powers of the modern world, but in the end to triumph over them."[33]

The tragedy of the "lost American," Wolfe suggests, is that they have "no door to enter, no room to dwell in, no single handsbreadth of certain, consecrated earth upon that continent of wild houseless space," and although his fiction is saturated with this loss—and the subsequent romanticizing of loss—there remains a unifying conception of "America," the "huge, single, and incomparable substance of America," toward which Wolfe's characters often direct their *Sehnsucht*.[34] Wolfe did not encounter fascism solely on the virtues of the "clean streets and trains on time" that he mentions in his notebook, but through the influence of those writers who described the fate of the lost man in the world and whose ideas became central to *völkisch* thought. As Mosse argues, "The intellectual and ideological character of *völkisch* thought was a direct product of the Romantic movement of nineteenth-century Europe. Like Romanticism, *völkisch* ideas showed a distinct tendency toward the irrational and emotional, and were focused primarily on man and the world."[35]

This romantic, "*völkisch*" quality of Wolfe's writing—both in Wolfe's idealization of the German homeland as well as in those passages that explore the profound experience of dislocation from community—were not foreign ideas within the U.S. imaginary.[36] Early in Wolfe's own studies, the author encountered this idea of the *Volk* through Frederick Koch, the professor of drama at UNC Chapel Hill who had set up a workshop in "folk drama" and established the Carolina Playmakers in 1918, of which Wolfe was a charter member. Koch identified his use of "folk play" as deriving from the German *Volk*, which he took to be "concerned with folk subject matter: with the legends, superstitions, customs, environmental differences, and the vernacular of the common people."[37] In the workshop, Wolfe composed his own mountaineer "folk play," *The Return of Buck Gavin* (1919), which Koch later included in his second collected volume of *Carolina Folk Plays*.[38] In a short essay from 1920, Wolfe wrote that Koch saw the folk play as "the regeneration of the degenerate modern stage," adding that "all real drama," according to Koch, "had to come from the soil."[39] Though Wolfe was highly conscious of the ersatz nature of his hastily written play, Richard Kennedy remarks that this experience with the playmakers introduced him to a writing method that used "the materials of [his] own experience in [his] writing," charting his own internal geography.[40]

Wolfe and German Artists

One essential component of Wolfe's relationship with Germany that is frequently overlooked in critical studies is the response by contemporary German writers to the author and his fiction, an omission that reflects the America-centric analysis that this book has elsewhere identified. In outlining some of these interactions with German authors, my hope is to illuminate the extent to which Wolfe was revered in Germany—predominantly by antifascist artists while also reflecting on the nature of Wolfe's hazy politics during a time where German artists were not afforded the same luxury of ambivalence. Wolfe was not an activist writer, though he intersected with many German artists that are today recognized as important critics of the Nazi regime. The fraught history of his investment in German myths, and his very real importance for German readers, reveals the peculiar complexity of writing and reading during the period of National Socialism in Germany.

In a lecture on Wolfe and the "bitter secret of life" ("*Thomas Wolfe und das bittere Geheimnis des Lebens*"; 1953), German author Heinrich Böll challenged the characterization of vitality in the author's fiction, arguing that Wolfe's insistence on the constant "shadow of death" tempered his apparent attraction to vitalism.[41] However, Böll was still skeptical of Wolfe's tendency to romanticize modern Germany, suggesting that Wolfe's description of Munich as a "*deutsche Himmelreich*" (German kingdom of Heaven) was characteristic of the sort of Romanticism evident in *Blubo* literature.[42] *Blubo* was a term coined by Austrian composer Ernst Krenek in 1935 as a "contemptuous contraction" of Hitler's nationalistic slogan "*Blut und Boden*" (blood and soil).[43] Ruth Sanders has written that the "ominous Blut und Boden" was used so often that it became shorthand for Nazi ideology; these notions of "genetic origin and national territory" became a marketing campaign to "popularize Nazi nationalism and racism."[44] In his essay "*Zwischen 'Blubo' und 'Asphalt*,'" Krenek warned Austrians that they could not maintain sympathy with Nazi ideology like the *völkisch Blubo* literature without threatening their independence, something that they eventually did relinquish: "Through the two similarly primitive and dangerous catchwords, the negative *Kulturbolschewismus* [cultural Bolshevism] and the positive *Bodenverwurzeltheit* [rootedness in the soil], both derived from the National Socialist vocabulary, our cultural life is in danger of hewing to a line that threatens most gravely to compromise the spiritual independence of Austria from the Third Reich."[45] Böll's identification of Wolfe's "heavenly" vision of Germany with *Blubo* literature reinforces my argument that Wolfe was most closely aligned to National Socialism while he was romanticizing the nation. However, Böll points out that he and his readers might be inclined to attach a special sympathy to Wolfe and forgive this failure of political savvy, adding that Wolfe's vision of America could provide a penetrating critique of Europe: its "sophistication and barbarism [. . .] sensitivity and stupidity."

Böll was one of many German artists attracted to this singular author, a seemingly unprecedented literary light with his "*unerschöpflich*" (inexhaustible) array of American characters.[46] A reference to Wolfe appears in Böll's *Ansichten Eines Clowns* (*The Clown*; 1963), in a ghostly reminder to Hans Schnier—Böll's clown—of his deserted lover Marie, who used to read aloud from "Thomas Wolfe's *Look Homeward, Angel*. [. . .] Here I was, lying completely deserted in this stupid terra cotta bathtub. [. . .] I missed Marie's voice."[47] Böll was too young to have met Wolfe in prewar Germany, but his stories of homecomers returning as outsiders to postwar German society mirror Wolfe's own narratives of lost and exiled Americans. Given Böll's apparently plain and concise stories, written in what Theodore Ziolkowski describes as "idiomatic dialogue, a style economical to the point of understatement," Böll and Wolfe make strange bedfellows.[48] But as Robert Conrad points out, Böll's "laconic plainness" did not prevent a "simple lyricism that appealed to a spiritual longing" from being conveyed through his terse narratives, and Böll identifies his own pleasure at the "wild [. . .] bitter [. . .] terrible and beautiful America," which he believed lay at the heart of Wolfe's narratives.[49] One story that is representative of Böll's simple lyricism, "Autumn Loneliness" (1948), opens with two men standing at a tram station, waiting in constant suspense as groups of people arrive and alight. The story's narrator—who presents events as if they are a strange memory—is held spellbound, "convinced that someone was about to come [. . .] whose homeward steps would force our own weary, aimless footsteps to keep up with the tempo of his happy excitement."[50] "Autumn Loneliness" contains many echoes of *Of Time and the River*, which also opens at a station on an autumn afternoon, filled with the "quietly suppressed excitement" that "seemed to infuse" the moment with an "electric vitality"—though for Wolfe it is "the thrill and menace of the coming train" rather than a tram.[51] In Böll's story, the narrative abruptly ends when the narrator realizes that his companion—with whom he has been traveling constantly for the previous two months—was "waiting for something quite specific," that the goal of the "arduous flight" and "journey lasting two months" was to meet with his own partner.[52] As the narrator hears a woman gasp and his friend rush forward with a "smothered cry," he recalls that "something like a shadow fell across the astonished void of my heart." The storyteller—recalling Wolfe's own heroes—had been waiting aimlessly, this tram station being "just another street corner, one of many thousand," and as he turns away he heads out toward "that Somewhere," surrounded by the "freshness of the falling light [. . .] permeated by the spicy smell of burning potato plants, the smell of childhood and of longing [*Sehnsucht*]."

This "smell of childhood and of longing" evokes the *Sehnsucht* so central to Wolfe's fiction, and Wolfe shared his artistic adherence to this expression of longing with another German writer, Hermann Hesse, who believed that the task of the artist was to "awaken *Sehnsucht*."[53] In 1933, in the kind of review that had incited Vesper's vitriol, Hesse wrote about *Look Homeward, Angel*: "Like a genial drinker, this enthusiast pours into himself all the juices of earth and life, eternally in love, eternally the artist—and what an artist!" For Hesse, Wolfe's "story of a buried life" was especially compelling because it combined "the lust for life" with "extreme despair," focusing on the "loneliness and lostness of every man, even in the midst of a visible community."[54] Writing in 1933, the year the Weimar Republic was uprooted and replaced with Hitler's regime, Hesse's generous review of Wolfe's novel is qualified by an expectation that the next volume "will have to lead the naïve young Siegfried to a spot where the beauty and the 'lostness' of the world are no longer compatible." For Hesse, like Böll, Wolfe's fiction contained evidence of the dangers of romanticizing youthfulness, pointing out that there must be "a painful sublimation, responsible search for meaning," since the book leaves its protagonist—by which Hesse indicates both Eugene and Wolfe—"with equal possibilities of becoming a genius or a scamp."[55]

Hesse's recommendation that Wolfe depart from this naïve Romanticism was informed by the cultural change Hesse was observing around him in the turbulent year of 1933, and it is important to note that Hesse perceived *Look Homeward, Angel* as concluding with "its hero still a youth" while, as Hesse observes, it is "beyond question [that] the hero is the author himself."[56]

Heinrich Ledig-Rowohlt, Wolfe's friend and chaperone during his visits to Germany, argued that discussions of Nazism and cultural change with Wolfe had the effect of emphasizing the "gulf that separated Germany from the democratic countries," noting that even as Wolfe wrote books that were "a source of encouragement [. . .] to German readers," the unalterable reality was that Wolfe was oblivious to the true horrors of National Socialism.[57] For Hesse, it was enough that Wolfe's novel seemed so wonderfully alive, "the most powerful piece of fiction from present-day America that I know of," suggesting that the "beauty and genius the book contains" ultimately transcend the novel's "profound problem" of unbridled Romanticism.[58] Like Böll, Hesse was willing to forgive Wolfe's political naïveté on the basis of his exuberant portrait of an American family, particularly since the young hero, with his "blossoming fantasy" and "enormous hunger for life," was certainly Wolfe himself.

In 1937 Thomas Mann noted in his diary that he had been reading *Look Homeward, Angel*, suggesting that it was "good, powerful," though unaware that eight years earlier Wolfe had listed Mann's two novels, *Buddenbrooks* (1901) and *The Magic Mountain* (1924), in his own journal as being among "the best novels written during this century."[59] In an interview with the *Greensboro Record* in 1941, following his immigration to the United States, Mann positioned Wolfe as being among the strongest voices in America, glossing over the author's relationship with Nazi Germany, though Mann was an outspoken critic of the regime and those writers he identified as capitulating to its expectations.[60] In the end it was Klaus Mann, Thomas's son, who most appreciated the resonance of Wolfe's novel for the Mann family following the collapse of Nazi Germany. Returning to Germany only one day after the armistice, Klaus was horrified by how his former homeland had been "morally mutilated, crippled," realizing that the fantasy of return for his family was merely an "illusion."[61] Writing to Thomas Mann, he warned his father not to return home: "It would be a very grave mistake on your part to return to this country. [. . .] Conditions here are too sad. All your efforts to improve them would be hopelessly wasted."[62] As Andrea Weiss notes, *You Can't Go Home Again*, "one of Klaus's favorite books," never had "more resonance than that May afternoon when Klaus drove up to his childhood home," only to discover that during the family's absence it had been converted by the Nazis into a *Lebensborn*, where "racially qualified young men and equally well-bred young women collaborated in the interest of the German nation," for the purpose of "the propagation of [the] Nordic race."[63]

Weiss notes that in an essay Klaus titled "An American Soldier Revisiting His Former Homeland"—which Klaus read over several radio stations while traveling through Europe—he would "invariably [end] the broadcasts with a declaration of his estrangement," reframing the famous title of *You Can't Go Home Again*.[64] Klaus's essay ends: "I felt a stranger in my former fatherland. There was an abyss separating me from those who used to be my countrymen. Wherever I went in Germany, the melancholy tune and nostalgic leitmotiv follow me: You can't go home again."[65] In 1939 Klaus published *Der Vulkan* (The Volcano), which charted what Hermann Rasche calls "the broad panorama of individual human fates and the ever-changing topography of exile."[66] This "Novel among Emigrants"—the book's subtitle—details the experiences of émigrés forced to flee Hitler's Germany, with Klaus anticipating the theme that he would be so drawn to in Wolfe: "Whoever has left his home, has done so for good. Things at home change, we cannot imagine how things at home are, we are not part of it anymore. We have become strangers."[67]

For the German playwright Carl Zuckmayer, Wolfe's theme of exile was similarly compelling. According to Gene Plunka in *Staging Holocaust Resistance* (2012), Zuckmayer's military satire *Der Hauptmann von Köpenick* (1931) provoked the ire of the Nazi party, forcing the writer to first leave Germany for Austria after his plays were banned following Hitler's rise to power, fleeing to Switzerland, then later to the United States after the Anschluss in 1938.[68] Zuckmayer was good friends with the German translator of Wolfe, Hans Schiebelhuth, and in his memoir, *A Part of Myself* (1970), he reflected on the familiar journey of exile—"the journey of no return" as Zuckmayer calls it—linking his and other German writers' experiences with the "self-exiled" Wolfe:

> Going into exile is "the journey of no return." Anyone who sets out on it dreaming of coming home is lost. He may return—but the place he will find is no longer the one he left, and he himself is no longer the one who left. He may return to people he missed, to places he loved and did not forget, to the region where his own language is spoken. But he never returns home. *You can't go home again* is the title of a book by the self-exiled America writer Thomas Wolfe. You cannot go back to the land of your childhood, where you were wholly at home; neither can you go back to a country you were forced to leave. For you want to find its former image, and that is gone forever.[69]

Beyond the suggestiveness of Wolfe's themes of exile and insatiable homesickness to a generation of exiled writers, the exuberance of the American author's work was also profoundly appealing to German artists and readers, who found themselves in a diminished artistic environment. According to Martha Dodd, daughter of the first U.S. ambassador to Nazi Germany: "To the desolateness of the intellectual life of Germany, Thomas Wolfe was like a symbol of the past when great writers were great men."[70] The sheer beauty contained in Wolfe's fiction, and the suggestions of a rich intellectual and cultural life that this work and his visits implied about America, was thrilling to the Germans who encountered him. Erich Franzen, writing for the *Berliner Börzen-Courier*, said of *Schau Heimwärts, Engel!*: "The brilliance of its presentation, the superb sweep of its spiritual outlook, and the almost fanatical verisimilitude of the whole thing, make the book one of the most significant of our time. It must be looked upon as the voice of the entire younger American generation, who became articulate here, in the most significant way, for the first time."[71] The early joy and anticipation of finding a "home" in Germany was reciprocated by the warmth and friendship that Wolfe experienced in his visits there, and, as Dodd points out, part of Wolfe's apparently uncritical attitude toward Nazism "can be explained by his own state of delirium."[72] Moreover, Stokes argues that since Wolfe's publisher Rowohlt Verlag had been nearly bankrupted by the impact of the Depression, losing "so many of its best-selling authors on account of Nazi political and racial persecution," by 1935 Wolfe had become "one of the most significant writers left on its list despite that sales of his first novel were quite modest in Germany."[73] The correspondence between Rowohlt Verlag and Wolfe, as well as what the publisher described as "an aggressive advertising campaign," provides evidence of this faith in Wolfe; Ledig-Rowohlt wrote to Wolfe that "even if we shall not grow rich being your German publisher we still enjoy very much and are proud of you as one of our most important authors."[74]

One contemporary German reader of Wolfe—the nationalist German author and filmmaker Ernst von Salomon—described reading Wolfe's books with "absorbed fascination," finding in them the "tide of American literature [reaching] its flood."[75] Von Salomon valorized Wolfe in his controversial book *Der Fragebogen* (The Questionnaire; 1951), an autobiographical work structured as a response to the Allied questionnaire that formed the basis of the de-Nazification program after World War II and which became a best seller in West Germany, selling over 250,000 copies.[76] Philipp Gassert points out that not only was von Salomon portraying the manifest failings of the unpopular program, but *Der Fragebogen* was "peppered with invectives against the Americans, whom he depicted as brutal, degenerate, dumb, and mean."[77] Von Salomon was an author with the Rowohlt publishing house—he knew both Martha Dodd and Ledig-Rowohlt—and he records the anticipation of Wolfe's arrival in Berlin, noting that "[Ledig] and Martha Dodd would put their heads together for hours and talk with ecstatic expressions about a certain Tommy. [. . .] This Tommy I took at first to be some dearly beloved friend whom they had, perhaps, both known as children, and it was a long time before I realized that the man was in fact that famous American writer, Thomas Wolfe, whom neither of them had yet met." For von Salomon, Wolfe was a "giant, arising from the Rocky Mountains" who had swallowed the "whole, huge American continent and was now spewing it out again," while his antipathy toward Americans found a symbol in the Romantic persona of Wolfe: "More even than the other great American story-tellers, Wolfe aroused in me a boundless admiration for the Americans' art and an equally heartfelt wish that I might never be compelled to live in their country."[78]

Wolfe and the Politics of Literature

It is impossible to be exact about how much Wolfe's popularity and warm reception within the German literary scene hindered his perceptiveness about National Socialism, but it is clear that he was surrounded by antifascists early on. Sinclair Lewis—who first introduced Wolfe to Rowohlt and helped secure his translation and success in Germany—was one of the many best-selling authors whom Rowohlt could no longer publish in translation after 1935. His 1935 political allegory, *It Can't Happen Here*—a work that has received new scrutiny in the wake of the election of Donald Trump as president of the United States—imagines a fascist takeover of the United States and, along with his criticism of the 1933 Nazi book burnings, ensured Lewis was numbered among the "decadent" authors banned by the Reich.[79] Lewis's book was published just after the sensational congressional testimony of Smedley Butler, a retired major general of the Marines who told a House committee that a New York bond salesman named Gerald MacGuire was conspiring to set up a fascist government in the United States—later known as the "Business Plot." As Arthur Schlesinger Jr. points out, "No one quite knew what to make of the Butler story," but "the House committee [. . .] declared itself able to verify all the pertinent statements made by Gerald Butler."[80] The committee's report concluded that "certain persons had made an attempt to establish a fascist organization in this country," and while the fascist dream in America was hardly concrete, Schlesinger adds that "what was clear in 1935 was the impression that new forces had somehow been released in American politics."

Fear of fascism in America was clearly apparent by the time *It Can't Happen Here* was published—which, incidentally, coincided with Wolfe's first publicized visit to Berlin—and Lewis's antifascist response to the threat differed starkly from Wolfe's.[81] *It Can't Happen Here* met with enormous success upon publication, with MGM Studios purchasing the film rights only to later drop the project, a decision that Lewis saw as being prompted by pressure from "movie industry czar Will Hays," who "feared a boycott of Hollywood films in Hitler's Germany and Mussolini's Italy."[82] Instead, *It Can't Happen Here* was turned into a play in 1936, produced by Roosevelt's Federal Theatre Project, which included a Yiddish version in New York and a Seattle production with an all-black cast. In Wolfe's case, there is a letter that reveals the author's problematic and deeply ambivalent political perspective; Wolfe's agent, Elizabeth Nowell, includes a letter from Mischa Mindess in her correspondence with Wolfe that asked for permission to translate "I Have a Thing to Tell You" into Yiddish in 1937, to which Wolfe replied: "As to the enclosed letter from Mischa Mindess [. . .] I am not so sure. I wouldn't mind at all having it done if it were not for the suggestion of propaganda it might attach to it. And frankly I do not think the story ought to be used in that way. It is a straight story, so far as I know it has no propaganda in it save that the reader wishes to supply for himself by inference."[83]

# # #

Returning to Wolfe's reception in Germany, it is clear that Rowohlt's support of Wolfe was significant. The publisher regularly promoted the author in house, including encouraging one of their main writers, Hans Fallada, to read *Von Zeit und Strom* (1936), the German translation of *Of Time and the River*. In response, Fallada wrote to Rowohlt: "This is something truly wonderful, and certainly the most beautiful and most poetic book that you have ever published. What Spirit! What a poet! To be able to write like this—surely this falls into the realm of the divine! Captivating! As I've said: simply wonderful!"[84] For Fallada—a German novelist who had chosen to continue publishing in Nazi Germany—writing was rife with complexity, such that Wolfe's unabashed lyricism without fear of suppression must have seemed exhilarating. Fallada had been among those writers who had chosen what novelist Frank Thiess called an "inner emigration"; opposed to the regime but remaining in Germany, he avoided confrontation with the Nazis by choosing inoffensive, apolitical themes.[85] Fallada achieved considerable fame worldwide with *Little Man, What Now?* (1932), which was accepted by the American Book-of-the-Month Club and turned into a 1934 American film of the same title, but he had also been imprisoned and placed on "undesirable" lists, before once again earning favor with the publication of his novel *Wolf among Wolves* (1937).[86] Fallada was a controversial figure in German literature; Erik Larson notes that he was "reviled in some quarters for his failure to stand up to the Nazis but defended in others for not choosing the safe path of exile."

Ultimately, Fallada's work is a case study in the complex politics of literature during Nazi Germany: following 1933, there were numerous bans and public book burnings, though as Jan-Pieter Barbian points out, "until the war German booksellers could offer numerous translations of French, British, and American literature," among which he names books by Proust, Steinbeck, Joyce, Tolstoy, Valéry, Conrad, Shaw, Faulkner, and Wolfe.[87] Thomas Mann criticized German novelists like Fallada, noting that "It may be superstitious belief, but in my eyes, any books which could be printed at all in Germany between 1933 and 1945 are worse than worthless and not objects one wishes to touch. A stench of blood and shame attaches to them. They should all be pulped."[88] However, Barbian notes that even Mann's works continued to be sold through the publisher S. Fischer after his emigration, only indexed when Mann was deprived of his citizenship at the end of 1936.[89]

Wolfe and Fallada track a similar trajectory in relation to Nazi Germany, where success sometimes implied either an apolitical outlook or fascist complicity, but both authors also left books that contained explicit criticisms of National Socialism, albeit novels that were only published after their death: Fallada with *Alone in Berlin* (1947) and Wolfe with *You Can't Go Home Again* (1940). While there is no evidence that Wolfe and Fallada ever met, both men shared the same German publisher, and both spent time in Germany with a circle of friends—specifically Ledig-Rowohlt, Martha Dodd, and Mildred Harnack—all of whom attempted to challenge the authors' perceptions about Germany and National Socialism. But their continued success in Nazi Germany, as Stokes notes of Wolfe, helps "illuminate the always perplexing situation of literature" and its production "within a would-be totalitarian dictatorship," particularly regarding the success of foreign authors.[90] Ledig-Rowohlt wrote to Hans Fallada in 1936—the year after he had first hosted Wolfe in Berlin—characterizing the Americans as "the only valve in this stuffy European air," a phenomenon Wolfe noted in his "Spanish Letter," which would later be incorporated into the "Dark Messiah" chapter of *You Can't Go Home Again*:

> The work of our younger writers was eagerly published, read, and judged as was the work of writers everywhere throughout the world. Even in 1936 when, after an absence of almost five years, I saw the country again, and for the first time under the regime of Adolph [*sic*] Hitler, the evidence of this noble enthusiasm, now submerged and mutilated, was still apparent in the most touching way. It has been said by some people that there are no more good books published in Germany, because good books can no longer be published or read. This is not true as so many things one reads about Germany today are not true. [. . .] Good books are still published where the substance and material of good books does not in any way controvert or either openly or by implication criticize the present regime. [. . .] For all these reasons, the eagerness, the curiosity, and the enthusiasm for Germans for the books which they are still allowed to read has been, if anything, movingly intensified. Their eagerness to find what is going on in the world, what is being written and published outside of Germany, their generous enthusiasm for such American writing as they are now allowed to read is as overwhelming as it is pathetic.[91]

Overwhelmingly, however, the Nazi period saw what Murray Hall has termed the "provincialization of literature," a stagnation effected by a lack of exchange with other literatures and the restricting of translation.[92] Barbian points out that despite the surprising numbers of books sold in National Socialist Germany, it is important to take into account the new "National Socialist mass book market" supplied predominantly by companies associated with the German Labor Front.[93] Addressing the reception of Faulkner in Germany, Peter Nicolaisen and Daniel Göske note that "the contingencies of translating and publishing serious foreign literature in the early years of the Nazi regime are difficult to imagine. [. . .] After July 1935, prior to publication, each translation of a foreign book needed official approval by Goebbels's Ministry of Propaganda." Faulkner had also been picked up by Rowohlt—*Light in August* (1932) was first translated in 1935—and his novels were among "some forty books by important American authors" Rowohlt published before the beginning of World War II.[94] The *Buchhändler im neuen Reich*—the official journal of the state-aligned booksellers' association—identified this "very strange and reprehensible tendency to value foreign literature" in a 1939 editorial: "National Socialism has combated this as an 'intellectual swamping' and clearly character-

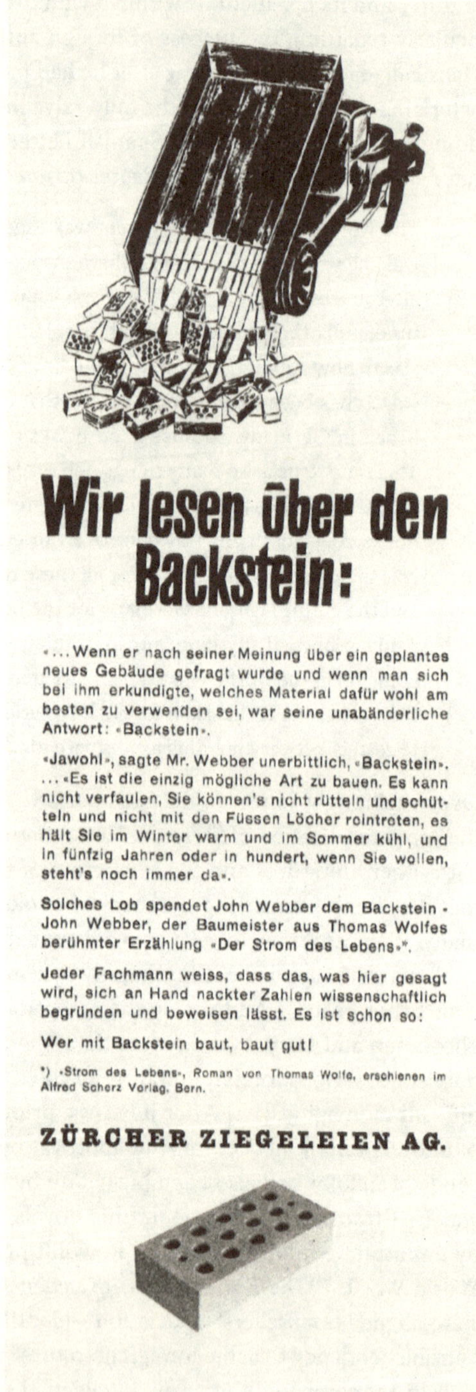

FIGURE 5.
Advertisement for Zürcher Ziegeleien, "Anzeigenseite," *Schweizerische Bauzeitung* 121, no. 7 (February 13, 1943). Zürcher Ziegeleien was a Swiss building materials company, and the text of the advertisement includes a quote from the German-language translation of *The Web and the Rock*, which features a short paean to brick.

ized it as the expression of the Volk's feeling of inferiority. Over the years since the National Socialist revolution, German literature itself has been thoroughly cleansed, and all the elements alien to the German character eradicated. But today we are faced with a development that tries, using the indirect route of foreign translated literature, to familiarize us with exactly the same negative values we have just managed to remove from German literature itself."[95]

While the regime's control was never fully complete, Kate Sturge notes that it was the "broad range of modernism and the works of authors either considered unacceptable in their style or content," or those who had spoken out against the Nazi Party, whose works were removed.[96] However, contemporary American literature, "generally undesirable in official eyes," did not completely disappear, and Sturge points out that some experimental or "decadent" work was published "surprisingly late in the period," highlighting Faulkner's *Absalom, Absalom!* in 1938 and Wolfe's *Strom des Lebens* (*The Web and the Rock*) in 1941 as examples.[97] In one unusual instance of this phenomenon, Wolfe's novel served a surprising function in Swiss newspapers during World War II, advertising bricks for the building materials company Zürcher Ziegeleien, which quoted from "Thomas Wolfe's famous story *Der Strom des Lebens*" in their half-page advertisement: "Brick. It's the only way to build. You can't rot it out, you can't rattle it or shake it, you can't kick holes in it, it will keep you warm in Winter and cool in Summer, and fifty years from now, or a hundred for that matter, it will still be here"[98] (figure 5).

Wavering Illusions

Despite Wolfe's seeming ambivalence, his friends in Germany recognized the privileged position of the American author and his problematic indifference—or even attraction—to German fascism, suggesting ways in which he could turn his pen to politics. Ledig-Rowohlt notes that as he became increasingly conscious of the German people's lack of freedom, he encouraged Wolfe to "write a great novel by which he as a writer, not as a political propagandist, should appeal to the conscience of mankind. [. . .] I begged him, for daily he experienced what a source of encouragement his books were to German readers. He had an obligation to these Germans."[99] Of those three people who had also visited Fallada—Ledig-Rowohlt, Martha Dodd, and Mildred Harnack—it was Harnack who was the most outspoken against the Nazi regime, a resistance that would later see her as the only American executed by the Nazi Party. Harnack had met with Fallada on May 27, 1934, attempting to sound him out, with Brysac noting that though she was conscious of his cowardice, she was intent that "he was not a Nazi, he is not hopeless."[100] Dodd later admitted that the meeting "made a permanent impression on me. [. . .] I saw the stamp of naked fear on a writer's face—for the first time."[101] Later, Brysac cites an unpublished memoir of Dodd's noting that Harnack had similarly worked to "develop Wolfe's later political understanding," helping change his mind about Germany.[102] Harnack was deeply moved by *Look Homeward, Angel* and had lectured on Wolfe at the American's Women's Club in 1933 and again in 1934 before an audience of German academics, while also publishing an essay on Wilder, Wolfe, and Faulkner.[103] Harnack and Wolfe had met in Berlin on May 8, 1935, at an embassy tea hosted by Martha Dodd. According to Anne Nelson, Martha had asked Harnack to assemble the German guest list, which comprised "writers, poets, publishers and magazine editors, many of whom were already involved in secret anti-Nazi activity."[104] Harnack had already drummed up enthusiastic German reception for Wolfe before his arrival and, following the dinner, interviewed Wolfe for the *Continental Post*—an English-language newspaper in Berlin.[105] After Wolfe left Germany in 1936 for the final time, Harnack wrote him a letter, asking: "Will triton ever blow his wreathed horn or Tom call me [. . .] for I'm only able to stay here till Thursday morning and there's a longing in me to know how you are."[106] Though Wolfe would never visit Berlin again, nor learn of Harnack's imprisonment and eventual execution, it is clear that these encounters with the resistance left a permanent impression on the author: Dodd recounts that it was during Wolfe's final trip to Germany, arriving "a much soberer person," that he "met with even more Germans than in the first year, learned what made the wheels go round, in the partisans as well as the non-partisans [. . .] his feeling for their tragic frustration left him no alternative but to stay away from present-day Germany."[107]

Wolfe and Martha Dodd had pursued a brief affair during his visit in 1935, and the author also spent time traveling with her to Weimar, visiting the home of Goethe and the tombs of both Schiller and Goethe. Dodd recalls visiting Die Wartburg—part of the "magical trip" that Wolfe had described exultantly to his editor—and feeling that the scene was "morbid and romantic, without some of the strange barbarism of Wagner, peopled with the dark heroes and legends of the new Nazi religion." Dodd felt that the trip was "a joy and a revelation," increasing her awareness of both the "deep, courageous chapters in the history of [German] literature and progress"—reinforced by Wolfe's Romantic impressions—but also of the "perversion of heroic Germanic legend" in Nazi symbolism and ideology.[108] Wolfe also developed a friendship with her father, William Dodd—the first American ambassador to Nazi Germany, who was ardently opposed to the growing threat of Nazism—and in one letter to Wolfe, Martha mentions "the Nazi-Hegel thing Dad gave you," another attempt to open the author's mind to the dangers of Nazi ideology.[109] In a letter to Perkins, Wolfe characterizes the Dodds' home as a bastion of free opinion: "Their home in Berlin has been a free and fearless harbor for people of all opinions," he writes, "and people who live and walk in terror have been able to draw their breath there without fear, and to speak their minds."[110] However, Wolfe's reticence to see the extent of the danger is evident in his very next lines:

> This I know to be true, and further, the dry, plain, homely unconcern with which the Ambassador observes all the pomp and glitter and decorations and the tramp of marching men would do your heart good to see. I wish you could have been there the other night in his house when he came back from attending Hitler's two hour and forty minute speech which was delivered to that group of automatic dummies that now bears the ironical title of the "Reichstag." [. . .] It was Emerson who said that if you heard the pop of a popgun not to believe it was anything else but a pop of a popgun, even if all the captains and kings of the earth told you it was the roar of a cannon.[111]

Wolfe had not yet developed the habit of calling Hitler "the dark Messiah," and in William Shirer's journal from Berlin of September 1936, he records meeting the young writer after a suggestion from Martha Dodd: "Wolfe is somewhat conscious of not being politically minded at a time when most writers are and indeed, we agreed, should be. He admitted the deficiency, but said he was learning."[112]

"Nun Will Ich Ihnen 'Was Sagen"

The extent to which Thomas Wolfe was able to reconcile his knowledge of Nazi ideology with his understanding of Germany is impossible to gauge. While he left behind at least two significant indictments of Germany during this period—"I Have a Thing to Tell You" and "The Spanish Letter"—there is also his unwillingness to proffer any substantial opinion on the Germany with which he was, by 1936, very familiar, along with his reticence to allow his work to publicly critique Hitler's regime. Dieter Meindl argues that "I Have a Thing to Tell You," as it appears as book 6 in *You Can't Go Home Again*, reveals "a modification of Wolfe's modernism" toward a deeper understanding of the social and political realities of National Socialism, suggesting that the "shock of recognition in Nazi Germany" gave momentum to Wolfe's new "political intuition and humane reflection" a "more moral modernism."[113] Leslie Field has similarly argued that, with the publication of this story, "Wolfe came to see the evil behind the mask of Germany and sensed at once that anti-Semitism and humanity were incompatible."[114] But these summaries of Wolfe's position are too reductive, not only with regard to Wolfe's enduring racialist thinking, but also in their suggestion that Wolfe's "shock of recognition" precipitated a new political outlook wedded to the author's "moral modernism." After "I Have a Thing to Tell You" was published, Wolfe still happily consented to letting *Scribner's*

Magazine publish a more subdued, though no less romantic, story about Germany titled "Oktoberfest" (1937), which details a night in a Munich beer hall spent with "four young people from the mass of life and from the heart of Germany," closing with the young protagonist scouring the streets of "the magic city of Munich" for "something priceless and unutterable," flushed with feelings of happiness and joy, certain of "impending happiness, of impossible delight, that was almost ours."[115] Later, this story was incorporated into *The Web and the Rock* (1939), in which Wolfe left further material detailing the "great Germanic dream" of Munich, a "kind of German heaven" that was for Wolfe's hero, George Webber, the "most haunting, the most exciting, the most undefined" city he had ever known.[116] It was this description of Munich that Böll likened to the *Blubo* literature championed by the Nazi party, as proof that Wolfe had not yet shaken off his *Sehnsucht* for Germany.

Nevertheless, book 6 of *You Can't Go Home Again*, "I Have a Thing to Tell You," remains Wolfe's most complete statement about Germany under National Socialism, detailing his crumbling Romantic vision in light of "the dark Messiah" and the "poisonous emanations of suppression, persecution, and fear" that "permeated the air like miasmic and pestilential vapors, tainting, sickening, and blighting the lives of everyone he met."[117] It is difficult to speculate on Wolfe's political intent with this narrative, given that the author anticipated a ban in Nazi Germany after the first publication of the story in 1937, yet also rejected a Yiddish translation that same year, with the suggestion that the narrative might be misconstrued as propaganda. But what is clear is that the 1937 story "I Have a Thing to Tell You," "The Spanish Letter," and Aswell's synthesis of these texts in book 6 of *You Can't Go Home Again* are mourning a Germany that Wolfe saw as "the dark, found Helen he had lost. [. . .] [H]e knew now, as he had never known before, the priceless measure of his loss."[118] This loss for Wolfe is described as a kind of exile, with the first-person voice of the earlier published story replaced with third-person narration, and it is obvious that the sentiment of loss is as much the author's as it is his character's. In the original story, as the train leaves Germany and enters Belgium, another traveler remarks, "We are so happy to be—*out*!" after which—in language he often employed in letters and journal entries—Wolfe writes his own reflection on being "out": "I too was 'out,' who was a stranger to her land, who never yet had been a stranger in it. I too was 'out' of that great land whose image had been engraved upon my spirit in my childhood and my youth, before I had ever seen it. I too was 'out' from that land which had been much more to me than land, which had been for me so much more than place. It was a geography of heart's desire. It was a soul's dark wonder, the haunting beauty of the magic land. It had been burning there forever, like the dark Helen burning in man's blood. And now, like the dark Helen, it was lost to me."[119]

Later, the novelist observes that leaving Germany was the "way of exile and of no return," astonishingly numbering himself among those authors who were forced to flee the nation they too had loved. Germany was a symbolic *homeland* for Wolfe, the "geography of heart's desire," and so leaving the nation that had been irrevocably marred by the evils of Nazism constituted a spiritual exile from a land that had been "so much more than place." Tellingly, though Wolfe had used the phrase "you can't go home again" in his Purdue lecture titled "Writing and Living" in connection with his return to his hometown of Asheville, Aswell chose to also incorporate this famous line within the context of the exile from Germany, where it is imbued with an entirely new meaning: one can neither go home to the past, back to the magical vision of Germany, back to a vision of a nation that seemed—naïvely—unblemished, nor return to the "old German land with all the measure of your truth, your glory, beauty, magic, and your ruin."[120]

The 1937 *New Republic* version of "I Have a Thing to Tell You" unsurprisingly did not find a German audience, save for Goebbels's propaganda machine, which Ledig-Rowohlt noted had "read and gutted" the magazine, meaning that there was no translation of the original story until 2004, where it appeared in Lubrich's *Reisen ins Reich*.[121] However, the longer version of this anti-Nazi narrative, in book 6 of *You Can't Go Home Again*, was published in Germany by Rowohlt as *Es führt kein Weg zurück* (1950), albeit after World War II. This German translation of Wolfe's novel, particularly this section of the narrative, was also appropriated by acclaimed director Rolf Hädrich in his telemovie *Erinnerung an einen Sommer in Berlin* (1972), which follows "*Schriftsteller und Nobelpreisträger Thomas Wolfe*" as he spends a summer in Berlin during the 1936 Olympics.[122] Hädrich used the narrative of "I Have a Thing to Tell You," as it appears in the novel, to construct a film about the Berlin Olympics and the specter of Nazism, following Wolfe's growing realization that the romance and pageantry of the summer Olympics hid the more insidious realities of life under Hitler. The movie intersperses early footage and modern interviews with Leni Riefenstahl, Ledig-Rowohlt, William Shirer, and Albert Speer with the dramatic narrative of Wolfe—played by Burt Nelson—to criticize the Romantic sympathies that Wolfe embodied and to reveal both the hidden terror and the magic allure that the Olympics embodied. Wolfe's biography, particularly as he came to interpret it in "I Have a Thing to Tell You," is here reimagined as emblematic of the broader response of Germans to the Olympic Games, useful for Hädrich as a critical lens to revisit a particular historical juncture and determine what it augured for the coming war and atrocities. Ironically, this movie is easier to find in Germany than *Es führt kein Weg zurück*—which has not been reprinted since 1995—since Studio Hamburg re-released the movie in its 2008 "Grosse Geschichten" collection.

Rudolf Frank and the Other Way

There is one final version of "I Have a Thing to Tell You" that has not received any critical attention, and that is the focus of the final section of this chapter. The few scholarly works addressing the contemporary publication of Wolfe's novels in Germany—most recently the centenary celebration of the Rowohlt publishing house, *100 Jahre Rowohlt* (2008)—all acknowledge that *Es führt kein Weg zurück* could not have been published in Nazi Germany, but that a translation into German was possible in neutral Switzerland.[123] Only Pusey notes that "the translator is given as Ernst Reinhard, while the publishers wrote me that Dr. Rudolf Frank made the translation," though Pusey has nothing to say about Frank and adds only that the translation is "unimaginative" as well as being "arbitrary and inaccurate."[124] Frank's version of *Es führt kein Weg zurück* (1942) was published in Bern by Alfred Scherz Verlag, several years after he had fled Austria—his first nation of exile—following the Anschluss in 1938. In engaging with this translation, I am extending Jeffrey Einboden's contention in *Nineteenth-Century U.S. Literature in Middle Eastern Languages* (2013) that the "intermediacy of expression and culture" present in translation "reveals as much as it obscures, acting not as a veil but as a lens, refracting implications latent within American texts themselves."[125] In the case of *Es führt kein Weg zurück*, what Einboden describes as the "translatory displacement" of Middle Eastern translations is recast as a political and ideological displacement, treating the excised, amended, and censored German translation as a means by which to reread Wolfe and to illuminate aspects of the politics of literature that otherwise remain hidden.

Rudolf Frank was actively involved in German theater in the early decades of the twentieth century; he performed in Max Reinhardt's *Deutsches Theatre* in Berlin and, as a director, Volkmar Zühlsdorff writes, "made Brecht famous by giving *Trommeln in der Nacht* (*Drums in the Night*) its premiere at the Munich *Kammerspiele* in 1922."[126] By 1931, Frank also was highly regarded in film and radio, though his most significant success came with the publication of the young-adult novel *Der Schädel des Negerhäuptlings Makaua* (1931), touted as a "war novel for the younger generation," which Frank described as "an antiwar novel to warn young people."[127] The book was highly acclaimed and has since been translated into English as *No Hero for the Kaiser* (1986), but after the transfer of power to the Nazis in 1933, Frank's book was blacklisted as "harmful and undesirable" and was among those books burned in May 1933.[128] In 1938 the American Guild for German Cultural Freedom—designed to "secure the freedom and continued existence, for the present and the future, of an artistic and scientific German culture which is not tied to any political party"[129]—sponsored a writing competition for exiles, in which Frank submitted a manuscript titled *Fair Play*. The novel, later published in 1998—sixty years after it was written—covers his experiences in Austria from 1936 to the Anschluss and openly criticizes the Nazi regime.[130]

By 1939 Frank had fled Austria, had his doctorate stripped, and began work in Switzerland publishing and translating under various pseudonyms, including Francis Ruddy, Albert Rudolph, and Ernst Reinhard, though this work would eventually cease in 1943 following the denunciation of a fellow writer, after which he was interned in various Swiss refugee camps until the end of World War II. Frank translated Daphne du Maurier and Pearl S. Buck, among others, though it was Wolfe's novel in which the writer—a Jewish exile—encountered the strongest critique of the ideology against which he was ardently opposed. Considering the long history of how Wolfe's anti-Nazi narrative has been read, this record of an exiled German Jew, deprived of all his rights and privileges and forced to work in secrecy, provides a unique insight into the politics of literature during the Nazi period and is a further example of the unexpected global trajectories that texts can follow. Unlike Wolfe's other novels, which were not roundly considered offensive to the Nazi regime, the explicit criticism in *Es führt kein Weg zurück* was tempered and altered in Frank's translation. Even though, as Frank's son Vincent C. Frank-Steiner points out, his duty as a translator was "less important than his fight against Nazism," Wolfe's novel provided obstacles for a wartime translation by a German émigré that could not be avoided.[131]

According to Vincent Frank-Steiner, Rudolf Frank considered Wolfe as one of the "very great authors—perhaps even the greatest of the U.S.," once suggesting to another Swiss publisher, Steinberg Verlag, that they consider including Wolfe's work among their publications.[132] Regardless of his admiration for Wolfe's work, however, Frank and his editor found it necessary to significantly alter the text of *You Can't Go Home Again* in order to successfully publish the work in the German language. The first alteration to book 6—"I Have a Thing to Tell You"—is the alteration of the title, presumably because Wolfe's original subtitle, "Nun Will Ich Ihnen 'Was Sagen," was attached to the 1937 story that had already attracted criticism from the Nazi party. The chapter's alternate title, "Der Andere Weg" (The Other Way), makes little sense as a direct translation, but it does contain an implicit reference to the theme of return in the novel, alluding to the other path that George Webber must take, renouncing the lure of fascism. The new title is also a direct echo of a short story by Ernst Zahn titled "*Der andere Weg*" (1912), which follows the return of a German businessman living in America.[133] The alterations to the text from this point are even more profound and reflect the translator's anxiety around transposing Wolfe's material. In the opening introduction—actually added by Aswell himself, though almost directly copying letters and notes Wolfe had left—there is a paragraph that details Webber's "intense longing for Germany," the country "which he liked the best" and whose "mystery and magic haunted him."[134] Finishing with "the very thought of Germany meant peace to his soul, and release, and happiness, and the old magic again," the entire section, roughly nine lines, is entirely omitted from Frank's translation.[135] It is possible that these omissions were made for structural or other reasons, but the overwhelming majority of changes—unsurprisingly—concern sections directly dealing with modern Germany and Hitler.

The following section, which comes under the heading "The Dark Messiah" in *You Can't Go Home Again*, bears the most marks of excision and alteration. Frank retitled this extract as "*Der amerikanische Homer*," referring to a later line in which Webber is dubbed "the American Homer."[136] This is a title Wolfe himself was given in Germany, and the title change reflects a deliberate shift away from Hitler and the specter of fascism, and instead toward the author's fame in Germany.[137] In "The Dark Messiah," Wolfe describes the atmosphere in Berlin during the Olympics, noting that "people were disturbed and anxious, and there seemed to be a sense of impending calamity in the air," but Frank's translation omits this line entirely, instead shifting the register away from fear and toward Webber's own political apathy:

> Ein Wechsel war eingetreten. George hatte davon gelesen; die Zeitungen waren voll davon, aber er schenkte ihren Berichten wenig Beachtung und noch weniger Glauben. Wichtigkeit maß er ihnen schon gar keine bei. Wozu auch? Es gab überall extreme Parteien, und so hielt er denn alles für übertrieben und anders, als man es in den Zeitungen darstellte.

> A change had occurred. George had read about it; the papers were full of it, but he paid little heed to their reports and did not attach any importance to them. Why should he? There were extremist parties everywhere and so he thought it was exaggerated and different from what you read in the papers.[138]

While this is almost a direct transliteration of Wolfe's own words, Frank's version leaves out an important qualifying statement from the original text: "He thought he knew Germany and the German people, and on the whole he was inclined to feel that the true state of affairs had been exaggerated and that things simply could not be as bad as they were pictured." As "The Dark Messiah" continues, Wolfe reflects on both the beauty and magnificence of the Olympics in the Berlin summer as well as on the darker spectacle of the SS and the "great displays of marching men."[139] Frank was careful to excise proper names, preferring "the capital city" over "Berlin," and when Wolfe finally names "the Leader's bodyguards, the Schutz Staffel units, the Storm Troopers, all the ranks and divisions in their different uniforms," Frank redacted the entire passage.[140]

At this point in the narrative, Wolfe introduces the most forbidding image of Hitler, the people waiting spellbound for "the Leader," a "little dark man with a comic-opera mustache, erect and standing, moveless and unsmiling, with his hand upraised, palm outward, not in Nazi-wise salute, but straight up, in a gesture of blessing such as the Buddha or Messiahs use." For Wolfe, this was the most enduring vision of Hitler, not in the fury of his oratory but as he appeared before "the masses of the nation, the poor ones of the earth, the humble ones of life," who waited for two brief moments in the day: "The moment when the Leader went out to the stadium, and the moment when he returned."[141] Frank describes this same throng of people but instead leaves them waiting outside the stadium, not in anticipation of Hitler's arrival but simply unable to afford the price of a ticket. The entire description of Hitler, which in Wolfe's eyewitness account serves, in part, to taint the ebullient descriptions of Berlin with the menace of Nazism, is missing in this version of *Es führt kein Weg zurück*. In fact, the very next line illustrates Frank's inability to faithfully render Wolfe's picture of National Socialism: whereas in English, Webber's friend Else is unwilling to discuss "anything even remotely connected with the Nazi regime," in Frank's German she refuses to discuss "politics" ("*Vom Anfang ihrer Bekanntscaft an hatte es Else abgelehnt, über Politik zu reden.*")[142] This word choice is aptly descriptive of the following section, in which Frank goes to great lengths to avoid directly mentioning Nazism or individuals connected with it. Rather than explicitly identifying what these "politics" are, Frank instead adds the caveat that "not all were as silent as Else," an extra line that illuminates Frank's hope of gesturing toward the problematic "politics" in Germany while still remaining constricted in what he could say:

> Aber nicht alle waren so schweigsam wie Else v. Kohler. Doch was sie auch sagten, und was er auch sah, alles ging im Überschwang seiner Empfindungen für die Geliebte und im Jubel seiner persönlichen Erfolge unter. Die Fröhlichkeit, mit der er das Volk, jetzt wie einst, Feste feiern sah, erschien ihm hell und gut. Nur eine Kleinigkeit fiel ihm auf, und auch die erst nach einiger Zeit. Sie war nicht mehr als ein Wölkchen am fernen Horizont.

> But not all were as silent as Else von Kohler. But whatever they said, and whatever he saw, everything was submerged in the exuberance of his feelings for his beloved, and in the jubilation of his personal successes. The joy with which he saw the people now celebrating, as they had before, seemed bright and good to him. Only one small thing occurred to him and even then, only after some time. It was nothing more than a cloud on the distant horizon.[143]

This section combines a number of paragraphs, intentionally omitting any problematic references to Nazism, with the resulting impression clearly being far from a direct translation, instead reflecting Frank's own admission—and criticism—that Germans were unreasonably slow to see and speak about political realities, but also that "not all were as silent." *Schweigsam*, Frank's alteration of Wolfe's "discreet," powerfully conveys the intentionality of silence for some Germans, a reality that Frank bore the fruits of in his forced exile, writing under his false names. The phrase "*ein Wölkchen am fernen Horizont*" (a cloud on the distant horizon) is Frank's own creation, an ironic formulation when compared with the sections Frank left untranslated: "Men in brown uniforms everywhere," "physical manifestations of a brutal and compulsive force," and "men in concentration camps," all of which gesture toward a truly horrific reality far from a mere small cloud in the distance.[144] As Webber finds himself embroiled in conversations about Hitler and the impact of Nazism on Germany, Frank's version contains many other excised passages, which instead focus on Wolfe's proclamation that "the roots of it were much more sinister and deep and evil than politics or even racial prejudice could be."[145] Frank translates this line as "the roots were much deeper and more harmful than politics ever seemed to be," and while Webber realizes, "for the first time in his life," that he had come upon "something full of horror he had never known before," the indications of spiritual malaise are rendered in only the most general terms in Frank's translation:

> Es waren Symptome einer seelischen Erkrankung, die nicht an Volks- oder Stammesgrenzen gebunden war. Es war die schleichende Paralyse des Mißtrauens, die alle Beziehungen zwischen Menschen und Völkern lahmlegt und verscheucht.

> These were symptoms of a spiritual illness that was not tied to national or tribal boundaries. It was the creeping paralysis of mistrust that paralyzes and spoils all relationships between a man and his fellow men.[146]

The final section of "The Dark Messiah" in Wolfe's original contains an indictment of Nazism's alteration and near-destruction of the "German spirit," the "once-mighty people" who, culturally, were the "first citizen[s] of Europe."[147] Wolfe suggests that the German nation "managed to survive only as drowning men survive—by clutching desperately at any spar that floated free from the wreckage of the ship." Nothing could have seemed plainer to Frank, whose own career epitomized this cultural richness; Frank's biographer wrote: "How to describe him? Theatre director, journalist, novelist, writer (or co-writer) of stage and radio plays, editor, translator: he was all of them."[148] Frank includes Wolfe's emphasis on Germans as the first citizens of Europe, locating, as Wolfe does, the articulation of this "world spirit" in the figure of Goethe, though the tragedy of this spirit—"movingly evident, in [. . .] devious and distorted ways" in Wolfe's version—is gone from the translation. The tragedy of loss balances Wolfe's picture of this residual spirit: when Wolfe noted that "good books were still published [in Germany] if their substance did not [. . .] criticize the Hitler regime or contravert [*sic*] its dogmas," Frank's translation is comparatively insipid and also tragic:

> Es wäre natürlich dumm, meinte George, zu behaupten, ein gutes Buch müsse unbedingt die Behörde kritisieren oder den amtlichen Grundsätzen widersprechen.
>
> It would of course be stupid, George said, to insist that a good book must necessarily criticize the authorities or contradict official principles.[149]

Frank's translation was evidence of a fundamental factor that Wolfe missed in this very equation: good books *were* published, but certainly not if you were a Jew, implying that Wolfe's declaration takes on an entirely new inflection via the translation of a writer in exile. Frank's conclusion to this section of the narrative benefits from Wolfe's own deliberate vagueness, though what serves as artistic elusiveness following a very clear criticism of Nazism comes across as far more ambiguous in its translation. In Wolfe's version, this section ends with: "Little by little it sank in on him through all the golden singing of that summer, until at last he felt it, breathed it, lived it, and knew it for the thing it was."[150] In the 1942 translation, Frank renders this passage as:

> Alles was er sah und fand und entdeckte, sickerte langsam tief in ihn ein. Durch das goldene Singen des Sommers senkte es sich auf ihn herab, bis er es einatmete und durchfühlte, erlebte und für das erkannte, was es war.
>
> Everything he saw and found and discovered slowly trickled deep into him. It sank down on him through the golden singing of the summer, until he breathed it, felt it, experienced it, and recognized it for what it was.[151]

Even though he meticulously excised references to Hitler and the Nazi party, no German citizen reading Frank's version would have failed to interpret these last lines, to have "recognized it for what it was." After labeling Frank's translation as unimaginative and arbitrary, Pusey suggests that neither the 1942 or 1943 edition of the *Halbjahrsverzeichnis*—the German book trade periodical of new releases—lists *Es führt kein Weg zurück*, while Carol Johnston's discussion of German reviews in *Of Time and the Artist* also mentions no contemporary response to Frank's translation.[152] After the war, Frank's translation was not reprinted; a new translation of *Es führt kein Weg zurück*, with all references to Nazism restored, was published by Rowohlt in 1950. However, in a letter to Maxwell Perkins, Alfred Scherz Verlag records that by the June 23, 1942, 2,930 copies of Frank's translation of *Es führt kein Weg zurück* had already sold from a first edition printing of 3,000, with payment receipts showing that, by August 1943, a second edition had also been printed.[153] For the German readers who did encounter Wolfe first through Frank's translation, it must have seemed like quiet resistance from an American author, nothing like the outright rejection Wolfe imagined would leave him permanently estranged from Germany. Investigating this version of Wolfe's anti-Nazi story thus reveals the true exigencies of publishing life in Europe during the war, even in a neutral country like Switzerland, and particularly for an exiled Jewish writer like Rudolf Frank. Furthermore, it provides insight into the actual life of one of those Germans with whom Wolfe professed kinship, and the ultimate insufficiency of his story to proffer hope to an author like Frank or to fully atone for what at times reads like complicity. Even with Wolfe's final, critical assessment of Nazi Germany, it took until well after the war for those Germans he admired to read his work—unaltered—in their native language.

PART 3 Endurance

CHAPTER FIVE

Dances with Wolfes

The Postwar Legacy, Transpacific Impact, and Martian Resurrection of Thomas Wolfe

In the summer of 1944 the Quaker novelist and short-story writer Jessamyn West resurrected Thomas Wolfe. In her story "Tom Wolfe's My Name," set in the final years of the 1930s, West tells the story of Mr. Madden, a California textbook salesman recounting his meeting with Tom Sterling, an enigmatic winemaker convinced he is Thomas Wolfe. Initially, Sterling's portrait is a gentle parody of the novelist—his exchange about the "million-footed roots" and "million-fingered tendrils" of his grapes is the kind of talk, West notes, that "makes you sit up and shake your ears"—but as the story progresses the impersonation grows increasingly uncanny.[1] Unable to shake his curiosity, Madden visits the home of the "phony" Wolfe and discovers the household clutter of the Wolfe legend: dirty clothes scattered about, a "jumble of frying pans and papers," and even the huge ledgers containing thousands of pages in longhand, all painstakingly copied.[2] Madden, thoroughly unnerved, reflects on the scene: "Believe me, I felt pretty funny. This guy was a phony. He had to be. But he had sure gone to a lot of trouble to be a phony. It's bad enough when you look at something that's not what it seems—but it's a hundred times worse when you get a load of something that seems to be what it's not. I guess that's just the same thing put backward. Anyway, here was this guy who talked Wolfe, lived Wolfe, even wrote Wolfe—but he wasn't Wolfe."[3]

West's story neatly elucidates two common and related responses to the work of Thomas Wolfe by those writers, most often in their youth, who were influenced by Wolfe's fiction. The first is embodied in those who "talked Wolfe, lived Wolfe, even wrote Wolfe," writers who—whether consciously or unconsciously composed big, "Wolfean" novels or impersonated his gushing, romantic prose. Beyond just influence, however, there is also the surprising recurrence of Wolfe's tangible presence in works of fiction, often—as in West's story—in the form of resurrection.

Wolfe's influence on the works of young authors and his palpable presence in later and varied works of fiction reflect two points of departure—

what might be simply understood as influence and direct citation—that act to tease out new significances in literary works as they operate within, and reflect on, the history of literary culture. It is not unusual to trace the impact of major novelists on the work of those subsequent authors who follow after them, but given the peripheral status of Wolfe's fiction in educational syllabuses, on bookstore shelves, and within the current critical dialogue, these threads of influence are reinscribed with special importance. Critics like Mark McGurl, who offer pronouncements of Wolfe's decline, have failed to identify Wolfe's enduring appeal among authors, where the novelist has never really gone away. This chapter explores a myriad of literary voices—most frequently young and male—that have borne the weight of Wolfe's influence and conjured the ghost of Wolfe in their fiction, arguing for a critical revaluation that acknowledges Wolfe's spectral presence within the field of American literature while attending to the peculiar uses these writers find for Wolfe. Importantly, this book has argued that the process of attentively tracing global connections is crucial to the interpretation of Wolfe's novels and his impact on global literary culture after his death, focusing particularly on Wolfe's complex relationship with Germany and its literary culture. The current chapter expands this discussion through the inclusion of an Australian voice. While Wolfe's work is still discussed within the context of the American South—though often only peripherally—there has been no significant discussion of Wolfe's reception across a transpacific axis. Focusing on Wolfe's impact on the first novel of Australian author Christopher Koch, *The Boys in the Island* (1958), this chapter demonstrates how Wolfe's novels of a young southern boy longing for the promise of the "enchanted North" served as a model for Koch's own vision of childhood and spiritual isolation in the "deep South" of Tasmania.

Finally, not content with extending the web of influence as far as the southernmost state of Australia, this chapter will end with an exploration of Ray Bradbury's appropriation of Wolfe within the realms of science fiction, even out as far as Mars. The resurrection of Wolfe provides the central conceit for Bradbury's short story "Forever and the Earth" (1950), in which the author literally brings Wolfe back from the dead and sends him to Mars, hoping that he might compose the great Martian romance. Taking the theme of this resurrection as a starting point, my argument here is that Bradbury's regenerative act preempts his own influential romance of Mars in *The Martian Chronicles*, which Ursula Le Guin notes was an early instance of a work of fiction that attempted to "mak[e] science fiction romantic."[4] As the editors of *Visions of Mars* (2011) note, "before Bradbury, most literate readers deemed 'science fiction' a disreputable popular genre," but Bradbury "transformed public opinion of the most crucial genre of our technological era in part by his gorgeous lyricism."[5] Unmooring Wolfe's work from the cloistered and exceptional "South" has been a large focus of this book, and this final chapter follows Rita Felski's simple proposition in *Uses of Literature* (2008) that "the meaning of literature lies in its use," engaging "the worldly aspects of literature in a way that is respectful rather than reductive, dialogic rather than high-handed."[6] Interrogating Wolfe's ghostly presence in the work of these authors—and thus the various "uses" to which the author and his work are put—this chapter works outward in time and space, highlighting the extent to which Wolfe's ghost lingered, and still lingers, in postwar literature.

He Do Wolfe in Different Voices

West's story "Tom Wolfe's My Name" provides twin examples of common responses to the fiction of Thomas Wolfe: Sterling's impersonation of Wolfe's voice is an instance of a young author writing under Wolfe's influence, and "Tom Wolfe's My Name" is itself an experiment in literally resurrecting the author. While pointing out that an author is frequently mimicked is not sufficient cause for investigation, the dearth of critical scholarship on Wolfe—as this book has frequently noted—does not align with the degree of Wolfe's influence. Looking at the Depression era in American literature, one might just as easily substitute other "forgotten" writers like Sinclair Lewis or Erskine Caldwell, but Wolfe's appeal—particularly as it is popularly identified with his overt romanticizing of youth—is often strongly associated with an author's earliest experiments in writing, influencing their very choice to become a professional writer. While Jack Kerouac is Wolfe's most famous acolyte, Walker Percy has remarked that for any young, southern male writing in his wake, Wolfe's presence was unavoidable: "Oh yes, Wolfe was THE writer when I was a young man. I almost thought it was in the nature of things that if a young Southern male wrote a novel in the 1930s, 40s or maybe 50s he would write a Thomas Wolfe novel: growing up in the South, coming to terms with life, school, in the same slightly inflated style of perhaps 'A stone, a leaf, a door' or 'O lost by the wind grieved' and that sort of thing, which sounded great at the time, which doesn't sound quite so good now."[7]

This response might be characterized as "writing under the influence," since the novelists who experienced it regularly characterized their "Wolfean" stage as a kind of youthful intoxication they soon renounced. According to Percy, *The Moviegoer* (1961) was "more or less a conscious revolt, or turnabout, an attempt to do something completely different, to get away from Southern rhetoric, the Wolfe-like concern with self." (There is, however, a brief nod to Altamont—the fictional hometown of Eugene Gant—that appears in *The Moviegoer* as the name of a neighborhood theatre.)[8] Readers of Kerouac's first published novel, *The Town and the City*—the very title of which betrays Wolfe's influence—quickly identified a new protégé of Wolfe, but, unlike Percy, a revolt from the "Wolfe-like concern with self" was far from the mind of the young author. In a letter to his friend Bill Ryan from 1943—several years before he began work on *The Town and the City*—Kerouac reflected on Wolfe's preeminence: "No one in America, notwithstanding, has ever said as much as Wolfe said. I am not going to discredit Wolfe, as so many fools are doing now in the light of contemporary history: it gives these fools a new sense of superiority to discredit the master, and it will last until they rediscover his essential greatness, which may be too late and may cause a great deal of mortification. Wolfe wrote about the essential and everlasting America, not the V-for-Victory America."[9]

Unlike the broadcasts and wartime editions that presented Wolfe as a vehicle for a democratic vision of America, Kerouac saw the novelist as transcending the "V-for-Victory" narratives popular during World War II, focused instead on something more essentially "American." Following the publication of *The Town and the City*, critics like Howard Mumford Jones took to lambasting Kerouac's book as "prodigious splashing about, general emotional appeals in the 'lost, lost, lost' cadence of Thomas Wolfe," and the London critics, according to Paul Maher, urged Kerouac to "move on and find a different style that did not emulate Wolfe so closely."[10] Ann Charters notes that following the collapse of his dream of "an easy literary success" with *The Town and the City*, Kerouac "wrestled with the problem of breaking free of the hold of his previous model, Thomas Wolfe," and in a letter to Neal Cassady shortly after the novel's publication, Kerouac wrote about this struggle:

> Wolfe—a great voice from the howling wilderness; and think, think, think, Neal, if Wolfe had lived and got hung up on this voice of his, and come right out and wrote a book in deliberate voice-from-the-howling-wilderness tones and substance-tale, what *that* would have been, such as, for instance, the voice of Wolfe himself walking on foot from Coast to Coast, which was undoubtedly his secretest, deepest thought, or among the deepest. [. . .] Well, since Mexico, I've been trying to find my voice. For a long time it sounded false, of course. For a long time I labored on several other variations. [. . .] What I'm going to do is let the voices speak for themselves.[11]

Kerouac would later tell Allen Ginsberg that replying to both Cassady's and Ginsberg's letters was where "all that sketching came out," helping him break him off from "American formalism *à la* Wolfe."[12] His desire to "let the voices speak for themselves" was ultimately realized in his famous novel, *On the Road* (1957), catapulting him into literary fame. After reading the roll manuscript of *On the Road*, which Kerouac completed in three weeks in 1951, John Clellon Holmes wrote in his journal that "[Kerouac] has made a decided improvement here, I believe, and now has his own style. There will certainly be no comparisons to Thomas Wolfe this time."[13]

Although Kerouac and Percy encountered Wolfe during the late 1930s and very early 1940s and might therefore have been expected to feel the influence of a "great" writer just deceased, the ghost of Wolfe prevailed well after World War II. In Philip Roth's *My Life as a Man* (1974), the character of Nathan Zuckerman—whom Margaret Smith characterizes as perhaps Roth's most distinctive literary voice and frequently the "subject of autobiographical inquest"[14]—captures a picture of youthful intoxication with Wolfe, followed almost immediately by the necessary "mature" rejection. In his youth, Zuckerman reads *Of Time and the River* and finds that it "verified something he had known in his bones all along, but in which he could not place his faith until it had been articulated by someone of indisputable moral prestige." Shortly after this satirized vision of a youthful encounter with the *Sehnsucht* of Wolfe, Roth adds blandly that Zuckerman "really could not read Thomas Wolfe any more" after his inability to stomach "facile hyperbole," and the sentimental, "unbridled flow of passion" is unavoidably developed through his training in New Criticism.[15] In the final section of his novel *Zuckerman Unbound* (1981), titled "Look Homeward, Angel," Roth again turns to Wolfe, this time to decry the youthful romanticism that the older Zuckerman now sees as a deceptive and impossible dream amidst the frenzy of literary fame and the impending death of his father:

> Zuckerman had been remembering that summer just twenty years ago [. . .] when he read three thousand pages of Thomas Wolfe straight through. [. . .] "He believed himself thus at the center of life; he believed the mountains rimmed the heart of the world; he believed that from all the chaos of accident the inevitable event came at the inexorable moment to add to the sum of his life." Inevitable. Inexorable. "Oh yes!" noted stifled Nathan in the margin of his copy of *Look Homeward, Angel*, unaware that the resounding privative clang of the Latinate adjectives wasn't necessarily so stirring when you ran into the inevitable and the inexorable at the center of your life. [. . .] All he wanted at sixteen was to become a romantic genius like Thomas Wolfe and leave little New Jersey and all the shallow provincials therein for the deep emancipating world of Art. As it turned out, he had taken them all with him.[16]

Years later, in response to a query about "The Book That Made Me a Reader" for the Center for Fiction, Roth admitted to the influence of Wolfe on his own youthful self: "In 1949, when I was sixteen, I stumbled on Thomas Wolfe [. . .] who made numerous adolescents aside from me devotees of literature for life. In Wolfe, everything was heroically outsized, whether it was the voracious appetite for experience of Eugene Gant [. . .] or of George Webber. [. . .] The hero's loneliness, his egocentrism, his sprawling consciousness gave rise to a tone of elegiac lyricism that was endlessly sustained by the raw yearning for an epic existence—for an epic American existence. And, in those post-war years, what imaginative young reader didn't yearn for that?"[17]

In his memoir, *Interior Landscapes: Autobiographical Myths and Metaphors* (1990), Anishinaabe poet and novelist Gerald Vizenor describes a similar youthful encounter with Wolfe—this time in a "barren military library" in Japan—but unlike Roth's Zuckerman, without the reticence of admission or desire to distance himself from his indebtedness to Wolfe.[18] Vizenor first read Wolfe in the collection *A Stone, a Leaf, a Door* (1945)—in which John S. Barnes had arranged some of Wolfe's prose into a poetic form—and he writes that "I have never overcome my wearisome want to raise the word from the page, to sound out the passion and the sacrifices of literature in the voice of the crane. Wolfe roamed an interior landscape and rounded boundaries on a prose run; his language was wild and immense."[19] In an interview with Joëlle Rostkowski, Vizenor said that at eighteen years of age he was "truly, literally transformed, actually transported by the novels of Thomas Wolfe."[20] Reflecting on his departure from Matsushima—and also his lover Aiko Okada—Vizenor's memoir quotes Wolfe's story "Dark in the Forest, Strange as Time": "People were speaking the universal language of departure, that varies not at all the whole world over. [. . .] And he saw and heard these familiar words and actions . . . the overwhelming loneliness of familiarity, the sense of the human identity that so strangely unites all the people in the world, and that is rooted in the structure of man's life, far below the tongue he speaks, the race of which he is a member."[21]

For Vizenor, the language of estrangement and unutterable loneliness he encountered in Wolfe gave expression to his own feelings of isolation. As he considers his dilemma that "I was leaving for home, but there was no home, no home was real to me then," he again defers to Wolfe, this time quoting from *Of Time and the River*: "For what is it that we Americans are seeking on this earth? Why is it we have crossed the stormy seas so many times alone, lain in a thousand alien rooms at night hearing the sounds of time, dark time, and thought until heart, brain, flesh and spirit were sick and weary with the thought of it; 'Where shall I go now? What shall I do?'"[22]

Later, while studying creative writing under Eda Lou Walton at New York University, Vizenor adds that he was encouraged to "shout and brush the wild nation with descriptions in the manner of Thomas Wolfe."[23] Vizenor's relation to Wolfe is therefore less ambivalent than that of both Kerouac and Roth in his insistence on the novelist's influence.

Even more recently, author George Saunders has written about the hold that Wolfe's voice had on him in a piece for *Slate* magazine, noting how the language of Wolfe's fiction had a way of imposing its form on a college kid's conception of the world:

> I liked him because he was epic and broken-hearted and sloppy and emotional and in love with the world and wrote sentence after sentence beginning with the word "O," as in "O Brooklyn, harbinger of cruel autumn," or "O mourned and never-to-be-regained Time" (though I'm pretty sure I just now made those two up). I loved his big-heartedness and the way, apparently, he had just taken his

> life and made a huge book out of it. But damn, his life was so much bigger and romantic than mine! He felt things so much more deeply, knew so many more Tragic Figures! So, soon I had developed the habit of pacing tragically around and phrasing my life in his terms: "O bitter Seven-Eleven of broken love, which, mourning, how many times have I paced by you, mad visions trumpeting my ravening brain, because of the lovely (FILL IN NAME OF GIRL) lost, no more to be Regained?" Finally I realized that my life didn't GO in that voice, and left the book behind, but sadly, with an affection I still feel. O Wolfe![24]

Unlike the aforementioned writers, Saunders's own voice—an idiosyncratic amalgam of jargon, neologism, and fractured dialogue that Adam Begley calls the "crippling incoherence of daily speech" filled with the "brutal solecisms of the American vernacular," which he "arrange[s] on the page with meticulous care"[25]—bears no resemblance to Wolfe's, but Saunders admits that Wolfe was "the first time that a literary author got under my skin."[26] On discovering the "brevity manifested in form" within Hemingway's *In Our Time*, Saunders describes encountering a stylistic antidote to Wolfe's vastness: "Before *In Our Time*, I'd thought that great art was just . . . big: long and expansive and uncontrolled, a sort of unmediated genius-rant ala Thomas Wolfe," yet, importantly, it was Wolfe whose voice he imitated in his earliest attempts at writing.[27] Responding to a question in *Guernica* magazine about those earliest writings, Saunders admits to hoping "they've mildewed into nothingness."[28] This voice of Wolfe to which Saunders refers does occasionally appear in his own short stories, in passages that demand self-consciously lyrical and expansive prose. In "Escape from Spiderhead," for instance, from Saunders's story collection *Tenth of December* (2013), convicted criminals are housed in a prison where they are guinea pigs for experimental pharmaceuticals. One drug, Verbaluce, improves linguistic fluency and lexical range, so instead of a garden looking "nice" and "super-clear" it begins to appear—under the influence of Verbaluce—as "a sort of embodiment of the domestic dreams forever intrinsic to human consciousness [. . .] to wit, I was sensing the eternal in the ephemeral."[29] Saunders on Verbaluce is Thomas Wolfe.

Speaking of a youthful attraction to Wolfe in high school, William H. Gass admitted to the *Paris Review* that though he was "basically a closet romantic, a tame wild man," over time the novelist had developed an aloof formalism: "I became detached; I emphasized technique; I practiced removal. I was a van. I took away things."[30] In the preface to his story collection *In the Heart of the Heart of the Country* (1968), Gass reiterated this fundamentally *youthful* interest in Wolfe, noting that in the years after his adolescence he "painfully advanced on Thomas Wolfe" and like him "made the world a Whitman Sampler and a list of sweets."[31] In the novelist's final novel, *Middle C* (2013), Wolfe operates as a metonym for rhetorical excess, ironically positioned in the novel through the young Joseph Skizzen's euphoric recitations to "corner[ed] schoolmates," to whom he reads aloud passages "with such heat and vehemence they were at first held in ear range by surprise and trepidation before annoyance released them."[32] Gass gives particularly laborious passages for Skizzen to fawn over, long and tedious lists from *You Can't Go Home Again* that are merely accumulations of declarative sentences: "The Chinese hate the Japanese, the Japanese the Russians, the Russians also hate the Japanese, and the hordes of India the English."[33] For Skizzen—drily reflecting Gass's own early enthusiasm as well as parodying other such Wolfean acolytes—these passages "struck such a chord, he could have been hearing an opera sung for the second time," and he advances on the unwilling listeners with increased gusto: "Just listen to this! Isn't this it? Really, isn't it? Just listen!" Gass's satire of the Wolfe-aficionado is aimed at the immature reader—Skizzen "failed Faulkner, he flunked Carlyle, he rejected Joyce, and at Hopkins simply blinked"—with Wolfe's bombast and romantic excess prompting Skizzen's admiration: "In the center of that future room, amid strips of bad news like shags of animal hair—dangles ready to applaud a bellow—cans to kick like points after touchdowns—Joseph Skizzen would call out Wolfe's words in the triumphant tones of 'I told you so.'"[34]

Write What You Know

Beyond this lingering influence and impersonation of Wolfe's voice, the second response to Wolfe that Jessamyn West's story identifies is the surprisingly frequent inclination of writers not only to write *like* Wolfe but to write Wolfe into their fiction, as if these authors are unable or unwilling to let the dead author rest. Harold Bloom has noted that "[t]he mighty dead return, but they return in our colors, and speaking in our voices," though Bloom's theory of revival does not account for the far more literal and visceral processes of resuscitation taking place in the work of Wolfe's followers.[35] The stories of Bradbury and West are not the only instances of this sort of resuscitation; Wolfe reappears as a spectral figure in a remarkable number of later fictional works. In an outline for an unpublished and unfinished 1942 story titled "Joe Doakes and the Immortals," a young Jack Kerouac sketched a story centered around Doakes, a gatekeeper who tends to the "immortals"—Homer, Wolfe, Dante, Goethe, Joyce, Shakespeare, and many others—as they arrive in the "Meadows" to enjoy the pleasures of an endless bacchanalic feast and the company of "scientists, actors, artists, statesmen, pharaohs, fabulous concubines and paramours, figures of fame!"[36] In the outline he writes: "And there sat Wolfe, at the head of the table, flushed, happy as any man has ever been, immense and great. From the very first, I knew the immortals liked him. There was a twinkle in old Homer's eye. Shakespeare looked upon him with rare grace." While "Joe Doakes" never saw the light of day, a number of similar works that incorporated Wolfe were published, with the most commercially successful of these being Herman Wouk's *Youngblood Hawke*, published in 1962.

Youngblood Hawke is a sprawling novel about a gifted young writer from Kentucky who descends on New York with his outsize manuscript in "a high pile of torn and dented blue typing-paper cartons" and becomes an overnight success. As critics at the time recognized, the novel is clearly a fictionalized account of Thomas Wolfe's life and career, and Wouk—intentionally evoking Wolfe's ghost—has his eponymous hero provide an explanation for the similarity: "The critics are going to compare me to Thomas Wolfe, I suppose, because I'm from the South and I write long books. Please don't think I'm crazy, but I think I can do better than Wolfe did. See, I can't touch his poetry, but I tell stories. All he did was write his memoirs. Beautiful, lyric, American, colossal, immortal memoirs."[37] Wouk's "popular" mode of writing attracted a lot of criticism at the time of publication, provoking a hatchet job from Stanley Edgar Hyman, who wrote that Wouk was pandering to an audience of "yahoos" and that *Youngblood Hawke* was "the most fraudulent and worthless novel I have read in many years," while David Boroff wrote that Wolfe's powerful and lyric novels loomed "inescapably" in the background, leaving Wouk's "bloated and prosy" novel to satisfy "ordinary" readers, who apparently constituted the majority of Wouk's large readership.[38] Like many of Wouk's best-seller novels, the novel made it to the screen in the form of Delmer Daves's 1964 film *Youngblood Hawke*, and Hawke/Wolfe enjoyed a revitalized life on screen, played by the television star James Franciscus.

Two years earlier, Wolfe had turned up in the massive autobiographical novel of his friend Vardis Fisher, titled *Orphans in Gethsemane: A Novel of the Past and Present* (1960), this time as David Hawke, the original name Wolfe had considered for the hero of his second novel before reverting to Eugene Gant. At nearly a thousand pages—and the final book in his monumental twelve-volume series, *Testament of Man* (1943–60)— *Orphans in Gethsemane* demonstrated Fisher's obsession with writing everything down, which led an exasperated John Peale Bishop to write: "Honesty does not consist in telling all. And that is just what Mr. Fisher does. He tells all."[39] Given its autobiographical bent, *Orphans in Gethsemane* provides an even more thinly veiled avatar of Wolfe than Wouk's novel, and David Hawke is introduced as "a huge man, fully six feet, six inches tall, with a great mass of bushy uncombed black hair," Wolfe's precise specifications. Furthermore, Fisher's description of Hawke's first novel as "a big amorphous chaos of words and emotions, a cyclone of power and rhetoric, a long paean to David Hawke," not only describes Wolfe's *Look Homeward, Angel* but recalls the familiar criticisms of autobiography that were so often leveled at Wolfe.[40] In using the very name that Wolfe had considered for his own autobiographical novel, Fisher's portrait is a strange mixture of the Wolfe he knew and his fictional doppelgänger Gant. Wolfe's frequent recourse to himself—which Mark McGurl labels as "autobardolatry"[41]—is here mirrored in the works of writers who chose him as their subject, though ultimately in both these instances the effect is a little like explaining a joke: the point is lost.

Particularly in the early stages of his career, Wolfe articulated a vision of fiction writing that amounted to a defense of his method, writing in his "To the Reader" note at the beginning of *Look Homeward, Angel* that "the author has written of experience which is now far and lost, but which was once part of the fabric of his life. If any reader, therefore, should say that the book is 'autobiographical' the writer has no answer for him: it seems to him that all serious work in fiction is autobiographical."[42] In a long letter to Julian Meade—a young writer preparing an article on Wolfe for publication in *The Bookman*—Wolfe identified his "Studies in the Romantic Poets" course at Harvard as providing the theoretical substrate for these assertions, writing:

> I get hot under the collar when the word autobiography is mentioned because the way people use it seems to me to have no sense or meaning whatever. [. . .] [N]owhere can you escape autobiography whenever you come to anything that has any real or lasting value in letters. [. . .] Lowes [in *The Road to Xanadu*] goes on to attempt to show that the thing that happened when Coleridge wrote [. . .] happens when the artist creates anything—in other words, that this use of experience which is sunken in the well of unconsciousness, or which is only half remembered, is a typical use of the creative faculty.
>
> Now what is this, Meade, except the most direct and natural use of autobiography, and how could Coleridge have written differently from the way he did write, and how could Joyce have written differently from the way he wrote, and how could Proust have written differently from the way he wrote? Coleridge's experiences came mainly from the pages of books and Joseph Conrad's experiences came mainly from the decks of ships; and finally, could anyone tell you that Joyce and Proust are either more or less autobiographical than Coleridge or Swift, and if they do tell you so, would you think their words any longer had meaning or were worthy of serious consideration?[43]

Viewing Wolfe's work as a useful tunnel into "the darker corners" of institutionalized creative writing programs, McGurl has noted that Wolfe's method involved the "reductio ad absurdum of the familiar call to *write what you know*," and Fisher's novel is an example of an inability to revive Wolfe without employing his method of "autobardolatry."[44] In fact, many of the youthful writers who were drawn to Wolfe subscribed to this same philosophy of writing: that fiction must be "the most direct and natural form of autobiography." As McGurl notes, "it is the young, above all others, who have proved most susceptible to his [Wolfe's] self-aggrandizing charms."[45] But far more suggestive are those stories where Wolfe's specter still looms, but without the jarring insistence on hiding the author behind alternatively named doppelgängers and without the obligation to write *everything you know*. West's story of the phony Wolfe ends with the simultaneous death of the real Thomas Wolfe and his phony double, managing to be at once a mocking portrait of Wolfe and a genuine elegy mourning his loss while also providing a prescient vision of the author's profound, lingering, and sometimes uncanny impact on his readers. Similarly, in *Sophie's Choice* (1979), William Styron—who at eighteen wrote that Wolfe was "the greatest writer of our time"[46]—uses Wolfe's novels (rather than Wolfe himself) to captivate the book-hungry Sophie with their "lyrical, tragic though optimistic and sweeping vision of America," a gesture to the impact Wolfe's novels had on readers during World War II, on both sides of the conflict.[47] In 1968 Styron wrote an article for *Harper's* in which he described the profound impact that Wolfe had on him as a young man:

> [I]t would be hard to exaggerate the overwhelming effect that reading Wolfe had upon so many of us who were coming of age during or just after the second world war. I think his influence may have been especially powerful upon those who, like myself, had been reared as Wolfe had in a small Southern town or city. [. . .] The sudden exposure to a book like *Look Homeward, Angel*, with its lyrical torrent and raw, ingenuous feeling, its precise and often exquisite rendition of place and mood, its buoyant humor and the vitality of its characters and, above all, the sense of youthful ache and promise and hunger and ecstasy which so corresponded to that of its eighteen-year-old reader—to experience such a book as this, at exactly the right moment in time and space, was for many young people like being born again into a world as fresh and wondrous as that seen through the eyes of Adam. Needless to say, youth itself was largely responsible for this feverish empathy [. . .] nonetheless, a man who can elicit such reactions from a reader at whatever age is a force to be reckoned with.[48]

In one interesting example of transnational Wolfean influence, Yugoslav writer Danilo Kiš employs Wolfe as a metonym for autobiographical writing. Kiš's play *A Wooden Trunk for Thomas Wolfe*, which was broadcast on Belgrade television in 1974, is concerned with memory, creativity, and the failure of people to find adequate language to articulate experience. The story centers on two characters: Solomon, an elderly doctor, and Jakov, a young would-be writer. Both men are Holocaust survivors, and both are struggling with a yearning for a book to exist that chronicles their experiences. It is Jakov who most obviously resembles Wolfe: he is full of self-assurance that suffering is adequate cause for literary genius, and he echoes Wolfe's own writerly conviction that "a man must use the experience of his own life if he is to create anything that has substantial value":[49]

JAKOV (*in the mirror, as if to himself*): I have put ten years of thought into my book, Doctor . . . Ten years of gloomy nightmares and insomnia!

DOCTOR (*in the semi-darkness, invisible save his tonsure*): How magnificently you said that: I see my mother as Lot's wife, turning into a pillar of salt. . . .

JAKOV (*to himself, in the mirror*): I subordinated everything to it! Everything! . . . The lives of a great number of people will go into that book. The experience of millions!

DOCTOR (*still invisible in the semi-darkness, from which his bald spot gleams*): You can write it! You must! You have a whole life-time ahead of you, Jakov . . .

JAKOV (*into the mirror, finishing his previous thought*): Yes, yes. My own life will go into it, too. My entire existence.[50]

Over the course of the play it becomes evident that Jakov is not up to being a writer: he is undisciplined, impatient, forgetful, and lacks the sufficient skill to write a book. The play ends in the agony of frustration and with the death of Solomon before his story can be preserved. Rather than referring to any of Wolfe's novels in particular, the inclusion of Wolfe in this play—including in the play's title—is primarily symbolic. Wolfe is a figure of promiscuous genius: productive but rough-hewn; powerfully expressive but overly verbose. The meaning of Wolfe's "wooden trunk" from the play's title is revealed in a scene where Jakov recalls a story of a publisher uncovering a Wolfe masterwork in a wooden crate of cast-off manuscripts:

JAKOV: Somewhere I read about how Thomas Wolfe used to work. You see, he had this trunk, a crate . . . made of wood. And he threw his manuscripts into it, stack after stack, year after year. Then one fine day a publisher drops in to visit him unannounced . . . It was one of the big guys. And he asks him, he asks Thomas Wolfe that is, what he'd been writing. "Nothing, sir," Wolfe says. "Say what? You've written nothing?" the publisher asks. "That's right. Nothing," says Wolfe. Then the publisher wonders out loud what's in the trunk there next to the desk. "My manuscripts," responds Wolfe. "For ten years now I've been tossing my manuscripts in there. My garbage! This chest, my good sir, is full of pages I've filled up, and on that paper is the largest part of my existence. [. . .] And all that, good sir, is pure, garden-variety pulp. Wasted, useless paper. [. . .] So the publisher says to Wolfe that he'd still like to see it . . . Just in case. Just to put his mind at ease. [. . .] He picked up the chest (the publisher, that is) and hauled it off, put all the pages of the manuscripts in order, read them, and went back to see the author a few weeks later . . . (*Pause.*) He took him a

> contract. And he told him: "Mr. Wolfe, you've written a work of genius!" (*Pause. Jakov turns to the doctor.*) That's all I wanted to say. The end.[51]

Here is a dream of the bad writer. A novel of genius literally pieced together from a trash pile of discards. While the story is mostly invented, it captures the essence of Wolfe's own telling of the acceptance of *Look Homeward, Angel* by Maxwell Perkins, in which the famed editor intuited originality amidst copious excess. That the play is named after this trunk of discards is telling: for Jakov, as with Wolfe, the trunk is experience, a receptacle for the castoffs of lived reality. But Jakov's life is too fraught with unspeakable anguish to make sense of his own trunk of experience, calling to mind Adorno's famous suggestion that "to write poetry after Auschwitz is barbaric." Jakov's story of Wolfe is thus a story of yearning for some interlocutor who might speak for him, an editor who might help articulate the inexpressible. In the case of Wolfe, the anguish of objectless yearning is the thing desired: *Sehnsucht* describes both infinite longing and the addiction to that longing that fuels Wolfe's creative project. Or, following Jakov's story: filling the trunk was the point for Wolfe. The play's wordless penultimate scene contains a moving expression of suffering that reveals Jakov's foolishness in choosing Wolfe as a model for writing his own chronicle of anguish:

> *It's 2 a.m. on the clock on the bedside table. Jakov is sitting at the desk. A blank sheet of paper is in the typewriter. [. . .] Next to the desk are empty beer bottles. The wooden trunk is still at its old post, also next to the desk but on the right side. The menorah stands on the trunk, its last candle now burning down. The flickering of the candle and the sizzling of the expiring flame are audible. Jakov stares, his face utterly devoid of expression, at the blank paper. Outside one can hear the drumming of the autumn rain. When the last candle on the menorah goes out, Jakov gets to his feet. He puts the menorah back in its former spot and then opens the trunk. Retrieves a crumpled sheet of paper from the empty chest, smooths it out with the palm of his hand, tosses it back into the chest. Then he slams the lid furiously and turns back to the table. All of a sudden he rests his head on the keys, his clenched fists stretched out on both sides of the typewriter. The keys rise to meet the paper. He sobs. His body shakes. The ticking of the alarm clock on the nightstand grows louder and louder, and this sound gradually transforms into the beating of a human heart. Fade to black.*[52]

Wolfean Fragments

When one starts looking, spectral traces of Wolfe abound, even in the most unlikely genres.[53] In one example, an apocryphal, forged Wolfe journal—*Thomas Wolfe's Western Journal: The Lost Pages*—serves as a prominent clue in

Joseph Hansen's *Death Claims* (1973), leading Dave Brandstetter, a burly insurance investigator styled as a private eye, to uncover a scholar's fraud.[54] In the epigraph to the published script for *Taxi Driver*, the loneliness of Travis Bickle, the taxi driver, is universalized through a reference to Wolfe's narrative essay, "God's Lonely Man" (1941): "The whole conviction of my life now rests upon the belief that loneliness, far from being a rare and curious phenomenon, is the central and inevitable fact of human existence."[55] In Glen Duncan's acclaimed *The Last Werewolf* (2011), Wolfe's words are unexpectedly given voice by Jake Marlowe—a "200-year-old, Kant-reading, chain-smoking aesthete" who also happens to be a werewolf—who gives the phrase "You Can't Go Home Again" added gravity, suggesting the impossibility of returning to the human community.[56] Scott Yarbrough has recently pointed out that Cormac McCarthy's *Suttree* (1979)—filled with "metaphysical hyperlinks that make use of literary shorthand to develop and signify themes, motifs and meaning"—uses the line "I Have a Thing to Tell You" as a reference to Wolfe's story of the same name.[57] McCarthy here summons Wolfe's theme of alienation as something universal: "I have a thing to tell you. I know all souls are one and all souls lonely."[58] In yet another material instance of Wolfe's resurgence, David Dalton describes the "truly awesome" contents of twenty-six-year-old Janis Joplin's purse that he witnessed while riding in a limousine with the singer: her "baglady's compulsion to carry her whole life with her" included Thomas Wolfe's *Look Homeward, Angel*.[59] (In terms of monumental memory, it is also interesting to consider the commemoration of Wolfe on a U.S. postage stamp in 2000, presumably in the midst of a long slump in popularity.) Perhaps my favorite example occurs in William Gay's novel *Provinces of Night* (2001), where Fleming Bloodworth—the novel's brooding young hero who wants to be a writer—loses patience with his uncle Brady (an addled soothsayer who is fond of hexes) and uses the sizable tome of *Of Time and the River* as a bludgeon: "He reached Fleming the book. Thomas Wolfe, the spine read. *Of Time and the River*. The boy flipped the pages. The only word his eyes registered was October. He suddenly drew the book back and slammed it as hard as he could into Brady's face. It struck with the force of a fist."[60]

The most recent example of Wolfe's resurgence—as of 2019—is in the Netflix Original show *Ozark*, which is about a family forced to leave the suburbs of Chicago following a failed laundering scheme by the father, Martin Byrde.[61] In the series the Byrdes relocate to Osage Beach, Missouri, and are forced by a Mexican cartel to set up an even larger laundering operation in the titular Ozarks. In episode 8 of the second season, Wyatt Langmore, a college-aged male who is part of a local criminal family, walks into a bookstore with Charlotte Byrde—the teenage daughter of Martin and his wife, Wendy—and the camera lingers on a first-edition copy of *Look Homeward, Angel* in a locked case. Wyatt is buoyed by the sight of the novel, and exclaims: "*Look Homeward, Angel*! That's like, my favorite American novel ever."[62] Unlike other pithier references to Wolfe, this extended scene dwells on Wyatt's love of the novel: he proceeds to tell Charlotte about Wolfe's height and his writing habits and in so doing reveals his own artistic sensitivity. As Wyatt walks off to take a call, the camera focuses on Charlotte, who eventually hides the book in her jacket pocket.

Later in the episode as they are driving from the store, Charlotte reveals her theft of the book to Wyatt, and the subsequent scene explores the unbridgeable gap between Wyatt—a Langmore—and Charlotte, an interloper in the community from a respectful family. Wyatt is forced to reject the gift of the first-edition book due to the likelihood of his imprisonment, which Charlotte—who is comfortably middle class—failed to register in the thrill of her petty crime. At the end of the scene, Charlotte, in anger, tosses the first edition out of the window before Wyatt turns the car around, presumably to retrieve it. Besides employing *Look Homeward, Angel* as a significant plot point, *Ozark*'s reference to Wolfe had one other unintended consequence. Following the release of the episode on August 31, 2018, bookseller AbeBooks reported that *Look Homeward, Angel* was the second most searched for book on their platform during September 2018.[63] It was not simply the inclusion of the novel in the show that sparked renewed interest but the exploration of the novel as an object of love. Wyatt's desire for the novel, and Charlotte's own desire to please Wyatt, revolves around the grip that Wolfe had on the young man's heart. For viewers of *Ozark*, the wish to own a first edition of *Look Homeward, Angel* is an example of how desire is transferable via the tangible object of a book: to own Wolfe's novel is to experience, in part, the yearning the novel inspired in Wyatt.

# # #

Wolfean fragments turn up in nearly every genre of fiction. In Howard Waldrop's "You *Could* Go Home Again" from the collection *Going Home Again* (1997), Wolfe is again revivified, though in this instance Waldrop is intent on avoiding the curse of imitation, noting in his afterword to the story that "when most people write about Wolfe, they try to write *like* Wolfe. I wasn't going to do that."[64] The Wolfe of Waldrop's story is a far soberer version of the novelist, suffering a distinct loss of vitality—and memory—since a brain operation that Waldrop invents to save Wolfe from the tuberculosis that killed him in 1938: "At times like this, Wolfe truly felt something was wrong. Not wrong with him—the doctors reassured him on that—but with everything else. The times. The world. His present life. Like there was something fundamentally wrong with the whole business of living."[65] "You *Could* Go Home Again" also contains a strange future vision of the author aboard a dirigible in 1940, an exercise in speculating what the world would look like had war been averted, Wolfe survived, and the United States been subsumed into a technocracy. The story is also a vehicle for various and unusual flights of fancy: Wolfe listens to Fats Waller and meets T. E. Lawrence, Nevil Shute, and J. D. Salinger. The fictionalized Wolfe also plans to make a return trip to Germany to see Thea Voelker, the artist with whom Wolfe fell in love during his final visit to Germany in 1936. For Waldrop, the impetus to write the story is ultimately located in the profound impact of Wolfe, of which he writes:

> Such an impact he had you can't imagine. [. . .] Here were books about the long-striding, world-engulfing, book-swallowing, drinking, eating, fighting, fearless and foulmouth days of a writer too large for any American-made chair. Some of it seems overblown and tortured now (a lot still holds up), but it didn't seem that way in 1929, and it sure as hell didn't to me in 1962. [. . .] Don't take our words for it; read them yourselves.[66]

A more sustained citation of Wolfe's work in recent times can be found in *The Dark Tower* series (1982–2012), Stephen King's monumental eight-volume, multigenre, (hyper)intertextual series of novels that Michael Agger aptly calls "Pulp Metafiction."[67] In *The Dark Tower*, Thomas Wolfe's presence abounds, so much so that after composing the first six volumes, King revised the first book of the series, *The Gunslinger* (1982; rev. 2003), and added the famous incantation of alienation from *Look Homeward, Angel* as its epigraph, responding to the growing importance Wolfe's fiction had taken on within the broader work:

> . . . a stone, a leaf, an unfound door; of a leaf, a stone, a door. And of all the forgotten faces.
>
> Naked and alone we came into exile. In her dark womb, we did not know our mother's face; from the prison of her flesh have we come into the unspeakable and incommunicable prison of this earth.
>
> Which of us has known his brother? Which of us has looked into his father's heart? Which of us has not remained forever prison-pent? Which of us is not forever a stranger and alone?
>
> . . . O lost, and by the wind grieved, ghost, come back again.[68]

In King's series, the mournful refrain of "a stone, a leaf, an unfound door" operates as a kind of incantation, and King weaves its symbols throughout the complex and meandering narrative maze of *The Dark Tower*. In *The Dark Tower V: Wolves of the Calla* (2003), the hero Roland retrieves a glass ball called "Black Thirteen" that operates in the story as a key between different fictional universes, a state of being King calls "todash."[69] "Black Thirteen" is a kind of ultimate hyperlink, allowing King to indulge the metafictive strategy by which *The Dark Tower* can include the countless intertextual links—everything from King

Arthur to Star Wars—all of which are painstakingly collected in Robin Furth's massive *Stephen King's* The Dark Tower: *The Complete Concordance* (rev. 2012).[70] In *Wolves of the Calla*, the glass ball called "Black Thirteen" is stored in a box that carries Wolfe's inscription "a stone, a leaf, an unfound door," and later in the narrative when "Black Thirteen" is used to open a door to another universe, carved on that door is the hieroglyph for "UNFOUND."[71]

In *The Dark Tower III: The Waste Lands* (1991), Wolfe's novel *You Can't Go Home Again* appears in one character's dream, and in an instance of King's intentional slippage between fiction and reality—King himself appears as a character at a number of points—the lines printed in Wolfe's novel are transformed into the opening lines from King's *The Gunslinger*, the first volume of the series: "He looked down at the book and was utterly unsurprised to find it was *You Can't Go Home Again*, by Thomas Wolfe. [. . .] He stopped for a moment, flipped the book open, and read the first line. *The man in black fled across the desert, Wolfe had written, and the gunslinger followed.*"[72] King's self-described magnum opus has inspired at least three dedicated critical studies—Bev Vincent's *The Road to the Dark Tower* (2004) and *The Dark Tower Companion* (2013) as well as Patrick McAleer's *Inside the Dark Tower Series* (2009)—not to mention dozens of online communities and blogs, including author Suzanne Johnson's three-year *Dark Tower* blog series for publisher and science fiction and fantasy site Tor.com.[73] In her important study *Dissecting Stephen King* (2005), Heidi Strengell compares King's active readers, popularly known as his "Constant Readers," with Stanley Fish's "interpretative communities," contending that they "share interpretative strategies not for reading [. . .] but for writing texts," as they closely interact with King and his fiction.[74] Wolfe, like King, is a palpable *presence* for many of his readers, and his texts operate as seeding narratives, constantly being rewritten and regenerated. Furthermore, the cycle of displacement that *Sehnsucht* points toward—a constant searching for something unreachable—remains for King, and others, one of the most compelling aspects of Wolfe's work.

Wolfe and the Global Deep South of Australia

One completely unexplored transnational relationship in the study of Thomas Wolfe—and an area of scholarly interest that is in its infancy more broadly—concerns his transpacific reception and influence. In a 1950 article on Wolfe published in *Woroni*—the journal of the Canberra University Student association—one Australian critic lamented that "it is somewhat astonishing that one of the few really great American novelists, perhaps the only one who possesses that indefinable quality of genius, should remain comparatively unknown and little read," encouraging the Australian readership—already unfamiliar with

Wolfe scarcely a decade after his death—that the novelist "must be read by all who would understand American literature and America itself."[75] Nearly twenty years later, in a column for the *Canberra Times*, another Wolfe aficionado praised Heinemann for finally reissuing Wolfe's four novels in Australia, writing that "for many years English and Australian readers have been able to buy only his first novel" and that Wolfe "is still damned with faint praise" in spite of "some recent attempts to revive his reputation."[76] Indeed, although a 1952 Heinemann edition of Maxwell Geismar's *Selections from Thomas Wolfe* introduced some of the author's other writing to an Australian audience, Wolfe's work was remarkably hard to find in Australia for years after the novelist's death and has remained scarce since.[77] Recently, however, the University of Adelaide Press has collected *Look Homeward, Angel*, *Of Time and the River*, and *You Can't Go Home Again* as ebooks in their online curated collection of classic, public-domain works, providing free access in Australia even though the novels remain under copyright in America. While most of the ephemera regarding Wolfe's life remains solely published in the United States, the growth of resources like Project Gutenberg and eBooks@Adelaide offer an unprecedented level of access to Wolfe's fiction in Australia, albeit at a time when the novelist is all but forgotten.

Despite such scarcity, Wolfe's literary influence does extend as far as Australia. In an essay from *Crossing the Gap* (1987) titled "The Novel as Narrative Poem," the Australian novelist Christopher Koch writes that "it was Thomas Wolfe who caused me to become a writer."[78] Like so many of the previously mentioned encounters, Koch saw in Wolfe an author who "carried one away, who said things that one had never believed anyone else could feel, let alone say" and, at sixteen, believed no one had "ever written of these secret things before." For Koch, the intense experiences of childhood and youth became the theme of his first novel, *The Boys in the Island* (1958), and his recollection of Wolfe's impact on his early reading life bears the signs of revelation: "Later in life we may admire greater literature, we may have better taste and discrimination; but never again will we know the intense excitement of those first revelations in print. This was how it was for me with Wolfe; and above all, he showed me what the novel could be: that it could do far more than tell a story; that it could weave the poetry of my world; my time."

In *Antipodean America* (2013), Paul Giles has argued that when relations between the United States and Australia are considered within the academic context, it is usually "in the context of the supposed 'Americanization' of the southern continent," ignoring the ways in which "Australasia has formed a shadow self in US national narratives" and also how the "cultural histories of the two countries" have "long been imbricated within each other."[79] This discussion of Wolfe's influence on Koch is not intended to simply uncover a hitherto unexamined shadow of the United States within the Australian imaginary, reinforcing what Giles identifies as "simple assumptions of unilateral, one-way cultural traffic," but rather to broaden the scope of Wolfe's reception and influence across the Pacific and outside of the narrow circle of "the South," arguing that the narrative of Eugene Gant's youthful flight from a small southern town is reimagined in Koch's tale of Francis Cullen, a young Tasmanian boy longing for the mainland. Koch's self-conscious transposition of Wolfe's themes of alienation and longing—so often characterized as endemic to U.S. literary culture—challenges an exceptionalist approach to both Australian and American literary studies, and offers a case study of how these "imbricated" literary cultures can be approached within a more reciprocal framework. A comparative reading not only situates Wolfe's involvement within the frequently overlooked cultural exchange between the literatures of America and Australia but also challenges any implicit regionalism in protecting *our* Australian literature from going "to buggery" (as Australian critic C. A. Cranston has written), instead identifying Koch's work as part of a global exchange of myths.[80]

# # #

When *The Boys in the Island* was first published in 1958, it received mildly enthusiastic reviews. The novel follows Francis Cullen, a young boy growing up in rural Tasmania, who charts his childhood longing for the "Otherland"—a mythical place that signifies his longing for escape and transformation—as well as the loss of first love, and ultimately the impossibility of the mainland ever satisfying his longing. On its release, *The Boys in the Island* was viewed as a vision of youthful Romanticism, particularly the opening chapters of Francis's childhood, which John Quinlem described as containing themes that "are lived by all men, consciously felt at the time by some, and remembered afterwards only by a few—the sensitive few [. . .] the equal of the type since Wordsworth."[81] Writing in 1959, Rosemary Wighton praised Koch's novel as bucking the trend of "realistic novels" in Australian literature, a convention that she saw as tacitly proposing that "a novel, to be truly Australian, *must* be 'realistic' in this sense." *The Boys in the Island,* according to Wighton, provided a subtle, poetic connection between "scenes and peoples as seen through Francis's eyes, and his inner desires and torments," and was therefore "a welcome contrast to the endless and pointless descriptions of objects complained of earlier."[82] As in Wolfe's *Look Homeward, Angel* and *Of Time and the River,* Koch's *The Boys in the Island* charts an internal geography—what Wolfe, following Matthew Arnold, called "The Buried Life"[83]—and, like Wolfe's novels, *The Boys in the Island* follows the movement from provincial to metropolitan space, signifying a transition from an unidentifiable longing to an ultimate dissatisfaction. It is this movement, and the corresponding *Sehnsucht* that such wandering evokes, where the connection between the two novels is most immediately obvious; indeed, Koch has written that Wolfe's story of a provincial youth longing for the city matched his own early experiences in Tasmania:

> No other writer will give me what he gave me, if only because the experience of which he wrote so uncannily corresponded to my own. A boy growing up in the cool hills of North Carolina in the early years of this century, dreaming of the great cities in the North that he would some day discover; a boy listening at night to the lonely cry of the train that would one day take him there: this was what Wolfe wrote of. And these things miraculously matched the dreams of a boy listening to the train-cry in the cool hills of Tasmania in the 1940s, imagining unknown cities on the mainland of Australia he would one day see. I don't doubt that Wolfe's evocation of longing and promise matched the experience and the dreams of country boys and small town boys everywhere; but few writers in this country then gave them utterance. Wonder and joy, the vision of optimism and innocence, came to me from the northern hemisphere.[84]

Like Eugene Gant, for whom the "Tantalus mocker of a city [. . .] duped his hunger with a thousand phantom shapes of impossible desire," Francis Cullen's childhood belief in the promise of the "Otherland"—sought after in *The Boys in the Island* via the mainland city of Melbourne—remains forever out of reach:

> It was the suffocation of all promise, slain on the gleaming St. Kilda tramlines of a sulky Sunday, on the empty Parade before the silent house whose faces did not know him.
>
> But even now he could not be free of a suspicion that another city, the city of the promise, lay locked just out of sight. The tough, implacable and utterly indifferent Mainland city he knew now he could never love had put on him a great melancholy, which was its own, masking the unfound pockets of joy. And yet, yet, there was something in this very melancholy, in the melancholy itself, to disturb him with the notion of something unfound, stirring in his bowels.
>
> He went down onto the beach, and out along a concrete sewerage pipe to the water's edge, and dropped a stone with an echoless plop into the oily water, and stared at the motionless wide-flung arm of Port Melbourne around the Bay, at the chirruping distance-dance there of the countless red and grey buildings; they chirruped softly and danced in the afternoon emptiness with a merciless cheery life. He watched them, and whispered to himself: "*Melbourne. Melbourne. Melbourne*," as though the name might unlock the withheld enigma; but nothing opened up, the afternoon continued timelessly, the suffocating, melancholy blanket did not lift from him.[85]

The resonances with Wolfe in this passage are manifold: the impossible promise of the city, the notion of something "unfound"—a word repeated six times in *Look Homeward Angel* as part of Wolfe's symbolic refrain "a stone, a leaf an unfound door"—even the desire stirring in "his bowels," echoing *Of Time and the River*, where "the bowels of youth are yearning with lost love."[86] An English reviewer for the *Times* suggested that there is "a kind of frustrated lyricism both in Francis and in the writing," and, interestingly, in later editions of *The Boys in the Island* this same passage is trimmed of many such "Wolfean" flourishes: "Promise lay slain on the St Kilda tram-lines of Sunday; but even now he could not be free of a suspicion that another city, the city of the promise, lay locked just out of sight. He went down onto the beach and walked to the water's edge and dropped a stone with an echoless plop into the oily water, and stared at the motionless, wide-flung arm of Port Melbourne, around the Bay. He whispered to himself: '*Melbourne, Melbourne, Melbourne*,'—as though the name might unlock something. But only melancholy made itself felt, containing the memory of another city just out of sight."[87]

Following this revision of "the city of promise," Koch also excised entire passages from the original novel, including some more ruminations on the nature of "melancholy": the "monstrous, faceless, yet almost poignant" melancholy that was "the memory of another city just out of sight. [. . .] The memory (not his own) of its meaning was all around him, but he could never get to it."[88] This reiteration of an unreachable and nameless desire—an evocation of Francis Cullen's alienation that mirrors Eugene Gant's, written in the style of Thomas Wolfe—still remains in Koch's revised edition, but without those verbal clues that point to the heritage of longing in *The Boys in the Island* as being closely aligned with Wolfe's *Sehnsucht*. Koch has written about the revisions he made to his first novel, noting that "the young man who wrote it, reveling in the excesses of youth, never used one word where ten would do."[89] Koch's renunciation of Wolfe's stylistic and thematic influence here is one more example of the way many other writers have described being in thrall to Wolfe at an early stage in their career, only to cast off his influence in later years.

"We Walked to School through London Fogs"

In *Australian Literature: Postcolonialism, Racism, Transnationalism* (2007), Graham Huggan argues that Koch's work—particularly his nonfiction—demonstrates a "customary cocktail of geographical determinism, racial essentialism, and gender-specific language" that makes for "highly questionable cultural politics."[90] Citing Koch's essay "The Lost Hemisphere" (1987)—"a writer can't finally escape his own country"[91]—Huggan argues that the author's work reflects a recurring anxiety about place, specifically the notion that there is a definable "Australian" or "Tasmanian" community whose character is best expressed and understood from within those communities.[92] This form of exceptionalism has been previously discussed in terms of the Southern Agrarian experiment in the 1930s, while new southern studies' arguments around the "inventedness" of "the South" are equally applicable to the figure of "Australia" or, in Koch's case, "Tasmania." Just as representations of "the South," as Greeson notes, are deeply connected to the "the needs and expectations of a broader American imaginary," Koch's "Tasmania" is characterized in opposition to "the Mainland." Peter Pierce suggests "no Tasmanian, writing of Tasmania, has more fully exposed, knowingly and subliminally, the attachments and repulsions that the place engenders; the binding emotional ties which war against the desire to venture away that the intense parochial experience of Tasmania also creates."[93] Back in the mid-1960s, Charles Higham wrote a "Letter from Sydney" to the New York–based *Hudson Review* in which he noted that "*The Boys in the Island*, set in the island state of Tasmania, shows how it is possible to be a colonial *within* an intellectual colony: the boys long to escape to the 'big city' of Melbourne."[94]

For Koch, Tasmania was a "peripheral" space defined by its geographic difference, both latitudinal—Tasmania is the southernmost state of Australia—and also by its island character. Lawrence Buell, discussing the "atlas of the provincial imaginary," has noted a swath of novels concerning "lives led in isolated locales remote from metropolitan centers imagined as culturally quaint and thin to the point of grotesquerie," and while *The Boys in the Island* does dwell on the provincialism and isolation of Tasmania—calling it "a fragment separated from the parent continent by a wide stretch of sea"[95]—the imprint of colonialism on Koch's Tasmania also reveals the complexly transnational nature of the island, configured as a displaced England.[96] A prominent concern of Koch's early work was the "semi-fiction" of the "Commonwealth" as something Australians took seriously in the 1950s, stemming from the cultural displacement he felt in being "both" Australian and British. In his essay "Crossing the Gap," Koch writes: "Like many another writer, I was concerned with dualities. Perhaps an Australian writer must be a little more concerned with them than others are, since he is bound to find duality deep within his spirit. A European, he is forever severed from Europe, and unlike an American, is even severed from his ancestral hemisphere."[97] In his novel *The Doubleman* (1985), Koch captures this internal contradiction through a description of Tasmania's geographic and climatic difference from mainland Australia:

> The whole of dry, Time-flattened Australia lies north of latitude forty, its climate Mediterranean and then sub-tropical. But small, mountainous Tasmania, filled with lakes and rivers, is south of latitude forty; and this makes it different. Politically, it is part of the Commonwealth of Australia; physically, it is not.
>
> The island lies in the track of the Roaring Forties, the westerly winds that

> blow from Cape Horn. In the upside-down frame of the Antipodes, it duplicates the Atlantic coast of Europe; and Brian Brady and I were children of a green, marine landscape: subjects of the stern winter cold. Our spirits were conditioned by the blood-thrilling Westerlies; snow fell in our mid-winters; we walked to school through London fogs.[98]

As Danielle Wood contends in "Writing Tasmania's 'Different Soul'" (2008), this theme of an isolated and marginalized Tasmania was "unproblematically available to writers writing about Tasmania in the middle of the twentieth century," much as some inventors of southern identity in the United States uncritically courted ideas of regional exceptionalism.[99] Paul Sharrad has argued that Koch's significance to Australian letters from this period lies in this contribution to national self-understanding of the "closeted collective psyche of 'fifties and 'sixties Anglo-Australia," attitudes that Sharrad also links to Koch's waning cultural status.[100]

Viewed from this perspective, Koch's engagement with Wolfe's fiction of estrangement and escape—particularly as he conceives "miraculous" resonances with the author's story of Eugene Gant—uncovers not only the hitherto undiscussed presence of Wolfe's "lost and lonely South" in *The Boys in the Island* but also points to a deeper antagonism in literary criticism toward fiction that documents unpalatable convictions that were, in their time, less contentious. In *Finding Purple America* (2013), Jon Smith, channeling Žižek, denounces "white southern melancholy" as a predominant failing of old southern studies, a desire for an object—usually for the "past" or some southern "essence"—that "leads us to desire it even as we may not know the reason for our desire."[101] Rather than simply forget these objects of desire—which lead to the object remaining "overpresent" and so still desired as a "lack"—Smith admonishes "southernists" to try and "understand what leads them to seek out such objects in the first place and invest so much in them." In light of Smith's caution, the value in my own comparative reading of Wolfe and Koch is not simply a rehearsal of melancholic desire—either the "South" of Wolfe or Koch's lonely island of Tasmania—but rather an investigation into the performance of melancholic desire as it is enacted in *The Boys in the Island.* Instead of vindicating or censuring Koch's provincialism in this early novel, it is far more productive to note the ways in which Koch approaches Wolfe's fiction—as many critics still do—as an ur-narrative of the provincial youth longing for escape, noting how Koch's nostalgic reminiscences of reading Wolfe as a young man impacts his own writing on adolescence. What Smith does not explicitly point out in his withering critique of "old southern studies" is the degree to which new southern studies remains skeptical of any texts—like Wolfe's—that have been tethered to this "melancholic" way of reading. My contention is that such antipathy can be similarly extended to the more recent disavowal of Koch in some circles of Australian literary studies, as a reaction against what Dixon and Birns see as a reliance on "nationalist tropes."[102]

Wolfe and the "Otherland"

Koch's earliest configuration of Tasmania not only reflected those colonial attitudes that he sees as "hidden in our unconscious," a response to the summons of the mother country that was "waited for as an adolescent waits for love," but, crucially, it was also conceived under the spell of Thomas Wolfe.[103] Paul Genoni rightly points out that "Koch's Tasmania is not England, any more than it is Australia," writing that "its temperament may be European, but its location is Antipodean, and it is therefore a hybrid 'other.'"[104] Adding to this "hybridity" are the looming shadows of the hills of North Carolina; Koch writes that his earliest impetus for creation came from the belief that, like Wolfe, "I could try, as Wolfe had tried, to tell what had never quite been told, to chart that dream-country which we all carry within us, and which, unattended, will dwindle on the horizon and disappear."[105] As previously quoted, Koch insistently saw his own experiences in light of Eugene Gant's, evoking the "cool hills of North Carolina" and "the cool hills of Tasmania," while in another piece Koch remarked that both he and Gant were "pent in by hills."[106] In *The Boys in the Island*, the first example of Wolfe's influence is in the description of Tasmania: "[It] is different from the hot Australian mainland; it has a different weather and a different soul, knowing as it does the sharp breath of the south, facing the Antarctic."[107] The "weathers of man's soul" is a Wolfean phrase, first used in *Of Time and the River*, and that novel's opening description of "two images" is equally applicable to Koch's picture of Tasmania: "These two images—call them rather lights and weathers of man's soul—of the world-far, lost and lonely South, and the fierce, the splendid, strange and secret North were swarming like a madness through his blood."[108]

Koch's description of early childhood is particularly influenced by *Look Homeward, Angel*; both heroes—Eugene Gant and Francis Cullen—have unusually cogent perceptions as children. It is in this state of inarticulate wonder that both boys learn to desire something beyond reach, laying the foundation for their later *Sehnsucht* for those things lost in childhood. In *Look Homeward, Angel*, Eugene glimpses something like the world of faery while riding in a train: "Eugene watched the sun wane and redden on a rocky river, and on the painted rocks of Tennessee gorges: the enchanted river wound into his child's mind forever. Years later, it was to be remembered in dreams tenanted with elvish and mysterious beauty."[109] Near the opening of *The Boys in the Island*, the young Francis is sitting alone in a car, listening to passing trains, and in this isolated moment Koch similarly reflects on the unseen within the real world:

> Here, in this long grey-bitumen road, with its lights going off forever, its clanging dangerous trams, and the important hoots of trains coming out of the dark from the station nearby, he suddenly smelt and knew of vast areas of otherness, the other places of the world he had not seen, beginning. They were all around, far yet near, areas high and amazing and unseen; areas of otherness but nearness. They were very near Gooree: here in Gooree was the closest you could get to them. Their fierce breath panted around him, through the dusk-blue screen of the pulsing outbreaks of night, a night on fire with unseen incredible cities beyond his six years, beyond the island.[110]

The hoot of the train in this passage is similarly evocative of Wolfe's writing on longing, and in his essay "The Novel as Narrative Poem," Koch notes that "listening to the train-cry" linked his own biography with Wolfe's Eugene.[111] Like "a stone, a leaf, an unfound door," the sound of the train's whistle in Wolfe's oeuvre is a romantic clarion call, as in *Of Time and the River* when Eugene finally leaves Altamont for "the North": "Down in the city's central web, the boy could distinguish faintly the line of the rails, and see the engine smoke above the railroad yards, and as he looked, he heard far off that haunting sound and prophecy of youth and of his life—the bell, the wheel, the wailing whistle—and the train."[112] Writing on this very connection to Wolfe, Koch noted that, "[l]ike Eugene Gant in *Look Homeward, Angel*, I had never in my life seen a big city. [. . .] I too lay awake at night gripped by joy and expectancy as the lone, drawn-out whistle of the steam train came across the dark, going north towards the world."[113] The specificity of this particular reproduction highlights both Koch's profound indebtedness and the extent to which Koch interpreted his own experiences through the lens of Wolfe's fiction.

It is in Koch's descriptions of youthful longing that the novelist comes closest to straight mimicry or impersonation of Wolfe, wherein he takes the model of what he calls Wolfe's "magic in commonplace things" to evoke Francis's grasping for the "Otherland." Like Wolfe's heroes, who are forever knocking at closed doors and constantly attempting to articulate what is finally "unutterable," Koch describes Francis's yearning for this other place through a series of sensuous images:

> But the Otherland near Gooree had no name, and was no place that could be explained: it was the sound of a tune, an afternoon light on the eastern hills, a car's far hum out in the deeps of night, or the wild, lonely cry of plover going over: he could not tell about that to Lewie. But Francis waited for it, for himself. And at times he glimpsed it, at night when in the rain-fresh dark of that winter, absorbed in their talk and plans, he and Lewie wandered talking through Gooree after the pictures, through street after little street, the excitement of their talk making tiredness impossible; he saw it then in the deserted byways of that final suburb as they stood one night on the railway tracks and the twin

> gleam of the lines shot into the darkness. He smelt it in the mixed tang of urine and weeds out by the toilet [. . .] the cool-breasted dark carrying the whole murmur of the suburb evening like a tune out into the flat nearby reaches of the country; it was then and there, for brief moments; the Otherland, the areas of otherness and nearness.[114]

In the revised version of this passage, Koch added in that Francis had "heard it in the thin-wired whistle of the train across the valley of Elimatta, calling as it had done all his life, bereft yet exultant, promising the world," as a clear homage to the same cry that calls to Eugene in *Of Time and the River:* "He heard the wailing cry of the great train, bringing to him again its wild and secret promises of flight and darkness, new lands and a shining city."[115] The choice of cascading images—descriptions of the commonplace that evoke the romantic yearning of Francis—very nearly mirrors a particular passage from *Of Time and the River:* "The sound of forest waters in the night, the rustling of cool corn-blades in the dark, the goat-cries of a boy into the wind, the pounding of great wheels upon a rail, the sound of quiet casual voices at a country station in the night, and the thorn of delight, the tongueless cry of ecstasy that trembles on the lips of the country kid as he lies awake for the first time in the night in the top berth of a Pullman car while the great wheels pound beneath him toward the city."[116]

Though this technique is common to Romantic literature, it is important to add that Koch himself identifies his use of "prose-poems" as originating with Wolfe, in his characterization of Wolfe as "a genius that produced sprawling, exuberant prose-poems about the U.S. that rival in their scope and lyric beauty the verse of Walt Whitman [. . .] dreams and emotions I had never imagined could be set down in words."[117] In "The Novel as Narrative Poem," Koch claimed that Wolfe "showed me what the novel could be: that it could do far more than tell a story; that it could weave the poetry of my world; my time."[118]

This Is Major Tom to Ground Control

There is one further and final imaginative territory where Wolfe's specter lingers: the unlikely world of science fiction. But while Wolfe's story titles have often provided fodder for science fiction authors—some examples include Alfred Bester's "Of Time and Third Avenue" (1951), Gregory Benford's *Of Space-time and the River* (1985), and Robert Silverberg's "Look Homeward, Spaceman" (1956)—only one pulp magazine saw Wolfe transported into the future. On the cover of the 1950 spring issue of American pulp science fiction magazine *Planet Stories,* a man dressed as a boy scout in Robin Hood tights grips onto a blonde-haired woman—resplendent in gold and clutching a shiny orb—both figures leaping through space trailing a stream of light behind them. The lead story,

"Flame-Jewel of the Ancients," is billed as "A Thrilling Space-Adventure Novel," precisely the kind of melodramatic space opera in which *Planet Stories* trafficked.[119] Despite the pulp heritage of *Planet Stories*—the adventures and planetary romances marked it off from the more scientifically plausible and "serious" science fiction of *Astounding Science Fiction* under the editorship of John W. Campbell—the magazine showcased works by writers such as Isaac Asimov and Theodore Sturgeon and was the first magazine to publish Philip K. Dick in 1952 with the story "Beyond Lies the Wub."[120] In *Storytelling in the Pulps, Comics, and Radio* (2004), Tim DeForest writes that *Planet Stories*' most important contribution to science fiction was "the many Ray Bradbury stories it published," and in 1950, nestled behind that garish cover for "Flame-Jewell of the Ancients," was Bradbury's "Forever and the Earth."[121] This story, replete with a full-page illustration of Thomas Wolfe's face hovering over the moon and a rocket flying behind him (figure 6), was accompanied by the following synopsis: "They brought that great blazing writer three hundred years into the future. They gave him the stars and planets and all space for his hungry pen. Then they tried to put Thomas Wolfe back in his grave."[122] "Forever and the Earth" centers on a scheme devised by Henry William Field, a multimillionaire and failed writer, who decides to bring Thomas Wolfe back from the dead to achieve what he believes no one else can—to write the great Martian romance: "I've called you because I feel Tom Wolfe's the man, the necessary man, to write of space, of time, huge things like nebulae and galactic war, meteors and planets, all the dark things he loved and put on paper were like this. He was born out of his time. He needed really *big* things to play with and never found them on earth."

"Forever and the Earth" is a literal embodiment of the desire to revive Wolfe through fictional representation, returning to September 15, 1938, before Wolfe died in a hospital in Baltimore. In an interview with Jonathan Eller in 2002, Bradbury reflected on Wolfe's influence on his writing and his desire, in turn, to give Wolfe a chance to write again:

> Thomas Wolfe was my madness when I was nineteen. And I got to thinking one day, "How do you encompass the future?" And in order to do it, you've got to get the proper man, so you go back and you get Tom Wolfe, and you send him out—little realizing I can do the job myself. I didn't have that kind of ego. So Tom Wolfe became my messenger, and I wrote a lot of things under his influence. [. . .] Most of my time-travel stories—well, starting with Thomas Wolfe, "Forever and the Earth"—are [written] to rescue my beloved writers from their destiny. To make Wolfe live again, to give him a new life, give him a chance to write more novels. So my motivation has always been to rescue. [. . .] I'm a lifesaver. I'm standing on the shore and I see all my favorite authors out there drowning, and I swim out to save them. So all those time-travel stories are the Salvation Army run by Ray Bradbury.[123]

FIGURE 6. Illustration for Ray Bradbury, "Forever and the Earth," *Planet Stories* 4, no. 6 (Spring 1950). Image retrieved from the Internet Archive.

In "Forever and the Earth," Bradbury writes that Wolfe is "the only man [who] could handle the sun without being burnt to a ridiculous cinder," and Wolfe becomes his messenger, writing "a book bigger and better in every way than anything [Wolfe] ever wrote" while he was alive, an account of space and the Red Planet that is finally equal to Wolfe's *Sehnsucht.* In the story, as Wolfe heads off in a rocket, his words are transmitted to a humming machine that scrawls a facsimile of Wolfe's "fevered hand a million miles away," and in an homage to the author's lyricism—piling phrase upon phrase building to a kind of revelry—Bradbury records his impressions of reading this new "Wolfean" cosmic chronicle:

> He read the words about space and time and travel, about a large man and a large journey and how it was in the long midnight and coldness of space, and how a man could be hungry enough to take all of it and ask for more. [. . .] Space was like October, wrote Thomas Wolfe. He said things about its darkness and its loneliness and man so small in it. The eternal and timeless October, was one of the things he said. And then he told of the rocket itself, the smell and the feel of the metal of the rocket, and the sense of destiny and wild exultancy to at last leave Earth behind, all problems and all sadnesses, and go seeking a bigger problem and a bigger sadness.[124]

Surprisingly, this Bradbury short story has attracted very limited attention from critics writing about Thomas Wolfe. In 1988 the *Thomas Wolfe Review* ran a short article by Morton I. Teicher titled "Ray Bradbury and Thomas Wolfe," which does little more than describe the story, reacting to "Forever and the Earth" as a kind of curio, a "triumphant efflorescence of fantasy."[125] More recently, Salvatore Proietti's "Beyond the Hills: Of Thomas Wolfe and Science Fiction" (2003) reads the story as an extension of Bradbury's "faith in fabulation as a means of boundless imaginative expansion," a subtext that Proietti sees as defining all of Bradbury's fiction: as a single, extended parable on "the disappearance of imagination from modern culture" and the need for "a new innocence" discovered on the frontiers of new planets.[126] This frontier argument is not a novel contribution to Bradbury studies; it is most clearly explicated in Gary K. Wolfe's frequently reprinted essay "The Frontier Myth in Ray Bradbury" (1980), which treats Bradbury's *The Martian Chronicles* (1950) as an exemplar of Frederick Jackson Turner's famous thesis on the American frontier.[127] Gary K. Wolfe argues that science fiction can be broadly understood as retaining, in part, "some sort of frontier experience"; the narrative of "Forever and the Earth" demonstrates the extent to which Bradbury believed this new frontier demanded the imaginative gifts of a writer like Wolfe, a case of romance over scientific realism.[128]

In this way, Bradbury's story speaks to the tension between the science fiction world and the broader reading public that was apparent as the 1940s drew to a close, a period Damon Knight recalls as "the floodtide of the cerebral story in science fiction": coming out of the so-called Golden Age of Science Fiction of the 1930s and '40s, Bradbury's lyrical and romantic stories represented a distinct shift away from the "hard" science fiction of his forebears while at the same time garnering a significant popular and critical reputation that cemented him as one of the preeminent practitioners of science fiction and fantasy for the next sixty years, beginning with *The Martian Chronicles* (1950).[129] Writing on the release of *The Martian Chronicles*, Jonathan Eller and William Touponce described its publication as a "pivotal event" in the "growing respectability" of American science fiction, as the first "science fiction book to find two distinct reading audiences," demonstrating that, as of May 1950, "science fiction was still seen as different from mainstream literature but no longer separate from it."[130] This "growing respectability" of science fiction has not been realized—at least not to any great extent—in critical work on southern fiction, a fact that is curious considering the history of regarding southern identity as a product of "place" and the ways in which science fiction charts a similar trajectory, leading John Moore to write that "Southern science fiction protocols maintain an uneven but perceptible dialogical relationship with Southern literature protocols."[131]

Interestingly, more recent criticism on science fiction produced in the South—following Gregory Benford's call for "more Southern spice and flavor in our future literary cuisine"[132]—has tended to elide new southern studies' skepticism toward the exceptional function of "the South," highlighting instead what John David Miles calls the "value of understanding the role of region in the production of a genre that so often makes a practice of distancing itself from physical geography."[133] What follows, then, is not an attempt to figure the South in space but rather an investigation of the ways in which Wolfe's *Sehnsucht* was, for Bradbury, the ideal expression of infinite desire that this new cosmic geography engendered. Given this book's interest in the spatial embodiment of that which can never, truly, be embodied, Bradbury's refiguring of "space" as space offers one suggestive way that Wolfe's *Sehnsucht* proved imaginatively productive for an American writer.

Published over the late 1940s and collected as *The Martian Chronicles* in 1950, Ray Bradbury's story cycle of the American colonization of Mars is his own fulfillment of the project set for Wolfe in "Forever and the Earth"—to write the great Martian romance. In *Becoming Ray Bradbury* (2011), Jonathan Eller has described the submission of *The Martian Chronicles* manuscript in 1949 as the "beginning of Bradbury's *Annus Mirabilis*," which stretches from the fall of 1949 to the fall of 1950, a period that also saw the submission for publication of *The Illustrated Man* (1951) and "The Fireman," the early novella form of *Fahrenheit 451* (1953).[134] Understandably, then, critics have tended to overlook "Forever and the Earth," only one of twenty-four new story appearances by Bradbury in 1950 and an unusually sentimental story, which George E. Slusser called "mawkish [. . .] literary body snatching."[135] The story obviously remained pertinent for Bradbury, however, who rewrote "Forever and the Earth" with Norman Corwin as a radio play in 1977, which was eventually published as *Forever and the Earth: Radio Dramatization* in 1984. The broadcaster was a significant influence on the young Bradbury, who describes Corwin as "burst[ing] on the airways of the world" with sound experiments that "stunned me into wondering who this experimenter was. [. . .] He fell on me like a shower of meteors."[136] The collaboration was, for Bradbury, the satisfaction of a dream that had solidified when Bradbury heard Corwin's adaptation of "bits and pieces of Thomas Wolfe" that "hooked [him] forever," and following the publication of Bradbury's first novel he sent a copy to Corwin with the invitation to drinks, sparking a long friendship. Corwin was a prominent figure during the late infancy of radio, producing more than two hundred original radio plays, while his work with CBS's *Columbia Workshop* is viewed by many critics as "radio's high water mark."[137] In 1941 *Columbia Workshop* offered Corwin the unprecedented opportunity to take over the program for six months to produce a series that ultimately became *Twenty-Six by Corwin*, comprising an astonishing twenty-six half-hour original programs that often bore little or no resemblance to those preceding them. It was during this series, on October 5, 1941, that Corwin broadcast "Wolfiana," a rhapsody for radio that adapted passages from *Look Homeward, Angel* and *Of Time and the River*.[138] Several years later, on June 13, 1944, Corwin revisited the figure of Wolfe in the second instalment of his "An American Trilogy," which featured Charles Laughton and the composer Bernard Hermann (better known for his collaborations with Alfred Hitchcock), and it was this broadcast in particular that so excited Bradbury and led to the eventual collaboration on *Forever and the Earth* more than thirty years later.[139]

The print publication of this radio dramatization in 1984 represents a labor of love for Bradbury. His love for Thomas Wolfe, according to the author's note for *Forever and the Earth*, "coincides with my love for Norman Corwin," and like the "shower of meteors" in Corwin's broadcasts, Wolfe's fiction "fell on [Bradbury] like an avalanche."[140] Speaking of his story in a letter to Marjorie Fairbanks—a friend of Wolfe's who was planning a biography of the novelist—Bradbury wrote that "I have always loved ["Forever and the Earth"] mainly, of course, for its theme. How did I get the idea? From reading Wolfe of course and feeling the great sense of loss at finding he had died so young."[141] In the early 1940s, Bradbury had also begun work on a poem, "October," which he told Eller was an example of how "Tom Wolfe became my messenger" in his younger years, suggesting that "that'll give you an idea of how mad I was."[142] October is the most evocative month for Wolfe, which he writes about most frequently; in *Of Time and the River*, October stands as an important symbol of *Sehnsucht*, a synecdoche for abundance and loss: "October had come again, and that year it was sharp and soon: frost was early, burning the thick green on the mountain sides to massed brilliant hues of blazing colors, painting the air with sharpness, sorrow and delight—and with October."[143] Wolfe repeats the refrain "October has come again" eight times in the novel, characterizes the month as "the season for returning" where "the bowels of youth are yearning with lost love," and proposes that "Spring has no language but a cry."[144] In Bradbury's poem, which even bears the title "October," Wolfe's influence is very clear; the poem begins with "October, the ripe, the golden month has come," and Bradbury similarly characterizes October as a time of return:

> Is not October the month of months?
> The soul shaking month
> When all memories are resurrected
> By the turn of Time's spade.[145]

Bradbury later called the poem "pure Tom Wolfe," a youthful experiment that bore the author's influence so heavily that it finally reads as a parodic pastiche of Wolfe's rhapsodic passages:

> October, the wild, sad month—
> [. . .]
> October.
> And the ghastly regions of the past,
> [. . .]
> Lo! The twenty billion dead are stirring in their tombs.
> Acorns are dropping,
> Horse chestnuts slick and brown and gleaming,
> Hard underfoot in the moonlight
> [. . .]
> Dogs are scampering in deserted dells,
> Baying,
> Setting up rhymed echoes,
> Whining in empty railway stations in little far off towns,
> Far, far away.[146]

Bradbury returned to this evocative month of October at other times in his fiction, and this early experiment in writing "pure Tom Wolfe" is again apparent in a later iteration of October, included in Bradbury's early story collection *The October Country* (1955). At the beginning of the collection, Bradbury writes that the "October Country" is "that country where it is always turning late in the year. That country where the hills are fog and the rivers are mist; where noons go quickly, dusks and twilights linger, and midnights stay. [. . .] Whose people passing at night on the empty walks sound like rain."[147] When Bradbury revised

"Forever and the Earth" for its radio dramatization, he expanded a section that in the original had opened with the line "space was like October," and in this later version Bradbury reimagines space *as* October, an idea given expression by Wolfe's proxy in the play: "Space seems that dear and old and lost October I so much loved to spell. Here are the darknesses of ten thousand autumn nights, the great attic where all the discarded summer toys of the Gods are kept. [. . .] It is the time of going away. It is the autumn with no spring. Space was and is and will forever be—October."[148] In 1976 Bradbury gave an interview to the *Paris Review* in which he explained that Wolfe was "a great romantic," a writer who can "open the doors of the world" to young writers, suggesting that "Wolfe is perfect when you're nineteen." Prompted by the interviewer's suggestion that *The Martian Chronicles* is filled with "intensely lyrical" passages, Bradbury replied that sometimes he would "get an old copy of Wolfe and cut out paragraphs and paste them in my story, because I couldn't do it, you see."[149] In both forms of "Forever and the Earth," this technique of pasting passages into his stories occurs figuratively through the voice of the rescued Wolfe and explicitly demonstrates Bradbury's recourse to Wolfe's *Sehnsucht* in comprehending stellar spaces and the mystery of Mars. Though this story has been nearly forgotten, Bradbury's seminal collection *The Martian Chronicles* also bears signs of writing "under his influence," extending the romance of Wolfe's America beyond its original planetary bounds.[150] The popularity of Bradbury's brand of lyrical science fiction in the 1950s is connected, in part, to this early narrative of Wolfe's resurrection, and the author's influence remained apparent for Bradbury during his career. In one of the final stories Bradbury published, "Miss Appletree and I" (2009), Wolfe's presence still looms large in an aging man's reflections on the melancholy passage of time: "You know me, I'm a moody old dog. I'm the son of Thomas Wolfe, O Time, O River, oh, the grieving of the winds, lost, lost, forever lost."[151] In *The Bradbury Chronicles* (2005), Sam Weller notes this continuing impact of Wolfe on Bradbury: "Later in his career when Ray gave lectures, he shared his approach to writing: 'Throw up in the morning and clean it up in the afternoon!' he coached at the top of his lungs. He credited Thomas Wolfe for teaching him this approach. 'Wolfe taught me how to throw up. His books were immense upchuckings. Not much plot, but he was wild about life and he tore into it and he jumped up and down and he yelled.'"[152]

"The Huge Chronicle of the Billion Forms"

In his essay "Is Mars Heaven?" (2011), Eric S. Rabkin identifies Bradbury's story cycle, *The Martian Chronicles*, as a "milestone in the history of science fiction in specific and American literature in general," arguing that "today's readers may not appreciate the widespread ignorance and disparagement of science fiction then," and that "for an American audience in the early 1950s, *The Martian Chronicles* offered literary continuity and mythic redemption without any real science at all."[153] The amenability of Bradbury's fiction to earlier critical frameworks partially explains why *The Martian Chronicles* was, according to Rabkin, "the first [book] to gain a putatively SF author extended treatment in the *New York Times*," and also inspired the first interview that the *New York Times* ever ran with an acknowledged science fiction writer "who interested the newspaper precisely because he was an SF writer."[154] The difficult path for science fiction writers in attaining critical legitimacy within discussions of American capital-L "Literature" has been one factor in the contentious branding of Bradbury, linking the author with Wolfe's own struggle for acceptance in light of the normative assumptions of canon-builders in the postwar period. In Eller and Touponce's *Ray Bradbury: The Life of Fiction* (2004), the authors broaden the generic label for Bradbury, calling him a "fantasist, a mythmaker, and a writer of moral fables," while Steven Kagle's essay "Homage to Melville" (1992) contends that "when we finally try to categorize Ray Bradbury's place as a writer we will ultimately place him beside Herman Melville. [. . .] In placing him with Melville I am [. . .] asserting that Bradbury's place in literary history is closer to that of Melville and other nineteenth-century writers of the prose romance than it is to twentieth-century writers of science fiction."[155] Meanwhile, Adam Lawrence has noted that, on the other "side" as it were, critics of Bradbury's science fiction credentials in *The Martian Chronicles* have read "the book's failure to depict the Red Planet plausibly and scientifically" as a sign of Bradbury's "nostalgic, inward-looking vision" and failure in inventing worlds that do not "estrange but rather reaffirm a comfort zone."[156] Adding to this confusion is the ever-present sense of embarrassment when discussing any science fiction text within the broader critical climate, a phenomenon that Fredric Jameson describes in his *Archaeologies of the Future* (2005):

> The conventional high-cultural repudiation of SF—its stigmatization of the purely formulaic (which reflects the original sin of the form in its origins in the pulps), complaints about the absence of complex and psychologically "interesting" characters [. . .] a yearning for original literary styles which ignores the stylistic variety of modern SF [. . .] is probably not a matter of personal taste, nor is it to be addressed by way of purely aesthetic arguments, such as the attempt to assimilate selected SF works to the canon as such. We must here identify a kind of generic revulsion, in which this form and narrative discourse is the object of psychic resistance as a whole and the target of a kind of literary "reality principle."[157]

Whether or not the lack of "generic revulsion" toward *The Martian Chronicles* can be read as evidence of its marginal science fiction status, what remains unacknowledged is the extent to which this new, lyrical rendering of Mars owes a clear debt to Thomas Wolfe.

Structurally, critics have been quick to note that in 1944, Bradbury read both Sherwood Anderson's *Winesburg, Ohio* (1919) and John Steinbeck's *Red Pony* (1937), providing a model for the stories that would ultimately be collected in *The Martian Chronicles*.[158] Although twelve of the fifteen stories had been previously published before the novel's release, Eller writes in "The Body Eclectic" (2010) that beyond simply drawing together existing materials through a form of bricolage, Bradbury's revision of the stories, the addition of three new stories in the original edition, as well as eleven new "bridging" passages, constituted the creation of "an entirely new book" that transcended the "limitations of pre-existing materials."[159] As a novel, however, *The Martian Chronicles* (1950) still reads like an assemblage of stories, and critics have spent time variously positing an overarching narrative: a nostalgic backward glance to small-town America, a frontier myth for pioneering Americans, or an oblique sermon on colonization and race relations via a narrative of invasion and settlement on Mars, among others.[160] Recently, Adam Lawrence has suggested that contrary to these popular readings of *The Martian Chronicles* as "a nostalgic yearning for days of innocence and for an Edenic return to the agrarian pioneer settlement era," or even as chastising the expansionist ideology and destruction of indigenous culture, one particular story, "Night Meeting," points to "*something new*."[161] In explicating this "something new," Lawrence turns to Lévinas's expression of "metaphysical desire," described by the philosopher in his work *Totality and Infinity* (1961) as a desire for "a land not of our birth."[162] Linking with my own conceptualization of *Sehnsucht* and metaphysical desire, "Night Meeting" also reveals the lingering influence of Wolfe, particularly as he also shares in this longing for "a land not of our birth."

In "Night Meeting," one of the new stories Bradbury added to *The Martian Chronicles*, Tomás Gomez—an amiable traveler whose lack of suspicion and willingness to embrace Mars as wholly alien distinguishes him from the other colonists—encounters Muhe Ca, a Martian or apparition of a Martian, and together they both travel across the deserted landscape. As the story progresses the two characters soon realize that, though they can see the other, they are unable to touch, and the landscape they perceive around them differs dramatically, not only in kind, but also in "Time": Tomás sees a dead Martian landscape and new signs of American civilization while Muhe Ca perceives a Martian city and carnival lights and the "canals [. . .] full of lavender wine."[163] Unlike previous encounters between colonists and Martians, the meeting is wholly hospitable, and their separation from each other—a distance that is determined as much by Time as "otherness"—leads to a form of thoughtful contemplation, which Lawrence calls "a philosophical contemplation of the self-other encounter."[164] Tomás tells Muhe Ca that "the ruins prove it! They prove that *I* am the Future," to which the Martian retorts: "What does it matter who is Past or Future, if we are both alive, for what follows will follow, tomorrow or in ten thousand years."[165] Walter Mucher reads the story as an exploration of the self-other encounter, suggesting that "Tomás and Muhe, Earthling and Martian, are the two poles of this identity dyad. Each represents the other's reality by projecting its negation unto the other."[166] For Lawrence, the encounter between Earthling and Martian is an instance of a Lévinasian ethical substitution, "in which the self is overwhelmed by the presence of an Other that cannot be pre-determined." Conceived as such, the self-other meeting in "Night Meeting" is concerned with what Lévinas calls "the otherwise than being," while the promise of such Martian encounters is one of the "defamiliarizing or estranging effects" that lead to new vision, not merely nostalgia for an Edenic return.[167]

Lawrence's comparison of Bradbury with Lévinas in this story is fruitful in considering the lingering influence of Wolfe, particularly in further theorizing the overlap with Wolfe's own aesthetic and ontology of longing. In *Totality and Infinity*, Lévinas writes that metaphysics is turned toward the "'elsewhere' and the 'otherwise' and the 'other'" and that therefore the "metaphysically desired" tends toward "*something else entirely*"; it is not a satisfiable need, "a nostalgia [or] a longing for return," but rather it "desires beyond everything that can simply complete it." As with "goodness," for Lévinas, "the Desired does not fulfill it, but deepens it."[168] The clearest appropriation of Wolfe's expression of longing in "Night Meeting" is present in Bradbury's discussion of time, which dwells, like Wolfe, on its tangible qualities. As Tomás drives into "darkness and hills," he passes through a faery landscape: Mars is "quieter tonight than any other," the "deserts and the empty seas [swing] by him" and the mountains are held in stark relief against the stars.[169] Surrounding Tomás is "a smell of Time in the air," and Bradbury slips into the lyrical rhythms of Wolfe's prose in describing the makeup of time: "What did Time smell like? Like dust and clocks and people. And if you wondered what Time sounds like it sounded like water running in a dark cave and voices crying and dirt dropping down upon hollow box lids, and rain. And, going further, what did Time look like? Time looked like snow dropping silently into a black room or it looked like a silent film in an ancient theatre, one hundred billion faces falling like those New Year balloons, down and down into nothing. That was how Time smelled and looked and sounded. And tonight [. . .] tonight you could almost touch Time."[170]

It is not only the rhetorical questioning and polysyndeton that mirrors Wolfe's writing on time but also the nature of time that both writers describe. In *Of Time and the River*, Eugene is similarly captivated by what Wolfe calls the earth's "moveless silence," "far-off hills receding into time as haunting as a dream." Furthermore, "time's sanded drop," like Bradbury's drops of dirt, is described as a river "flowing forever from our desperate grasp even as a river flows," much like the sound of water that Tomás hears.[171] Tomás and Muhe Ca both experience the play of time like a chill on their skin—as a "strangeness," as though they are entirely alone in the world—while the encounter of the "other" is seen as a dream for Tomás and a vision for Muhe Ca.[172] Likewise, in *Of Time and the River,* the "murmurous sound of time," which is "remote and everlasting," distilled out of "all the movement, frenzy, and unceasing fury of our unresting lives," provides the "still sad music of humanity," a moment of encounter among the "million passing lives" fixed in eternal time."[173] The strangeness both characters acknowledge in *The Martian Chronicles* "has to do with Time," Muhe Ca concludes, while the overwhelming solitude that each feels connected to this experience of time echoes Wolfe's "strange spirit of time and solitude," which he describes with the lyricism that Bradbury would later try to evoke: "[T]he strange spirit of time and solitude that hovered above [the earth] eternally, and which can never be described, but which may be evoked by a cow-bell broken by the wind in distant valleys, the lonely whistle of a departing train, or simply a sinuous gust of wind that smokes its way across coarse mountain grasses when spring comes."[174]

In *Longing for the Other* (2009), Dalton suggests that just as *Sehnsucht* expresses "the potency within human life to act and to move [. . .] to move upward as it were, out beyond the immediate and toward that which seems to lie beyond our lives," Lévinas's "metaphysical desire" is directed toward the transcendent; in *Totality and Infinity,* it is "trans*ascendence*," where one feels "ascendant, elevated, lifted up, over and beyond not only oneself, but everything which is horizontally immediate and available." Lévinas distinguishes this desire from nostalgia, which is "a longing for return" or, as Dalton writes, "the restoration of a lost immanence," and instead notes its fundamentally *insatiable* nature: like *Sehnsucht,* it is situated in a realm "beyond satisfaction and nonsatisfaction."[175] Lévinas's theory thus deepens my conceptualization of *Sehnsucht,* employed in this book as an interpretive lens for exploring Wolfe's ontology of longing, extending it into the infinity of space: just as Bradbury determines that Wolfe's romance was hindered by the confines of earth in "Forever and the Earth," his story "Night Meeting" appropriates Wolfe's lyrical vision of landscape, while his mystical rendering of time is used to explore "a land not of our birth." Just as McCullers wrote in 1940 that "Americans are homesick most for the places we have never known," Bradbury's Martian romance shows how his postwar experiment in science fiction provides a new way of expressing a sense of exile and estrangement. It is precisely this expression of longing that similarly marks Koch's *The Boys in the Island* as having been written under Wolfe's influence: the romantic lens through which Wolfe viewed America—and Germany in his later novels—is transposed onto both Koch's deep "South" of Tasmania and Bradbury's distant Mars. The inextricably related impulses to both impersonate and revive Wolfe that have been explored throughout the chapter speak to the seductive power of his Romantic vision, which has endured long after his death. While critical discussions have dwindled in recent years, the legacy of the novelist's vision remains imprinted in the works of numerous writers who came after him, evidence that while critics might have exiled Wolfe to the "literary boondocks," he has never really gone away.

CONCLUSION

In 1938, when Margaret Mitchell learned of Wolfe's early death, she wrote to a friend to express a "distinct feeling of shock," suggesting that "if ever there was a comet in these Southern skies, [Wolfe] was it."[1] Mitchell's metaphor is emblematic of the way in which many contemporary critics perceive Wolfe's decline: as a curious and luminous blaze in American literary history that disappeared abruptly, vanishing soon after it arrived. Many who argue for his enduring significance have reinforced Mitchell's designation of "Southern skies"—Wolfe as the southern man of letters or as a "product of Appalachia"[2]—and this impulse to cloister the novelist within a tradition of regional exceptionalism, or to predict his final and ultimate exile from literary debate, has led to the current critical disavowal, perpetuating a profound mishandling of the facts of Wolfe's reputation and influence. My broader aim in this book has been to reinterpret Wolfe from the perspective of an outsider; eschewing what Giles has termed "monolithic national narratives," I have instead advocated for a new critical perspective on Wolfe that seeks to historicize his work within its cultural context and attend to its manifold uses, repositioning the novelist as a globally significant author in light of a series of complex global traversals and exchanges.[3] Following Brian T. Edwards's suggestion that the American "text artifact" must be understood as taking part in an "explosion of de-centerings," this book has also identified the myriad ways in which both Wolfe and his fiction have been used, reworked, reimagined, and even revived, in a conscious attempt to move beyond stable boundaries like "the South" and "America" in order to explore Wolfe's complicated literary legacy.[4]

Another overarching argument of this book is that a vital aspect of Wolfe's writing is his ontology of longing, a sustained and obsessive investigation into the nature of yearning and desire that manifests in his fiction as romance and despair, both of which are infinite and incoherent. By reading Wolfe's fiction in light of my own theorization of the German term *Sehnsucht*, I have argued that such expressions situate his work within both philosophical discourses on the nature of being and various German intellectual and literary traditions, problematizing the countless critical readings that narrowly define the object of Wolfe's longing as something quintessentially "nostalgic" or "American." Beyond being merely a recurring thematic concern of Wolfe's fiction, *Sehnsucht* was also what Wolfe's work evoked for many readers; the book's final chapter linked such expressions of *Sehnsucht* with his enduring appeal for those authors who wrote "under the influence" of Wolfe in their youth, laboring under his literary authority as though it was an addiction. Although *Sehnsucht* has only been discussed in relation to Wolfe and some of his most ardent acolytes, the term also has broader interpretive potential for the analysis of American literature. Going beyond what Jon Smith has described as "circling endlessly around the Lost Loved Object," a "melancholic state [. . .] whose object-cause is infinitely receding," my use of *Sehnsucht* incorporates the inward-focus of longing *for the sake of longing* while always looking forward and outward: *Sehnsucht* is thus a longing addiction that is not directed toward a definable locus-point like *home* but rather one that displaces the very object of desire, existing simultaneously as a pleasure and a torment.[5] While Smith might reply that this is precisely melancholy's "Lacanian drive," whose source of enjoyment, according to Žižek, is the "repetitive movement of this closed circuit," the fundamental nature of *Sehnsucht* is not to endlessly repeat these desires but rather to point toward the possibility of transcendence: in Heidegger's words, to show that "man is something other than only a man."[6]

Conceiving of longing in Wolfe's fiction as something more nearly related to Lévinas's "metaphysical desire," rather than reifying ideas of "memory" or "nostalgia" that, according to Smith, endure as a critical posture in "nearly any work of old southern studies," this discussion of *Sehnsucht* opens up new territory for examining those expressions of loss and desire that abound in American literature—so much so that Carson McCullers saw them as endemic. Indeed, McCullers herself would be an ideal candidate for a critical reassessment in light of *Sehnsucht*: the lonesome Mick Kelly in *The Heart Is a Lonely Hunter* (1940) is constantly beset by an aimless yearning that was "a whole lot worse than being hungry for any dinner, yet it was like that. I want—I want—I want—was all that she could think about—but just what this real want was she did not know."[7] Importantly, this is not to suggest that *Sehnsucht* be merely incorporated into the American literary historian's toolkit, offering another way to express a distinctly national phenomenon. Instead, the very nature of *Sehnsucht* as an infinite, objectless yearning describes a more profoundly human phenomenon, still embedded in a European philosophical and literary tradition but gesturing toward something fundamentally *global*. For Wolfe studies, such a critical repositioning constitutes an essential renunciation of what this book has suggested is an almost single-minded insistence on "American" or "southern" designations. This shift is not intended to devalue these identifiers—in which Wolfe himself had significant investments—but rather to treat such uncritical labels with increased scrutiny.

In highlighting Wolfe's centrality to developing notions of culture during the 1930s, my book has proposed a new path of critical inquiry, treating Wolfe and his fiction as objects of cultural relevance that went far beyond mere aesthetic evaluations. While it important to note Wolfe's frequent tendency to produce turgid and overwrought prose on a large scale, it is also true that his work was widely considered to have constituted the pinnacle of modern American literature by both critics and general readers, an estimation that is clearly visible in the multitude of ways his voice endured, both in America and abroad. By examining the social and intellectual life of the 1930s, it is clear that Wolfe's work intertwined with the mass project of cultural "domestication" as well as with the more rarefied debates around the South and literature's role in politics, since the very act of omitting his writing from the literary canon was imbricated within the process of canon invention. Rather than treating aspects of Wolfe's fiction as inherently American or southern, *Look Abroad, Angel* has demonstrated how these labels were applied to his work within their particular American context: as both a great American hope and spiteful southerner during the early 1930s, as a voice for democracy during the war period, as a swollen rhetorician with the advent of New Criticism, and then rebirthed as a voice of "the South" in the postwar period.

My book's focus on a broader, transnational relationship between Wolfe and Germany reinforces Wolfe's inherently global character, revealing what Dimock describes as the "weaving in and out of other geographies" that American literature always enacts.[8] This reframing of Wolfe is not only crucial in light of an increasingly cloistered critical dialogue around his work but also because it reveals the true status of Wolfe's fiction, repositioning him within what David Damrosch has called world literature's endless "mode of circulation and reading," encompassing literary works that have "circulate[d] beyond their culture of origin [. . .] actively present within a literary system beyond that of its original culture."[9] While I have been predominantly interested in the circulation and reception of Wolfe in Germany in the first half of the twentieth century, it is important to note that since 2009, Manesse Verlag—a German-language publisher—has released four new translations of Wolfe's work: *Oktoberfest* (2010), *Die Party bei den Jacks* (2011), as well as the novels *Schau heimwärts, Engel* (2009) and *Von Zeit und Fluss* (2014).[10] These latter two translations remain the only critically annotated editions of Wolfe's first and second novel in any language.[11] More recently, Oliver Hilmes's *Berlin 1936: Sechzehn Tage im August* (2016)—which relies heavily on Wolfe's final visit to Germany as source material for its creative rendering of a year in Berlin—concludes with the suggestive association of Wolfe's death on September 15, 1938, and Neville Chamberlain's maiden flight on his way to negotiate, unsuccessfully, with Adolf Hitler.[12]

As Brinkmeyer points out, "perhaps no southern writer was influenced as deeply as Thomas Wolfe by the rise of Nazi Germany," and my investigation of this complex and reciprocal relationship sheds light on the interplay between German and American literature during the 1930s and 1940s, extending Moore's claim that Wolfe is an important case study in exploring the American imagining of Nazi Germany.[13] Specifically, my book has contributed to this discussion through two significant interventions: first, by carrying out a detailed examination of Wolfe's indebtedness to German literature and his *Sehnsucht* for an imagined Germany, my book has provided concrete evidence for Wolfe's appropriation of German myths, locating one expression of his longing in an alternate homeland. Moving beyond the regional configuration of Brinkmeyer's *Fourth Ghost*, I have suggested that Wolfe was not only haunted by his "deeply ingrained thoughts and feelings about race [. . .] made manifest in the Nazi system" but also by his reading of such writers as Goethe and Schiller, drawing on a deeply seductive vision of Germany that would similarly come to inform Nazi constructions of *Heimat*.[14]

Look Abroad, Angel has also explored the actual German response to Wolfe, examining his influence and reception among German writers, both in exile and at home. One of the shortcomings of studies arguing for Wolfe's relevance in the study of American literature is their inevitable lack of engagement with non-American writers, instead focusing solely on Wolfe's perspective on Germany as if viewed through a one-way mirror. This strategy links with the wider intention of this book to "look abroad," arguing that one of the most obvious and productive avenues for developing an appreciation of Wolfe's global importance—looking at his overseas reception—remains relatively unexplored. Beyond establishing that Wolfe was an important figure for writers such as Hermann Hesse, Heinrich Böll, and Klaus Mann, among others, this book has also carried out a detailed interpretation of the previously unexamined translation of *You Can't Go Home Again* by Rudolf Frank, opening up discussion around Wolfe's relationship with the literary politics of Germany under National Socialism as well as exploring the potential of such translations, in Einboden's words, as "substitute centres of gravity within this extensive and evolving tradition of reception."[15] In the same way that earlier chapters repositioned Wolfe and his fiction as objects of cultural relevance—deeply implicated in the cultural politics of Depression-era America—tracing this transatlantic relationship has made it possible to illuminate the complex interactions taking place between American and German culture between 1933 and 1945, highlighting Wolfe's privileged and often problematic role in this exchange.

The enduring appeal of Wolfe in the work of writers following his death challenges suggestions of Wolfe's slow descent into insignificance, highlighting the failure of Wolfe critics to recognize the myriad of literary voices that still bear the weight of his influence. Although far from comprehensive, this book has emphatically demonstrated that Wolfe's peripheral status in the critical dialogue does not reflect his surprising recurrence in fictional works, providing a timely intervention in the field just as critics such as McGurl are preparing to dismiss Wolfe as a "footnote."[16] Importantly, my book has also introduced a previously unexamined transpacific axis into the discussion of Wolfe and American literature, examining Wolfe's presence in the work of Christopher

Koch and arguing, along with Giles, for wider acknowledgment of the ways in which the "cultural histories" of Australia and the United States have "long been imbricated within each other."[17] By introducing the hitherto invisible axis of Australia into a discussion of Wolfe, my book thus intersects with a burgeoning field of critical inquiry identified by Dixon and Birns in *Reading across the Pacific*, who suggest that Australian literature, just as American literature, is "best seen in a series of relations with other literatures, not least American."[18] Following on from my argument that Wolfe's ghostly presence should be understood as moving outward in time and space, the final chapter examined Wolfe's "Martian" resurrection, arguing that Ray Bradbury's literary resuscitation of Wolfe—together with his continued recourse to the *Sehnsucht* Wolfe evokes—is evidence of Wolfe's romantic vision extending beyond earthly boundaries and into the realm of science fiction. The study of Wolfe's impact on Koch and Bradbury provides a final example of the range of Wolfe's influence, tracing the "geography" of *Sehnsucht* beyond the hills of North Carolina to the "deep South" of Koch's Tasmania and to the forlorn alien landscape of Bradbury's *Martian Chronicles*.

While Thomas Wolfe currently attracts little sustained debate outside of a single dedicated journal, the reasons for his current obscurity ultimately reflect a complex history of critical treatment that belies many of the actual details of his earliest reception and appropriation—both in America and abroad—as well as the sustained interest in his life and fiction by numerous writers and thinkers. By historicizing Wolfe, theorizing the idea of *Sehnsucht* in his work, attentively tracing his various global connections, contemplating how his work was read and repurposed, and uncovering his ghostly presence in the work of later writers, my book has resituated the novelist as a writer of global significance, whose work not only had, but continues to have, profound relevance for an understanding of American literature that is, in Giles's formulation, "embodied within the orbit of the planet."[19] Interpreting Wolfe in this manner, the phrase "you can't go home again" is not a simple statement about the impossibility of return but a realization that home is not "the South," or "America," or even "*Heimat*"; home is always displaced, always nebulous and uncertain—an indistinct spot on a distant and ever-receding horizon. Like Wolfe, American literature cannot go home again, so long as home is fixed within an exceptionalist framework within inflexibly nationalistic parameters, so long as its yearning is turned inward. This critical reassessment of Wolfe is an attempt at looking both homeward and abroad, altering our interpretive perspective in order to reposition Wolfe as an American novelist of global importance.

NOTES

Introduction

1. "Worst Stock Crash Stemmed by Banks," *New York Times*, October 25, 1929, 1.

2. Meyers, "Hemingway's Achievement."

3. McGurl, *The Program Era*, 79.

4. Idol, "Thomas Wolfe," 20.

5. Barr, "The Dandridges and the Gants," 310.

6. Duck, "What Was the New Southern Studies?"

7. Giles, "Transnationalism and Classic American Literature," 63.

8. Kazin, *On Native Grounds*, 475.

9. The relationship between Wolfe and the South will be the focus of chapter 2, but for a representative discussion of Wolfe as a distinctly "southern" writer see Holman, *The Loneliness at the Core*. For a discussion of Wolfe and literary modernism see Holliday, *Thomas Wolfe and the Politics of Modernism*.

10. Felski, *Uses of Literature*, 8.

11. Felski, *Uses of Literature*, 10.

12. Dimock, "A Theory of Resonance," 1061.

13. Atkinson, *Faulkner and the Great Depression*, 5–7.

14. Dimock, *Through Other Continents*, 3.

15. Ibid., 11.

16. Bone, *The Postsouthern Sense of Place*, 51–52.

17. Lloyd, *Rooting Place, Rooting Memory*, 146. I owe Scott Romine special thanks for this insight on the Agrarians' prediction of forms of longing that have proved relevant and persuasive for writers and scholars interested in the South.

18. Wolfe scholars enjoy reminding people that this famous phrase was pulled from a lecture Wolfe gave at Purdue University titled "Writing and Living" and was only later incorporated into the posthumously released *You Can't Go Home Again* (1940) by the editor, Edward Aswell. Despite this fastidiousness, the sentiment is echoed throughout Wolfe's writing and remains an apt summary of his impossible longing for return.

19. Dontnod Entertainment, *Life Is Strange*.

20. J. Smith, *Finding Purple America*, 35.

21. McCullers, "Look Homeward, Americans," in *The Mortgaged Heart*, 217.

22. Even in studies that sought to link *Sehnsucht* with the expression of ideas like "lostness" and desire in American literature, *Sehnsucht* is treated as a useful descriptive term for a distinctly American phenomenon, severing the German Romantic heritage of the word and treating it instead as an expression of a more nuanced form of spiritual longing. See, for example, Kehl, "Writing the Long Desire," 309–19. For a similar simplification of *Sehnsucht* as the "key to the secret of life" see Bitzer, "*Sehnsucht*." More recently, Joseph Grant Bain has argued that Wolfe's vision of alienated and "lost" individuals ties the novelist to a distinctly southern mode of gothic fiction. See Bain, "Disturbing Signs," 86–111.

23. S. Stewart, *On Longing*, x.

24. Lévinas, *Totality and Infinity*, 34.

25. Wolfe, *Of Time and the River*, 90.

26. *Oxford English Dictionary Online*, 2nd ed., s.v. "long, v.1."

27. *Oxford English Dictionary Online*, 2nd ed., s.v. "longing, n.1."

28. Drew M. Dalton, *Longing for the Other*, 6.

29. *Oxford English Dictionary Online*, 2nd ed., s.v. "long, v.1."

30. *American Heritage Dictionary of the English Language*, 4th ed., s.v. "longing."

31. Matt, *Homesickness*, 5–6.

32. Flatley, *Affective Mapping*, 28.

33. J. Allen, *Homelessness in American Literature*, 4.

34. Twain, *Adventures of Huckleberry Finn*, 99–100.

35. Matt, *Homesickness*, 194–95.

36. For examples of this see Mishra, *Loneliness in Modern American Fiction*; Whalen, "Home and Homelessness"; Brown, "The Road Home," 23–48; George, *The Politics of Home*; and J. Allen, *Homelessness in American Literature*.

37. Wolfe, *Of Time and the River*, 856.

38. Ibid., 857, 869.

39. Schneidau, *Walking Giants*, 182.

40. The figure of "the South" in Wolfe, and the critical tradition that has branded Wolfe as a regionalist writer, will be explored at length in chapter 2. For a discussion of home and uprootedness, see Jackson, *At Home in the World*.

41. Wolfe, *Look Homeward, Angel*, 522, 527.

42. Wolfe, *Of Time and the River*, 858.

43. Wolfe, *The Starwick Episodes*, 62.

44. Canby, "The River of Youth," 529–30.

45. Matt, *Homesickness*, 5.

46. Boym, *The Future of Nostalgia*, 6.

47. Matt, *Homesickness*, 5.

48. Starobinski, "The Idea of Nostalgia," 85.

49. Boym, *The Future of Nostalgia*, 3.

50. Ibid., 12.

51. Bishop, "The Sorrows of Thomas Wolfe," 13.

52. Boym, *The Future of Nostalgia*, xiii; McCullers, "Look Homeward, Americans," in *The Mortgaged Heart*, 217; "Thomas Wolfe from North Carolina," interview by Marion L. Starkey, in *Thomas Wolfe Interviewed*, 16.

53. Fiedler, *Love and Death*, 469, 470.

54. M. Roth, *Memory, Trauma, and History*, 30–31. For further discussion of nostalgia as pathology see Austin, *Nostalgia in Transition*.

55. MacDonell, "Alley-Ways of America," 6; DeVoto, "Genius Is Not Enough," 4. For a psychological treatment of Wolfe's longing see Mijuskovic, *Loneliness*. For a recent psychoanalytical treatment see Hamilton, *Life and Art*, 253–82.

56. Wolfe, *Of Time and the River*, 541–42, 606.

57. Ibid., 139, 706.

58. For examples of this rehabilitation of nostalgia see Lowenthal, *The Past Is a Foreign Country*; Boym, *The Future of Nostalgia*; Funchion, "Divisible Pasts"; Malpas, "Philosophy's Nostalgia," 87–101; Duyvendak, *The Politics of Home*; M. Roth, *Memory, Trauma, and History*; Illbruck, *Nostalgia*; and Lowenthal, "Nostalgic Dreams and Nightmares," 28–54.

59. Scott, "You Can't Go Home Again," 7.

60. J. Smith, *Finding Purple America*, 30.

61. Heidegger, *The Fundamental Concepts of Metaphysics*, 5; Heidegger, *Hölderlin's Hymn "The Ister,"* 49.

62. Schelling, *Philosophical Investigations*, 29–30.

63. Ibid., 29–30, 124. For further discussion of Schelling's use of *Sehnsucht* see Wirth, *The Conspiracy of Life*.

64. Clark, "Heidegger's Cravings," 16.

65. Heidegger, *Schelling's Treatise*, 125.

66. Heidegger, "*Bauen, wohnen, denken*," quoted and translated in Blickle, *Critical Theory*, 7.

67. *Deutsches Wörterbuch Online*, s.v. "Sehnen."

68. *Deutsches Wörterbuch Online*, s.v. "Sucht."

69. Norman, "A Rare Form of Mental Disease (Grübelsucht)," 62.

70. James, "II.—On the Function of Cognition," 37.

71. Hesse, "Thomas Wolfe," 346–47.

72. Ibid., 349.

73. W. O'Brien, *Novalis*, 111. Frederick C. Beiser notes that "[o]ne of the most remarkable traits of [. . .] German romantics was their belief in the metaphysical stature of art." See Beiser, *The Romantic Imperative*, 73.

74. Baker, "Loss and Expectation," 64.

75. Helmreich, "Sehnsucht," in Apter and Cassin, *Dictionary of Untranslatables*, 940.

76. Wurth, "The Musicality of the Past," 222.

77. Wolfe, *Look Homeward, Angel*, 345, Wolfe's italics. This translation is from Goethe, *Wilhelm Meister's Apprenticeship*, 83. All subsequent references in English are from this version, which uses Hal Draper's 1989 translations of the two songs of Mignon that are explored in this book.

78. Gaston, *Impossible Mourning*, 66.

79. Ibid., 67–68, 66.

80. Wurth, *Musically Sublime*, 48, 49.

81. Hoffmann, *Life and Opinions*, 53–54.

82. Wolfe, *Of Time and the River*, 857.

83. Bergo, "The Birth Pangs of the Absolute," 106–7.

84. Woenesser, *Heidegger in America*, 279.

85. Hegeman, *Patterns for America*.

Chapter 1. Unearthing the Buried Life

1. Maxwell Perkins to Thomas Wolfe, August 28, 1930, in *Editor to Author*, 70.

2. For two brief mentions of Wolfe in studies of Depression fiction see Cashman, *America in the Twenties and Thirties*, 120–23, and Solomon, *Literature, Amusement, and Technology*, 244n.34, 248n.29.

3. Wolfe, *Look Homeward, Angel*, 2.

4. For examples of this see Wolfe, *O Lost*, ed. Arlyn and Matthew J. Bruccoli; Bruccoli and Bucker, *To Loot My Life Clean*; T. Mitchell, *Thomas Wolfe*; Mauldin, *When Do the Atrocities Begin?*; Wolfe, *The Four Lost Men*, ed. Arlyn and Matthew J. Bruccoli.

5. McGurl, *The Program Era*, 15.

6. Johnston, *Thomas Wolfe*, 9–10.

7. Donald, *Look Homeward*, 222. The actual sales figures of *A Farewell to Arms* (1929) were even more impressive. Published in late September 1929, the book had sold 33,000 copies by October 22, 1929. See Wagner-Martin, *Ernest Hemingway's A Farewell to Arms*, 43.

8. West, *American Authors*, 108.

9. Parker, "The Artist's Reward," 28.

10. Wallace, "A Novel of Provincial American Life," 4.

11. Fearing, "A First Novel of Vast Scope."

12. Latimer, "The New American Family," 21.

13. Wallace, "A Novel of Provincial American Life," 4.

14. Turnbull, *Thomas Wolfe*, 150.

15. Fearing, "A First Novel of Vast Scope." Fearing had published his first collection of poems, *Angel Arms* (1929), that same year.

16. Stutman, *My Other Loneliness*, 146.

17. Display Ad 166, "Look Homeward, Angel," *New York Times*, January 12, 1930, 71.

18. Ibid., emphasis mine.

19. Gardner, *Reviewing the South*, 2.

20. Gardner, *Reviewing the South*, 5.

21. "Recent Publications," *Scribner's Catalogue* (Spring 1930), in *To Loot My Life Clean*, 31.

22. Wolfe, "To the Reader," in *Look Homeward, Angel*, n.p.

23. Adams, "Amazing New Novel," 1.

24. Ibid.

25. Donald, *Look Homeward*, 216; Turnbull, *Thomas Wolfe*, 146.

26. McGurl, *The Program Era*, 82.

27. Thomas Wolfe to Julia Wolfe, November 6, 1929, in *The Letters of Thomas Wolfe to His Mother*, 155.

28. Ibid., 155–56.

29. See McGurl, *The Program Era*, 77–125. This argument will be more fully addressed in chapter 5, looking particularly at Wolfe's legacy in the work of later writers.

30. Dewey, "Individualism, Old and New," 123.

31. Hegeman, *Patterns for America*, 3. For further discussion of the development of ideas of culture in America during this period, also see Bradley, *Making American Culture*.

32. Susman, *Culture as History*, 154.

33. J. DeForest, "The Great American Novel."

34. Maxwell Perkins to Thomas Wolfe, June 3, 1930, in *Editor to Author*, 68.

35. Butcher, "Best Sellers of Year," 14, emphasis mine.

36. "Books and Yet More Books for the Christmas Buyer: A List of Suggestions for Those Who Will Solve the Holiday Problem in the Good Old Way," *New York Times Book Review*, December 1, 1929, 7.

37. C. Wilson, *The Labor of Words*, 2.

38. Butcher, "Best Sellers of Year," 14.

39. West, *American Authors*, 124.

40. "PUBLISHING: Mass-Produced Culture," *Time* 47, no. 11 (March 18, 1946): 80.

41. Hellman, review of *Look Homeward, Angel*, by Thomas Wolfe, 122.

42. Wolfe, *Look Homeward, Angel: A Story of the Buried Life* (London: Heinemann, 1930).

43. Wolfe, *Schau heimwärts, Engel!: eine Geschichte vom begrabnen Leben*, trans. Hans

Schiebelhuth (Berlin: Rowohlt, 1932); Wolfe, *Look Homeward, Angel: A Story of the Buried Life* (New York: Modern Library, 1934).

44. Satterfield, *The World's Best Books*, 2.

45. "The literary or artistic field is at all times the site of a struggle between the two principles of hierarchization: the heteronomous principle, favourable to those who dominate the field economically and politically (e.g. 'bourgeois art') and the autonomous principle (e.g. 'art for art's sake'), which those of its advocates who are least endowed with specific capital tend to identify with a degree of independence from the economy, seeing temporal failure as a sign of election and success as a sign of compromise." Bourdieu, "The Field of Cultural Production," 40.

46. Satterfield, *The World's Best Books*, 137.

47. Ibid., 126. Anderson's *Winesburg, Ohio* (1919) was also released in a Modern Library edition in 1922.

48. Thomas Wolfe to Julia Wolfe, March 8, 1934, in *The Letters of Thomas Wolfe to His Mother*, 223.

49. Johnston, *Thomas Wolfe*, 11. For further discussion of the American literary marketplace in the first part of the twentieth century, see West III, *American Authors*.

50. Gurko, *The Angry Decade*, 29.

51. Miss Stella F. Brewster to Thomas Wolfe, January 29, 1934, bMS Am 1883.1 (729), William B. Wisdom Collection of Thomas Wolfe, Houghton Library, Harvard University.

52. Mrs. Dorothy C. Carroll to Thomas Wolfe, September 8, 1935, bMS Am 1883.1 (729), William B. Wisdom Collection of Thomas Wolfe, Houghton Library, Harvard University.

53. William Cooke to Thomas Wolfe, undated, bMS Am 1883.1 (729), William B. Wisdom Collection of Thomas Wolfe, Houghton Library, Harvard University; Jemima Saiz to Thomas Wolfe, July 26, 1933, bMS Am 1883.1 (729), William B. Wisdom Collection of Thomas Wolfe, Houghton Library, Harvard University.

54. Lily Anne Hough to Thomas Wolfe, July 5, 1936, bMS Am 1883.1 (729), William B. Wisdom Collection of Thomas Wolfe, Houghton Library, Harvard University.

55. Blair, "Main Street Reading *Main Street*," 145.

56. Eleanor Bodkin to Thomas Wolfe, November 30, 1936, bMS Am 1883.1 (729), William B. Wisdom Collection of Thomas Wolfe, Houghton Library, Harvard University.

57. Luiz Calero to Thomas Wolfe, May 20, 1945, bMS Am 1883.1 (730), William B. Wisdom Collection of Thomas Wolfe, Houghton Library, Harvard University.

58. Nancy Tubiash to Thomas Wolfe, March 16, 1935, bMS Am 1883.1 (729), William B. Wisdom Collection of Thomas Wolfe, Houghton Library, Harvard University.

59. Lessing, "Thomas Wolfe, Myth-Maker," 9.

60. Jack Kerouac, journal entry, holograph notebook "1940" (53.1), Jack Kerouac Papers, Henry W. and Albert A. Berg Collection of English and American Literature, New York Public Library.

61. Kerouac, "The Minimization of Thomas Wolfe," 71.

62. Ibid., 75–76.

63. Jack Kerouac, typescript essay, untitled (7.11), Jack Kerouac Papers, Henry W. and Albert A. Berg Collection of English and American Literature, New York Public Library.

64. Kerouac, "The Minimization of Thomas Wolfe," 75–76.

65. Brinkley, introduction to *The Town and the City*.

66. Kerouac, *On the Road*, 48.

67. Berrigan, "Interview with Jack Kerouac," in Plimpton, *Beat Writers at Work*, 117.

68. Wolfe, *Of Time and the River*, 623.

69. M. Bradbury, *The Modern American Novel*, 60–61.

70. Thomas Wolfe to Sherwood Anderson, September 22, 1937, in *The Letters of Thomas Wolfe*, 656.

71. Wolfe, *Look Homeward, Angel*, 442.

72. For a discussion of Lewis's fading star, particularly in relation to New Criticism, see Hutchisson, *The Rise of Sinclair Lewis*, 2–8.

73. Hutchisson, *The Rise of Sinclair Lewis*, 2.

74. DeVoto, "Review of *Arrowsmith*," quoted in Schorer, "Sinclair Lewis," in *Seven Modern American Novelists*, 58.

75. Schorer, "Sinclair Lewis," 67.

76. S. Lewis, "Nobel Lecture."

77. Ibid., emphasis mine.

78. Wolfe, *You Can't Go Home Again*, 537–39.

79. Furthermore, as H. M. Ledig-Rowohlt writes, Lewis had "drawn his German publisher's attention to the young writer's work, and Ernst Rowohlt had eagerly accepted Wolfe's novel after another important Berlin house had just turned it down." Ledig-Rowohlt, "Thomas Wolfe in Berlin," 185. The significance of Wolfe's reception in Germany will be discussed in subsequent chapters.

80. Cowley, *And I Worked*, 96.

81. Deleuze and Guattari, *What Is Philosophy?*, 171–72.

82. S. Lewis, "Press Conference," 27.

83. William Saroyan to Thomas Wolfe, December 31, 1935, bMS Am 1883.1 (568), William B. Wisdom Collection of Thomas Wolfe, Houghton Library, Harvard University.

84. "Books and Authors," *New York Times Book Review*, April 26, 1931, 6.

85. Thomas Wolfe to Maxwell Perkins, July 31, 1930, in *The Letters of Thomas Wolfe*, 246.

86. Aldington, "American Novelists," 6.

87. Ibid.

88. Ibid.

89. See particularly Rothman, "Thomas Wolfe and James Joyce," 52–77; Church, "Thomas Wolfe," 85–104; Durr, "*Look Homeward, Angel*," 54–68; Harper, *The Aristocracy of Art*; and Holliday, *Thomas Wolfe*.

90. Unsigned review of *Look Homeward, Angel*, by Thomas Wolfe, *Times Literary Supplement*, July 24, 1930, 608.

91. DeVoto, "Genius Is Not Enough," 3.

92. Hugh Walpole, interview by H. Allen Smith, January 7, 1930, quoted in *The Letters of Thomas Wolfe*, 222.

93. For a discussion of Walpole in the United States see Steele, *Sir Hugh Walpole*.

94. Thomas Wolfe to Maxwell Perkins, March 31, 1935, in *To Loot My Life Clean*, 139.

95. Ibid., 139–40.

96. Cross, "The Secret City," 315–16.

97. Thomas Wolfe to Maxwell Perkins, March 31, 1935, in *To Loot My Life Clean*, 140. For a discussion of the rise of "middlebrow" literature see Humble, *The Feminine Middlebrow Novel*.

98. Leavis, *Fiction and the Reading Public*, 22–24.

99. Humble, *The Feminine Middlebrow Novel*, 45.

100. "Obituaries," *The Times*, June 2, 1941, 6.

101. An exception to Walpole's out-of-print work is the recently reissued four volumes of *The Herries Chronicle* by publishing house Frances Lincoln, the latest of which was released in November 2011. An example of one of the very few recent pieces of critical work on Walpole is the excellent article by Nicola Wilson, "Virginia Woolf, Hugh Walpole, the Hogarth Press, and the Book Society," 237–60, which explores the rather unexpected relationship between Woolf and Walpole, including the involvement of Hogarth Press with the Book Society and, more broadly, the relationship between highbrow and middlebrow literary culture in 1930s Britain.

102. Humble, *The Feminine Middlebrow Novel*, 1.

103. Woolf, *The Death of the Moth*, 115.

104. Humble, *The Feminine Middlebrow Novel*, 2–3.

105. Cowley, *Exile's Return*, 289.

106. Cowley, "The Forty Days of Thomas Wolfe," 163–64.

107. Cowley, *Exile's Return*, 9.

108. Ibid., 292.

109. Young, "In Search of a Lost Generation," in *American Fiction, American Myth*, 208.

110. For further discussion of the ambiguity of this term see Dolan, *Modern Lives*. For a discussion of the sometimes overlooked relationship between Wolfe and Paris in the 1920s, see Thurner, "'It Is Evil,'" 289–310.

111. Monk, *Writing the Lost Generation*, 3.

112. See, for example, Cowley, *Exile's Return*; McCormick, *American Literature*;, Dolan, *Modern Lives*; Fitch, *Sylvia Beach and the Lost Generation*; and Monk, *Writing the Lost Generation*.

113. Monk, *Writing the Lost Generation*, 4, 10.

114. Thomas Wolfe to Alfred Dashiell, November 1930, in *To Loot My Life Clean*, 61–62.

115. In a recent work comparing American expatriate understanding of exile and the experience of Palestinians following the creation of the Israeli state, Ahmad Rasmi Qabaha points out that the authenticity of Wolfe's attachment to America was gauged through his *choice* of exile. See Qabaha, *Exile and Expatriation*, 171.

116. Lerner, *America as a Civilization*, 791.

117. Lerner, *America as a Civilization*, 949.

118. Wolfe, "A Letter on Homelessness," Series I. bMS Am 1883 (1126), William B. Wisdom Collection of Thomas Wolfe, Houghton Library, Harvard University.

119. Wolfe, *Autobiography*, 105.

120. I'm indebted to Scott Romine for pointing out this distinction between the two authors' peculiar forms of longing. Romine further suggested Fitzgerald's longing might be directed in such a way because of the author's consumerist poetics. It is difficult to say whether this accounts, at least in part, for Fitzgerald's enduring popularity.

121. Frow, "Tourism and the Semiotics of Nostalgia," 135.

122. Wolfe, *Of Time and the River*, 859.

123. Rabinowicz, *American Pulp*, 128.

124. For this discussion see Davis, *Two-Bit Culture;* and Cole, *Books in Action*.

125. Rabinowicz, *American Pulp*, 129–30.

126. Hench, *Books as Weapons*, 52.

127. Ibid., 2.

128. Ibid., 4–5.

129. Holliday, *Thomas Wolfe*, 127.

130. Kazin, *On Native Grounds*, ix.

131. Wolfe, *Of Time and the River*, 160; Kazin, *On Native Grounds*, ix.

132. Kazin, *On Native Grounds*, 475.

133. Wheelock, introduction to *The Face of a Nation*, v.

134. CBS to Maxwell Perkins, May 16, 1939, bMS Am 1883.12, William B. Wisdom Collection of Thomas Wolfe, Houghton Library, Harvard University.

135. Wolfe, *Of Time and the River*, 155.

136. Wolfe, "The Face of America," 143.

137. Stokes, "Thomas Wolfe in Nazi Concentration Camps," 27.

138. M. Moore, *Know Your Enemy*, xiii.

139. "Novels of the Day," *Sydney Morning Herald*, September 5, 1930, 7.

140. This rather prudish sensitivity was reflected in policy by the Irish Free State Censorship Board, which banned Wolfe's novel in 1931. The *New York Times Book Review* adds ironically that "somebody must have told the board that the book is not so devotional as its title might lead one to believe." See "Books and Authors," *New York Times Book Review*, April 26, 1931, 8.

141. "Books of the Week," *Brisbane Courier*, October 4, 1930, 20.

142. "America and Her Writers," *Queenslander*, December 17, 1931, 44.

143. "Some Recent Fiction," *West Australian*, September 13, 1930, 4.

144. Zacharasiewicz, *Images of Germany*; Brinkmeyer, *The Fourth Ghost*.

145. This positioning of the book's argument intersects with recent interests in the transpacific connections of U.S. literature, most comprehensively explored by Paul Giles in *Antipodean America* (2013) and discussed at length in chapter 5.

146. Kodaira and Tsunemoto, *Studies in Thomas Wolfe*; Wang, "Thomas Wolfe Studies in China," 138–41, 235.

147. Gellert, "Sensitive Giant," 8.

148. "Look Homeward, Angel," *Goulburn Evening Post*, March 20, 1945, 1; Douglas Wilkie, "As I See It," *Advertiser* (Adelaide, SA), May 9, 1950, 2.

149. For an extended discussion of Wolfe's influence on Koch as well as on the Australian poet Dorothy Hewett, see Evans, "Thomas Wolfe," 7–24.

150. McGurl, *The Program Era*, 80–81.

151. Ibid., 79–80.

152. Ibid., 125.

153. Ibid., xi.

154. It is important here to mention Faulkner's clarification of his original statement—which he often repeated in letters and interviews—that he rated Wolfe first because "we were all failures" and "I rated the authors on the basis of their splendid failure to do the impossible." See Schmidt, *The Novel*, 763–64.

155. Jameson, "Dirty Little Secret," 39.

Chapter 2. Homesick for Unknown Places

1. Wolfe, "Notes from the Harvard Years," in *The Notebooks of Thomas Wolfe*, 5.

2. Mencken, "The Sahara of the Bozart," 143.

3. Wolfe, "Notes from the Harvard Years," 7.

4. Woodard, *The Burden of Southern History*, 28–29.

5. Kreyling, *Inventing Southern Literature.*

6. J. Smith, *Finding Purple America*, 35.

7. One example of this is the previously mentioned special issue of *Appalachian Heritage* from 2007, which was dedicated to Thomas Wolfe's enduring legacy as a regional author in southern Appalachia. See Holliday, "Thomas Wolfe (1900–1938)," 8–71.

8. Woodard, *The Burden of Southern History*, 27–31.

9. Denning, *The Cultural Front*, 35.

10. Mencken, "The Sahara of the Bozart," 136.

11. Duck, *The Nation's Region*, 7.

12. McPherson, *Reconstructing Dixie*, 9–10.

13. Twelve Southerners, *I'll Take My Stand*, 1.

14. Duck, *The Nation's Region*, 61.

15. Ibid., 245.

16. Donald, *Look Homeward*, 359.

17. See Davidson, *Regionalism and Nationalism.*

18. Donaldson, introduction to *I'll Take My Stand*, xxxii.

19. Davidson, "Farewell—and Hail!"

20. Davidson, *Regionalism and Nationalism*, 12.

21. Greeson, "The 'Mysteries and Miseries' of North Carolina," 285.

22. Gardner, *Reviewing the South*, 52.

23. Davidson, "Farewell—and Hail!"

24. Wolfe, *Look Homeward, Angel*, 589.

25. Davidson, "Farewell—and Hail!"

26. Donald Davidson to Allen Tate, July 29, 1929, in *The Literary Correspondence of Donald Davidson and Allen Tate*, 228.

27. Kreyling, *Inventing Southern Literature*, 9–10.

28. Wolfe, *Look Homeward, Angel*, 626.

29. John Duvall notes that, while the *Southern Review* was losing money by the time it ceased publication in 1942, the journal was known early on for "publishing some of the best fiction and poetry of its day." Importantly, the editor often only accepted "certain kinds of writing" that conformed to his regionalist project. See Duvall, "New Criticism's Major Journals," 931.

30. Wade, "The Life and Death of Cousin Lucius," in *I'll Take My Stand*, 265–301.

31. Wolfe, *Of Time and the River*, 23–24.

32. Wade, "Prodigal," in *Thomas Wolfe: The Critical Reception*, 70. See Ransom, *God without Thunder.*

33. Wade, "Prodigal," 72.

34. Wolfe, *Of Time and the River*, 114.

35. Ibid.

36. Ibid., 366–67; Wade, "Prodigal," 73.

37. Wade, "Prodigal," 74.

38. McCullers, "Loneliness . . . An American Malady," in *The Mortgaged Heart*, 285.

39. McCullers, "Look Homeward, Americans," in *The Mortgaged Heart*, 217.

40. Whisnant, *All That Is Native and Fine*, 7, 260.

41. Romine, *The Real South*, 2–3.

42. M. O'Brien, "Place as Everywhere," 271–73.

43. Thomas Wolfe to Dixon Wecter, March 5, 1937, in *The Letters of Thomas Wolfe*, 613.

44. Thomas Wolfe to Stark Young, March 7, 1936, in *The Letters of Thomas Wolfe*, 495.

45. Donald, *Look Homeward*, 361.

46. Wolfe, *The Web and the Rock*, 228.

47. Ibid., 229.

48. Grammer, "Reconstructing Southern Literature," 129.

49. Wolfe, *The Web and the Rock*, 230.

50. Mencken, "The South Astir," quoted in *American Georgics*, 285.

51. Wolfe, *The Web and the Rock*, 230.

52. Ibid., 231. Jonathan Daniels wrote that in *Look Homeward, Angel*, "North Carolina, and the South are spat upon." See Daniels, "Wolfe's First Is Novel of Revolt," 2.

53. M. O'Brien, "Place as Everywhere," 272, 288.

54. Wolfe, *Of Time and the River*, 808.

55. Tate and Bishop, *American Harvest*, 10.

56. Underwood, "Autobiography and Ideology," 35.

57. Bishop, "The Sorrows of Thomas Wolfe," 17.

58. Tate and Bishop, *American Harvest*, 16–17; *History of the Office of the Coordinator of Inter-American Affairs*, 94.

59. Richard, *Censorship and Hollywood's Hispanic Image*, 274.

60. Allen Tate to John Peale Bishop, July 22, 1942, in *The Republic of Letters*, ed. Young and Hindle, 189.

61. Wolfe, *Of Time and the River*, 859.

62. CBS Radio Workshop, "1489 Words," February 10, 1957.

63. This section of Wolfe's work was also collected as "The Names of the Nation" in Carl Van Doren's *An Anthology of World Prose* (1935), and a truncated section was included in John Bartlett's collection *Familiar Quotations* (1937), of which Wolfe owned a copy. See Wolfe, "The Names of the Nation," in *An Anthology of World Prose*, ed. Carl Van Doren, 1158–1562; and "Thomas Wolfe," in *Familiar Quotations*, ed. John Bartlett, 932–33.

64. The line "Blow, bugle, blow, set the wild echoes flying" is from Tennyson's long narrative poem *The Princess*, which was originally published in 1847 but had the "Bugle song" added in the 1850 edition. See Alfred Tennyson, *The Princess* (London: Edward Moxon, 1850).

65. Wolfe, *Of Time and the River*, 868. The line "Sweete *Themmes* runne softly, till I end my Song" is from *Prothalamion* (1596). See Edmund Spenser, *Prothalamion or A Spousall Verse Made by Edm. Spenser*, 2.

66. Wolfe, *Of Time and the River*, 868.

67. Ibid., 869.

68. Ibid., 868.

69. Wolfe included a list of "potential fascist literary groups and individuals" in a notebook that included the Southern Agrarians. See Wolfe, "Pocket Notebook 32" [n.d.], in *The Notebooks of Thomas Wolfe*, 887.

70. Reeves, *Thomas Wolfe's Albatross*, 6.

71. Brinkmeyer, *The Fourth Ghost*, 151.

72. Wolfe, *You Can't Go Home Again*, 740, 175.

73. Wolfe, *The Web and the Rock*, 36–37.

74. "ON MURDERER'S TRAIL," *Washington Post*, November 15, 1906, 3.

75. Epstein, "Urban Governance and Tolerance," 689.

76. "OUTLAW DIES FIGHTING," *Washington Post*, November 16, 1906, 1.

77. Wolfe, "The Child by Tiger," in *The Complete Short Stories of Thomas Wolfe*, 345.

78. "Harris Not Lynched," *Washington Post*, January 9, 1907, 11.

79. Finnegan, *A Deed So Accursed*, 132.

80. Wolfe, "The Child by Tiger," 348.

81. Sitkoff, *A New Deal for Blacks*, 59; Wolfe, *You Can't Go Home Again*, 743; *New York Herald Tribune*, September 29, 1941.

82. White, *A Rising Wind*.

83. Brinkmeyer, *The Fourth Ghost*, 152.

84. Stern, *Eugenic Nation*, 16; Wolff, *Mendel's Theatre*, 3.

85. In *Defending the Master Race* (2009), Jonathan Spiro notes: "With Nordicism becoming so popular in American society, it did not take long for leading politicians to associate themselves with the movement. [. . .] In October of 1921, President Harding publicly endorsed Stoddard's *Rising Tide of Color* in a major speech in Birmingham, Alabama." See Spiro, *Defending the Master Race*, 177–78.

86. "Want More Babies in Best Families," *New York Times*, September 25, 1921, 16.

87. Mehler, "History," 40.

88. Kühl, *The Nazi Connection*, 20–21.

89. Stoddard, *Into the Darkness*, 190.

90. Stoddard, "How to Keep Out," 327–21; Thomas Wolfe, "The Sun and the Rain," 358–59.

91. Fitzgerald, *The Great Gatsby*, 13.

92. J. Higham, *Strangers in the Land*, 265.

93. English, *Unnatural Selections*, 14. For a discussion of the lingering policy implications of the American eugenics movement see Ordover, *American Eugenics*.

94. For examples of this see Cobb, *Away Down South;* and Duck, *The Nation's Region*.

95. Duck, *The Nation's Region*, 7.

96. McPherson, *Reconstructing Dixie*, 11.

97. Duck, *The Nation's Region*, 7.

98. Barr, "The Dandridges and the Gants," 310.

99. Geismar called it simply "the accident of birth." See Geismar, *Writers in Crisis*, 196. For a refutation of Geismar's statement that reinforces Wolfe's "southern" status, see Gray, *The Literature of Memory*, 133–34.

100. Kreyling, *Inventing Southern Literature*, xxii; Greeson, *Our South*, 3.

101. Barr, "The Dandridges and the Gants," 310.

102. Ibid., 313.

103. Cash, *The Mind of the South*, 379.

104. R. King, "Allegories of Imperialism," 148.

105. See, for example, McKee and Trefzer, preface to "Global Contexts, Local Literatures"; Duck, *The Nation's Region*; Romine, *The Real South*; Stecopoulos, *Reconstructing the World*; Greeson, *Our South*; and J. Smith, *Finding Purple America*.

106. McKee and Trefzer, "Global Contexts, Local Literatures," 678.

107. Greeson, *Our South*, 10, 1.

108. Ibid., 2, 291n.3.

109. Stecopoulos, *Reconstructing the World*, 8.

110. Duck, *The Nation's Region*, 9.

111. Kreyling, "Toward 'A New Southern Studies,'" 5.

112. Kreyling, *The South That Wasn't There*, x, 2.

113. J. Smith, *Finding Purple America*, 30.

114. Benson, *Disturbing Calculations*, 48–49, 51.

115. T. Powell, *The Intellectual*, 15.

116. Greeson, *Our South*, 4.

117. Starkey, "Thomas Wolfe from North Carolina," 16–17.

118. McCullers, "Look Homeward, Americans," in *The Mortgaged Heart*, 217.

119. For a study of homesickness in American culture see Matt, *Homesickness*. For studies on nostalgia see particularly Starobinski, "The Idea of Nostalgia," 81–103; Boym, *The Future of Nostalgia*; and M. Roth, *Memory, Trauma, and History*.

120. Wolfe, *Of Time and the River*, 601.

121. Heidegger, *Schelling's Treatise*, 124.

122. Heidegger, *Hölderlin's Hymn "The Ister,"* 49.

123. Wolfe, *You Can't Go Home Again*, quoted in Bloch, *The Principle of Hope*, 3:1370.

Chapter 3. "The Measureless Realm of Elfland"

1. Thomas Wolfe to Maxwell Perkins, May 23, 1935, in *To Loot My Life Clean*, 160.

2. Thomas Wolfe to Aline Bernstein, November 8, 1926, in *My Other Loneliness*, 118.

3. Brinkmeyer, *The Fourth Ghost*, 146.

4. M. Moore, *Know Your Enemy*, xiii.

5. Zacharasiewicz, *Images of Germany*, 105, 113.

6. Bloch, *The Principle of Hope*, 3:1376.

7. It is important to recognize that Bloch's idea of grasping oneself—the self-encounter—is tied to his Marxist politics. Alina Vaisfeld notes that the "homeland" of Bloch implies "social justice [. . .] married to an openness to change and to the future," rather than a more mystical or nationalistic conception of a "German" homeland located in a mythic past. See Vaisfeld, "Ernst Bloch," 75.

8. For a discussion of *Heimat* in German cinema, see Moltke, *No Place Like Home;* and Strzelczyk, "Far Away, So Close," 109–10.

9. Confino, *Germany as a Culture of Remembrance*, 27–28.

10. Applegate, *A Nation of Provincials*, 6.

11. For a detailed discussion of *Heimat* also see Boa and Palfreyman, *Heimat*; Blickle, *Heimat;* Eigler and Kugele, *Heimat;* and Szejnmann and Umbach, *Heimat, Region, and Empire*.

12. Szejnmann and Umbach, introduction to *Heimat, Region, and Empire*, 7.

13. Higgs, Manning, and Miller, *Appalachia Inside Out*, xv.

14. Ibid., 313, xv.

15. Applegate, "Senses of Place," 49–50.

16. Szejnmann and Umbach, *Heimat, Region, and Empire*, 4.

17. Wolfe, "Pocket Notebook 3, August 24, 1928," in *Notebooks*, 166.

18. Szejnmann and Umbach, *Heimat, Region, and Empire*, 2.

19. Wolfe, *Of Time and the River*, 29.

20. Lukács, *Soul and Form*, 111.

21. Hönnighausen, "European Culture in Southern Literature," 38–39. Klaus Lanzinger notes that the Rhine, for Wolfe, was "the very essence of the romantic fairyland image of Germany." See Lanzinger, *Jason's Voyage*, 182.

22. A representative example can be found in *Thomas Wolfe and the Politics of Modernism*: "Even though Wolfe loved Germany and acknowledged it as his ancestral home, he felt

he had no choice but to choose the idealism of American democracy over ruthless Nazi ideology." Holliday, *Thomas Wolfe and the Politics of Modernism*, 76. Also see Field, "Thomas Wolfe's Attitudes," 180–85; Strauss, "You Can't Go Home Again," 107–16; Meindl, "Thomas Wolfe and Germany," 6–23, 207; and Godwin, "You Can't Go Home Again," 24–31, 206.

23. Brinkmeyer, *The Fourth Ghost*, 166.

24. Wolfe, *The Web and the Rock*, 611.

25. Ibid. Wolfe uses the German word "*Unendlichkeit*," which translates as infinity.

26. Wolfe, "Dark in the Forest, Strange as Time," 275–76.

27. Stein, "Musical Settings," 125–26. The English translation of the lines is from Goethe, *Wilhelm Meister's Apprenticeship*, translated by Eric A. Blackall and Victor Lange (1995).

28. Hoffmann, "Beethoven's Instrumental Music," 96.

29. Ibid., 98, 102.

30. Thomas Wolfe to Aline Bernstein, November 25, 1928, in *My Other Loneliness*, 280.

31. Wolfe, *Look Homeward, Angel*, 345.

32. Ibid., 593.

33. Ibid., 592–93.

34. Thomas Wolfe to John Hall Wheelock, July 23, 1929, in *To Loot My Life Clean*, 19–20.

35. Wolfe's Everyman's Library copy of Carlyle's translation of *Wilhelm Meister's Apprenticeship* is held at the Houghton Library, Harvard University.

36. Goethe, *The Sufferings of Young Werther*, 8. For a study of Wolfe's novels as bildungsromans see Kohl, *The Wilhelm Meister Pebble*.

37. Stein, "Musical Settings," 125.

38. Goethe, *Wilhelm Meister's Apprenticeship*, 83.

39. Wolfe, *Of Time and the River*, 24.

40. Coleridge was also taken by the beauty of *Kennst du das Land* and had produced a translation of the first two stanzas before apparently giving up—the only translation from *Wilhelm Meister* he attempted. See Mays, *Poetical Works I*, 1017–18.

41. Thomas Wolfe to Frank Wells, August 29, 1921, in Donald, *Look Homeward*, 25.

42. Wolfe, *Look Homeward, Angel*, 308.

43. Ibid., 308–9.

44. Ibid., 217, 319.

45. Zwingmann, *"Heimweh" or "Nostalgic Reaction,"* 19–20; Rousseau, *A Complete Dictionary of Music*, 266–67.

46. Goethe to Schiller, January 13, 1804, quoted and trans. in Illbruck, *Nostalgia*, 81.

47. Illbruck, *Nostalgia*, 82. For Baudrillard's use of "absolute otherness" see Baudrillard, *The Transparency of Evil*, 122–55.

48. Schiller, *William Tell*, 5.

49. Wolfe, *Of Time and the River*, 366.

50. Hönnighausen, "European Culture in Southern Literature," 35–36.

51. Wolfe, "Pocket Notebook 15," August 12, 1930, in *The Notebooks of Thomas Wolfe*, 498. The translation is from the *Notebooks*.

52. See *The Notebooks of Thomas Wolfe*, 158, 209, 237, 247, 261, 265.

53. Wolfe, *Look Homeward, Angel*, 588.

54. Wolfe, *O Lost*, 685. Arlyn and Matthew J. Bruccoli wrongly title the poem "*Die Heimfehr*" and incorrectly identify it as the forty-fifth poem in the cycle (when in fact it is the forty-seventh) in their emendations to *O Lost*. See *O Lost*, 685. The line originally appears in Wolfe, *Look Homeward, Angel*, 319.

55. Wolfe, *Look Homeward, Angel*, 314.

56. Thomas Wolfe to Aline Bernstein, November 9, 1926, in *My Other Loneliness*, 118.

57. Heine, *The Homecoming*, 2.9–12, 24, in *The Complete Poems of Heinrich Heine*, 76–77.

58. Thomas Wolfe to Aline Bernstein, August 27, 1928, in *My Other Loneliness*, 200.

59. Dennis, *Inhumanities*, 110.

60. Heine, *Der Rabbi von Bacherach;* cited in Skolnik, *Jewish Pasts, German Fictions*, 49.

61. Wolfe, *The Party at Jack's*.

62. Wolfe, *The Party at Jack's*, 16.

63. Ibid., 29.

64. Ibid., 16–17.

65. Stutman and Idol, introduction to *The Party at Jack's*, xxviii.

66. Wolfe, *The Party at Jack's*, 24.

67. Ibid., 24–25.

68. Ibid., 24, 25.

69. See the above discussion of food and nostalgia in my introduction.

70. See L. Wolfe, *The Literary Gourmet*; B. Allen, *Food*, 34–36, 187, 232–33; and O'Neill, *American Food*, 182–86. In her unfinished autobiography, *Illumination and Night Glare* (1999), Carson McCullers wrote that "Thomas Wolfe is another author I love, partly because of his wonderful gusto in describing food." See McCullers, *Illumination and Night*, 59.

71. Ibid., 611–12.

72. Thomas Wolfe to Aline Bernstein, November 9, 1926, in *My Other Loneliness*, 118.

73. Wolfe, *Of Time and the River*, 613.

74. Arnold, "The Buried Life," in *The Poems of Matthew Arnold*, 273.

75. Ibid., 274.

76. Dunsany, *The King of Elfland's Daughter*, 139.

77. Thomas Wolfe to Aline Bernstein, September 7, 1928, in *My Other Loneliness*, 202, 208.

78. Wolfe, *O Lost*, 144–45.

79. Arnold, *On the Study of Celtic Literature*, 154.

80. James, *The Varieties of Religious Experience*, 383. One other curious exception from Wolfe's period of writing can be found in the autobiography of Marie the Queen Consort of Romania, first serialized in the *Saturday Evening Post* between 1933 and 1934 and later published in three volumes by Charles Scribner's Sons, beginning with *The Story of My Life* (1934). Musing about the loss of the enchanted time of youth while in Romania awaiting her wedding day, Marie writes about her *Sehnsucht*: "For months and months afterwards, devoured by loneliness and home-sickness in that far land [. . .] filling me with intolerable pain and *Sehnsucht* so that often I had to smother my mouth in my pillow not to call out with grief and longing." See Marie, Queen Consort of Ferdinand I, *The Story of My Life*, 290.

81. James, *The Varieties of Religious Experience*, 383, 383n.1.

82. For recent examples of the prevalence of *Sehnsucht* in discussions of Lewis, see especially Connolly, *Inklings of Heaven*; Bruce L. Edwards, *C. S. Lewis*; Jasper, "*The Pilgrim's Regress* and *Surprised by Joy*," 223–36; Jacobs, "The Chronicles of Narnia," 265–80; and McGrath, *C. S. Lewis*.

83. Lewis, *Surprised by Joy*, 14. See Carnell, *Bright Shadow of Reality*. Andrew Walker notes that *Sehnsucht* was "perhaps Lewis's favourite Romantic motif." See Walker, "Scripture, Revelation and Platonism," 25.

84. Lewis, *The Pilgrim's Regress*, 24.

85. Ibid., 7–8.

86. Ibid., 9–10.

87. Lewis, "The Weight of Glory," 98–99.

88. Lewis, "Christianity and Culture," 23.

89. Ibid., 23n.1.

90. Lewis, *Surprised by Joy*, 22.

91. Burwick, *The Damnation of Newton*, 109; Novalis, *Henry von Ofterdingen*, 1.

92. Lewis, preface to *George MacDonald*, 33.

93. Ibid., 33–34.

94. Ibid., 34–35.

95. "*In einem echten Märchen muss alles wunderbar, geheimnisvoll und unzusammenhängend sein; alles belebt. Jedes auf eine andre Art. Die ganze Natur muss wunderliche mit der ganzen Geisterwelt gemischt sein; herr tritt die Zeit der Anarchie, der Gesetzlosigkeit, Freiheit, der Naturstand der Natur, die Zeit vor der Welt ein . . . Die Welt des Märchens ist die, die Welt der Welt durchaus entgegengesetzte, und eben darum ihr so durchaus ähnlich, wie das Chaos der vollendeten Schöpfung ähnlich ist*," quoted in MacDonald, *Phantastes*. "In a true fairy tale everything must be marvelous—mysterious and unconnected—everything must be animated. Everything in a different fashion. The whole of Nature must be interwoven in a wondrous manner with the entire spirit world. The age of general anarchy—lawlessness—freedom—the *natural state* of *Nature*—the age prior to the *world* . . . The world of fairy tales is the *absolutely opposite* world to the world of truth (history)—and for this reason so *remarkably similar* to it—as *chaos* is to *completed creation*." Translation from Novalis, *Notes for a Romantic Encyclopaedia*, 34. The original quotation can be found in *Novalis Schriften*, 326–27.

96. Dearborn, *Baptized Imagination*, 40.

97. Novalis, *Hymns to the Night*, in *Rampolli*, ed. and trans. George MacDonald.

98. C. S. Lewis to Arthur Greeves, August 13, 1930, in *The Collected Letters of C. S. Lewis*, 1:922.

99. MacDonald, *Phantastes*, 313.

100. Lewis, *Mere Christianity*, 106.

101. C. S. Lewis to Mary Van Deusen, June 6, 1952, in *The Collected Letters of C. S. Lewis*, 3:199. In an earlier letter to Mary from May 5, 1952, Lewis wrote that "The landscape lures one into it. I long to be tramping over those wooded – or, what is better, half wooded hills. I'm as sensitive as a German to the spell of *das Ferne* and all that." See *The Collected Letters of C. S. Lewis*, 3:186.

102. Davidman, "The Longest Way Round," 88.

103. It seems likely that Davidman—who once described herself as "as a sort of editor-collaborator like Max Perkins"—would have introduced Lewis to Wolfe, if not explicitly then certainly through this published confession of her conversion that Lewis had read and in which his own influence had played a large part. See Dorsett, *And God Came*, 130.

104. Brinkmeyer, *The Fourth Ghost*, 151.

105. H. H., "*Wir sprachen Thomas Wolfe*," *Berliner Tageblatt*, August 5, 1936, 66.

106. Durst, *Weimar Modernism*, xv.

107. Dodd, *My Years in Germany*, 84.

108. P. Gay, *Weimar Culture*, 77.

109. Thomas Wolfe to Maxwell Perkins, May 23, 1935, in *To Loot My Life Clean*, 160–61.

110. P. Gay, *Weimar Culture*, 77.

111. Lepenies, *Seduction of Culture*, 9.

112. Wolfe, *Look Homeward, Angel*, 347.

113. Wolfe, *O Lost*, 687.

114. See Lenz, *The Tutor and The Soldiers*, 11.

115. Wolfe, *Schau heimwärts, Engel*, trans. Irma Wehrli, 751n.431. It is also unlikely that Wolfe, who was far from fluent in German, would have read a German translation of a work in French.

116. Werfel, *Wir Sind.*

117. Weissenberger, "Performing the Poem," 205.

118. Wagener, *Understanding Franz Werfel*, 1, 2.

119. Franz Kafka to Felice Bauer, December 1912, quoted in Wagener, *Understanding Franz Werfel*, 1; Rainer Maria Rilke, "On the Young Poet," quoted in Wagener, *Understanding Franz Werfel*, 1.

120. Thomas Wolfe to Aline Bernstein, December 15, 1926, in *My Other Loneliness*, 137. See Wolfe, *Notebooks*, 158, 209, 226, 244.

121. Jungk, *Franz Werfel*, 217.

122. Steiman, *Franz Werfel*, 2.

123. Ibid., 3, 3–4.

124. M. Moore, *Know Your Enemy*, xviii.

Chapter 4. "The Geography of Heart's Desire"

1. M. Moore, *Know Your Enemy*, 52.

2. Thompson, "The Last Time I Saw Berlin," 9.

3. Wolfe, *Schau heimwärts, Engel!*

4. Pusey, "The German Vogue of Thomas Wolfe," 136.

5. Brysac, *Resisting Hitler*; M. Moore, *Know Your Enemy*; Larson, *In the Garden of Beasts*; Nagorski, *Hitlerland.*

6. Lubrich, *Travels in the Reich*, 98. While Lubrich is correct in noting that the exact novella form of "I Have a Thing to Tell You" as it appeared in the *New Republic* was not translated into German until it appeared in his anthology, Wolfang Klimke had produced a German translation, edited and collected from *You Can't Go Home Again* in 1958, which he titled *I Have a Thing to Tell You*. See Wolfe, *I Have a Thing to Tell You*, ed. Wolfgang Klimke (Paderborn: Schöningh, 1958).

7. M. Moore, *Know Your Enemy*, 341.

8. Wolfe, *Es führt kein Weg zurück: Roman*, trans. Ernst Reinhard (Bern: Scherz, 1942).

9. Pusey was the first to note this translation in "The German Vogue of Thomas Wolfe," and since then most commentaries on the German reception have followed his dismissal of the translation as unimaginative and arbitrary without engaging with the actual text. One notable exception is E. D. Johnson's article "On Translating Thomas Wolfe," where the author appears to have seen Frank's translation, but Johnson refers to the translator only as Ernst Reinhard—Frank's pseudonym—and then simply to note that it "follows Wolfe closely, almost word for word," a statement that grossly misrepresents the actual excisions and alterations discussed in chapter 4. See Pusey, "The German Vogue of Thomas Wolfe," 135; and Johnson, "On Translating Thomas Wolfe," 100.

10. See "'. . . ein sehr lebhaftes Vielerlei': Der Theatermann und Schriftseller Rudolf Frank, 1886–1979."

11. Brinkmeyer, *The Fourth Ghost*, 151.

12. Ibid., 160.

13. Wolfe, "Pocket Notebook 31," September 2, 1936, in *Notebooks*, 829.

14. Brinkmeyer, *The Fourth Ghost*, 162.

15. Wolfe, "Pocket Notebook 31," September 7, 1936, in *Notebooks*, 829–30.

16. Wolfe, "The Spanish Letter," in *The Complete Short Stories of Thomas Wolfe*, 618.

17. Thomas Wolfe to Elizabeth Nowell, September 14, 1936, in *Beyond Love and Loyalty*, 46.

18. Stokes, "Translation and Publication," 30.

19. Preston, *Thomas Wolfe*, 71.

20. Vesper, "*Unsere Meinung*," quoted in Stokes, "Translation and Publication," 170. See also Pusey, *The German Vogue of Thomas Wolfe*, 147.

21. Hermann Hesse to Thomas Mann, February 13, 1936, and Thomas Mann to Hermann Hesse, February 16, 1936, in *The Hesse/Mann Letters*, 57, 59.

22. Brinkmeyer, *The Fourth Ghost*, 165.

23. Wolfe, "I Have a Thing to Tell You (*Nun Will Ich Ihnen 'Was Sagen*)," in *The Short Novels of Thomas Wolfe*, 274. This is a reprint of the 1937 story published in the *New Republic*. All subsequent references to this version of the story are from this edition.

24. Wolfe, "I Have a Thing to Tell You (*Nun Will Ich Ihnen 'Was Sagen*)," 132–36; 90, 159–64; 90, 202–7.

25. Skipp, introduction to *The Complete Short Stories of Thomas Wolfe*, xxv.

26. Ledig-Rowohlt, "Thomas Wolfe in Berlin," 200–201.

27. Brinkmeyer, *The Fourth Ghost*, 166–67.

28. Thompson, "Dorothy Thompson Says," 12.

29. Brinkmeyer, *The Fourth Ghost*, 173.

30. Mosse, *The Crisis of German Ideology*, 4.

31. Wolfe, *You Can't Go Home Again*, 703–4.

32. Ibid., 741.

33. Einseidel, "*Romandichtung*," 841–44.

34. Wolfe, *Of Time and the River*, 858–59.

35. Mosse, *The Crisis of German Ideology*, 13.

36. Ibid., 75.

37. F. Koch, "Drama in the South," 10–11.

38. F. Koch, *Carolina Folk-Plays*.

39. Wolfe, "The Man Who Lives with His Idea," in *The Magical Campus*, 83.

40. Kennedy, *The Window of Memory*, 48.

41. Böll, "*Thomas Wolfe und das bittere Geheimnis des Lebens*," in *Erzählungen, Hörspiele, Aufsätze*, 351. For another analysis of Böll's interpretation of Wolfe see Hummel, *Intertexualität im Werk Heinrich Bölls*, 74–75.

42. Böll, "*Thomas Wolfe und das bittere Geheimnis des Lebens*," 351. Recently, Daniel Spoth has discussed the fiction of William Faulkner in light of Nazi *Blubo* literature, suggesting that there is a "spatial defamiliarization" in Faulkner's fiction that "echoes National Socialists' 'blood and soil' ideologies in disconcerting manners." See Spoth, "Totalitarian Faulkner," 249.

43. J. Stewart, *Ernst Krenek*, 183.

44. Sanders, *German*, 181.

45. Krenek, "*Zwischen 'Blubo' und 'Asphalt*,'" quoted and trans. in J. Stewart, *Ernst Krenek*, 184.

46. Böll, "*Thomas Wolfe*," 351, 349.

47. Böll, *The Clown*, 109.

48. Ziolkowski, "Heinrich Böll," 215.

49. Conrad, *Understanding Heinrich Böll*, 18; Böll, "*Thomas Wolfe und das bittere Geheimnis des Lebens*," 351.

50. Böll, "Autumn Loneliness," in *The Casualty*, 129.

51. Wolfe, *Of Time and the River*, 3.

52. Böll, "Autumn Loneliness," 131.

53. "*Die Aufgabe des Künstlers ist* [. . .] *das Wecken der Sehnsucht*." Hermann Hesse, *Mit Hermann Hesse durch das Jahr*, 64.

54. Hesse, *My Belief*, 347, 346.

55. Ibid., 347, 349.

56. Ibid., 347.

57. Ledig-Rowohlt, "Thomas Wolfe in Berlin," 196–97.

58. Hesse, *My Belief*, 347–49.

59. Wolfe, *Notebooks*, 310; Mann, *Thomas Mann Diaries*, 276.

60. Butler, "Interview with Thomas Mann," *Greensboro Record*, October 30, 1941, in *Frage und Antwort*, 261–64.

61. Weiss, *In the Shadow*, 209.

62. Klaus Mann to Thomas Mann, May 16, 1945, in Weiss, *In the Shadow*, 209.

63. Ibid., 211.

64. Ibid., 212–13.

65. Mann, "An American Solider Revisiting His Former Fatherland," quoted and trans. in Weiss, *In the Shadow*, 213.

66. Rasche, "Klaus Mann's Novel *The Volcano*," 93–94.

67. Mann, *Der Vulkan*, quoted and trans. in Rasche, "Klaus Mann's Novel *The Volcano*," 95.

68. Plunka, *Staging Holocaust Resistance*, 29.

69. Zuckmayer, *A Part of Myself*, 329.

70. Dodd, *My Years in Germany*, 81.

71. This translation can be found in a three-page document titled "Translations" located at bMS Am 2815 (16–17), William B. Wisdom Collection of Thomas Wolfe, Houghton Library, Harvard University. Carol Johnston suggests that this document is the series of German "excerpts" sent to Wolfe by Rowohlt Verlag as mentioned in a letter sent to Perkins by Wolfe on August 8, 1933, and as such would have corresponded to the release of *Schau Heimwärts, Engel!* See Johnston, *Of Time and the Artist*, 58.

72. Dodd, *My Years in Germany*, 82.

73. Stokes, "The Translation and Reception," 155.

74. Rowohlt Verlag to John Hall Wheelock, May 29, 1936, bMS Am 1883.1 (557) William B. Wisdom Collection of Thomas Wolfe, Houghton Library, Harvard University; Heinrich Maria Ledig-Rowohlt to Thomas Wolfe, June 23, 1936, bMS Am 1883.1 (557) William B. Wisdom Collection of Thomas Wolfe, Houghton Library, Harvard University.

75. Salomon, *The Answers of Ernst von Salomon*, 179.

76. Hannah, *Dark Territory in the Information Age*, 54–55.

77. Gassert, "Neither East Nor West," 630.

78. Salomon, *The Answers of Ernst von Salomon*, 178–79, 179.

79. Harris, "It Really Can Happen Here," *Salon*, September 30, 2105. See Karolides, *Banned Books*, 267. Following the 1933 book burnings, Lewis was reported as saying:

"Throughout the ages many of the greatest scientists and theologians have been uncomfortably honored by being burned at the stake. Apparently the Nazis are paying the same kind of honor to the noblest books that have been produced in Germany in the last twenty years. The authors should feel nothing save satisfaction at receiving this unintentional tribute from an organized mob. I trust that this action will serve to spread their reputation and glory in every land outside Germany, and that America, among other countries, will mark down for reading whatever books may be burnt." See "Let America Honor Books Nazis Burned," *Jewish Daily Bulletin* 10 (May 14, 1933).

80. Schlesinger, *The Age of Roosevelt*, 83.

81. Importantly, Benjamin Alpers notes that "*It Can't Happen Here* would almost certainly never have been written had it not been for Lewis's marriage to [Dorothy] Thompson." See Alpers, *Dictators*, 51–52.

82. Talbot, *Devil Dog*, 140.

83. Thomas Wolfe to Elizabeth Nowell, July 23, 1937, in *Beyond Love and Loyalty*, 65.

84. "*Das ist etwas ganz Herrliches und sicher das schönste und dichterischste Buch, das Sie je heraus—gegeben haben. Was für ein Atem! Was für ein Dichter! So schreiben zu können, das freilich liegt schon ganz im Bereich der Gnade! Hinreissend! Wie gesagt: einfach herrlich!*" Quoted in a letter from Heinrich Maria Ledig-Rowohlt to Thomas Wolfe, May 5, 1936, bMS Am 1883.1 (556), William B. Wisdom Collection of Thomas Wolfe, Houghton Library, Harvard University.

85. "The world from which we inner German emigrants sought support was an interior realm which Hitler, despite all his efforts, never succeeded in conquering." Open letter from Frank Thiess in *Stuttgarter Stimme*, August 17, 1945, quoted and trans. in Wilkinson, *The Intellectual Resistance in Europe*, 299n.6.

86. Larson, *In the Garden of Beasts*, 366.

87. Barbian, *The Politics of Literature*, 361.

88. Ritchie, *German Literature under National Socialism*, 115.

89. Barbian, *The Politics of Literature*, 359.

90. Stokes, "The Translation and Reception," 172.

91. Heinrich Maria Ledig Rowohlt to Hans Fallada, April 8, 1936, in Töteberg und Buck, *Hans Fallada*, 163; Wolfe, "The Spanish Letter," 617–18.

92. Murray Hall, *Der Paul Zsolnay Verlag*, quoted in Sturge, "'Flight from the Programme,'" 55.

93. Barbian, *The Politics of Literature*, 362.

94. Nicolaisen and Göske, "William Faulkner in Germany," 64, 63.

95. Editorial in *Buchhändler im neuen Reich*, quoted and trans. in Sturge, "Translations in Nazi Germany," 52.

96. Sturge, "Translations in Nazi Germany," 59.

97. Ibid. Although *Strom des Lebens* was published in Switzerland, Pusey notes that it "appears to have been known in Germany." See Pusey, "The German Vogue of Thomas Wolfe," 133.

98. Wolfe, *The Web and the Rock*, 2, quoted in advertising for Zürcher Ziegeleien under the title "*Wir lesen über den Backstein*." See "*Anzeigenseite*," *Schweizerische Bauzeitung* 121, no. 7 (February 13, 1943), 6. Three subsequent editions of the *Schweizerische Bauzeitung* also ran the advertisement in 1943.

99. Ledig-Rowohlt, "Thomas Wolfe in Berlin," 196.

100. Brysac, *Resisting Hitler*, 150.

101. Dodd, "In Memory," quoted in Brysac, *Resisting Hitler*, 150.

102. Brysac, *Resisting Hitler*, 178.

103. Ibid., 175; Harnack-Fish, "*Drei jung Dichter aus USA*."

104. Nelson, *Red Orchestra*, 91.

105. Magi, "Thomas Wolfe and Mildred Harnack-Fish," 103.

106. Mildred Harnack to Thomas Wolfe, January 29, 1937, bMS Am 1883.1 (293), William B. Wisdom Collection of Thomas Wolfe, Houghton Library, Harvard University.

107. Dodd, *My Years in Germany*, 84–85.

108. Ibid., 83–84, 84.

109. Martha Dodd to Thomas Wolfe, [n.d.] bMS Am 1883.1 (186), William B. Wisdom Collection of Thomas Wolfe, Houghton Library, Harvard University.

110. Thomas Wolfe to Maxwell Perkins, May 23, 1935, in *To Loot My Life Clean*, 161.

111. Ibid., 161–62.

112. Shirer, *Berlin Diary*, 66.

113. Dieter Meindl, "Thomas Wolfe and Germany," 207.

114. Field, "Thomas Wolfe's Attitudes," 180.

115. Wolfe, "Oktoberfest," 27–31.

116. Wolfe, *The Web and the Rock*, 602.

117. Wolfe, *You Can't Go Home Again*, 633.

118. Ibid., 704.

119. Wolfe, "I Have a Thing to Tell You," 277.

120. Wolfe, *You Can't Go Home Again*, 704.

121. Lubrich, *Reisen ins Reich*.

122. *Erinnerung an einen Sommer in Berlin*, directed by Rolf Hädrich.

123. "*Der Roman konnte in Nazi-Deutschland nicht verlegt warden; eine erste Übersetzung erschien 1942 in Bern*." See Gieselbusch et al., *100 Jahre Rowohlt*, 129.

124. Pusey, "The German Vogue of Thomas Wolfe," 135.

125. Einboden, *Nineteenth-Century U.S. Literature*, 2.

126. Zühlsdorff, *Hitler's Exiles*, 153.

127. Quoted in Frank, *No Hero for the Kaiser*, [n.p.].

128. I am indebted to Dr. Vincent C. Frank-Steiner, Rudolf Frank's son, for insight into his father's life as well as to Wilfried Weinke, who curated the 2013 Rudolf Frank Exhibition "'*. . . ein sehr lebhaftes Vielerlei': Der Theatermann und Schriftseller Rudolf Frank*, 1886–1979," http://www.rudolf-frank.net (accessed October 25, 2013).

129. *Die Stunde* (Vienna), October 30, 1936, quoted in Zühlsdorff, *Hitler's Exiles*, 36.

130. Rudolf Frank, *Fair Play*.

131. Vincent C. Frank-Steiner, email message to author, November 11, 2013. I am indebted to Robert Brown and Vera Meyer for help with the following translations of *Es führt kein Weg zurück*.

132. Vincent C. Frank-Steiner, email message to author, November 11, 2013.

133. Zahn, "*Der andere Weg*," in *Was das Leben zerbricht*.

134. Wolfe, *You Can't Go Home Again*, 620.

135. Ibid.; Wolfe, *Es führt kein Weg zurück*, trans. Ernst Reinhard, 628.

136. Wolfe, *You Can't Go Home Again*, 623.

137. Ibid.; Wolfe, *Es führt kein Weg zurück*, 629.

138. Wolfe, *Es führt kein Weg zurück*, 629.

139. Wolfe, *You Can't Go Home Again*, 621, 627.

140. Wolfe, *Es führt kein Weg zurück*, 634–35.

141. Wolfe, *You Can't Go Home Again*, 628, 627–28.

142. Wolfe, *You Can't Go Home Again*, 628; Wolfe, *Es führt kein Weg zurück*, 635.

143. Wolfe, *Es führt kein Weg zurück*, 635.

144. Ibid.; Wolfe, *You Can't Go Home Again*, 628.

145. Wolfe, *You Can't Go Home Again*, 631.

146. Ibid.; Wolfe, *Es führt kein Weg zurück*, 636.

147. Wolfe, *You Can't Go Home Again*, 633.

148. Cited in Zühlsdorff, *Hitler's Exiles*, 153.

149. Wolfe, *You Can't Go Home Again*, 632; Wolfe, *Es führt kein Weg zurück*, 638.

150. Wolfe, *You Can't Go Home Again*, 633.

151. Wolfe, *Es führt kein Weg zurück*, 638.

152. Pusey, "The German Vogue of Thomas Wolfe," 135; Johnston, *Of Time and the Artist*, 157.

153. Alfred Scherz Verlag to Maxwell Perkins, June 23, 1942, bMS Am 1883.12 (3), William B. Wisdom Collection of Thomas Wolfe, Houghton Library, Harvard University.

Chapter 5. Dances with Wolfes

1. Jessamyn West, "Tom Wolfe's My Name," in *Love, Death, and the Ladies' Drill Team*, 77.

2. Ibid., 85.

3. Ibid., 86–87.

4. Le Guin, "Ursula K. Le Guin," interview by Geek's Guide to the Galaxy.

5. Hendrix, Rabkin, and Slusser, introduction to *Visions of Mars*, 4.

6. Felski, *Uses of Literature*, 7–8.

7. Starr, "Interview," *The State* (Columbia, SC), November 5, 1980, in *Conversations with Walker Percy*.

8. Percy, *The Moviegoer*, 75.

9. Jack Kerouac to Bill Ryan, January 10, 1943, in *Jack Kerouac: Selected Letters*, ed. Ann Charters, 37.

10. Jones, "Back to Merrimac," 18; Maher, *Kerouac*, 211. Expressing his interest in this "lostness" of Wolfe's characters in a journal entry from December 2, 1949, Kerouac equated Wolfe's "'brother loneliness'" with "[t]he thing [. . .] central to our existence [. . .] our everlasting companion. [. . .] It's also every man's 'mystery' and deepest being." See Kerouac, *Windblown World*, 249.

11. Jack Kerouac to Neal Cassady, October 6, 1950, in *Jack Kerouac: Selected Letters*, 232–33.

12. Jack Kerouac to Allen Ginsberg, December 26, 1956, in *Jack Kerouac and Allen Ginsberg*, 337.

13. Holmes, "Journal Entry," April 27, 1951, quoted in *Brother-Souls*, 195.

14. M. Smith, "*My Life as a Man*," 86.

15. Roth, *My Life as a Man*, 16–17, 24.

16. Roth, *Zuckerman Unbound*, 180.

17. Roth, "The Book That Made Me a Reader."

18. Vizenor, *Interior Landscapes*, 144.

19. Ibid. See Thomas Wolfe, *A Stone, a Leaf, a Door*.

20. Rostkowski, *Conversations*, xliii.

21. Ibid., 149. Originally in Wolfe, "Dark in the Forest, Strange as Time," in *From Death to Morning*, 103.

22. Ibid., 148, 154. Originally in Wolfe, *Of Time and the River*, 90.

23. Ibid., 158.

24. Saunders, "My First Literary Crush," interview by College Week, Slate.com, November 15, 2005.

25. Begley, "Beautiful Losers," *The Guardian*, August 5, 2000.

26. Saunders, "George Saunders," interview by Joel Whitney.

27. Saunders, "The Book That Made Me a Reader."

28. Whitney, "George Saunders."

29. Saunders, "Escape from Spiderhead," in *The Tenth of December*, 46.

30. Gass, "William H. Gass," 17.

31. Gass, preface to *In the Heart of the Heart of the Country*, xxiii.

32. Gass, *Middle C*, 81.

33. Wolfe, *You Can't Go Home Again*, quoted in Gass, *Middle C*, 81.

34. Gass, *Middle C*, 80–81, 81, 83.

35. Bloom, *The Anxiety of Influence*, 141.

36. Jack Kerouac, "Typescript and holograph notes, 'Notes: Joe Doakes and the Immortals.'" Series 1, Box 6.59, Jack Kerouac Papers, Henry W. and Albert A. Berg Collection of English and American Literature, New York Public Library.

37. Wouk, *Youngblood Hawke*, 13, 28.

38. Hyman, "A Novelist of Great Promise," 23; Boroff, "Hillbilly Literary Tycoon," 36.

39. Bishop quoted in Canada, "Vardis Fisher," 212.

40. Fisher, *Orphans in Gethsemane*, 644, 645.

41. McGurl, *The Program Era*, 77–125.

42. Wolfe, *Look Homeward, Angel*, n.p. For a more recent discussion of Wolfe and autobiography see Boyle, "Thomas Wolfe and the Genre Question."

43. Thomas Wolfe to Julian Meade, February 1, 1932, in *The Letters of Thomas Wolfe*, 320–21.

44. McGurl, *The Program Era*, 80–82.

45. Ibid., 80.

46. William Styron to William C. Styron Sr., September 28, 1943, in *Selected Letters of William Styron*, 5.

47. Styron, *Sophie's Choice*, 95.

48. Styron, "The Shade of Thomas Wolfe," 98.

49. Wolfe, *The Story of a Novel*, 21.

50. Kiš, *A Wooden Trunk for Thomas Wolfe*, in *Night and Fog*, 83.

51. Ibid., 96.

52. Ibid., 113.

53. There has been a tendency in Wolfe scholarship to move beyond actual, evidential traces into wild speculation. In one recent example, Vivian Casper describes intertextual links between Eugene O'Neill's *Long Day's Journey* and Wolfe's *Look Homeward, Angel* that rely on "O'Neill's inferred borrowings" and "seemingly echoed epithets, allusions, and exact dialogue" that Caspar admits are purely speculative: "Whether O'Neill's echoes of Wolfe are conscious or unconscious is impossible to know." See Casper, "Thomas Wolfe and Eugene O'Neill," 79–93.

54. Hansen, *Death Claims.*

55. Wolfe, "God's Lonely Man," in *The Hills Beyond*, 186. See Blake, "Inside Bickle's Brain," 139–51, for a fuller discussion of this connection.

56. Cronin, "A Melancholy Werewolf's Existential Howl," *New York Times*, BR11; G. Duncan, *The Last Werewolf*, 224.

57. Yarbrough, "The Intertextual *Suttree*," 103–20.

58. McCarthy, *Suttree*, 553.

59. David Dalton, *Piece of My Heart*, 24.

60. W. Gay, *Provinces of Night*, 280.

61. I am indebted to Kayla Pressley Seay at the Thomas Wolfe Memorial for alerting me to this episode.

62. "The Big Sleep," *Ozark*, season 2, episode 8. Directed by Alik Sakharov. Written by David Manson. Netflix, August 31, 2018.

63. AbeBooks, "How Netflix's *Ozark* Sparked Interest in a 1929 First Edition," *Medium*, September 27, 2018.

64. Waldrop, afterword to "You *Could* Go Home Again," in *Going Home Again*, 54.

65. Waldrop, "You *Could* Go Home Again," 36.

66. Waldrop, afterword to "You *Could* Go Home Again," 50.

67. Michael Agger, "Pulp Metafiction," *New York Times Book Review*, October 17, 2004, 14.

68. King, *The Gunslinger*, xxvii. Originally from Wolfe, *Look Homeward, Angel*, 2. In her novel *Pitch Dark* (1983), Renata Adler has remarked that Gertrude Stein's "A rose is a rose is a rose" was not, in spirit, "so remote from [Wolfe's] a stone, a leaf, an unfound door," writing that there is "a great hollow wind [that] blows through both of them, and both are on the verge, undeniably, of tears." See Adler, *Pitch Dark*, 115.

69. King, *The Dark Tower V*, 161.

70. Furth, *Stephen King's the Dark Tower.*

71. King, *The Wolves of Calla*, 317, 513.

72. King, *The Dark Tower III*, 67. Italics in original.

73. Vincent, *The Road to the Dark Tower;* Vincent, *The Dark Tower Companion*; McAleer, *Inside the Dark Tower Series.*

74. Strengell, *Dissecting Stephen King*, 6.

75. A. Powell, "Thomas Wolfe," 6.

76. Dunlevy, "A Giant Despite His Faults," 14.

77. See Geismar, *Selections from Thomas Wolfe.*

78. Koch, "The Novel as Narrative Poem," in *Crossing the Gap*, 144.

79. Giles, *Antipodean America*, 5.

80. Cranston, review of *Water from the Moon*, 117–21.

81. Quinlem, "The Sensitive Clod," 538.

82. Wighton, "The Realistic Novel," 61, 3.

83. Arnold, "The Buried Life," 271–75.

84. Koch, "The Novel as Narrative Poem," 144–45.

85. Koch, *The Boys in the Island*, 203–4.

86. Wolfe, *Of Time and the River*, 332.

87. "New Fiction," *Times* (London), January 22, 1959, 13; Koch, *The Boys in the Island*, 178.

88. Koch, *The Boys in the Island*, 204.

89. Koch, "Author's Note," in *The Boys in the Island*, vii–viii.

90. Huggan, *Australian Literature*, 12.

91. Koch, "The Lost Hemisphere," in *Crossing the Gap*, 103.

92. Huggan, *Australian Literature*, 13.

93. Greeson, "The 'Mysteries and Miseries' of North Carolina," 285; Pierce, "Defection and Dislocation," 55.

94. C. Higham, "Letter from Sydney," 649.

95. Koch, *The Boys in the Island*, 15.

96. Buell, "Antipodal Propinquities?" 4.

97. Koch, *Crossing the Gap*, 12.

98. Koch, *The Doubleman*, 23.

99. Wood, "Writing Tasmania's 'Different Soul,'" 156.

100. Sharrad, review of *Water from the Moon*, 3.

101. J. Smith, *Finding Purple America*, 34.

102. Birns and Dixon, *Reading across the Pacific*, xvi. For a discussion of Koch's absence in Australian literary studies, see Gaile, "'Going Double,'" 151–56; Vernay, *Water from the Moon*; Carr, "Overdue Study of Multifaceted Writer," 224–25; Gare, "Death by Silence," 28–37; and Pierce, "Home Truths," 18.

103. Koch, *Crossing the Gap*, 32.

104. Genoni, "Girt By Sea," 127.

105. Koch, "The Novel as Narrative Poem," 146.

106. Koch, "Treasures in the Basement," *Weekend Australian*, November 9, 2002.

107. Koch originally added this phrase, "different weather and a different soul," in his 1974 revision of the novel. Koch, *The Boys in the Island* [2013], 10.

108. Wolfe, *Of Time and the River*, 24.

109. Wolfe, *Look Homeward, Angel*, 53.

110. Koch, *The Boys in the Island*, 68.

111. Koch, "The Novel as Narrative Poem," 145.

112. Wolfe, *Of Time and the River*, 86.

113. Koch, "Treasures in the Basement," 4.

114. Koch, *The Boys in the Island*, 68.

115. Koch, *The Boys in the Island* [2013], 58; Wolfe, *Of Time and the River*, 404.

116. Wolfe, *Of Time and the River*, 422.

117. Koch, "Treasures in the Basement," 4.

118. Koch, "The Novel as Narrative Poem," 144.

119. *Planet Stories* 4, no. 6 (Spring 1950), 1.

120. Dick, "Beyond Lies the Wub," 69–73.

121. T. DeForest, *Storytelling in the Pulps*, 76.

122. Bradbury, "Forever and the Earth," 26.

123. Bradbury, interview by Jonathan Eller, 2002, Los Angeles.

124. Bradbury, "Forever and the Earth," 31, 32.

125. Teicher, "Ray Bradbury and Thomas Wolfe," 19. Also see Holliday, *Thomas Wolfe*, 125–26, for a brief discussion of this story.

126. Proietti, "Beyond the Hills," 80.

127. See G. Wolfe, "The Frontier Myth in Ray Bradbury," 33–54.

128. G. Wolfe, "The Frontier Myth in Ray Bradbury," 35.

129. Knight, "When I Was in Kneepants," 3. On this periodization of the "Golden Age" see Robert Silverberg's essay "Science Fiction in the Fifties," where he argues that 1950s sci-

ence fiction—including works by Bradbury—constituted the real "Golden Age" of science fiction. See Silverberg, "Science Fiction in the Fifties," 163–72.

130. Eller and Touponce, *Ray Bradbury*, 105.

131. J. Moore, "Shifting Frontiers," 62. For a later articulation of this position, see A. Duncan, "It's All SF," 59–69.

132. Benford, "The South and Science Fiction," 390.

133. Miles, "Science Fiction and Fantasy," 332. One other example of this is in *Crossroads: Tales of the Southern Literary Fantastic* (2004), where the authors note that "what southern literature and the literature of the fantastic share is a rootedness in the particularity of place." See Cox and Duncan, *Crossroads*, 12.

134. Eller, *Becoming Ray Bradbury*, 206.

135. Slusser, *The Bradbury Chronicles*, 50.

136. Bradbury, *Forever and the Earth: Radio Dramatization*, 9.

137. Sterling, *Biographical Encyclopedia of American Radio*, 70.

138. CBS Columbia Workshop, *Twenty-Six by Corwin*, "Wolfiana," directed by Norman Corwin, October 10, 1941.

139. CBS, "An American Trilogy: Thomas Wolfe," *Columbia Presents Norman Corwin*, directed by Norman Corwin with Charles Laughton, June 13, 1944. Laughton later released an anthology of stories he had read aloud titled *Tell Me a Story* that included three selections from Wolfe and three from Bradbury. See Laughton, *Tell Me a Story*.

140. Bradbury, *Forever and the Earth*, 9.

141. Ray Bradbury to Marjorie Fairbanks, Series I, MS Am 1883.9 (5), Marjorie C. Fairbanks Correspondence and Notes on Thomas Wolfe, Houghton Library, Harvard University.

142. Ray Bradbury, interview by Jonathan Eller, 2002, Los Angeles.

143. Wolfe, *Of Time and the River*, 327. This section had originally appeared in the story "No Door" (1933) that was extracted from the manuscript of *Of Time and the River* for *Scribner's Magazine*, though it is most likely that Bradbury encountered the October motif in the novel form. See Wolfe, "No Door," 46–56.

144. Wolfe, *Of Time and the River*, 52, 205, 327–29, 332–33.

145. Ray Bradbury, "October," ca. 1940–41, unaccessioned typescript, Bradbury Albright Collection (cabinet 24), Bradbury Memorial Archive, Center for Ray Bradbury Studies, Indiana University School of Liberal Arts, IUPUI (Indianapolis).

146. Ray Bradbury, interview by Jonathan Eller, 2002, Los Angeles; Bradbury, "October."

147. Bradbury, *The October Country*, 1. The title story of that collection was not included in *The October Country* and was instead finally published as the novel *Something Wicked This Way Comes* (1962), where, as Bradbury notes, the story collected "midnights and funeral trains." See Bradbury, foreword to *The October Country*, viii. Also see Bradbury, *Something Wicked This Way Comes*.

148. Bradbury, *Forever and the Earth: Radio Dramatization*, 33.

149. Ray Bradbury, interview by *Paris Review*, ca. 1976, in *Listen to the Echoes*, 361, 361–62.

150. The following discussion of Bradbury's breakout novel should be understood in the context of a growing critical appreciation of Bradbury over the last few decades. The last few years alone have yielded Bloom, *Ray Bradbury;* Eller, *Becoming Ray Bradbury*; Rabkin, "Is Mars Heaven?" 95–104; McMillan, *Orbiting Ray Bradbury's Mars*; as well as *The New Ray Bradbury Review* (2010), a journal released in partnership with Kent State Univer-

sity Press, and Indiana University's Center for Ray Bradbury Studies, which was founded in 2007.

151. Bradbury, "Miss Appletree and I," in *We'll Always Have Paris*, 197.

152. Weller, *The Bradbury Chronicles*, 92.

153. Eric S. Rabkin, "Is Mars Heaven?" 98.

154. Ibid., 96–98.

155. Eller and Touponce, *Ray Bradbury*, 2; Kagle, "Homage to Melville," 19.

156. Lawrence, "A 'Night Meeting' in the Southwest," 70–71.

157. Jameson, *Archaeologies of the Future*, xivn.9.

158. See Eller, *Becoming Ray Bradbury*, 204–6.

159. Eller, "The Body Eclectic," 165.

160. See Rabkin, "Is Mars Heaven?" 95–104; Slusser, *The Bradbury Chronicles*, 4; G. Wolfe, "The Frontier Myth in Ray Bradbury," 33–54; Harlow, "Martian Legacy," 311–14; and Leonard, "Race and Ethnicity in Science Fiction," 253–63.

161. Lawrence, "A 'Night Meeting' in the Southwest," 72.

162. Lévinas, *Totality and Infinity*, 33–34.

163. Bradbury, *The Martian Chronicles*, 107.

164. Lawrence, "A 'Night Meeting' in the Southwest," 72.

165. Bradbury, *The Martian Chronicles*, 109–10.

166. Mucher, "Being Martian," 182.

167. Lawrence, "A 'Night Meeting' in the Southwest," 75, 83.

168. Lévinas, *Totality and Infinity*, 33, 34.

169. Bradbury, *The Martian Chronicles*, 103.

170. Ibid., 103–4.

171. Wolfe, *Of Time and the River*, 569, 551.

172. Bradbury, *The Martian Chronicles*, 109–10.

173. Wolfe, *Of Time and the River*, 245.

174. Bradbury, *The Martian Chronicles*, 109; Wolfe, *Of Time and the River*, 366.

175. Drew M. Dalton, *Longing for the Other*, 21, 20.

Conclusion

1. Margaret Mitchell to Helen Dowdey, September 16, 1938, in *Margaret Mitchell's Gone with the Wind Letters*, 231.

2. Inscoe, *Race, War, and Remembrance*, 10n.12.

3. Giles, *Virtual Americas*, 256.

4. Brian T. Edwards, "The Word, the Text, and the Americanist," 233–34.

5. J. Smith, *Finding Purple America*, 40–41.

6. J. Smith, *Finding Purple America*, 32; Žižek, *Looking Awry*, 5; Heidegger, *Schelling's Treatise*, 124.

7. McCullers, *The Heart Is a Lonely Hunter*, 50.

8. Dimock, *Through Other Continents*, 3.

9. Damrosch, *What Is World Literature?*, 4–5.

10. Wolfe, *Oktoberfest eine Erzählung*, trans. Horst Maria Lauinger; Wolfe, *Die Party bei den Jacks*, trans. Susanne Höbel; Wolfe, *Schau heimwärts, Engel*, trans. and annotated Irma Wehrli; Wolfe, *Von Zeit und Fluss*, trans. and annotated Irma Wehrli. Unsurprisingly,

the new film *Genius* (2016), centering on the relationship between Maxwell Perkins and Thomas Wolfe, premiered at the Berlin Film Festival.

11. This is excluding the 2000 release of *O Lost*, which was derived from Wolfe's carbon copy of his original manuscript and thus does not reflect the published version of *Look Homeward, Angel*.

12. Hilmes, *Berlin 1936*, 280.

13. Brinkmeyer, *The Fourth Ghost*, 146; M. Moore, *Know Your Enemy*, xiii–xviii.

14. Brinkmeyer, *The Fourth Ghost*, 151.

15. Einboden, *Nineteenth-Century U.S. Literature*, 9.

16. McGurl, *The Program Era*, 79.

17. Giles, *Antipodean America*, 5.

18. Dixon and Birns, *Reading across the Pacific*, xiii.

19. Giles, *Antipodean America*, 492.

BIBLIOGRAPHY

Adams, Walter S. "Amazing New Novel Is Realistic Story of Asheville People." *Asheville Times*, October 20, 1929, 1.

Adler, Renata. *Pitch Dark*. 1983. Reprint, New York: New York Review of Books, 2013.

Aldington, Richard. "American Novelists." *Sunday Referee*, July 6, 1930, 6.

Allen, Brigid. *Food: An Oxford Anthology*. Oxford: Oxford University Press, 1994.

Allen, John. *Homelessness in American Literature: Romanticism, Realism, and Testimony*. New York: Routledge, 2004.

Alpers, Benjamin Leontief. *Dictators, Democracy, and American Public Culture: Envisioning the Totalitarian Enemy, 1920s–1950s*. Chapel Hill: University of North Carolina Press, 2003.

Applegate, Celia. *A Nation of Provincials: The German Idea of Heimat*. Berkeley: University of California Press, 1990.

———. "Senses of Place." In *The Oxford Handbook of Modern German History*, edited by Helmut Walser Smith, 49–70. Oxford: Oxford University Press, 2011.

Apter, Emily, and Barbara Cassin, eds. *Dictionary of Untranslatables: A Philosophical Lexicon*. Translated by Steven Rendall. Princeton, NJ: Princeton University Press, 2014.

Arnold, Matthew. *On the Study of Celtic Literature*. London: Smith, Elder, 1867.

———. *The Poems of Matthew Arnold*. Edited by Kenneth Allott. London: Longmans, Green, 1965.

Atkinson, Ted. *Faulkner and the Great Depression: Aesthetics, Ideology, and Cultural Politics*. Athens: University of Georgia Press, 2006.

Austin, Linda M. *Nostalgia in Transition, 1780–1917*. Charlottesville: University of Virginia Press, 2007.

Bain, Joseph Grant. "Disturbing Signs: Southern Gothic from Poe to McCullers." PhD diss., University of Arkansas, 2010.

Baker, John M., Jr. "Loss and Expectation: Temporal Entwinement as Theme and Figure in Novalis, Wordsworth, Nerval, and Leopardi." In *Romantic Poetry*, edited by Angela Esterhammer, 63–90. Philadelphia: John Benjamins, 2002.

Barbian, Jan-Pieter. *The Politics of Literature in Nazi Germany: Books in the Media Dictatorship*. Translated by Kate Sturge. London: Bloomsbury Academic, 2013.

Barr, Stringfellow. "The Dandridges and the Gants." *Virginia Quarterly Review* 6, no. 2 (April 1930): 310–13.

Bartlett, John, ed. *Familiar Quotations: A Collection of Passages, Phrases, and Proverbs Traced to Their Sources in Ancient and Modern Literature*. Boston: Little, Brown, 1937.

Baudrillard, Jean. *The Transparency of Evil: Essays on Extreme Phenomena*. Translated by James Benedict. London: Verso, 1993.

Beiser, Frederick C. *The Romantic Imperative: The Concept of Early German Romanticism*. Cambridge, MA: Harvard University Press, 2003.

Benford, Gregory. "The South and Science Fiction." *Science Fiction Studies* 27, no. 3 (2000): 385–90.

Benson, Melanie. *Disturbing Calculations: The Economics of Identity in Postcolonial Southern Literature, 1912–2002*. Athens: University of Georgia Press, 2008.

Berg, A. Scott. *Maxwell Perkins: Editor of Genius*. New York: E. P. Dutton, 1978.

Bergo, Bettina. "The Birth Pangs of the Absolute: Longing and Angst in Schelling and Kierkegaard." In *Philosophy's Moods: The Affective Grounds of Thinking*, edited by Hagi Kenaan and Ilit Ferber, 105–22. Dordrecht: Springer, 2011.

Birns, Nicholas, and Robert Dixon, eds. Introduction to *Reading across the Pacific: Australia–United States Intellectual Histories*, xiii–xxi. Sydney: Sydney University Press, 2010.

Bishop, John Peale. "The Sorrows of Thomas Wolfe." *Kenyon Review* 1, no. 1 (Winter 1939): 7–17.

Bishop, John Peale, and Allen Tate. *The Republic of Letters: The Correspondence of John Peale Bishop and Allen Tate*. Edited by John J. Hindle and Thomas Daniel Young. Lexington: University Press of Kentucky, 1981.

———, eds. *American Harvest: Twenty Years of Creative Writing in the United States*. 1942. Reprint, Garden City, NY: Garden City Publishing, 1943.

Bitzer, Barbara. "*Sehnsucht:* The Key to the Secret of Life, as Illustrated in Selected Modern American Novels." PhD diss., Arizona State University, 1994.

Blair, Amy L. "Main Street Reading *Main Street*." In *New Directions in American Reception Study*, edited by Philip Goldstein and James L. Machor, 139–58. Oxford: Oxford University Press, 2008.

Blickle, Peter. *Heimat: A Critical Theory of the German Idea of Homeland*. Rochester, NY: Camden House, 2002.

Bloch, Ernst. *The Principle of Hope*. Translated by Neville Plaice, Stephen Plaice, and Paul Knight. 3 vols. Oxford: Basil Blackwell, 1986.

———. *The Spirit of Utopia*. Translated by Anthony A. Nassar. Stanford, CA: Stanford University Press, 2000.

Bloom, Harold. *The Anxiety of Influence: A Theory of Poetry*. 2nd ed. Oxford: Oxford University Press, 1997.

———, ed. *Thomas Wolfe*. New York: Chelsea House, 1987.

Boa, Elizabeth. "Some Versions of *Heimat:* Goethe and Hölderlin around 1800, Frenssen and Mann around 1900." In *Heimat: At the Intersection of Memory and Space*, edited by Friederike Eigler and Jens Kugele, 34–52. Berlin: De Gruyter, 2012.

Boa, Elizabeth, and Rachel Palfreyman. *Heimat—A German Dream: Regional Loyalties and National Identity in German Culture, 1890–1990*. Oxford: Oxford University Press, 2000.

Böll, Heinrich. *The Casualty*. Translated by Leila Vennewitz. New York: Farrar, Straus and Giroux, 1986.

———. *The Clown*. Translated by Leila Vennewitz. London: Weidenfeld and Nicolson, 1965.

———. *Erzählungen, Hörspiele, Aufsätze*. Köln: Kiepenheuer und Witsch, 1961.

Bone, Martyn. *The Postsouthern Sense of Place in Contemporary Fiction*. Baton Rouge: Louisiana State University Press, 2005.

Boroff, David. "Hillbilly Literary Tycoon." *Saturday Review of Literature* 45, no. 20 (May 19, 1962): 36.

Bourdieu, Pierre. *The Field of Cultural Production: Essays on Art and Literature*. Edited by Randal Johnson. Cambridge: Polity Press, 1993.

Boyle, Gwendolen Aoife. "Thomas Wolfe and the Genre Question: Beyond the 'Charge of Autobiography.'" PhD diss., University College Cork, 2013.

Boym, Svetlana. *The Future of Nostalgia*. New York: Basic Books, 2001.

Bradbury, Malcolm. *The Modern American Novel*. Oxford: Oxford University Press, 1992.

Bradbury, Ray. "Forever and the Earth." *Planet Stories* 4, no. 6 (Spring 1950): 26–35. https://archive.org/details/Planet_Stories_Volume_4_Number_6_.

———. *Forever and the Earth: Radio Dramatization*. Athens, Ohio: Croissant, 1984.

———. *Listen to the Echoes: The Ray Bradbury Interviews*. Edited by Sam Weller. Brooklyn, NY: Melville House, 2010.

———. *The Martian Chronicles*. 1950. Reprint, Garden City, NY: Doubleday, 1952.

———. *The October Country*. 1955. Reprint, New York: Ballantine Books, 1996.

———. *Something Wicked This Way Comes*. New York: Simon and Schuster, 1962.

———. *We'll Always Have Paris: Stories*. New York: HarperCollins, 2009.

Bradley, Patricia. *Making American Culture: A Social History, 1900–1920*. New York: Palgrave Macmillan, 2009.

Brinkmeyer, Robert H., Jr. *The Fourth Ghost: White Southern Writers and European Fascism, 1930–1950*. Baton Rouge: Louisiana State University Press, 2009.

Brown, Russell. "The Road Home: Meditation on a Theme." In *Context North America: Canadian/U.S. Literary Relations*, edited by Camille R. La Bossière, 23–48. Ottawa: University of Ottawa Press, 1994.

Brysac, Shareen Blair. *Resisting Hitler: Mildred Harnack and the Red Orchestra*. Oxford: Oxford University Press, 2000.

Buell, Lawrence. "Antipodal Propinquities? Environmental (Mis)Perceptions in American and Australian Literary History." In *Reading across the Pacific: Australia–United States Intellectual Histories*, edited by Nicholas Birns and Robert Dixon, 3–22. Sydney: Sydney University Press, 2010.

Burwick, Frederick. *The Damnation of Newton: Goethe's Color Theory and Romantic Perception*. Berlin: Walter de Gruyter, 1986.

Butcher, Fanny. "Best Sellers of Year Reported by Publishers." *Chicago Daily Tribune*, December 21, 1929, 14.

Canada, Mark. "Vardis Fisher: An Essay in Bibliography." In *Rediscovering Vardis Fisher: Centennial Essays*, edited by Joseph M. Flora, 209–34. Moscow: University of Idaho Press, 2000.

Canby, Henry Seidel. "The River of Youth." *Saturday Review of Literature* 11, no. 34 (March 9, 1935): 529–30.

Carnell, Corbin Scott. *Bright Shadow of Reality: Spiritual Longing in C. S. Lewis*. Grand Rapids, MI: William B. Eerdmans, 1974.

Carr, Richard. "Overdue Study of Multifaceted Writer." Review of *Water from the Moon: Illusion and Reality in the Works of Australian Novelist Christopher Koch*, by Jean-François Vernay. *Antipodes* 23, no. 2 (December 2009): 224–25.

Cash, W. J. "The Mind of the South." *American Mercury* 18 (October 1929): 185–92.

———. *The Mind of the South*. New York: Vintage Books, 1941.

Cashman, Sean Dennis. *America in the Twenties and Thirties: The Olympian Age of Franklin Delano Roosevelt*. New York: New York University, 1989.

Casper, Vivian. "Thomas Wolfe and Eugene O'Neill: Intertextual References." *Eugene O'Neill Review* 35, no. 1 (2014): 79–93.

CBS. "An American Trilogy: Thomas Wolfe." *Columbia Presents Norman Corwin*. Directed by Norman Corwin with Charles Laughton. June 13, 1944.

CBS Columbia Workshop. "Wolfiana." *Twenty-Six by Corwin*. Directed by Norman Corwin. October 10, 1941.

Charters, Anne, and Samuel Charters, eds. *Brother-Souls: John Clellon Holmes, Jack Kerouac, and the Beat Generation*. Jackson: University Press of Mississippi, 2010.

Church, Margaret. "Thomas Wolfe: Dark Time." In *Thomas Wolfe: Three Decades of Criticism*, edited by Leslie A. Field, 85–104. New York: New York University Press, 1968.

Clark, David L. "Heidegger's Cravings: Being-on-Schelling." *Diacritics* 27, no. 3 (Autumn 1997): 8–33.

Cobb, James C. *Away Down South: A History of Southern Identity*. Oxford: Oxford University Press, 2005.

Cohn, Deborah, and Jon Smith, eds. Introduction to *Look Away! The U.S. South in New World Studies*, 3–13. Durham, NC: Duke University Press, 2004.

Cole, John Y., ed. *Books in Action: The Armed Services Editions*. Washington, DC: Library of Congress, 1984.

Coleridge, Samuel Taylor. *Poetical Works: Poems (Reading Text)*. Vol. 1 of *The Collected Works of Samuel Taylor Coleridge*. Edited by J. C. C. Mays. Princeton, NJ: Princeton University Press, 2001.

Confino, Alon. *Germany as a Culture of Remembrance: Promises and Limits of Writing History*. Chapel Hill: University of North Carolina Press, 2006.

Conn, Peter. *The American 1930s: A Literary History*. Cambridge: Cambridge University Press, 2009.

Connolly, Sean. *Inklings of Heaven: C. S. Lewis and Eschatology*. Leominster, Herefordshire: Gracewing, 2007.

Conrad, Robert C. *Understanding Heinrich Böll*. Columbia: University of South Carolina Press, 1992.

Cotkin, George. *Existential America*. Baltimore, MD: Johns Hopkins University Press, 2003.

Cowley, Malcolm. *And I Worked at the Writer's Trade: Chapters of Literary History, 1918–1978*. New York: Viking, 1978.

———. *Exile's Return*. Rev. ed. 1951. Reprint, Harmondsworth: Penguin Books, 1976.

———. "The Forty Days of Thomas Wolfe." *New Republic* 82, no. 1059 (March 20, 1935): 163–64.

Cox, F. Brett, and Andy Duncan, eds. *Crossroads: Tales of the Southern Literary Fantastic*. New York: Tor Books, 2004.

Cranston, C. A. Review of *Water from the Moon: Illusion and Reality in the Works of Australian Novelist Christopher Koch*, by Jean-François Vernay. *Journal of the Association for the Study of Australian Literature* 7 (March 2008): 117–21.

Cross, Anthony. "The Secret City: Hugh Walpole, Russia, and His Novel about Petrograd (1919)." *Journal of European Studies* 35, no. 3 (September 2005): 315–37.

Dalton, David. *Piece of My Heart: A Portrait of Janis Joplin*. New York: Da Capo, 1991.

Dalton, Drew M. *Longing for the Other: Levinas and Metaphysical Desire*. Pittsburgh, PA: Duquesne University Press, 2009.

Damrosch, David. *How to Read World Literature*. Chichester, UK: Wiley-Blackwell, 2009.

———. *What Is World Literature?* Princeton, NJ: Princeton University Press, 2003.

Davidman, Joy. "The Longest Way Round." In *Out of My Bone: The Letters of Joy Davidman*, edited by Don W. King, 83–98. Grand Rapids: William B. Eerdmans, 2009.

Davidson, Donald. "Farewell—and Hail!" *Nashville Tennessean*, February 16, 1930.

———. *Regionalism and Nationalism in the United States: The Attack on Leviathan*. 1938. Reprinted with an introduction by Russell Kirk. New Brunswick, NJ: Transaction, 1991.

———. *The Spyglass: Views and Reviews, 1924–1930*. Edited by John Tyree Fain. Nashville, TN: Vanderbilt University Press.

Davidson, Donald, and Allen Tate. *The Literary Correspondence of Donald Davidson and Allen Tate*. Edited by John Tyree Fain and Thomas Daniel Young. Athens: University of Georgia Press, 1974.

Davis, Kenneth C. *Two-Bit Culture: The Paperbacking of America*. Boston, MA: Houghton Mifflin, 1984.

Dearborn, Kerry. *Baptized Imagination: The Theology of George MacDonald*. Aldershot, UK: Ashgate, 2006.

DeForest, John William. "The Great American Novel." *The Nation*, January 9, 1868.

DeForest, Tim. *Storytelling in the Pulps, Comics, and Radio: How Technology Changed Popular Fiction in America*. Jefferson, NC: McFarland, 2004.

Deleuze, Gilles, and Félix Guattari. *What Is Philosophy?* Translated by Hugh Tomlinson and Graham Burchell. New York: Columbia University Press, 1994.

Denning, Michael. *The Cultural Front: The Laboring of American Culture in the Twentieth Century*. London: Verso, 1996.

Dennis, David B. *Inhumanities: Nazi Interpretations of Western Culture*. Cambridge: Cambridge University Press, 2012.

DeVoto, Bernard. "Genius Is Not Enough." *Saturday Review of Literature* 13, no. 26 (April 25, 1936): 3–4, 14–15.

Dewey, John. "Individualism, Old and New. Part 5: The Crisis in Culture." *New Republic* 62 (March 19, 1930): 123–26.

Dimock, Wai Chee. "A Theory of Resonance." *PMLA* 112, no. 5 (1997): 1060–71.

———. *Through Other Continents: American Literature across Deep Time*. Princeton, NJ: Princeton University Press, 2006.

Dodd, Martha. *My Years in Germany*. London: Victor Gollancz, 1939.

Dolan, Marc. *Modern Lives: A Cultural Re-Reading of "The Lost Generation."* West Lafayette, IN: Purdue University Press, 1996.

Donahue, Brian, Sara M. Gregg, and Edwin C. Hagenstein, eds. *American Georgics: Writings on Farming, Culture, and the Land*. New Haven, CT: Yale University Press, 2011.

Donald, David Herbert. *Look Homeward: A Life of Thomas Wolfe*. London: Bloomsbury, 1987.

Donaldson, Susan V. Introduction to *I'll Take My Stand: The South and the Agrarian Tradition*, by Twelve Southerners, ix–xl. Baton Rouge: Louisiana State Press, 2006.

Dontnod Entertainment. *Life Is Strange*. Tokyo: Square Enix, 2012.

Dorsett, Lyle W. *And God Came In: The Extraordinary Story of Joy Davidman*. Peabody, MA: Hendrickson, 2009.

Duck, Leigh Anne. *The Nation's Region: Southern Modernism, Segregation, and U.S. Nationalism*. Athens: University of Georgia Press, 2006.

———. "What Was the New Southern Studies?" *Society for the Study of Southern Litera-*

ture Newsletter 41, no. 1 (Spring 2013). http://southernlit.org/society-for-the-study-of-southern-literature-newsletter-47-1-spring-2013.

Duncan, Andy. "It's All SF: Science Fiction, Southern Fiction, and the Case of Murray Leinster." *Foundation* 29 (2000): 59–69.

Duncan, Glen. *The Last Werewolf.* New York: Knopf, 2011.

Dunlevy, Maurice. "A Giant Despite His Faults." *Canberra Times*, December 20, 1969, 14.

Dunsany, Lord. *The King of Elfland's Daughter.* 1924. Reprint, New York: Ballantine, 1999.

Durr, Jimmie Carol Still. "*Look Homeward, Angel,* Thomas Wolfe's *Ulysses.*" *Southern Studies* 24, no. 1 (1985): 54–68.

Durst, David C. *Weimar Modernism: Philosophy, Politics, and Culture in Germany, 1918–1933.* Lanham, MD: Lexington Books, 2004.

Duvall, John N. "New Criticism's Major Journals." In *North America, 1894–1960.* Vol. 2 of *The Oxford Critical and Cultural History of Modernist Magazines*, edited by Peter Brooker and Andrew Thacker, 928–43. Oxford: Oxford University Press, 2012.

Duyvendak, Jan Willem. *The Politics of Home: Belonging and Nostalgia in Western Europe and the United States.* New York: Palgrave Macmillan, 2011.

Edwards, Brian T. "The Word, the Text, and the Americanist." *American Literary History* 25, no. 1 (Spring 2013): 231–46.

Edwards, Bruce L., ed. *C. S. Lewis: Life, Works, and Legacy.* 4 vols. Westport, CT: Praeger, 2007.

Eigler, Friederike, and Jens Kugele, eds. *Heimat: At the Intersection of Memory and Space.* Berlin: De Gruyter, 2012.

Einboden, Jeffrey. *Nineteenth-Century U.S. Literature in Middle Eastern Languages.* Edinburgh: Edinburgh University Press, 2013.

Einseidel, Wolfgang von. "Romandichtung." *Europäische Umschau* 12 (October 1936): 841–44.

Eller, Jonathan R. *Becoming Ray Bradbury.* Urbana: University of Illinois Press, 2011.

———. "The Body Eclectic: Sources of Ray Bradbury's *Martian Chronicles.*" In *Ray Bradbury*, edited by Harold Bloom, 141–72. New York: Bloom's Literary Criticism, 2010.

Eller, Johnathan R., and William F. Touponce, eds. *Ray Bradbury: The Life of Fiction.* Kent, OH: Kent State University Press, 2004.

English, Daylanne K. *Unnatural Selections: Eugenics in American Modernism and the Harlem Renaissance.* Chapel Hill: University of North Carolina Press, 2004.

Epstein, Seth. "Urban Governance and Tolerance: The Regulation of Suspect Spaces and the Burden of Surveillance in Post–World War I Asheville, North Carolina." *Journal of Urban History* 43, no. 5 (2017): 683–702.

Erinnerung an einen Sommer in Berlin. Directed by Rolf Hädrich. 1972. Hamburg: Studio Hamburg, 2008.

Evans, Jedidiah. "Thomas Wolfe and the Really Deep South." *Thomas Wolfe Review* 38, no. 1–2 (2014): 7–24.

Fearing, Kenneth. "A First Novel of Vast Scope: 'Look Homeward, Angel' an American Saga in Southern Setting." *New York Evening Post*, November 16, 1929.

Felski, Rita. *Uses of Literature.* Oxford: Blackwell, 2008.

Fiedler, Leslie. *Love and Death in the American Novel.* 1960. Reprint, London: Jonathan Cape, 1967.

Field, Leslie A., ed. *Thomas Wolfe: Three Decades of Criticism.* New York: New York University Press, 1968.

———. "Thomas Wolfe's Attitudes toward Germany and Jews." *Journal of Modern Literature* 11, no. 1 (March 1984): 180–85.

Finnegan, Terence. *A Deed So Accursed: Lynching in Mississippi and South Carolina, 1881–1940*. Charlottesville: University of Virginia Press, 2013.

Fisher, Vardis. *Orphans in Gethsemane: A Novel of the Past and Present*. Denver: A. Swallow, 1960.

Fitch, Noel Riley. *Sylvia Beach and the Lost Generation: A History of Literary Paris in the Twenties and Thirties*. New York: W. W. Norton, 1985.

Fitzgerald, F. Scott. *The Great Gatsby*. 1925. Reprint, New York: Scribner, 2004.

Flatley, Jonathan. *Affective Mapping: Melancholia and the Politics of Modernism*. Cambridge, MA: Harvard University Press, 2009.

Frank, Rudolf. *Fair play, oder, Es kommt nicht zum Krieg: Roman einer Emigration in Wien*. Berlin: Aufbau-Verlag, 1998.

———. *No Hero for the Kaiser*. Translated by Patricia Crampton. New York: Lothrop, Lee and Shepard, 1986.

Frow, John. "Tourism and the Semiotics of Nostalgia." *October* 57 (Summer 1991): 123–51.

Funchion, John Richard. "Divisible Pasts: Nostalgia and Narrative in American Literature and Culture, 1848–1900." PhD diss., Brown University, 2008.

Furth, Robin. *Stephen King's the Dark Tower: The Complete Concordance*. Rev. ed. New York: Scribner, 2012.

Gaile, Andreas. "'Going Double': Exploring Contradictions of Australianness in Christopher Koch's *Out of Ireland*." *Antipodes* 16, no. 2 (December 2002): 151–56.

Gare, Shelley. "Death by Silence in the Writers' Combat Zone." *Quadrant* 54, nos. 7–8 (July–August 2010): 28–37.

Gass, William H. *Middle C*. New York: Vintage International, 2013.

———. Preface to *In the Heart of the Heart of the Country, and Other Stories*, xiii–xlvi. Rev. ed. Boston: David R. Godine, 2007.

———. "William H. Gass: The Art of Fiction LXV." Interview by Thomas LeClair. In *Conversations with William H. Gass*, edited by Theodore G. Ammon, 17–38. Jackson: University Press of Mississippi, 2003.

Gassert, Philipp. "Neither East Nor West: Anti-Americanism in West Germany, 1945–1968." In *1945–1968*. Vol. 1 of *The United States and Germany in the Era of the Cold War, 1945–1990: A Handbook*, edited by Detlef Junker, 627–34. Cambridge: Cambridge University Press, 2004.

Gaston, Sean. *The Impossible Mourning of Jacques Derrida*. London: Continuum, 2006.

Gay, Peter. *Weimar Culture: The Outsider as Insider*. 1968. Reprint, Westport, CT: Greenwood Press, 1981.

Gay, William. *Provinces of Night*. London: Faber and Faber, 2001.

Geismar, Maxwell. *Writers in Crisis: The American Novel, 1925–1940*. Boston: Houghton Mifflin, 1942.

Gellert, Leon. "Sensitive Giant." *Sydney Morning Herald*, December 27, 1947, 8.

Genoni, Paul. "Girt by Sea: Islands in the Novels of Thea Astley and Christopher Koch." In *Australian Literary Studies in the 21st Century: Proceedings of the 2000 ASAL Conference Held at University of Tasmania, Hobart, 6–9 July 2000*, edited by Philip Mead, 121–27. Hobart: Association for the Study of Australian Literature, 2001.

George, Rosemary Marangoly. *The Politics of Home: Postcolonial Relocations and Twentieth-Century Fiction*. Berkeley: University of California Press, 1999.

Gieselbusch, Hermann, et al. *100 Jahre Rowohlt: Eine Illustrierte Chronik.* Reinbek bei Hamburg: Rowohlt, 2008.

Giles, Paul. *Antipodean America: Australasia and the Constitution of U.S. Literature.* Oxford: Oxford University Press, 2013.

———. "Transnationalism and Classic American Literature." *PMLA* 118, no. 1 (January 2003): 62–77.

———. *Virtual Americas: Transnational Fictions and the Transatlantic Imaginary.* Durham, NC: Duke University Press, 2002.

Godwin, Rebecca. "You Can't Go Home Again: Does Nazism Really Transform Wolfe's Romanticism?" *Thomas Wolfe Review* 33, nos. 1–2 (2009): 24–31, 206.

Goethe, Johann Wolfgang von. *The Sufferings of Young Werther.* Translated by Stanley Corngold. New York: W. W. Norton, 2012.

———. *Wilhelm Meister's Apprenticeship.* Edited and translated by Eric A. Blackall and Victor Lange. Princeton, NJ: Princeton University Press, 1995.

Göske, Daniel, and Peter Nicolaisen. "William Faulkner in Germany: A Survey." *Faulkner Journal* 24, no. 1 (Fall 2008): 63–81.

Grammer, John M. "Reconstructing Southern Literature." *American Literary History* 13, no. 1 (2001): 126–40.

Gray, Richard. *The Literature of Memory: Modern Writers of the American South.* London: Edward Arnold, 1977.

Greeson, Jennifer Rae. "The 'Mysteries and Miseries' of North Carolina: New York City, Urban Gothic Fiction, and *Incidents in the Life of a Slave Girl.*" *American Literature* 73, no. 2 (June 2001): 277–309.

———. *Our South: Geographic Fantasy and the Rise of National Literature.* Cambridge, MA: Harvard University Press, 2010.

Gromer, Crystal. "Werfel Discovered." *Commonweal* 117, no. 13 (July 13, 1990): 425–32.

Gurko, Leo. *The Angry Decade.* New York: Dodd, Mead, 1947.

Hackett, Alice Payne. *70 Years of Best Sellers, 1895–1965.* New York: R. R. Bowker, 1967.

Hamilton, James W. *Life and Art: The Creative Synthesis in Literature.* London: Karnac, 2009.

Hannah, Matthew G. *Dark Territory in the Information Age: Learning from the West German Census Controversies of the 1980s.* Burlington, VT: Ashgate, 2010.

Hansen, Joseph. *Death Claims.* 1973. Reprint, Madison: University of Wisconsin Press, 2004.

Harlow, Morgan. "Martian Legacy: Ray Bradbury's *The Martian Chronicles.*" *War, Literature and the Arts: An International Journal of the Humanities* 17, nos. 1–2 (November 2005): 311–14.

Harnack-Fish, Mildred. "Drei jung Dichter aus USA: Thornton Wilder, Thomas Wolfe und William Faulkner." *Berliner Tageblatt,* August 5, 1934.

Harper, Margaret Mills. *The Aristocracy of Art in Joyce and Wolfe.* Baton Rouge: Louisiana State University Press, 1990.

Hegeman, Susan. *Patterns for America: Modernism and the Concept of Culture.* Princeton, NJ: Princeton University Press, 1999.

Heidegger, Martin. *The Fundamental Concepts of Metaphysics: World, Finitude, Solitude.* Translated by William McNeill and Nicholas Walker. Bloomington: Indiana University Press, 1995.

———. *Hölderlin's Hymn "The Ister."* Translated by William McNeill and Julia Davis. Bloomington: Indiana University Press, 1996.

———. *Schelling's Treatise on the Essence of Human Freedom.* Translated by Joan Stambaugh. Athens: Ohio University Press, 1985.

Heine, Heinrich. *The Complete Poems of Heinrich Heine: A Modern English Version.* Edited and translated by Hal Draper. Cambridge, MA: Suhrkamp/Insel, 1982.

Hellman, Geoffrey T. Review of *Look Homeward, Angel,* by Thomas Wolfe. *New Republic* 61, no. 785 (December 18, 1929): 122.

Hench, John B. *Books as Weapons: Propaganda, Publishing, and the Battle for Global Markets in the Era of World War II.* Ithaca, NY: Cornell University Press, 2010.

Hendrix, Howard V., Eric S. Rabkin, and George E. Slusser, eds. Preface to *Visions of Mars: Essays on the Red Planet in Fiction and Science,* 1–8. Jefferson, NC: McFarland, 2011.

Hesse, Hermann. *Mit Hermann Hesse durch das Jahr.* Frankfurt am Main: Suhrkamp, 1976.

———. *My Belief: Essays on Life and Art.* Translated by Denver Lindley. London: Jonathan Cape, 1976.

Hesse, Hermann, and Thomas Mann. *The Hesse/Mann Letters: The Correspondence of Hermann Hesse and Thomas Mann, 1910–1955.* Edited by Anni Carlsson and Volker Michels. New York: Harper and Row, 1975.

Hicks, Granville. "Living with Books." *New Leader* 41, no. 4 (January 27, 1958): 20–22.

Higgs, Robert J., Ambrose N. Manning, and Jim Wayne Miller, eds. *Appalachia Inside Out.* Knoxville: University of Tennessee Press, 1995.

Higham, Charles. "Letter from Sydney." *Hudson Review* 19, no. 4 (Winter 1966–67): 645–52.

Higham, John. *Strangers in the Land: Patterns of American Nativism, 1860–1925.* New Brunswick, NJ: Rutgers University Press, 2002.

Hilmes, Oliver. *Berlin 1936: Sechzehn Tage im August.* München: Siedler Verlag, 2016.

History of the Office of the Coordinator of Inter-American Affairs. Washington: U.S. Govt. Printing Office, 1947.

Hoffmann, E. T. A. "Beethoven's Instrumental Music." In *E. T. A. Hoffmann's Musical Writings: Kreisleriana, the Poet and the Composer, Music Criticism,* edited by David Charlton and translated by Martyn Clarke, 96–103. Cambridge: Cambridge University Press, 1989.

———. *The Life and Opinions of the Tomcat Murr, Together with a Fragmentary Biography of Kapellmeister Johannes Kreisler on Random Sheets of Waste Paper.* Translated by Anthea Bell. Harmondsworth: Penguin, 1999.

Holliday, Shawn. *Thomas Wolfe and the Politics of Modernism.* New York: Peter Lang, 2001.

———, ed. "Thomas Wolfe (1900–1938)." Special issue of *Appalachian Heritage* 35, no. 4 (Fall 2007): 8–71.

Holman, C. Hugh. *The Loneliness at the Core.* Baton Rouge: Louisiana State University Press, 1975.

Hönnighausen, Lothar. "European Culture in Southern Literature: Thomas Wolfe and William Faulkner." In *Transatlantic Exchanges: The American South in Europe – Europe in the American South,* edited by Richard Gray and Waldemar Zacharasiewicz, 33–50. Vienna: Verlag der Österreichischen Akademie der Wissenschaften, 2007.

Huggan, Graham. *Australian Literature: Postcolonialism, Racism, Transnationalism*. Oxford: Oxford University Press, 2007.

Humble, Nicola. *The Feminine Middlebrow Novel, 1920s to 1950s: Class, Domesticity, and Bohemianism*. Oxford: Oxford University Press, 2004.

Hummel, Christine. *Intertexualität im Werk Heinrich Bölls*. Trier: WVT Wissenschaftlicher Verlag, 2002.

Hutchisson, James M. *The Rise of Sinclair Lewis, 1920–1930*. University Park: Pennsylvania State University Press, 1996.

Hyman, Stanley Edgar. "A Novelist of Great Promise." *New Leader* 45, no. 12 (June 11, 1962): 11–22.

Idol, John L., Jr. "Thomas Wolfe: A Biographical Sketch." *Appalachian Heritage* 35, no. 4 (Fall 2007): 13–21.

Illbruck, Helmut. *Nostalgia: Origins and Ends of an Unenlightened Disease*. Evanston, IL: Northwestern University Press, 2012.

Inscoe, John C. *Race, War, and Remembrance in the Appalachian South*. Lexington: University Press of Kentucky, 2008.

Jackson, Michael. *At Home in the World*. Durham, NC: Duke University Press, 1995.

Jacobs, Alan. "The Chronicles of Narnia." In *The Cambridge Companion to C. S. Lewis*, edited by Robert MacSwain and Michael Ward, 265–80. Cambridge: Cambridge University Press, 2010.

James, William. "II.—On the Function of Cognition," *Mind* 10, no. 37 (January 1885): 27–44.

———. *The Principles of Psychology*. Vol. 1. 1890. Reprint, New York: Cosimo, 2007.

———. *The Varieties of Religious Experience: A Study in Human Nature*. New York: Longmans, Green, 1902.

Jameson, Fredric. *Archaeologies of the Future: The Desire Called Utopia and Other Science Fictions*. London: Verso, 2005.

———. "Dirty Little Secret." *London Review of Books* 34, no. 22 (November 22, 2012): 39–42.

Jasper, David. "*The Pilgrim's Regress* and *Surprised by Joy*." In *The Cambridge Companion to C. S. Lewis*, edited by Robert MacSwain and Michael Ward, 223–36. Cambridge: Cambridge University Press, 2010.

Johnson, E. D. "On Translating Thomas Wolfe." *American Speech* 32, no. 2 (May 1957): 95–101.

Johnston, Carol Ingalls. *Of Time and the Artist: Thomas Wolfe, His Novels, and the Critics*. Columbia, SC: Camden House, 1996.

———. *Thomas Wolfe: A Descriptive Bibliography*. Pittsburgh, PA: University of Pittsburgh Press, 1987.

Jones, Howard Mumford. "Back to Merrimac." Review of *The Town and the City*, by Jack Kerouac. *Saturday Review of Literature* 33, no. 10 (March 11, 1950): 18.

Jungk, Peter Stephan. *Franz Werfel: A Life in Prague, Vienna, and Hollywood*. Translated by Anselm Hollo. New York: Grove Weidenfeld, 1990.

Kagle, Steven E. "Homage to Melville: Ray Bradbury and the Nineteenth-Century American Romance." In *Ray Bradbury's Fahrenheit 451*, edited by Harold Bloom, 19–30. Philadelphia: Chelsea House, 2001.

Karolides, Nicholas J. *Banned Books: Literature Suppressed on Political Grounds*. Rev. ed. New York: Facts on File, 2006.

Kazin, Alfred. *On Native Grounds*. New York: Harcourt, Brace and World, 1942.

Kehl, D. G. "Writing the Long Desire: The Function of *Sehnsucht* in *The Great Gatsby* and *Look Homeward, Angel*." *Journal of Modern Literature* 24, no. 2 (Winter 2000–2001): 309–19.

Kennedy, Richard S. *The Window of Memory: The Literary Career of Thomas Wolfe*. Chapel Hill: University of North Carolina Press, 1962.

———. "Wolfe's *Look Homeward, Angel* in the Literary Marketplace." *Thomas Wolfe Review* 6 (Fall 1982): 23–26.

Kerouac, Jack. *Jack Kerouac: Selected Letters, 1940–1956*. Edited by Ann Charters. New York: Viking, 1995.

———. "The Minimization of Thomas Wolfe in His Own Time." In "Memoir: The Young Kerouac," by Elbert Lenrow. *Narrative* 2, no. 1 (January 1994): 71–76.

———. *On the Road*. 1957. Reprint, New York: Penguin, 1991.

———. *The Town and the City*. 1950. Reprinted with an introduction by Douglas Brinkley. London: Penguin, 2000.

———. *Vanity of Duluoz: An Adventurous Education, 1935–1946*. 1968. Reprint, London: Penguin, 1994.

———. *Windblown World: The Journals of Jack Kerouac, 1947–1954*. Edited by Douglas Brinkley. New York: Penguin, 2006.

Kerouac, Jack, and Allen Ginsberg. *Jack Kerouac and Allen Ginsberg: The Letters*. Edited by Bill Morgan and David Stanford. New York: Viking, 2010.

King, Richard H. "Allegories of Imperialism: Globalizing Southern Studies." *American Literary History* 23, no. 1 (2010): 148–58.

King, Stephen. *The Dark Tower III: The Waste Lands*. London: Sphere, 1991.

———. *The Dark Tower V: The Wolves of Calla*. New York: Simon and Schuster, 2003.

———. *The Gunslinger*. Rev. ed. London: New English Library, 2003.

Kiš, Danilo. *Night and Fog: The Collected Dramas and Screenplays of Danilo Kiš*. Edited and translated by John K. Cox. Budapest: Central European University Press, 2014.

Knight, Damon. "When I Was in Kneepants: Ray Bradbury." In *Ray Bradbury*, edited by Harold Bloom, 3–8. Philadelphia: Chelsea House, 2001.

Koch, Christopher. *The Boys in the Island*. London: Hamish Hamilton, 1958.

———. *The Boys in the Island*. Rev. ed. Sydney: HarperCollins, 2013.

———. *Crossing the Gap: A Novelist's Essays*. London: Chatto and Windus, 1987.

———. *The Doubleman*. 1985. Reprint, Pymble, UK: Angus and Robertson, 1992.

———. "Treasures in the Basement." *Weekend Australian*, November 9, 2002. http://search.proquest.com/docview/356565830.

Koch, Frederick H., ed. *Carolina Folk-Plays, Second Series*. New York: Henry Holt, 1924.

———. "Drama in the South." In *Pioneering a People's Theatre*, edited by Archibald Henderson, 7–19. Chapel Hill: University of North Carolina Press, 1945.

Kodaira, Takashi, and Hiroshi Tsunemoto, eds. *Studies in Thomas Wolfe: A Tribute from Japan to Thomas Wolfe's Centennial*. Tokyo: Kinseido, 2000.

Kohl, Martina. *The Wilhelm Meister Pebble: Bildungsromanelemente in Thomas Wolfes Look Homeward, Angel (1929), Of Time and the River (1935), The Web and the Rock (1939) und You Can't Go Home Again (1940)*. Würzburg: Königshausen und Neumann, 1994.

Korstvedt, Benjamin M. *Listening for Utopia in Ernst Bloch's Musical Philosophy*. Cambridge: Cambridge University Press, 2010.

Kreyling, Michael. *Inventing Southern Literature*. Jackson: University Press of Mississippi, 1998.

———. *The South That Wasn't There: Postsouthern Memory and History*. Baton Rouge: Louisiana State University Press, 2010.

———. "Toward 'A New Southern Studies.'" *South Central Review* 22, no. 1 (Spring 2005): 4–18.

Kühl, Stefan. *The Nazi Connection: Eugenics, American Racism, and German National Socialism*. Oxford: Oxford University Press, 1994.

Laderman, Gary. *A Cultural History of Death and the Funeral Home in Twentieth-Century America*. Oxford: Oxford University Press, 2003.

Lanzinger, Klaus. *Jason's Voyage: The Search for the Old World in American Literature. A Study of Melville, Hawthorne, Henry James, and Thomas Wolfe*. New York: Peter Lang, 1989.

Larson, Erik. *In the Garden of Beasts: Love and Terror in Hitler's Berlin*. 2011. Reprint, London: Black Swan, 2012.

Latimer, Margery. "The New American Family." *New York Herald Tribune Books*, November 3, 1929, 21.

Laughton, Charles. *Tell Me a Story: An Anthology*. New York: McGraw-Hill, 1957.

Lawrence, Adam. "A 'Night Meeting' in the Southwest: Hospitality in *The Martian Chronicles*." In *Orbiting Ray Bradbury's Mars: Biographical, Anthropological, Literary, Scientific and Other Perspectives*, edited by Gloria McMillan, 70–87. Jefferson, NC: McFarland, 2013.

Le Guin, Ursula K. "Ursula K. Le Guin: Still Battling the Powers That Be." Interview by Geek's Guide to the Galaxy. *Wired*, July 25, 2012, www.wired.com/underwire/2012/07/geeks-guide-ursula-k-le-guin.

Leavis, Q. D. *Fiction and the Reading Public*. London: Chatto and Windus, 1939.

Ledig-Rowohlt, Heinrich Maria. "Thomas Wolfe in Berlin." *American Scholar* 22, no. 2 (Spring 1953): 185–201.

Lenz, J. M. R. *The Tutor. The Soldiers*. Translated by William E. Yuill. Chicago: University of Chicago Press, 1972.

Leonard, Elizabeth Anne. "Race and Ethnicity in Science Fiction." In *The Cambridge Companion to Science Fiction*, edited by Edward James and Farah Mendlesohn, 253–63. Cambridge: Cambridge University Press, 2003.

Lepenies, Wolf. *The Seduction of Culture in German History*. Princeton, NJ: Princeton University Press, 2006.

Lerner, Max. *America as a Civilization: Life and Thought in the United States Today*. New York: Simon and Schuster, 1957.

Lessing, Doris. "Thomas Wolfe, Myth-Maker." *Manchester Guardian*, October 3, 1958, 9.

Lévinas, Emmanuel. *Totality and Infinity: An Essay on Exteriority*. Translated by Alphonso Lingis. The Hague: Martinus Nijhoff, 1979.

Lewis, C. S. "Christianity and Culture." In *Christian Reflections*, edited by Walter Hooper, 12–36. London: Geoffrey Bles, 1967.

———. *Family Letters, 1905–1931*. Vol. 1 of *The Collected Letters of C. S. Lewis*. Edited by Walter Hooper. New York: HarperCollins, 2004.

———. *Narnia, Cambridge and Joy*. Vol. 3 of *The Collected Letters of C. S. Lewis*. Edited by Walter Hooper. New York: HarperCollins, 2007.

———. *Mere Christianity*. London: Geoffrey Bles, 1952.

———. *The Pilgrim's Regress: An Allegorical Apology for Christianity, Reason, and Romanticism*. Rev. ed. London: Geoffrey Bles, 1943.

———. *Surprised by Joy*. London: Geoffrey Bles, 1955.
———. "The Weight of Glory." In *Essay Collection: Faith, Christianity and the Church*, Edited by Lesley Walmsley, 96–106. London: HarperCollins, 2000.
———, ed. *George MacDonald: An Anthology*. 1946. Reprint, London: Collins, 1983.
Lewis, Sinclair. "Nobel Lecture: The American Fear of Literature." www.nobelprize.org/nobel_prizes/literature/laureates/1930/lewis-lecture.html (accessed August 27, 2013).
———. "Press Conference on Winning the Nobel Prize." *New York Times*, November 6, 1930, 27.
Lim, David C. L. *The Infinite Longing for Home: Desire and the Nation in Selected Writings of Ben Okri and K. S. Maniam*. New York: Rodopi, 2005.
Lloyd, Christopher. *Rooting Place, Rooting Memory: Regionalism in the Twenty-First-Century American South*. New York: Palgrave Macmillan, 2015.
Lowenthal, David. "Nostalgic Dreams and Nightmares." *Change over Time* 3, no. 1 (Spring 2013): 28–54.
———. *The Past Is a Foreign Country*. Cambridge: Cambridge University Press, 1985.
Lubrich, Oliver, ed. *Reisen ins Reich, 1933 bis 1945: Ausländische Autoren berichten aus Deutschland*. Frankfurt am Main: Eichborn, 2004.
———. *Travels in the Reich, 1933–1945: Foreign Authors Report from Germany*. Translated by Kenneth J. Northcott, Sonia Wichmann, and Dean Krouk. Chicago: University of Chicago Press, 2010.
Lukács, György. *Soul and Form*. Edited by John T. Sanders and Katie Terezakis. Translated by Anna Bostok. New York: Columbia University Press, 2010.
MacDonald, George. *Phantastes: A Faerie Romance for Men and Women*. London: Smith, Elder, 1858.
———, ed. *Rampolli*. London: Longmans, Green, 1897.
MacDonell, A. G. "Alley-Ways of America." *Observer*, August 18, 1935, 6.
Magi, Aldo P. "Thomas Wolfe and Mildred Harnack-Fish: The 1935 Berlin Interview." *Thomas Wolfe Review* 27, no. 1–2 (2003): 100–114.
Maher, Paul. *Kerouac: The Definitive Biography*. Lanham, MD: Taylor, 2004.
Malpas, Jeff. "Philosophy's Nostalgia." In *Philosophy's Moods: The Affective Grounds of Thinking*, edited by Hagi Kenaan and Ilit Ferber, 87–101. Dordrecht: Springer, 2011.
Mann, Thomas. *Frage und Antwort: Interviews mit Thomas Mann, 1909–1955*. Edited by Volkmar Hansen and Gert Heine. Hamburg: Albrecht Knaus, 1983.
———. *Thomas Mann Diaries, 1918–1939*. Edited by Hermann Kesten. Translated by Richard Winston and Clara Winston. London: Robin Clark, 1984.
Marie, Queen Consort of Ferdinand I. *The Story of My Life*. New York: Charles Scribner's Sons, 1934.
Marr, Timothy. "Melville's Planetary Compass." In *The New Cambridge Companion to Herman Melville*, edited by Robert S. Levine, 187–201. Cambridge: Cambridge University Press, 2013.
Marx, Leo. *The Machine in the Garden: Technology and the Pastoral Ideal in America*. Oxford: Oxford University Press, 1964.
Matt, Susan J. *Homesickness: An American Malady*. Oxford: Oxford University Press, 2011.
Mauldin, Joanne Marshall. *When Do the Atrocities Begin?* Knoxville: University of Tennessee Press, 2007.
McAleer, Patrick. *Inside the Dark Tower Series: Art, Evil, and Intertextuality in the Stephen King Novels*. Jefferson, NC: McFarland, 2009.

McCarthy, Cormac. *Suttree*. 1979. Reprint, London: Picador, 2010.

McCormick, John. *American Literature, 1919–1932: A Comparative History*. London: Routledge and Kegan Paul, 1971.

McCullers, Carson. *The Heart Is a Lonely Hunter*. 1940. Reprint, London: Cresset Press, 1953.

———. *Illumination and Night Glare*. Edited by Carlos L. Dews. Madison: University of Wisconsin Press, 1999.

———. *The Mortgaged Heart*. Edited by Margarita C. Smith. Harmondsworth: Penguin Books, 1975.

McGrath, Alister. *C. S. Lewis—A Life: Eccentric Genius, Reluctant Prophet*. Carol Stream, IL: Tyndale House, 2013.

McGurl, Mark. *The Program Era: Postwar Fiction and the Rise of Creative Writing*. Cambridge, MA: Harvard University Press, 2009.

McKee, Kathryn, and Annette Trefzer, eds. Preface to "Global Contexts, Local Literatures: The New Southern Studies." Special issue of *American Literature* 78, no. 4 (2006): 677–90.

McPherson, Tara. *Reconstructing Dixie: Race, Gender, and Nostalgia in the Imagined South*. Durham, NC: Duke University Press, 2003.

Mehler, Barry. "A History of the American Eugenics Society, 1921–1940." PhD diss., University of Illinois at Urbana-Champaign, 1988.

Meindl, Dieter. "Thomas Wolfe and Germany: Modernism and Anti-Anti-Semitism in 'Dark in the Forest, Strange as Time' and 'I Have a Thing to Tell You.'" *Thomas Wolfe Review* 33, nos. 1–2 (2009): 6–23, 207.

Mencken, H. L. *Prejudices: Second Series*. London: Jonathan Cape, 1921.

Meyers, Jeffrey. "Hemingway's Achievement." *Wall Street Journal*, June 30, 2011.

Mijuskovic, Ben Lazare. *Loneliness in Philosophy, Psychology, and Literature*. 3rd ed. Bloomington, IN: iUniverse, 2012.

Miles, John David. "Science Fiction and Fantasy." In *A History of Virginia Literature*, edited by Kevin J. Hayes, 322–34. New York: Cambridge University Press, 2015.

Mishra, A. K. *Loneliness in Modern American Fiction: With Special Reference to Sherwood Anderson, Ernest Hemingway and Thomas Wolfe*. Delhi: Authors Guild, 1984.

Mitchell, Margaret. *Margaret Mitchell's Gone with the Wind Letters, 1936–1949*. Edited by Richard Harwell. New York: Macmillan, 1976.

Mitchell, Ted, ed. *Thomas Wolfe: An Illustrated Biography*. New York: Pegasus Books, 2006.

Moltke, Johannes von. *No Place Like Home: Locations of Heimat in German Cinema*. Berkeley: University of California Press, 2005.

Monk, Craig. *Writing the Lost Generation: Expatriate Autobiography and American Modernism*. Iowa City: University of Iowa Press, 2008.

Moore, John. "Shifting Frontiers: Mapping Cyberpunk and the American South." *Foundation* 66 (1996): 59–68.

Moore, Michaela Hoenicke. *Know Your Enemy: The American Debate on Nazism, 1933–1945*. Cambridge: Cambridge University Press, 2010.

Morrison, Gail M. "The Composition of *The Sound and the Fury*." In *William Faulkner's The Sound and the Fury*, edited by Harold Bloom, 3–30. New York: Infobase, 2008.

Mosse, George L. *The Crisis of German Ideology: Intellectual Origins of the Third Reich*. London: Weidenfeld and Nicolson, 1966.

Mucher, Walter. "Being Martian: Spatiotemporal Self in Ray Bradbury's *The Martian Chronicles*." *Extrapolation: A Journal of Science Fiction and Fantasy* 43, no. 2 (Summer 2002): 171–87.

Nagorski, Andrew. *Hitlerland: American Eyewitnesses to the Nazis Rise to Power*. New York: Simon and Schuster, 2012.

Nelson, Anne. *Red Orchestra: The Story of the Berlin Underground and the Circle of Friends who Resisted Hitler*. New York: Random House, 2009.

Norman, Conolly. "A Rare form of Mental Disease (Grübelsucht)." *Transactions of the Royal Academy of Medicine in Ireland* 6, no. 1 (December 1888): 62–71.

Novalis. *Henry von Ofterdingen: A Novel*. Translated by Palmer Hilty. New York: Frederick Ungar, 1964.

———. *Notes for a Romantic Encyclopaedia*. Edited and translated by David W. Wood. Albany: State University of New York Press, 2007.

———. *Novalis Schriften*. Edited by Ludwig Tieck and Friedrich von Schlegel. Paris: Baudry, 1840.

O'Brien, Michael. "Place as Everywhere: On Globalizing the American South." In *Creating Citizenship in the Nineteenth-Century South*, edited by William A. Link, David Brown, Brian Ward, and Martyn Bone, 271–90. Gainesville: University Press of Florida, 2013.

O'Brien, William Arctander. *Novalis: Signs of Revolution*. Durham, NC: Duke University Press, 1995.

O'Neill, Molly. *American Food Writing: An Anthology with Classic Recipes*. New York: Library of America, 2007.

Ordover, Nancy. *American Eugenics: Race, Queer Anatomy, and the Science of Nationalism*. Minneapolis: University of Minnesota Press, 2003.

Parker, Dorothy. "The Artist's Reward." *New Yorker* 5, no. 41 (November 30, 1939): 28–31.

Percy, Walker. *Conversations with Walker Percy*. Edited by Victor A. Kramer and Lewis A. Lawson. Jackson: University Press of Mississippi, 1993.

———. *The Moviegoer*. 1961. Reprint, London: Methuen, 2003.

Perkins, Maxwell. *Editor to Author: The Letters of Maxwell E. Perkins*. Edited by John Hall Wheelock. New York: Charles Scribner's Sons, 1950.

Perkins, Maxwell, and Thomas Wolfe. *To Loot My Life Clean: The Thomas Wolfe–Maxwell Perkins Correspondence*. Edited by Matthew J. Bruccoli and Park Bucker. Columbia: University of South Carolina Press, 2000.

Phillipson, John S., ed. *Critical Essays on Thomas Wolfe*. Boston: G. K. Hall, 1985.

———. *Thomas Wolfe: A Reference Guide*. Boston: G. K. Hall, 1977.

Pierce, Peter. "Defection and Dislocation: The Fiction of Christopher Koch." *Westerly* 35, no. 2 (June 1990): 47–55.

Plimpton, George, ed. *Beat Writers at Work: The Paris Review*. New York: Modern Library, 1999.

Plunka, Gene A. *Staging Holocaust Resistance*. New York: Palgrave Macmillan, 2012.

Powell, A. "Thomas Wolfe: Little Known Genius." *Woroni*, July 19, 1950, 6–7.

Powell, Tara. *The Intellectual in Twentieth-Century Southern Literature*. Baton Rouge: Louisiana State University Press, 2012.

Preston, George R., Jr. *Thomas Wolfe: A Bibliography*. New York: C. S. Boesen, 1943.

Proietti, Salvatore. "Beyond the Hills: Of Thomas Wolfe and Science Fiction." In *Look Homeward and Forward: Thomas Wolfe, an American Voice across Modern and Contemporary Culture*, edited by Agostino Lombardo, Mario Faraone, Monica Melloni, and

Igina Tattoni, 77–86. Rome: Casa Editrice Università degli Studi di Roma La Sapienza, 2003.

Qabaha, Ahmad Rasmi. *Exile and Expatriation in Modern American and Palestinian Writing*. Cham, Switzerland: Palgrave Macmillan, 2018.

Quinlem, John. "The Sensitive Clod." Review of *The Boys in the Island*, by Christopher Koch. *Observer* 2, no. 17 (August 22, 1959): 538.

Rabinowicz, Paula. *American Pulp: How Paperbacks Brought Modernism to Main Street*. Princeton, NJ: Princeton University Press, 2014.

Rabkin, Eric S. "'Is Mars Heaven?' *The Martian Chronicles, Fahrenheit 451* and Ray Bradbury's Landscape of Longing." In *Visions of Mars: Essays on the Red Plant in Fiction and Science*, edited by Howard V. Hendrix, George Slusser, and Eric S. Rabkin, 95–104. Jefferson, NC: McFarland, 2011.

Ransom, John Crowe. *God without Thunder: An Unorthodox Defense of Orthodoxy*. New York: Harcourt, Brace, 1930.

Rasche, Hermann. "Klaus Mann's Novel *The Volcano*." In *Exiles and Migrants: Crossing Thresholds in European Culture and Society*, edited by Anthony Coulson, 91–100. Brighton: Sussex Academic Press, 1997.

Reeves, Paschal. *Thomas Wolfe's Albatross: Race and Nationality in America*. Athens: University of Georgia Press, 1968.

———, ed. *Thomas Wolfe: The Critical Reception*. New York: David Lewis, 1974.

Richard, Alfred Charles, Jr. *Censorship and Hollywood's Hispanic Image: An Interpretative Filmography, 1936–1955*. Westport, CT: Greenwood Press, 1993.

Ritchie, James MacPherson. *German Literature under National Socialism*. London: C. Helm, 1983.

Roberts, Terry. "Resurrecting Thomas Wolfe." *Southern Literary Journal* 33, no. 1 (Fall 2000): 27–41.

Romine, Scott. *The Real South: Southern Narrative in the Age of Cultural Reproduction*. Baton Rouge: Louisiana State University Press, 2008.

Rostkowski, Joëlle. *Conversations with Remarkable Native Americans*. Albany: State University of New York Press, 2012.

Roth, Michael. *Memory, Trauma, and History: Essays on Living with the Past*. New York: Columbia University Press, 2012.

Roth, Philip. "The Book That Made Me a Reader." The Center for Fiction. http://centerforfiction.org/for-readers/the-book-that-made-me-a-reader-archives/the-writer-who-made-me-a-reader (accessed February 11, 2014).

———. *My Life as a Man*. London: Jonathan Cape, 1974.

———. *Zuckerman Unbound*. New York: Farrar, Straus and Giroux, 1981.

Rothman, Nathan L. "Thomas Wolfe and James Joyce." In *A Southern Vanguard*, edited by Allen Tate. New York: Prentice-Hall, 1947, 52–77.

Rousseau, Jean-Jacques. *A Complete Dictionary of Music*. Translated by William Waring. New York: AMS Press, 1975.

Rubin, Louis D., Jr., ed. *Thomas Wolfe: A Collection of Critical Essays*. Englewood Cliffs, NJ: Prentice-Hall, 1973.

Sakharov, Alik, dir. "The Big Sleep." Episode 8, season 2 of *Ozark*. August 31, 2018.

Salomon, Ernst von. *The Answers of Ernst von Salomon*. Translated by Constantine Fitzgibbon. London: Putnam, 1954.

Sanders, Ruth H. *German: Biography of a Language*. Oxford: Oxford University Press, 2010.

Satterfield, Jay. *The World's Best Books: Taste, Culture, and the Modern Library*. Amherst: University of Massachusetts Press, 2002.

Saunders, George. "The Book that Made Me a Reader." The Center for Fiction. http://centerforfiction.org/for-readers/the-book-that-made-me-a-reader-archives/the-writer-who-made-me-a-reader. (accessed February 17, 2014).

———. "George Saunders: Dig the Hole." Interview by Joel Whitney. *Guernica*, August 11, 2006, www.guernicamag.com/interviews/dig_the_hole.

———. "My First Literary Crush." Interview by College Week. *Slate*, November 15, 2005, www.slate.com/articles/news_and_politics/college_week/2005/11/my_first_literary_crush.single.html.

———. *The Tenth of December*. New York: Random House, 2013.

Schelling, Friedrich Wilhelm Joseph von. *Philosophical Investigations into the Essence of Human Freedom*. Translated by Jeff Love and Johannes Schmidt. Albany: State University of New York Press, 2006.

Schiller, Friedrich von. *William Tell*. Translated by W. F. Mainland. Chicago: University of Chicago Press, 1972.

Schlesinger, Arthur M., Jr. *The Age of Roosevelt: The Politics of Upheaval, 1935–1936*. Boston: Houghton Mifflin, 1960.

Schmidt, Michael. *The Novel: A Biography*. Cambridge, MA: Harvard University Press, 2014.

Schorer, Mark. "Sinclair Lewis." In *Seven Modern American Novelists*, edited by William Van O'Connor, 46–80. Minneapolis: University of Minnesota Press, 1959.

Schneidau, Herbert N. *Walking Giants: The Presence of the Past in Modernism*. Oxford: Oxford University Press, 1991.

Scott, Jennifer A. "You Can't Go Home Again: Re-Constructing Nostalgia in the American Imagination." PhD diss., Ohio University, 2006.

Sharrad, Paul. Review of *Water from the Moon: Illusion and Reality in the Works of Australian Novelist Christopher Koch*, by Jean-François Vernay. *Postcolonial Text* 3, no. 4 (2007): 1–3.

Shirer, William L. *Berlin Diary: The Journal of a Foreign Correspondent, 1934–1941*. New York: Knopf, 1941.

Silverberg, Robert. "Science Fiction in the Fifties." In *Nebula Awards Showcase 2010*, edited by Brett Fawcett, 163–72. New York: ROC, 2010.

Sitkoff, Harvard. *The Depression Decade*. Vol. 1 of *A New Deal for Blacks: The Emergence of Civil Rights as a National Issue*. Oxford: Oxford University Press, 1978.

Skolnik, Jonathan. *Jewish Pasts, German Fictions: History, Memory, and Minority Culture in Germany, 1824 – 1955*. Stanford, CA: Stanford University Press, 2014.

Slusser, George Edgar. *The Bradbury Chronicles*. San Bernardino, CA: Borgo Press, 1977.

Smith, Jon. *Finding Purple America: The South and the Future of American Cultural Studies*. Athens: University of Georgia Press, 2013.

Smith, Margaret. "*My Life as a Man*: 'The Surprises Manhood Brings.'" In *Philip Roth: New Perspectives on an American Author*, edited by Derek Parker Royal, 75–87. Westport, CT: Praeger, 2005.

Solomon, William. *Literature, Amusement, and Technology in the Great Depression*. Cambridge: Cambridge University Press, 2002.

Spenser, Edmund. *Prothalamion or A Spousall Verse Made by Edm. Spenser*. London: Printed by J. Orwin for William Ponsonby, 1596.

Spiro, Jonathan Peter. *Defending the Master Race: Conservation, Eugenics, and the Legacy of Madison Grant*. Burlington: University of Vermont Press, 2009.

Spoth, Daniel. "Totalitarian Faulkner: The Nazi Interpretation of *Light in August* and *Absalom, Absalom!*" *ELH* 78, no. 1 (Spring 2011): 239–57.

Starobinski, Jean. "The Idea of Nostalgia." Translated by William S. Kemp. *Diogenes* 14, no. 54 (1966): 81–103.

Stearns, Monroe M. "The Metaphysics of Thomas Wolfe." *College English* 6, no. 4 (January 1945): 193–99.

Stecopoulos, Harilaos. *Reconstructing the World: Southern Fictions and U.S. Imperialisms, 1898–1976*. Ithaca, NY: Cornell University Press, 2008.

Steele, Elizabeth. *Sir Hugh Walpole and the United States: A Novelist's View of 1919–1936 America*. New York: Edwin Mellen, 2006.

Steiman, Lionel B. *Franz Werfel, the Faith of an Exile: From Prague to Beverly Hills*. Waterloo, ON: Wilfrid Laurier University Press, 1985.

Stein, Jack M. "Musical Settings of the Songs from *Wilhelm Meister*." *Comparative Literature* 22, no. 2 (Spring 1970): 125–46.

Sterling, Christopher H., ed. *The Biographical Encyclopedia of American Radio*. New York: Routledge, 2011.

Stern, Alexandra Minna. *Eugenic Nation: Faults and Frontiers of Better Breeding in Modern America*. Berkeley: University of California Press, 2005.

Stewart, John L. *Ernst Krenek: The Man and His Music*. Berkeley: University of California Press, 1991.

Stewart, Susan. *On Longing: Narratives of the Miniature, the Gigantic, the Souvenir, the Collection*. Durham, NC: Duke University Press, 1993.

Stoddard, Lothrop. *Into the Darkness: Nazi Germany Today*. New York: Duell, Sloan and Pierce, 1940.

Stokes, Lawrence D. "Thomas Wolfe in Nazi Concentration Camps." *Thomas Wolfe Review* 31, nos. 1–2 (2007): 22–36.

———. "Translation and Publication: Bringing Thomas Wolfe's Works to Germany." *Thomas Wolfe Review* 23, no. 2 (Fall 1999): 29–38.

———. "The Translation and Reception of Thomas Wolfe's Works in Nazi Germany, 1933–1938." In *Look Homeward and Forward: Thomas Wolfe, an American Voice across Modern and Contemporary Culture*, edited by Agostino Lombardo, Mario Faraone, Monica Melloni, and Igina Tattoni, 153–72. Rome: Casa Editrice Università degli Studi di Roma La Sapienza, 2003.

Strauss, Albrecht B. "You Can't Go Home Again—Thomas Wolfe and I." *Southern Literary Journal* 27, no. 2 (Spring 1995): 107–16.

Strengell, Heidi. *Dissecting Stephen King: From the Gothic to Literary Naturalism*. Madison: University of Wisconsin Press, 2005.

Strzelczyk, Florentine. "Far Away, So Close: Carl Froelich's *Heimat*." In *Cultural History through a National Socialist Lens: Essays on the Cinema of the Third Reich*, edited by Robert C. Reimer, 109–32. Rochester, NY: Camden House, 2000.

Sturge, Kate. "'Flight from the Programme of National Socialism?' Translations in Nazi Germany." In *Translation under Fascism*, edited by Christopher Rundle and Kate Sturge, 51–83. New York: Palgrave Macmillan, 2010.

Stutman, Suzanne, ed. *My Other Loneliness: Letters of Thomas Wolfe and Aline Bernstein.* Chapel Hill: University of North Carolina Press, 1983.

Styron, William. *Selected Letters of William Styron.* Edited by Rose Styron. New York: Random House, 2012.

———. "The Shade of Thomas Wolfe." In *Thomas Wolfe: A Collection of Critical Essays*, edited by Louis D. Rubin Jr., 97–107. Englewood Cliffs, NJ: Prentice-Hall, 1973.

———. *Sophie's Choice.* 1979. Reprint, New York: Vintage International, 1992.

Susman, Warren I. *Culture as History: The Transformation of American Society in the Twentieth Century.* New York: Pantheon Books, 1984.

Szejnmann, Claus-Christian W., and Maiken Umbach, eds. *Heimat, Region, and Empire: Spatial Identities under National Socialism.* New York: Palgrave Macmillan, 2012.

Talbot, David. *Devil Dog: The Amazing True Story of the Man Who Saved America.* New York: Simon and Schuster, 2010.

Tate, Allen, ed. *A Southern Vanguard.* New York: Prentice-Hall, 1947.

Teicher, Morton I. "Ray Bradbury and Thomas Wolfe: Fantasy and the Fantastic." *Thomas Wolfe Review* 12 (1988): 17–19.

Tennyson, Alfred. *The Princess: A Medley.* London: Edward Moxon, 1850.

Thompson, Dorothy. "Dorothy Thompson Says: Anniversary." *Reading Eagle* 59 (March 27, 1942): 12.

———. "The Last Time I Saw Berlin." *Saturday Review of Literature* 30, no. 11 (March 15, 1947): 9–10.

Thurner, Bettina. "'It Is Evil; It Is Beautiful; It Is Fascinating, It Is Bewildering': Thomas Wolfe's Paris of the 1920s." In *Rive Gauche: Paris as a Site of Avant-Garde Art and Cultural Exchange in the 1920s*, edited by Elke Mettinger, Margarete Rubik, and Jörg Türrschmann, 289–310. Amsterdam: Rodopi, 2010.

Töteberg, Michael, and Sabine Buck, eds. *Hans Fallada, Ewig auf der Rutschbahn: Briefwechsel mit dem Rowohlt Verlag.* Reinbel: Rowohlt, 2008.

Turnbull, Andrew. *Thomas Wolfe.* New York: Charles Scribner's Sons, 1967.

Twain, Mark. *Adventures of Huckleberry Finn.* 1885. Reprinted with an introduction by George Saunders. New York: Modern Library, 2001.

Twelve Southerners. *I'll Take My Stand: The South and the Agrarian Tradition.* 1930. Reprint, Gloucester, MA: Peter Smith, 1976.

Underwood, Thomas A. "Autobiography and Ideology in the South: Thomas Wolfe and the Vanderbilt Agrarians." *American Literature* 61, no. 1 (March 1989): 31–45.

Vaisfeld, Alina. "Ernst Bloch: The Thinker of Utopia's Reading of Kierkegaard." In *German and Scandinavian Philosophy.* Vol. 1 of *Kierkegaard's Influence on Philosophy,* edited by Jon Stewart, 67–84. Surrey: Ashgate, 2012.

Vernay, Jean-François. *Water from the Moon: Illusion and Reality in the Works of Australian Novelist Christopher Koch.* Youngstown, NY: Cambria Press, 2007.

Vincent, Bev. *The Dark Tower Companion: A Guide to Stephen King's Epic Fantasy.* New York: New American Library, 2013.

———. *The Road to the Dark Tower: Exploring Stephen King's Magnum Opus.* New York: New American Library, 2004.

Vizenor, Gerald. *Interior Landscapes: Autobiographical Myths and Metaphors.* Minneapolis: University of Minnesota Press, 1990.

Wade, John Donald. "Prodigal: An Essay on Thomas Wolfe." *Southern Review* 1, no. 1 (July 1935): 192–98.

Wagener, Hans. *Understanding Franz Werfel.* Columbia: University of South Carolina Press, 1993.

Wagner-Martin, Linda. *Ernest Hemingway's A Farewell to Arms: A Reference Guide.* Westport, CT: Greenwood Press, 2003.

Waldrop, Howard. *Going Home Again.* Perth: Eidolon, 1997.

Walker, Andrew. "Scripture, Revelation and Platonism in C. S. Lewis." *Scottish Journal of Theology* 55, no. 1 (2002): 19–35.

Wallace, Margaret. "A Novel of Provincial American Life." *New York Times Book Review,* October 27, 1929, 4.

Wang, Lan-Ming. "Thomas Wolfe Studies in China." *Thomas Wolfe Review* 34, nos. 1–2 (2010): 138–41, 235.

Warren, Robert Penn. *The Southern Review Years, 1935 – 1942.* Vol. 2 of *Selected Letters of Robert Penn Warren.* Edited by William Bedford Clark. Baton Rouge: Louisiana State University Press, 2001.

Weiss, Andrea. *In the Shadow of the Magic Mountain: The Erika and Klaus Mann Story.* Chicago: University of Chicago Press, 2008.

Weissenberger, Klaus. "Performing the Poem: Rituals of Activism in Expressionist Poetry." In *A Companion to the Literature of German Expressionism,* edited by Neil H. Donahue, 185–228. Rochester, NY: Camden House, 2005.

Weller, Sam. *The Bradbury Chronicles: The Life of Ray Bradbury.* New York: William Morrow, 2005.

Werfel, Franz. *Wir Sind: Neue Gedichte.* Leipzig: K. Wolff, 1913.

West, James L. W., III. *American Authors and the Literary Marketplace since 1900.* Philadelphia: University of Pennsylvania Press, 1988.

———. "F. Scott Fitzgerald, Professional Author." In *A Historical Guide to F. Scott Fitzgerald,* edited by Kirk Curnutt, 49–68. Oxford: Oxford University Press, 2004.

West, Jessamyn. *Love, Death, and the Ladies' Drill Team.* New York: Harcourt, Brace, 1955.

West, Rebecca. Review of *Winesburg, Ohio,* by Sherwood Anderson. *New Statesman* 29, no. 484 (July 22, 1922): 443–44.

Whalen, Brian Joseph. "Home and Homelessness in the American Imagination." PhD diss., University of Dallas, 1988.

Whisnant, David E. *All That Is Native and Fine: The Politics of Culture in an American Region.* Chapel Hill: University of North Carolina Press, 1983.

White, Walter Francis. *A Rising Wind.* Garden City, NY: Doubleday, Doran, 1945.

Wighton, Rosemary. "The Realistic Novel." *Australian Letters* 2, no. 3 (December 1959): 61–64.

Wilkinson, James. *The Intellectual Resistance in Europe.* Cambridge, MA: Harvard University Press, 1981.

Wilson, Christopher P. *The Labor of Words: Literary Professionalism in the Progressive Era.* Athens: University of Georgia Press, 1985.

Wilson, Nicola. "Virginia Woolf, Hugh Walpole, the Hogarth Press, and the Book Society." *ELH* 79, no. 1 (Spring 2012): 237–60.

Winchell, Mark Royden. *Cleanth Brooks and the Rise of Modern Criticism.* Charlottesville: University of Virginia Press, 1996.

Wirth, Jason M. *The Conspiracy of Life: Meditations on Schelling and His Time.* Albany: State University of New York Press, 2003.

Woenesser, Martin. *Heidegger in America.* Cambridge: Cambridge University Press, 2011.

Wolfe, Gary K. "The Frontier Myth in Ray Bradbury." In *Ray Bradbury*, edited by Martin Harry Greenberg and Joseph D. Olander, 33–54. New York: Taplinger, 1980.

Wolfe, Linda. *The Literary Gourmet: Menus from Masterpieces*. New York: Simon and Schuster, 1989.

Wolfe, Thomas. *The Autobiographical Outline for Look Homeward, Angel*. Edited by Lucy Coniff and Richard S. Kennedy. Baton Rouge: Louisiana State University Press, 2004.

———. *The Autobiography of an American Novelist*. Edited by Leslie Field. Cambridge, MA: Harvard University Press, 1983.

———. *The Complete Short Stories of Thomas Wolfe*. Edited by Francis Skipp. New York: Charles Scribner's Sons, 1987.

———. "Dark in the Forest, Strange as Time." *Scribner's Magazine* 96, no. 5 (November 1934): 273–78.

———. *Es führt kein Weg zurück: Roman*. Translated by Ernst Reinhard. Bern: Scherz, 1942.

———. "The Face of America." In *The Treasury Star Parade*, edited by William A. Bacher, 139–50. New York: Farrar and Reinhart, 1942.

———. *The Face of a Nation: Poetical Passages from the Writings of Thomas Wolfe*. Edited by John Hall Wheelock. New York: Literary Guild of America, 1939.

———. *The Four Lost Men: The Previously Unpublished Long Version*. Edited by Arlyn and Matthew J. Bruccoli. Columbia: University of South Carolina Press, 2008.

———. *From Death to Morning*. New York: Charles Scribner's Sons, 1935.

———. *The Hills Beyond*. New York: Sun Dial Press, 1943.

———. *I Have a Thing to Tell You*. Edited by Wolfgang Klimke. Paderborn, Germany: Schöningh, 1958.

———. "I Have a Thing to Tell You." In *The Short Novels of Thomas Wolfe*, edited by C. Hugh Holman, 233–78. New York: Charles Scribner's Sons, 1961.

———. *The Letters of Thomas Wolfe*. Edited by Elizabeth Nowell. New York: Charles Scribner's Sons, 1956.

———. *The Letters of Thomas Wolfe to His Mother*. Edited by C. Hugh Holman and Sue Fields Ross. Chapel Hill: University of North Carolina Press, 1968.

———. *Look Homeward, Angel: A Story of the Buried Life*, 1929. Reprint, New York: Charles Scribner's Sons, 1936.

———. *Look Homeward, Angel: A Story of the Buried Life*. London: Heinemann, 1930.

———. *Look Homeward, Angel: A Story of the Buried Life*. New York: Modern Library, 1934.

———. *The Magical Campus: University of North Carolina Writings, 1917–1920*. Edited by Matthew J. Bruccoli and Aldo P. Magi. Columbia: University of South Carolina Press, 2008.

———. "The Names of the Nation." In *An Anthology of World Prose*, edited by Carl Van Doren, 1158–1562. New York: Reynal and Hitchcock, 1935.

———. "No Door: A Story of Time and the Wanderer." *Scribner's Magazine* 93, no. 1 (July 1933): 7–12, 46–56.

———. *The Notebooks of Thomas Wolfe*. Edited by Richard S. Kennedy and Pascal Reeves. 2 vols. Chapel Hill: University of North Carolina Press, 1970.

———. *O Lost: A Story of the Buried Life*. Edited by Arlyn and Matthew J. Bruccoli. Columbia: University of South Carolina Press, 2000.

———. *Of Time and the River: A Legend of Man's Hunger in His Youth*. New York: Charles Scribner's Sons, 1935.

———. "Oktoberfest." *Scribner's Magazine* 101, no. 6 (June 1937): 27–31.

———. *The Party at Jack's*. Edited by Suzanne Stutman and John L. Idol Jr. Chapel Hill: University of North Carolina Press, 1995.

———. *Schau heimwärts, Engel! Eine Geschichte vom begrabnen Leben*. Translated by Hans Schiebelhuth. Berlin: Rowohlt, 1932.

———. *Schau heimwärts, Engel: Eine Geschichte vom begrabenen Leben*. Translated by Irma Wehrli. Zürich: Manesse Verlag, 2009.

———. *Selections from Thomas Wolfe*. Edited by Maxwell Geismar. London: Heinemann, 1952.

———. *The Starwick Episodes*. Edited by Richard Kennedy. Baton Rouge: Louisiana State University Press, 1994.

———. *The Story of a Novel*. New York: Charles Scribner's Sons, 1936.

———. "Thomas Wolfe from North Carolina: A Young American Writer Who Leaped into Fame with His First Novel." Interview by Marion L. Starkey. In *Thomas Wolfe Interviewed, 1929–1938*, edited by Aldo P. Magi and Richard Walser, 12–20. Baton Rouge: Louisiana State University Press, 1985.

———. *The Web and the Rock*. 1939. Reprint, London: William Heinemann, 1947.

———. *You Can't Go Home Again*. New York: Harper and Row, 1940.

Wolfe, Thomas, and Elizabeth Nowell. *Beyond Love and Loyalty: The Letters of Thomas Wolfe and Elizabeth Nowell*. Edited by Richard S. Kennedy. Chapel Hill: University of North Carolina Press, 1983.

Wolff, Tamsen. *Mendel's Theatre: Heredity, Eugenics, and Early Twentieth-Century American Drama*. New York: Palgrave Macmillan, 2009.

Wood, Danielle. "Writing Tasmania's 'Different Soul.'" *Island Studies Journal* 3, no. 2 (2008): 153–62.

Woodward, C. Vann. *The Burden of Southern History*. 3rd ed. Baton Rouge: Louisiana State University Press, 1993.

Woolf, Virginia. *The Death of the Moth and Other Essays*. London: Hogarth Press, 1942.

Wordsworth, William. *The Prelude; or, Growth of a Poet's Mind: An Autobiographical Poem*. London: Edward Moxon, 1850.

Wouk, Herman. *Youngblood Hawke*. Sydney: Collins, 1962.

Wurth, Kiene. "The Musicality of the Past: *Sehnsucht*, Trauma, and the Sublime." *Journal of the Philosophy of History* 1, no. 2 (2007): 219–47.

———. *Musically Sublime: Indeterminacy, Infinity, Irresolvability*. New York: Fordham University Press, 2009.

Yarbrough, Scott D. "The Intertextual *Suttree*: Walker Percy, Cummings, and Community." *Southern Literary Journal* 45, no. 2 (2013): 103–20.

Young, Philip. *American Fiction, American Myth: Essays*. University Park: Pennsylvania State University Press, 2000.

Zacharasiewicz, Waldemar. *Images of Germany in American Literature*. Iowa City: University of Iowa Press, 2007.

Zahn, Ernst. *Was das Leben zerbricht, ein Buch*. Stuttgart: Deutsche Verlags-Anstalt, 1912.

Ziolkowski, Theodore. "Heinrich Böll: Conscience and Craft." *Books Abroad* 34, no. 3 (Summer 1960): 213–22.

Žižek, Slavoj. *Looking Awry: An Introduction to Lacan through Popular Culture*. Cambridge, MA: MIT Press, 1991.

Zuckmayer, Carl. *A Part of Myself.* Translated by Richard and Clara Winston. London: Secker and Warburg, 1970.

Zühlsdorff, Volkmar. *Hitler's Exiles: The German Cultural Resistance in America and Europe.* London: Continuum, 2004.

Zwingmann, Charles A. A. "'Heimweh' or 'Nostalgic Reaction': A Conceptual Analysis and Interpretation of a Medico-Psychological Phenomenon." PhD diss., Stanford University, 1959.

INDEX

Page numbers in *italics* refer to illustrations.

THE NEW SOUTHERN STUDIES

The Nation's Region: Southern Modernism, Segregation, and U.S. Nationalism
BY LEIGH ANNE DUCK

Black Masculinity and the U.S. South: From Uncle Tom to Gangsta
BY RICHÉ RICHARDSON

Grounded Globalism: How the U.S. South Embraces the World
BY JAMES L. PEACOCK

Disturbing Calculations: The Economics of Identity in Postcolonial Southern Literature, 1912–2002
BY MELANIE BENSON TAYLOR

American Cinema and the Southern Imaginary
EDITED BY DEBORAH E. BARKER AND KATHRYN MCKEE

Southern Civil Religions: Imagining the Good Society in the Post-Reconstruction Era
BY ARTHUR REMILLARD

Reconstructing the Native South: American Indian Literature and the Lost Cause
BY MELANIE BENSON TAYLOR

Apples and Ashes: Literature, Nationalism, and the Confederate States of America
BY COLEMAN HUTCHISON

Reading for the Body: The Recalcitrant Materiality of Southern Fiction, 1893–1985
BY JAY WATSON

Latining America: Black-Brown Passages and the Coloring of Latino/a Studies
BY CLAUDIA MILIAN

Finding Purple America: The South and the Future of American Cultural Studies
BY JON SMITH

The Signifying Eye: Seeing Faulkner's Art
BY CANDACE WAID

Sacral Grooves, Limbo Gateways: Travels in Deep Southern Time, Circum-Caribbean Space, Afro-creole Authority
BY KEITH CARTWRIGHT

Jim Crow, Literature, and the Legacy of Sutton E. Griggs
EDITED BY TESS CHAKKALAKAL AND KENNETH W. WARREN

Sounding the Color Line: Music and Race in the Southern Imagination
BY ERICH NUNN

Borges's Poe: The Influence and Reinvention of Edgar Allan Poe in Spanish America
BY EMRON ESPLIN

Eudora Welty's Fiction and Photography: The Body of the Other Woman
BY HARRIET POLLACK

Keywords for Southern Studies
EDITED BY SCOTT ROMINE AND JENNIFER RAE GREESON

The Southern Hospitality Myth: Ethics, Politics, Race, and American Memory
BY ANTHONY SZCZESIUL

Navigating Souths: Transdisciplinary Explorations of a U.S. Region
EDITED BY MICHELE GRIGSBY COFFEY AND JODI SKIPPER

Where the New World Is: Literature about the U.S. South at Global Scales
BY MARTYN BONE

Red States: Indigeneity, Settler Colonialism, and Southern Studies
BY GINA CAISON

The Whole Machinery: The Rural Modern in Cultures of the U.S. South, 1890–1946
BY BENJAMIN S. CHILD

www.ingramcontent.com/pod-product-compliance
Lightning Source LLC
LaVergne TN
LVHW090754230826
846195LV00038B/201